AUTHORS AND AUTHORITY

The Social Foundations of Aesthetic Forms

The Social Foundations of Aesthetic Forms
A SERIES OF COLUMBIA UNIVERSITY PRESS

AUTHORS AND AUTHORITY

English and American Criticism 1750–1990

Patrick Parrinder

Columbia University Press
New York

Columbia University Press
New York

© Chapters 1–4 Patrick Parrinder 1977, 1991
© Chapters 5–7 Patrick Parrinder 1991

Chapters 1–4 of this book were first published in a slightly
different form as *Authors and Authority: A Study of English
Literary Criticism and its Relation to Culture 1750–1900* by
Routledge and Kegan Paul 1977

All rights reserved
Casebound editions of Columbia University Press
books are Smyth-sewn and printed on permanent and
durable acid-free paper

Printed in Hong Kong

c   10 9 8 7 6 5 4 3 2 1
p   10 9 8 7 6 5 4 3 2 1

Library of Congress Cataloging-in-Publication Data
Parrinder, Patrick.
     Authors and authority : English and American criticism 1750–1990 /
Patrick Parrinder.
         p.   cm.—(Social foundations of aesthetic forms)
     Includes bibliographical references and index.
     ISBN 0–231–07646–0—ISBN 0–231–07647–9 (pbk.)
     1. Criticism—Great Britain—History.   2. Criticism—United
States—History.   3. English literature—History and criticism—
Theory, etc.   4. American literature—History and criticism—
Theory, etc.   I. Title.   II. Series: Social foundations of
aesthetic forms series.
     PR63.P3   1991
     801'095'0941—dc20   90–28520
                                                                                    CIP

Contents

Preface

The first four chapters of *Authors and Authority*, with the subtitle 'A Study of English Literary Criticism and its Relation to Culture 1750–1900', were published by Routledge and Kegan Paul in 1977. The book was not originally meant to stop at 1900, so that the present, greatly enlarged edition represents the fulfilment of my original plan. At the same time, Chapters 5, 6 and 7 have been written in the very different intellectual climate of the late 1980s. One of the changes to be recorded is that nobody today discusses the 'decline of English' in the resigned, elegiac tone that was common fifteen years ago. Criticism and English studies have not only revealed great reserves of vitality, but there is a renewed sense of their cultural and educational importance. The relationship of literature to literacy, and the place of English in the national education systems of the English-speaking countries, have continued to be hotly contested.

Another major change is in the currency of the word 'authority', which in 1977 had scarcely risen to the surface of literary discussion. In the year that the earlier part of *Authors and Authority* appeared the journal *Daedalus* published a translation of Jean Starobinski's essay 'Criticism and Authority', a brief history of the concept of criticism in France. E. D. Hirsch, Jr's *Validity in Interpretation*, published ten years earlier, had been one of the first books to bring the terms 'author' and 'authority' together for rhetorical purposes, and by the early 1980s, in the aftermath of the post-structuralist inquisitions into the Death of the Author and the Myth of the Author, this coupling had become a commonplace. Where Hirsch's theory of reading seeks to reinstate the authority of the author's intention, many of the more recent discussions of literary authority either register its loss or, where it is judged to have survived, they seek to undermine it. The ironies involved were neatly illustrated by a conference of the 'Literature Teaching Politics' group, held in England in 1984: the conference took 'Authority' as its main theme and one of the topics offered was 'The absence of authority as itself authoritative'.

Chapters 1 to 4 have been considerably revised for the present edition. The new Chapters 5, 6 and 7 discuss twentieth-century literary criticism written in English, so I have been forced to omit, or to cite in very summary fashion, a good deal of the criticism viii *Preface*

and theory that is currently discussed in university English departments; in some cases this is because I judge it to be ephemeral, but much of the material concerned is either not primarily literary, or is read in translation. Readers chiefly interested in multinational literary theory will find structuralism and deconstruction discussed in Chapter 6, and feminism and cultural theory in Chapter 7, with emphasis on the major English-language critics in each field. The future of a strictly literary criticism is also questioned – and re-affirmed – in these chapters.

For Chapters 5, 6 and 7 I am grateful for the encouragement provided by Beverley Tarquini and Caroline Egar at Macmillan, and the resources of the universities of Reading and California (Santa Barbara), where they were written. Coral Howells and Jenny Taylor gave generous encouragement and support, as well as stern criticism of my attempts to deal with feminist theory. Above all, I must thank Lilian Argrave for her patience and expertise during many hours of word-processing, and Jenny Bevan for her assistance. My debts to family, friends, colleagues and students, in a book first conceived at the University of Cambridge nearly two decades ago, are quite simply too numerous to mention. I would like, however, to dedicate this edition of *Authors and Authority* to the memory of three former colleagues and mentors, Ian Fletcher, Graham Hough and Raymond Williams. Each of them is present at particular moments in this book but, at a deeper level, their very different lives and outlook embodied the critical vocation as I understand it.

PATRICK PARRINDER
Reading, October 1990

Introduction

He points the deathbone and the quick are still.
He lifts the lifewand and the dumb speak.

James Joyce

Prophet or pedant; interpreter or judge; the critic stands, often uncomfortably, between Joyce's two aphorisms. Criticism of literature occupies the space between our modern concepts of 'author' and 'authority' – concepts which in the romance languages share the same root in the Latin verb *augeo*. There is a primal sense, perhaps, in which the *auctor* or creator, whether of narratives, laws or merchandise, possessed all the 'authority' that there was to be had. But as civilisation proceeded by the progressive division of labour, one kind of authority came to be pitted against another. The native force of the maker or originator was brought up against the common standards of society. Scholars find the origins of literary criticism in scattered comments on writers and texts; perhaps the first substantial critic is Aristophanes, who discusses the relative merits of Aeschylus, Sophocles and Euripides.[1] But the traces of a still earlier situation are present in the first document of criticism which still has a living force: the discussion of poetry and poets in Plato's *Republic*. Plato speaks of the 'old quarrel between philosophy and poetry'. In Book Three, he examines poetry from the standpoint of the interests of the state, and gives the classical exposition of the theory of censorship. In Book Ten, as if dissatisfied with this, he returns to the subject and discusses the intrinsic nature of art in terms of representation. But Plato himself has traditionally been understood as the most poetic and imaginative of philosophers. If this is accepted, he can be seen to fulfil all three of the possible roles of author, of spokesman for external (and ultimately political) authority, and of critic or aesthetician occupying the middle ground. In the latter role, he acknowledges the seductive 'natural magic' of poetry, but balances this against the demands of the reason before concluding that poetry ought to be banned. Of course, Plato's Republic is an imaginary city, a pattern laid up in heaven. But in the last two hundred and fifty years literary criticism, or the activity of rationalising the creative practice of

1

literature, has lost its innocence and acquired a political dimension. Its modern history involves the history of culture itself, and of the idea of culture, as well as of particular individuals, doctrines and approaches.

So far we have seen 'authority' as a property of the individual creator or of the community to whose standards he is expected to conform. The process of social specialisation which leads to the emergence of critical, historiographical, legal and other separate areas of intellectual discourse endows the occupants of these areas with a local and, as it were, delegated authority. As classical criticism took shape, a number of modes of authority emerged in critical discourse, which were to define the limits of the discipline until the time of Johnson. To do justice to the nature of traditional criticism lies outside the scope of this book. The kinds of authority which the critics exercised may, however, be briefly indicated by a contrast of the three major Greek and Roman commentators on literature: Aristotle, Horace and Longinus.

Aristotle in the *Poetics* relies on the rigorous prosecution of an intellectual method. He is able to show poetic phenomena as ordered and systematic by the use of a technique of logical analysis applicable to the human world as a whole. It was because he had already demonstrated the technique elsewhere that he could enter so swiftly and confidently into the first principles of poetics. At the same time, this trenchancy of method would be of little account were it not for the empirical relevance of his distinctions and his ability to support them with appropriate examples. But the intrinsic grounds of the appeal that he makes remain wholly intellectual, consisting in his scientific methodology and command of his material. The gulf between the language of his treatise and that of the tragedies it surveys is as wide as any to be found in Greek, or any subsequent culture.

Horace writes as an established poet. Since his 'Art of Poetry' takes the form of advice to beginners this alone would make his words impressive. It is the expression in verse of a cultivated and learned mind, full of shrewdness and good sense. His observations draw upon his individual experience both as writer and as audience, and the value of his criticism stands or falls by his personal adequacy in each of these roles. Longinus, by contrast, was so far from being a prominent intellectual that we do not know who he was. He also presents himself as an 'intelligent reader', but without Horace's magisterial complacency; for he is neither a celebrity nor a pioneer. 'On the Sublime' begins with a critique of an earlier treatment of its subject; it acknowledges itself as one work among many in a common convention of literary discussion. The more technical aspect of the convention derives from the discipline of rhetoric, but this is the source of a limited rather than an exhaustive methodology. Longinus' analytic, unlike Aristotle's, is derivative and structures only part of his treatise. What is outside it includes some vivid practical criticism on texts from the established canon, as well as general observations drawn from a shared stock of critical axioms, which the author shows a faint embarrassment about repeating.

At the risk of being over-schematic, then, each of the three critics assumes a different basis for his authority. Aristotle relies on the consistency of an intellectual method and its verifiability; Horace principally on the force of his literary personality; and Longinus on the cogent manipulation of methods and assumptions which are shared. In a sense it could be argued that these three provide permanent models for literary-critical activity, so that all subsequent critics could be loosely ranged behind one or the other of them. Coleridge, I. A. Richards and Northrop Frye are would-be Aristotelians. The English neoclassical critics and today's exponents of continental literary theory are for the most part content to remain as Longinian underlabourers. The traditional strength of English criticism, however, has lain in the Horatian mode. The major critics have been major, or at least important, poets: they are Sidney, Jonson, Dryden, Dr Johnson, Wordsworth, Coleridge, Arnold and T. S. Eliot. We might add two critic-novelists, Henry James and Virginia Woolf. For some of these, poetic and critical concerns were arguably separable, but the majority exploited their creative standing to give extra conviction to their criticism. It was Eliot who gave the best justification for this, when he wrote that 'The important critic is the person who is absorbed in the present problems of art, and who wishes to bring the forces of the past to bear upon the solution of these problems.'[2] The 'forces' of the past include the tradition of English criticism itself, since the major critics have invariably been closely and jealously aware of their predecessors' work. Setting out to create the taste by which they and their associates were to be enjoyed, they have played a crucial part in the revolutions of modern poetic history.

The study of criticism, then, is an approach to the dynamics of modern literary development, and especially the development of poetry. At the same time, criticism exhibits the inertia of any established intellectual discipline. The field is at once an index of literary change, and an accumulative, partially autonomous branch of knowledge; in the broadest sense, a science. In considering the relation between the historian's view of criticism and the ordinary critic's sense of his function at a particular time, I believe that it is useful to take account of recent debates on the history and sociology of science.

In *The Structure of Scientific Revolutions* (1962), Thomas Kuhn argued that a field of enquiry becomes a science when it possesses a generally accepted 'paradigm'. Paradigms are defined as authoritative models of cognitive practice, such as Newton's investigation of optics, which are capable of generating fruitful and coherent traditions of research. Once accepted by the scientific community, the paradigm establishes both a methodology and a delimited field of phenomena, conceived as problems or 'puzzles', to which the methodology may be applied. Phenomena which do not fit this field are treated as anomalous and their scientific significance is discounted. 'Normal science', in Kuhn's definition, is the activity of filling in the gaps, or exhaustively articulating the theories and phenomena which the paradigm identifies; and this term covers the greater part of scientific activity. In the end, however, the anomalies and areas of intractability can no longer be ignored, and the science enters a crisis-period which can only be resolved by paradigm change – the 'scientific revolution' of Kuhn's title.

In applying this set of ideas to literary criticism, we at once meet the irony that normal science is opposed by Kuhn to 'critical discourse'. Critical discourse is a relatively chaotic state of enquiry in which different schools compete with one another and there is no common body of belief. The individual worker is thus obliged to state and defend his basic assumptions, and has very limited scope for building on the work of others. Progress, therefore, is fragmentary and questionable. Such a state is found in non- or pre-scientific fields, and only reappears in science itself at moments of imminent paradigm change. Like most philosophers of science, Kuhn looks on the transition of a field of enquiry into a science as being desirable in itself. But not all his colleagues share this satisfaction with the humdrum and intellectually conformist pursuit of 'normal science', and one, Paul Feyerabend, has strongly re-stated the Kantian position that 'critical discourse' is a more humane and dignified process of enquiry.[3] If we look frankly at modern literary criticism, however, we shall surely discover that a good deal of it has the intellectual and sociological characteristics of a 'normal science'.

This parallel, if it is accepted, is something more than a diagnostic convenience. It is my hope that in considering criticism as it is and has been, readers will consider what it one day should be. My own view is that it is during the revolutionary periods in the arts, when criticism and new creation come closest together, that criticism realises its full potential as 'critical discourse'. Yet the shortcomings as well as the achievements of the romantic and modernistic literary revolutions are now increasingly manifest to us. Today it seems that a whole phase of literary authority, in which poet and critic were masters of the 'forces of the past', may be coming to an end. Does this mean, as some have suggested, the diminution or disappearance of the literary-critical function as we have known it? That issue will be debated in this book's final section.

1 Samuel Johnson: The Academy and the Market-Place

Neoclassicism: Dryden and Pope

Samuel Johnson was the first English author to practise criticism as a major literary genre. He did so in writings that are pungent and direct, with a force of argument and a sweep of generalisation that still speak to us vividly. And yet for all that his criticism is not easily understood. The voice is stentorian and unmistakable, but the words reflect not only his personality, but the age in which he felt so confidently at home. Johnson's criticism, in fact, offers a unique point of entry into the imagination of a lost literary age.

The greater part of his methods, language and assumptions as a critic were drawn from the movement that we now call neoclassicism. This term is the subject of continuing debate and confusion. In the chauvinistic view of the historian of criticism J. W. H. Atkins, neoclassicism was a narrow and vicious critical outlook imported from the Continent at the time of the Restoration. In the English setting it was characterised by the half-baked dogmatism of Rymer and Dennis, and the obsequious deference that even Dryden sometimes expressed towards second-rate French critics such as Rapin and Bossu. Gradually in the eighteenth century native empiricism and national pride (epitomised, of course, by Johnson) reawakened and struggled out from under the yoke. It is true that the early neoclassical doctrines came by way of France, where Corneille, Boileau and their followers had reduced the authority of Aristotle and Horace to a rigid system of rules. But the superficiality of Atkins's account was shown up by R. S. Crane, who argued that neoclassicism may be properly understood, not as an alien group of doctrines, but as the dominant temper of a whole century of English literary thought. Despite increasing divergences of doctrine and focus, it is possible to trace a common language and a common conceptual scheme in criticism from the Restoration to the death of Johnson. Crane defines neoclassicism as 'a large but historically distinguishable aggregate of commonplace distinctions, of a highly flexible and ambiguous kind, out of which many variant critical systems and doctrines could be constructed'.[1] Within the field of neoclassical debate we may then distinguish separate periods and separate national traditions; thus the English form looks back to Rome rather than Greece, and favours the authority of Horace over that of Aristotle. Crane's thesis, in effect, is that English neo-classicism is the critical language of 'Augustan' culture as a whole. Perhaps the relative homogeneity of eighteenth-century criticism will not seem surprising when we consider the degree of continuity in Augustan verse, from Dryden to Goldsmith and Cowper.

Some questions are certainly begged by this; notably, the relation between neoclassicism in literature and the other arts. But the emphasis on neoclassicism as a language, a shared set of ways of formulating and solving literary problems, is a helpful one. It should not be allowed to obscure the conflicts that do occur; the fact that Rapin and, say, Bishop Hurd 'talked a common critical language' does not mean that they agreed. Crane's 'structural' view of neo-classicism has a close affinity with the account of scientific development given by Kuhn, whose work was discussed in the Introduction. What he does, in effect, is to define neoclassicism in terms which suggest it may be considered as a Kuhnian 'paradigm'. A critical literature guided by common norms of discourse and a common range of problems is certainly on the way to becoming a 'normal science'. And since Augustan criticism represents the rationalisation of, and the prescription for, a large part of contemporary poetic practice, the scientific analogy might even be extended to the art of poetry itself. This analogy shows its relevance when we consider one of the most puzzling and even repellent features of Restoration and Augustan literature: the writers' arrogance about their own relation to the recent past. The eighteenth century believed that a decisive change had recently occurred, in poetry as well as in literary theory. English verse had just emerged from barbarity. As it happens, an important component of this change was the emergence of the scientific attitude as a major cultural force. Sprat's *History of the Royal Society* (1667) was a manifesto both for experimental science and for the rationalisation of literary style.

In his book *The Burden of the Past and the English Poet*, W. J. Bate not only calls this change a revolution, but argues that it was the only genuine revolution in English literary history.[2] In chronological terms it virtually coincides with the only political event in English history which is traditionally called a revolution: the Glorious Revolution of 1688 which consecrated the new society in which Augustanism flourished. Yet it is difficult to conceive of a meaningful revolution in politics, art or science without an 'ancien régime' to overthrow, and where, in the case of neoclassi-cism, was that 'ancien régime'? The metaphysical poets and Jacobean dramatists whose work was supplanted after the Restoration hardly constituted an active opposition. The London theatres had been closed for nearly two decades, and the Civil War had put a stop to metropolitan culture. After the hiatus Dryden did not risk unpopularity when he 'modernised' the plays of Shakespeare, while the rise of Waller's reputation as one of the poets who harmonised English versification and 'reformed our numbers' was rapid and complete. He was first singled out in Soames's translation of Boileau (1683);[3] his claims as pioneer were rapidly endorsed by Rymer and Dryden, and still held the field in Johnson's *Lives of the Poets*. Waller died in 1687; few minor poets can have made such an easy conquest of posthumous fame. The 'strong lines' of the metaphysicals were abandoned, by Dryden among others, as a vein that had been worked out, and a new generation grew up for whom Herbert and Marvell were hardly even names.

It would seem, then, that the victory of neoclassicism resembles not so much a revolution ('paradigm change') as the creation of a 'normal science'. The Augustans were not faced with concerted opposition in the way that the romantics were, and so theirs was not a literary revolution on the modern pattern. In criticism, the end of the seventeenth century saw the schematisation and rationalisation of what had earlier been a far less organised and self-conscious group of activities. The discussion of writing was no longer confined to textbooks of rhetoric and to a largely oral tradition. We know virtually nothing about the arguments at the Mermaid Tavern, or between the Elizabethan dramatist and the other members of his company of actors. Something of the seventeenth-century poet's assumptions may be reconstructed from isolated texts like Ben Jonson's notebooks or Carew's elegy on Donne. But it was a very important advance that led to the proliferation of critical writing as a separate branch of intellectual activity, and also to the convention of the critical preface in which the writer stated his premises and defended his work. With neoclassicism, criticism ceased to be a largely private and oral activity and became a recognised intellectual discipline, playing its part in the rational pursuit of knowledge. The proliferation of critical activity in the eighteenth century is illustrated by any bibliography of the period. To take two popular genres: editions of Shakespeare were compiled by Rowe (1709), Pope (1725), Theobald (1735), Hanmer (1744), Warburton (1747), Johnson (1765), Capell (1768), Steevens (1773) and Malone (1790). Authors of essays on taste include Addison (1712), Hutcheson (1725), Hume (1757), Burke (1757), Gerard (1759), Kames (1762) and Alison (1790). It is this development, decisively affecting the nature of literature itself, which gives the scientific analogy for neoclassical criticism its validity.

The change did not happen at once. The critical texts of Dryden and Rymer do not themselves lay claim to any very high intellectual status; that was a construction that would be put upon them slightly later. Dryden, the first of the major English poet-critics, is relaxed, well-informed and opportunistic; he discovered in the critical preface a new and congenial way of commending his work to its readers. Rymer in *The Tragedies of the Last Age* (1677), with his extraordinarily crude and bumptious manner, is still quicker to assure us that he is 'not cut out for writing a Treatise, nor have a genius to pen anything exactly'. Whatever their other differences, both are far removed from the formality and self-discipline of scientific and philosophical discourse. And yet it is clear that Rymer, Dryden and their contemporaries thought of the new order they were introducing in literature as rational and scientific. Their manner might be informal, but the doctrines they were imparting to their readers had the sanction of the ancients and the prestige of acceptance throughout polite Europe. The practice of writing was henceforth to be guided by rules and precedents – rules which were 'Nature methodiz'd', as Pope was later to put it, and precedents stamped with the authority of Aristotle, Horace and their many translators and commentators. English versification was already being harmonised and regularised, and the history of English literature had to be formulated and shown as a prehistory – a slow ascent from darkness to the daylight of the present in which, for the first time, the perfection of English writing could be realised.

The neoclassical paradigm, then, was drawn from the received interpretations of Aristotle, Horace, Longinus, Quintilian and others. Its practical embodiment was found in the various classical literary forms, especially Greek tragedy and Roman satire, supported by the body of modern literature on strict critical principles such as French neoclassical tragedy. The elasticity of the system was greatly augmented by the variety of the classical forms from which precedents could be drawn. In England, however, the attempt to rationalise the literary tradition quickly ran into a major anomaly. It was not necessary to overthrow the foundations of Elizabethan drama in favour of the new principles, since those foundations had been almost entirely oral and implicit; in fact the neoclassical critics constructed a rationale of the native drama for the first time. Their difficulty was in making the rationale consistent, and, above all, in determining the place of Shakespeare within it.

Among those who adopted a rational standard was Sprat, who in the *History of the Royal Society* attacked allegorical and fanciful writing as a mode of superstition. There was Thomas Rymer, who, though impressive in his command of Greek tragedy, took it as a universal scientific norm, the 'straight line' against which the English dramatists were shown to have drawn woefully 'crooked' lines. Rymer's homely imagery and truculent appeals to common sense are notable; he follows Aristotle, but disclaims the pretensions of a learned 'Doctor of Subtilties'. He gives the impression of a provincial magistrate who sees the national veneration of Shakespeare and Beaumont and Fletcher as – like witchcraft or sorcery – popular superstitions to be rooted out. His second book, *A Short View of Tragedy* (1692), is a good deal more inquisitorial than *The Tragedies of the Last Age*, and contains his notorious onslaught on *Othello*. In the wake of the romantic idolisation of Shakespeare, Macaulay was to call Rymer 'the worst critic that ever lived', and his whole performance was an ignominious defeat for rationalism when applied to poetry. He could produce any number of arguments to ridicule Shakespeare, but was quite incapable of explaining the sources of tragic power, even in the classical dramas he set up as models.

Rymer was the kind of pioneer who never gets his due because he gives the whole discipline a bad name. His example reveals how important it was for the neoclassical critics to establish a conventional attitude to the literature of the past. Sneering superiority was not enough, and Johnson, eighty years afterwards, could put down Rymer simply by observing that he was a critical bully.[4] Dryden, however, was less sure-footed in his response. His disagreements with *The Tragedies of the Last Age* were stated, even in the private notes known as the 'Heads of an Answer to Rymer', with a good deal of deference. It was only after *A Short View*, fifteen years later, that he spoke out against Rymer's tone and motivation:

> But there is another sort of Insects, more venomous than the former. Those who manifestly aim at the destruction of our Poetical Church and State. Who allow nothing to their Countrymen, either of this or of the former Age. These attack the Living by raking up the Ashes of the Dead. Well knowing that if they can subvert their Original Title to the Stage, we who claim under them, must fall of course. Peace be to the Venerable Shades of Shakespear, and Ben Johnson: None of the Living will presume to have any competition with them: as they were our Predecessours, so they were our Masters.

Even this passage from the Dedication of *Examen Poeticum* can hardly be read without a suspicion of humbug; it is addressed to a patron and is but one of the twists and turns of Dryden's career, as he veers between reverent and debunking attitudes to his Jacobean predecessors. Dryden himself wanted the credit for the revision of English drama, and feared a venomous critic who might well go on to 'attack the Living'. The relation between the Jacobeans and his own generation was a question that worried him incessantly, and it was he who established the convention whereby a great predecessor is simultaneously revered and patronised, professions of love being accompanied by an ostentatious tolerance and a careful enumeration of faults. This is the norm in English criticism down to Johnson's 'Preface to Shakespeare' (it is even unconsciously parodied in Coleridge's criticism of Wordsworth); the result is an elegant compromise between the rational, scientific attitude that favours the contemporary, and the recognition of poetry as a liberal art with an emotive basis and a duty to honour its founding fathers.[5]

Though he eventually rejected Rymer, Dryden did not reject the rationalistic outlook that I have sketched. He was no theoretician himself, but his mind was immensely well-stocked with the theories of others, whose authority he assiduously invoked; he defended the propositions of the essay *Of Dramatick Poesie* (1668), for example, as 'derived from the authority of Aristotle and Horace, and from the rules and examples of Ben Jonson and Corneille'. Dryden's attitude is very different from that of Johnson,who defended his predecessor against charges of casuistry with the memorable remark that 'Reason wants not Horace to support it'. For Dryden, reason did want Horace. Submissiveness to authority, however, did not prevent him from reflecting the explicitly scientific element in Restoration criticism, notably in the essay *Of Dramatick Poesie*, where he relies upon Baconian and Ptolemaic arguments at two crucial points. The four speakers in the *Essay* engage in successive debates between the ancients and the moderns, French drama and English, and blank verse and rhyme. Crites, speaking first in defence of the ancients, describes the intellectual context in which all these debates take place. Natural science, he argues, has been revolutionised in the past hundred years, and 'more Noble Secrets in Opticks, Medicine, Anatomy, Astronomy, [have been] discover'd, than in all those credulous and doting Ages from Aristotle to us.' What then should happen to literature? Crites himself raises the scientific analogy only to deflect it; writers can best succeed in copying Nature by copying the ancients. But Eugenius, his opponent, does not miss his opportunity:

for if Natural Causes be more known now than in the time of
Aristotle, because more studied, it follows that Poesie and other
Arts may with the same pains arrive still nearer to perfection. . . .

Later on, Lisideius argues that French drama is superior to the
English because the French writers have observed the rules,
and the rules, after all, are nature methodised. English drama,
on the other hand, bears all the marks of its lowly origins as
popular entertainment. The English stage, with its duels and
battles, is 'too like the Theaters where they fight Prizes'. The
most important rules, in the Aristotelian tradition, are those
concerning the plot, and it is here that Elizabethan drama seems
most easily faulted. Neander defends it, however, on the grounds
that it is closer to nature, and one of the arguments he uses
is distinctly ingenious. It consists of a complicated analogy in
which the multiple subplots of the English drama are compared
to the Ptolemaic systems of the universe in which 'contrary motions
may be found ... to agree', and 'a Planet can go East and
West at the same time'. The use of Ptolemaic cosmology (the
complexities of which are also explored by Milton and Donne)
suggests a more sophisticated notion of artistic harmony than
the straightforward Aristotelian one. If the rules are on the
side of the French, the actual study of natural science is on
the side of the English.

It is important that Dryden should have voiced such arguments,
but it is far from clear that he held them with full conviction. There
are other features of the *Essay* and of Dryden's criticism in general
which point in a very different direction. Dryden is a fine example
of the practitioner-critic, the first English poet to have left vivid
discussions of versification and the poet's craft. It was also he who
turned English criticism into an artistic genre in its own right, since
whatever we may think of the arguments of the *Essay*, it is rarely
less than a pleasure to read. The imaginary setting is that of a
boat-trip down the Thames to witness a naval engagement with
the Dutch. This is criticism as the polite conversation of gentlemen
(leading not to discord but to mutual compromise) on a patriotic
social occasion. The result is confused and unsystematic, and yet
it is the nearest that Dryden ever came to a methodical treatise.
The best of his criticism is found not in such things as the 'Examen'
of Ben Jonson's *The Silent Woman* – though this has been predictably cried up as the ancestor of modern practical criticism[6] – but
in his more relaxed and conversational writing, for example in
the remarks on translation in several of his essays which bring
together his experience as a poet and his classical learning.

Dryden's intellectual opportunism and his increasing diffuseness prevent him from being a critic of the first rank, but his work is a unique expression of the English literary mind becoming conscious of itself.

To become conscious of itself was to declare its independence of natural science. A generation after Dryden, Swift satirised the scientists of Laputa, and Pope mocked the flower-growers and butterfly-hunters in the *Dunciad*. Neoclassical criticism had turned away from the intellectual purism of a Sprat or a Rymer to define its own ideal of rationality. The result was a social as well as a literary ideal, associating poetic excellence with a particular understanding of 'culture' as refinement, decorum and polish. In Dryden's prefaces to his plays, for example, we are at once aware of the dramatist (unlike Shakespeare) professionally seeing his work through the press, and of his self-projection as a man of gentility and learning far superior to those of his actors. The way was now opened for the definition of the 'standard of taste' and the identification of literature with cultivated enjoyment that were so widespread in the eighteenth century. The test of pleasure, indeed, played a significant part in the essay *Of Dramatick Poesie*, where the argument between French and English drama became a contrast of French tragedy and English tragicomedy – the former high art, and the latter closer to mere entertainment. Dryden's notion of tragedy was a highly secular one, reducing it to a matter of theatrical technique with no more powerful emotional impact than could be contained within the category of pleasure; and the result was that he discussed it on equal terms with comedy, and favoured the latter, English, form. (Later, under the short-lived influence of Rymer, he reverted to the classical notion of tragic dignity.)

Taste, as the Augustans defined it, was essentially a comparative exercise. David Hume, in what is perhaps the classic essay on the 'Standard of Taste' (1742), saw it as the prerogative of 'one accustomed to see and examine and weigh the several performances, admired in different ages and nations'. The operation is evidently an objective one, suggesting the availability of critical microscopes, forceps and balances. In order to achieve objectivity the critic had to free the mind of prejudice. When Hume discusses what it is to be free of all prejudice, he not only concludes that 'few are qualified to give judgment on any work of art' but makes out these few to be such paragons of virtue that it would seem a tragic waste for them to devote their time to literary criticism. The ideal Man of Taste would no doubt be Plato's philosopher-king, but it is ludicrous to pretend that this has much to do with the actual judging of literary works. Given the belief in a universal standard of taste, no wonder a man of the world such as Addison took a short cut and declared that the best works were those which had the sanction of the ages and of the 'Politer Part of our Contemporaries'.[7]

For Addison and Pope, the equation of literature and polite learning was quite explicit. Addison's critical papers in the *Spectator* (1711–14) were dedicated to raising the general level of public taste. Central to his purpose was the series of essays which definitively established *Paradise Lost* as a great classic. His commentary on the poem follows an orthodox Aristotelian procedure, and its literary intention is plainly to elevate Milton to a place beside Homer and Virgil. At the same time, Milton was an English Christian poet, and Addison's essays, which appeared on Saturdays, were meant as edifying literature suitable for reading on Sundays. This result was achieved by direct hints at the poem's devotional value, together with a liberal use of the term which would come to express the idea of tragic and epic dignity in Augustan writing – the adjective 'sublime'. The category of sublimity, deriving from Longinus's treatise and its translation by Boileau, helped bridge the gap between the moralistic attitude of Rymer and the hedonism of Dryden; it denotes a mode of pleasure or amazement which both edifies and exalts. Addison's stress on sublimity and the faculty of taste foreshadows the movement from objective to subjective and psychological criteria which – all observers are agreed – is the main development of eighteenth-century aesthetics. But although taste is in some sense inborn, he stresses the objective means by which it may be cultivated and improved; prominent among these are 'Conversation with Men of a Polite Genius', and reading the critics.

The air of genteel decorum is even stronger in Pope's 'Essay on Criticism' (1711). Both Addison and Pope introduced a new subject-matter, which reflects the growing volume of critical activity. They discuss the qualifications of the critic, the faults and prejudices to which he is subject and the ideal conduct of his discipline. Pope's poem is in fact a series of versified instructions to young critics, where Horace's 'Ars Poetica' consisted of instructions to young poets. As the critic's qualifications, Pope proposes Truth and Candour in addition to the conventional triad of Taste, Judgment and Learning. Above all, he should conduct himself as a gentleman, 'Tho' learn'd, well-bred; and tho' well-bred, sincere.' The theme of good manners dominates Pope's thumbnail sketches of the 'Happy Few' who make up the history of criticism. Horace, for example,

still charms with graceful Negligence,
And without Method talks us into Sense,
Will like a Friend familiarly convey
The truest Notions in the easiest way.

Among the moderns is Roscommon, the translator of Horace's
'Art of Poetry' (1680):

not more learn'd than good,
With Manners gen'rous as his Noble Blood;
To him the Wit of Greece and Rome was known,
And ev'ry Author's Merit, but his own

– a winning combination of the classical virtues and native British
modesty. Such modesty is fitting in a culture which holds that standards are already fixed and that the common sense of mankind
is already enshrined in the literary tradition. Pope memorably
defined wit ('What oft was thought, but ne'er so well expressed')
in such a way as to virtually exclude innovation, and Addison,
in his review of the 'Essay on Criticism', endorsed this: 'Wit and
fine Writing doth not consist so much in advancing Things that
are new, as in giving Things that are known an agreeable Turn.'
Now this must mean that while current literary discourse is confined
to the pursuit of ever-increasing politeness, it was not always so;
and the way is open for the growth of that pervasive inferiority
complex which W. J. Bate has called 'the burden of the past'.
Pope writes of the modern poet who 'Glows while he reads, but
trembles as he writes', and his panegyric of the ancients verges
on the bardolatry of Gray and Collins:

Hail Bards Triumphant! born in happier Days;
Immortal Heirs of Universal Praise!
Whose Honours with Increase of Ages grow,
As Streams roll down, enlarging as they flow!
Nations unborn your mighty Names shall sound,
And Worlds applaud that must not yet be found!

The implication is that the unborn nations and undiscovered worlds
will equally respond to the classical poets who have expressed the
universal truths of human nature. In the same passage the ancients
are seen as altars to which the learned of today bring their tribute
of incense. This was still, however, deliberate hyperbole; it had
not yet become an inescapable way of understanding the literary
past.

Apart from venerating the ancients, what could the neoclassical poet do? He could cultivate new genres (the various forms of mock-epic, topographical and descriptive verse); he could 'imitate' and translate; and he could shoulder that sense of social responsibility for literature which is so notable in Pope and the other Augustan poets. Dryden translated Virgil and Ovid; Pope translated Homer and edited Shakespeare; Johnson abandoned poetry for editorial and lexicographical tasks; Pope and Gray projected histories of English poetry, and Johnson projected a history of criticism. These were congenial and, at times, financially rewarding tasks; Pope received over £5000 for his translation of Homer. It was unfortunate that the poets could not always fulfil what they promised, so that the history of poetry was left to Thomas Warton (1774–81), and that of criticism to Harris's *Philological Enquiries* (1781). But such tasks increasingly demanded a degree of specialised application which a major writer could not undertake. Pope's and Johnson's editions of Shakespeare, for example, broached problems which could only be solved by academic textual scholarship.The idea that poets themselves should be responsible for consolidating their art as one of the branches of learning could not be expected to last long. But the Augustans' zeal for this was certainly remarkable.

There were urgent reasons for it. If Dryden or Pope did not step in to translate the classics, the job would be botched by some-body else; it was already being botched by somebody else. It was necessary, not only to create the series of authoritative editions and institutional handbooks that English literature so badly needed, but to snatch this task out of the hands of servile pedants and unscrupulous hacks. Dryden and Pope were concerned at once to raise the intellectual dignity of literature and to impose con-ditions of fair dealing (both between authors and publishers and between authors and public) on the literary market. The fact that these two concerns went together suggests that the gentility and decorum of neoclassical criticism was always something of a façade. The Man of Taste reflected the ethos of the patrons rather than of the authors themselves. To take their doctrines only at face value would be to forget that their ultimate source lay not so much in the Roman Empire, as in the writer's precarious position in eighteenth-century society.

Early neoclassicism held that with the Restoration English litera-ture had reached a pitch of refinement which would at last permit it to aspire to perfection. That position was maintained for a long time – certainly by Johnson – and yet with increasing misgivings. On the one hand, writing was seen as a gentlemanly pursuit, and the ideal Man of Taste defined by Addison and Hume was a being to be regarded with reverence. But then David Hume was one of many writers who were convinced by the 1740s that cultural refinement entailed artistic decadence; and long before this, for writers less bland and financially secure than the Scottish philosopher, literature had been degraded to a servile trade. The conditions of sweated literary labour are vividly portrayed in works like Fielding's *The Author's Farce* (1730), though hack writing was no new phenomenon of the Augustan age. What was new, however, was the intrusion of the concepts of writing for hire, of the author's economic status and also of the parasitic and uncreative quality of much literary work into almost every level of literary consciousness. It is because the 'Essay on Criticism' shuts out such consciousness, and makes literature preternaturally respectable, that it is such a thin work, badly needing to be complemented by a *Dunciad*. The sociology of Augustan writing, and in particular the vast expansion of fiction, journalism and other sub-literary forms which sustained an author like Defoe, are of very great relevance here. The level of economic competition promoted a new atmosphere of mercantilism and gang-warfare in literature, comparable to the Paris of Balzac's *Illusions Perdues* a century later. The greatest writers of the period reflect this in the sense of a fallen and degraded culture which is found in Pope's *Dunciad*, and in the antics of the Scriblerus Club out of which the *Dunciad* and *Gulliver's Travels* emerged.

Martinus Scriblerus, according to the *Memoirs* concocted by Pope and Gay (1741), was the son of Cornelius, a Walter Shandy-like figure devoted to the ancients and determined to provide the perfect upbringing for his son. Young Martin, however, was led astray by Crambe, his fellow-pupil, and gave himself up to the vanities and follies of the moderns. The first evidence of this was the treatise *Peri Bathous*, written in youth and carefully hidden from his father. *Peri Bathous: or, of the Art of Sinking in Poetry*, published by Pope in 1727, is in fact a satire containing its own succinct assessment of the Grub-Street dilemma. Literature is traditionally understood as a contest of excellence, with the honours going only to the few who reach the top of Parnassus. But what if it is now revealed in its true colours as a trade – a woefully labour-intensive industry? Isn't it reasonable for a trade-union attitude, demanding equal rewards for all, to be adopted? The goal can be achieved – for all but a few surly Parnassians – by the simple expedient of redefining the standard of excellence as the 'Bathos'. This solution is something more than a Tory satire on trendy mediocrity, for Pope's view of Dulness is ultimately aimed not at individual opponents but at the Age, and the Age will be found to include himself.

Scriblerus went on to become a great critic, as well as a great traveller, scientist and mathematician. He is the academic rather than the Grub Street critic, and is alleged to be the real author of Richard Bentley's notorious commentary on *Paradise Lost*. Later he emerges as the protean editor, explicator, annotator and presiding genius of the *Dunciad*, and as the theoretician of the genre of Dunciad or 'little epic'. Now Pope, the creator of Scriblerus, himself entertained the lifelong ambition of writing a major epic; one of his plans for this turned upon 'civil and ecclesiastical government'.[8] Not only are his great productions mock-epics, but they establish a literary context in which true epic no longer seems possible. And yet, though one cannot build a horse in the age of the steam-engine, horse-power can be put to new purposes. The *Dunciad* begins by parodying the *Aeneid*, it runs through innumerable borrowings from Virgil and Milton, and comes to us as a Variorum already encrusted with glosses and commentaries: the perfect synthetic ancient text. By its degraded incorporation of the great epics it reduces them to the status of discarded commodities; as if after Scriblerus has taken his pickings, they are no more than the abandoned shells of secondhand cars. The *Dunciad* may have exceeded Pope's intentions in its debunking of the aura which surrounded the classical epics and was already thickening around Milton. As for contemporary poetry, it is unnecessary to enumerate the multitude of ways in which the *Dunciad* reveals it as a mug's game, a fecund anarchy of knaves and humbugs, buffoons and sharks. Beyond Pope's attacks on his enemies we can sometimes glimpse the inexorable bathos of authorship itself:

> While pensive Poets painful vigils keep,
> Sleepless themselves, to give their readers sleep.

Poetry is not the expression of sublimity, heroism or good manners, it would seem, but the musty product of bookshop and printing-press, library and garret. Pope could pen a salute to the 'Bards Triumphant' of ancient times like any of his contemporaries, but he reflected his age far more profoundly in his epic of scribblers and critics. Johnson was his heir in confronting the thinness and blandness of so much neoclassical theorising; with insights as pungent as Pope's, he was to write criticism that took account of the full experience of writing in his time.

Minim, the *Dictionary* and the *Life of Savage*

Samuel Johnson went to London to seek his fortunes in 1773, at the age of twenty-eight. For some years he lived in extreme poverty, producing, among other things, fictitious reports of parliamentary debates for the printer Edward Cave. His *Life of Mr Richard Savage* attracted notice in 1744 (the year of Pope's death), and a year later he published a pamphlet of *Miscellaneous Observations on the Tragedy of Macbeth*. Soon afterwards he began work on the monumental *Dictionary*, not published until 1755, and although many of his critical views were first outlined in his periodical essays for the *Rambler* (1750–2), he did not embark upon a sustained literary–critical project until his edition of Shakespeare, published in 1765. By the time he received the commission for the *Lives of the Poets* in 1777, he had spent nearly forty years in literary London and had risen from Grub Street hack to the dominant man of letters of his day.

Johnson did not make his name by literary criticism, and he had a low enough opinion of those who did. The scientific analogy invoked at the start of this chapter assumed that there was a kind of journeyman practice of neoclassical criticism analogous to 'normal science'. In fact it was Johnson, in two brief essays in the *Idler* (1759), who drew the most devastating portrait we have of the critic as normal scientist. Dick Minim is an opportunist who takes advantage of the rapid development of criticism as a profession. After working as a brewer's apprentice, he picks up his critical knowledge orally, by listening to the talk in coffee-houses, and supplements this with some desultory reading. Having thus conversed with men of polite genius and read the critics, he has acquired the qualifications of Addison's Man of Taste, and launches himself as a critic. His reputation is made with a few precepts cribbed from the classical authorities, and a fine art of circumlocution and temporising when it comes to actually passing judgment. His success is so great that by the end he is majestically receiving pupils:

He then puts on a very serious air; he advises the pupil to read none but the best authors, and, when he finds one congenial to his own mind, to study his beauties, but avoid his faults, and, when he sits down to write, to consider how his favourite author would think at the present time on the present occasion. He exhorts him to catch those moments when he finds his thoughts expanded and his genius exalted, but to take care lest imagination hurry him beyond the bounds of nature. . . . He tells him, that every man has his genius, and that Cicero could never be a poet. The boy retires illuminated, resolves to follow his genius, and to think how Milton would have thought; and Minim feasts upon his own beneficence till another day brings another pupil.

The pupil might be imagined as a future critic or man of taste, in which case Minim is taking good care to make his own profession more of a closed shop than when he was a boy. But though the pupil may turn out a critic, he seems to have gone to Minim for advice on becoming a poet – and with this in mind, Johnson's paragraph is one of the deadliest satires ever written on literary education. The modern reader is not alone in being made uncomfortable by it; scholars have pointed out that, while most of Minim's pronouncements are the small change of neoclassicism, and some are Johnson's peculiar *bêtes noires*, others express opinions of his own.[1] Something may also be deduced from the restrained and muted tone of the essay on Minim. It is not so much that of a writer flaying the dunces who are his political and literary enemies, as that of a critic listening appalled to something not unlike the sound of his own voice. 'He whom nature has made weak, and idleness keeps ignorant, may yet support his vanity by the name of a critick': in this we may detect the note of self-laceration that we find in Johnson's private diaries and prayers.

While this is conjectural, there is certainly a problem about what Minim stands for. Reynolds in a subsequent number of the *Idler* referred to Johnson's 'ridicule of those shallow criticks, whose judgment, tho' often right as far as it goes, yet reaches only to inferior beauties, and who . . . from thence determine the merit of extensive works'.[2] It is true that the specimen of Minim's textual explications that we are given is so close to some aspects of modern critical practice that one wonders how many present-day students have ever been told to read the essay. But Minim is more than a finical mediocrity – he is a social and cultural phenomenon. First of all, he is a rentier, having been set free to become a 'man of wit and humour' by a large inherited fortune – a type that Johnson, with his Grub Street experience and lifelong class-consciousness,[3] bitterly detested. Second, he is a would-be academician, a middleman whose aim is to increase the pomp and prestige of the critical Establishment so that he can shine ever brighter in the reflected glory of the poets and sages. Johnson – as he had made clear in the *Life of Roscommon* (1748) – hated the idea of an English Academy. Minim's real reason for supporting it, he implies, is that he sees himself as its President, since he enjoys the next best thing in his presidency of a 'critical society elected by himself, where he is heard without contradiction'. In this society he occupies the 'chair of criticism' (it is obvious what sort of chair he would occupy today).

Criticism, then, has become a career, and writing has entered a new stage of institutionalisation. Johnson's position, shielded by the deadpan irony of the essays on Minim, remains a puzzling one. As biographer, editor and lexicographer he himself was one of the major institutionalising forces in English literature, yet he was also powerfully iconoclastic.

Johnson believed in cultural progress – he felt he had seen it in his own lifetime – and the great labours of his career were undertaken in the cause of such progress: they were the *Dictionary* (described by his friend and biographer Arthur Murphy as 'the MOUNT ATLAS of English literature'), the *Rambler*, the *Lives of the Poets* and the edition of Shakespeare. These works made their author into a national figure and led to his presiding over a literary circle which might well have become the nucleus of an English Academy. Johnson's Club was founded in 1764, and its members were such men as Reynolds, Burke, Goldsmith, Garrick, the Wartons, Adam Smith, Fox, Sheridan and Gibbon – the leading intellectuals of the age. The Club has far more of an institutional air than the Scriblerus clique of Pope, Swift and their allies, not to speak of the literary kangaroo court of Dick Minim. The degree of unity among its members was a good deal less than could be found in most academic communities today; Johnson himself was not above remarking that some of his colleagues deserved hanging for their political and religious views.[4] The exact nature of Johnson's authority over this dining club is hard to determine, since we rely so heavily on Boswell's glowing accounts. There is no doubt, however, that the legend of the Club contributed to the hardening of his reputation as a literary dictator after his death. Boswell showed him as the victor in innumerable exchanges, and when the neoclassical consensus had been abandoned it became easy to caricature him, as Wordsworth did in the 'Essay Supplementary', lording it over 'the little senate to which he gave laws'. We owe a considerable amount of his reputation as a tyrant to the impressionability of Boswell and the propaganda of the romantics.

The same causes have tended to trivialise Johnson's iconoclasm, which came to be seen as the splenetic outbursts of an English eccentric, lovable when he was kicking the stone, and hateful when he did the same to Milton's 'Lycidas'. But Johnson's opposition to an academy – his argument was that it would either fail to agree, or to exact obedience in respect of whatever it had agreed upon – reflects a fundamental suspicion of certain kinds of authority that may be traced throughout his thought. In directly political terms, he stated his position in a pamphlet on *The Bravery of the English Common Soldiers* (1767). Here he argued that English soldiers were braver than the French because of the degree of civil liberty and independence that they enjoyed. Englishmen, thanks to their legal and economic advantages, were naturally anarchists, but 'their insolence in peace is bravery in war'. A cohesive society, in other words, is one that gives the widest scope to plurality and independence, using coercion only as a last resort. The implicit model here is evidently that of Hanoverian constitutional monarchy as against the absolutism of the French. Johnson's charity toward plebeian insolence did not extend to 'surly and acrimonious' republicans such as Milton.

Johnson's letter to Lord Chesterfield (1755) dispensing with his patronage is his own most famous display of anti-authoritarian insolence. In fact, the manner of his rupture with Chesterfield sums up his intellectual as well as his personal relations with the patron who had looked to him as a 'dictator' to correct and purify the English tongue.[5] Chesterfield was the successor of Roscommon, Swift and others in proclaiming the need for the stabilisation of English, after the manner of the French Academy. Johnson, however, came to see the lexicographer's task as predominantly descriptive rather than prescriptive. Without wholly disappointing those who would look to his *Dictionary* for authority and direction, he sought to convey his sense of the inherent uncertainty and fluctuation of language. The task – conceived in accordance with the 'spirit of English liberty' – was not to fix, but to conserve.[6] Johnson's outlook, in fact, was that of an emergent Tory nationalism, resolutely opposing the authoritarianism of Academies just as it opposed French absolutism and 'popery'.

This resentment of absolutism is very strikingly found in his attitude to the literary tradition. Johnson was full of scorn for those who unnecessarily increased the 'burden of the past', seeing them as part of a 'general conspiracy of human nature against contemporary merit'.[7] His brisk reminder that 'reason wants not Horace to support it' has already been cited; and at the core of his opposition to most forms of literary antiquarianism and ancestor-worship there is his awareness of the tremendous power conferred by the 'sanction of antiquity':

> The faults of a writer of acknowledged excellence are more dangerous, because the influence of his example is more extensive; and the interest of learning requires that they should be discovered and stigmatized, before they have the sanction of antiquity conferred upon them, and become precedents of indisputable authority.   (*Rambler* no. 93)

Johnson's writings contain many statements like this, and many expressions of wariness and suspicion when he confronts a writer of 'acknowledged excellence'. Nor does he shirk the consequence of this, that no authority shall be indisputable in the light of reason – in literature at least. In ethics and theology, as we shall see, it is another matter.

In several ways, Johnson's forthright adherence to 'reason' in critical matters[8] is linked to his adherence to 'nature'. Both terms signalise his emphatically non-specialist approach to literature. He constantly resolves what we might think of as purely aesthetic problems – such as the value of tragicomedy, the unities, or Milton's pastorals – by a down-to-earth resort to standards of verisimilitude and common sense. Such standards do not suggest the need for any special literary expertise, and they reveal Johnson's steadfast opposition to those who sought to raise the qualifications for literary judgment out of reach of the common reader. Addison had implied that taste could be easily and docilely acquired by cultivating the classics, but later writers such as Hume (and eventually Wordsworth) saw its acquisition as an arduous and exacting discipline. Johnson, however, would have agreed with his friend Burke that 'the true standard of the arts is in every man's power'.[9] This means that some blunt and plain-spoken criticism must be expected, and Johnson's refusal to allow Milton to allegorise (or, in plain language, to tell lies) about shepherds and flocks in 'Lycidas' was a blow struck against literary sophistication and critical gentility which continues to reverberate. Johnson's view of the literary world in general is that such blows ought to be struck. The individual should make his voice heard. His own experience as self-made writer, victim of patronage and despiser of well-heeled mediocrity lies behind the overtly dispassionate conclusion to his discussion of academies in the *Life of Roscommon*: 'The present manners of the nation would deride authority, and therefore nothing is left but that every writer should criticise himself.' The only guidelines he would offer, where literature alone is at issue, are those of reason and nature.

The dialectic of authority and iconoclasm in Johnson's thought led him to seek an accommodation between individualist and institutional views of culture; and I have suggested that the model for this lay in the idea of constitutional monarchy. What do we actually mean, however, by these different ways of looking at culture? The question of the Academy which exercised Johnson is part of the problem with which we are concerned. Another part, of which he may not have been conscious, is the meaning of the word 'literature' itself.

According to the *New English Dictionary*, the modern sense of 'literature' as 'literary productions as a whole; the body of writings produced in a particular country or period' is of very recent emergence. In Johnson's *Dictionary* the word is only defined in the older sense of 'learning; skill in letters'. Johnson in fact saw 'learning', 'letters' and 'literature' as a triad of concepts to be defined in terms of one another. 'Literature' in this sense may be either the attribute of a learned individual (a frequent Johnsonian usage) or of a group or nation; one of the illustrations of the *Dictionary* sense is Bacon's assertion that 'This kingdom hath been famous for good Literature.' In both cases, however, the word has an active sense, denoting a type of human attainment. During the later eighteenth century – a period which, as Raymond Williams has shown,[10] saw decisive changes in the meanings of 'art', 'class', democracy', 'culture' and 'industry' – 'literature' came to be used in a passive, institutional sense, to denote a body of works already in existence. The *NED* gives an intermediate, active/ passive sense of 'literary work or production; the activity or profession of a man of letters; the realm of letters', first instanced in Johnson's 'Life of Cowley' (1779). Johnson, whether he knew it or not, played an important part in the change of meaning, and he was also influential in propagating the neologism 'literary'. This word does not figure in the *Dictionary* (1755). But in 1756 Johnson was connected with the *Literary Magazine*, and in 1779, after the death of Garrick, his own Club was christened the Literary Club. Johnson used 'literature' occasionally in the *Lives of the Poets* in a sense incompatible with his *Dictionary* definition, and – more importantly – he had much earlier shown a liking for the word in an elevated and patriotic context, as in this famous sentence from the Preface to the *Dictionary*:

> The chief glory of every people arises from its authors: whether I shall add any thing by my own writings to the reputation of English literature, must be left to time . . .

Relevant, too, is the fact that the *Dictionary* itself was the first English literary encyclopaedia. Its range of reference and wealth of quotation are astonishing, and between its covers 'the body of writings produced in a particular country' seems to have become a palpable reality for the first time. On the single page 'Listless – Litter', for example, we find quotations from Dryden, Pope, Swift, Locke, Taylor, Addison, Hooker, Browne, Bacon, Boyle, Milton, Shakespeare, Clarendon, Donne, Evelyn and others. The labour of filling two thick volumes with such – semantically classified – quotations defies description. Johnson himself understood that his work had a significance far beyond the bounds of lexicography as we would now see it. The Preface to the *Dictionary* challenges for it a central and permanent place in the productions of the English mind. That centrality is a function of its Englishness; Johnson implicitly connects the genius of our language and literature to the 'spirit of English liberty'. The emergence of the modern sense of 'literature' is indeed part of the rise of cultural nationalism.

In Johnson's time, then, 'literature', the new nationalistic conception, was succeeding 'learning', the international body of knowledge founded upon the classics. Scholars and literary historians were beginning to point out the antiquity of English poetry, and yet for most purposes, both for the conservative nationalist Johnson and for the public served by his edition of the English poets, its historical span remained brief. There were few authoritative reputations, and even fewer critical vested interests to spring to their defence. Johnson in the 'Preface to Shakespeare' (1765) speaks of his subject as one who has at last attained 'the dignity of an ancient', but he also stigmatises Shakespeare's, and later Milton's, faults with a severity that the nineteenth century was to find intolerable. Far from worshipping the dead, Johnson introduced his discussion of Shakespeare's faults with the highly rationalistic assertion that 'no question can be more innocently discussed than a dead poet's pretentions to renown.' This seems to imply both that what is at issue – poetic merit – is something less than momentous, and that it is in his discussion of the living that the critic is more conspicuously on trial.

In speaking of the 'innocence' of criticism, Johnson did not mean to deny the squabbling and spite of critical scholarship or the tradition of the venomous footnote. What emerges from his review of his editorial predecessors in the 'Preface to Shakespeare' is that scholarly acrimony flourishes in inverse proportion to the magnitude of the questions under discussion. The general reputation of a dead poet's work can hardly be altered by the scholar, since it is established by the repeated consent of generations of readers largely unaffected by criticism. Johnson's well-known criterion of literary survival exempts the reputations of dead poets from the fluctuations of contemporary fashion, and so drastically limits the jurisdiction of the individual critic.

It is very different when he is dealing with the living. Johnson's essays on the subject of contemporary writing and criticism are to be found among his periodical contributions to the *Rambler*, the *Adventurer* (1753–4) and the *Idler* (1758–60): a key text on the nature of criticism is *Rambler* no. 93. While the periodicals contain a number of set-piece excursions into critical theory and analysis of classic texts (notably *Paradise Lost* and *Samson Ago-*

nistes), these essays are heavily outnumbered by those devoted to general problems of authorship and the literary life. The focus is not upon 'literature' as an achieved body of works, but upon the arduous and gruelling activity of authorship. Johnson uses the 'life of writing'[11] as a kind of running synecdoche for the moral struggles of life in general. In this context, it is the psychology and motivation of the critic that concern him, and he implies that wrong judgments are not so much the signs of bad taste as of laziness, envy and vanity. The critic's verdict has far more influence when he is discussing the living, his personal prejudices are brought into play, and – above all – criticism of one's contemporaries is virtually a face-to-face transaction. An author, Johnson tells us, 'may be considered as a kind of general challenger',[12] and the contest is joined in a small literary world in which, as we know, both personal vilification and physical assault were rife (Johnson himself was threatened by Macpherson, the forger of 'Ossian'). In such a world, the periodical essays suggest, it is the critic's capacity for moral behaviour that is tested, rather than his ability to read a text.

Johnson, then, seems to consider reviewing, the discussion of the living, as a more exacting task than the study of the dead. But in fact the great bulk of his critical output was concerned with a special group of writers with a foot in both camps – the recently dead. To some extent this is the result of chance – the commissioning of the *Lives of the Poets* in 1777, when he was nearly seventy – but his interest in biography was lifelong, and he had completed the *Lives* of Savage and Roscommon while in his thirties. None of the subjects of the *Lives* can be said to have attained the 'dignity of an ancient', as Shakespeare had; they are poised between the twin states of authorship and literature. Johnson's aim as biographer–critic is at once to recount their careers as authors, and to pass judgment on their standing as literature. The first of these aims is predominant in his early critical biography, the *Life of Mr. Richard Savage* (1744).

Richard Savage, poet, Bohemian and convicted murderer, died in 1743; the *Life* was rushed out by his former drinking companion in the following year. Although incorporated in the *Lives of the Poets* forty-five years later, this was the first of Johnson's major works, written while he was still a starving and virtually unknown hack. It relates the most turbulent and dissipated literary career imaginable, and yet the themes that Johnson brings out suggest a series of affinities with those other, more resplendent biographies – of Cowley, Milton, Dryden, Addison and Pope – which are the core of the later *Lives*.

The explicit morals that Johnson extracts from Savage's story are these: first, that 'those are no proper Judges of his Conduct who have slumber'd away their Time on the Down of Abundance', and second, that 'nothing will supply the Want of Prudence'. The latter, aimed at Savage himself, was probably inserted to give an appearance of judicious impartiality, since the *Life*, for all its detachment and irony, is really a prolonged apology for Savage's conduct. His story exemplifies all the misfortunes that could be heaped upon an Augustan writer *in extremis*. It begins with an act of monstrous injustice, for Savage, we are told, is disowned by his own mother, the Countess of Macclesfield, and must suffer her persecutions continually. No sooner has he begun to overcome this disadvantage, than his name is tarnished by a tavern brawl in which he kills an opponent. Savage is convicted, imprisoned and later freed by royal pardon to continue the literary life. He is taken up by a patron and abruptly dropped. He writes fawning dedications to men with whom he will quarrel as soon as they are in print. He is promised positions, including the Laureateship, which he will never receive. His best poem is bought by the book-seller for a pittance, and one of its successors sells only seventy-two copies; and his chronic poverty leads to critical neglect and con-tempt. Friends organise a subscription for him, but the amount is insufficient, and his dream of a rural retreat proves a mirage. Finally, he is arrested on a debt of £8, and dies in prison. Savage is a spendthrift who soon dissipates such good fortune as comes his way, but his literary reverses are common to any struggling writer, and it is perhaps only his natural imprudence that prevents him from eventually winning through to a modest prosperity. Pope, who sensibly used his publisher's advance for the *Iliad* to buy an annuity, is the great representative of such prosperity, and it was he who eventually became Savage's benefactor, to the tune of £20 a year. But that prosperity, as Johnson showed it in the 'Life of Pope', was bought at the price of becoming the archetypal bour-geois poet, obsessed by money and property and the attentions of the great. Savage is the anti-bourgeois, stigmatised from birth, outlawed and victimised, and yet retaining to the last the 'insur-mountable obstinacy of his spirit'.

Savage's cheerfulness and conviviality, and even his fitful bril-liance as a poet, are what we should expect of such a Bohemian, maverick hero. His obstinacy, however, is more unusual. He will reject a gift of clothes or money if there is a hint of condescension or high-handedness in the way it is given; this, surely, was the side of him which appealed to Johnson. The contempt for those who have slumbered away on the down of abundance is Johnson's own, and throughout Savage's story we are made to feel constant resentment against the aristocracy, 'those little creatures whom we are pleased to call the Great'. Johnson is much more understanding when the burgesses of Bristol find themselves unable to tolerate Savage, for these are businessmen with work to do. What Johnson and the Bristol merchants have in common is presumably their independence – their ability to stand on their own feet unaided by patronage. Here Johnson reveals his commitment to the positive values of bourgeois individualism. Yet Savage's story is that of a writer trapped by its negative aspect, the reduction of his relationship with his patrons to a cash-nexus (not for him the 'liberall boord' and 'plentie of meate' that Ben Jonson enjoyed at Penshurst). He was trapped, but he did not give in. In later *Lives*, Johnson was to have little mercy for Dryden's servility and flattery of his patrons, or for Pope's spiritual bondage to snobbery and affectation. He found as much in the life of Savage as in the lives of these men to inspire a code of professional ethics.

The explicit themes of the *Life* set Savage apart from writers such as Dryden and Pope and show him, for better or worse, as a social outcast. But it is striking to learn from Boswell that Johnson himself may have been Savage's dupe in the matter of his parentage; his hero had, in all probability, entered upon the literary scene not as an outcast but as an impostor. Johnson, however, is well aware of the theme of confidence-trickery which runs through many other events of Savage's life, even if he does not draw any moral from it. When his patron accuses him of upsetting his household and stealing his books, the poet's friends 'easily credited both these Accusations', for he was one who had 'been obliged from his first Entrance into the World to subsist upon Expedients'. His most spectacular literary expedient results from his disappointment over the Laureateship. He decides to publish a poem every year on the Queen's birthday entitled the 'Volunteer Laureat', and for this effrontery receives an annual fifty guineas from the royal purse. When pay-day came round, Johnson tells us,

> His Conduct with regard to his Pension was very particular. No sooner had he changed the Bill, than he vanished from the Sight of all his Acquaintances, and lay for some Time out of the Reach of the Enquiries that Friendship or Curiosity could make after him; at length he appeared again pennyless as before, . . .

Savage is not only an ingenious scrounger and parasite, but an actor consciously fostering his own public image.

Pope's *Dunciad* was a monumental sociological satire on the life of the writer; the *Life of Savage* is a profound psychological examination. Every writer is a 'Volunteer Laureat', a 'general challenger' for social attention and approbation; every poetic career contains some species of pretence or imposture. That is why Savage's life, wild and crooked as it seems, is in a sense the prototype for the major biographies in the *Lives of the Poets*. The biographies of Dryden, Addison and Pope in particular are full of tales of flattery and trickery, of the poets' ingenuity of self-advertisement and their assiduity in procuring favours. These writers' need for self-assertion led them time and again to 'subsist upon Expedients', and their careers, when separated from their works, come to seem as degraded as those of Pope's Dunces. Even their works, under Johnson's scrutiny, reveal a fair amount of imposture. Cowley wrote 'The Mistress' though he had never had a love-affair. Pope claimed that the *Dunciad* had a moral design, but Johnson was 'not convinced'. And what of Dryden and Davenant's attempt to improve upon Shakespeare's *Tempest*?

> The effect produced by the conjunction of these two powerful minds was, that to Shakespeare's monster Caliban is added a sister-monster Sicorax; and a woman, who, in the original play, had never seen a man, is in this brought acquainted with a man that had never seen a woman.

At one level the *Life of Savage* implies that such impostures are caused by the economic insecurity of the writer, his mercenary existence in capitalist society and his low professional status. More explicitly, Johnson related them to permanent factors of human nature, and particularly to the writer's desire for fame and his unwillingness to pay its honest price in human effort. To the moralist the lives even of major poets are a muddied spectacle of confusion and imperfection, relieved, however, by dry humour and the thought that this brings them closer to the jurisdiction of the common man. It is only with time that imposture can be detected and the true merit of a writer's works revealed. Johnson would probably have agreed with Hume, who wrote of the poetic genius that 'the longer his works endure, and the more wide they are spread, the more sincere is the admiration which he meets with.'[13] It is only when this posthumous sifting has begun that the turbulent life of an author gives place to an achieved and immutable 'literature'.

Milton, Shakespeare and the *Lives of the Poets*

The writer, as Johnson sees him, has only a limited capacity to rise above his society. The prevalence of expedience and imposture reflects his subjugation by his environment and ultimately the fallen state of man himself. In this light, the *Lives of the Poets* might be read as a series of cautionary tales on a text from Johnson's poem *The Vanity of Human Wishes*:

> Nor think the Doom of Man revers'd for thee:

Johnsonian biography constantly reveals the muddle of human affairs, and the melancholy discrepancy of intention and fulfilment. It is not difficult to see how the gloom of his moral vision was linked to the anxieties and neuroses of his own life, and especially, in literary terms, to the interminable drudgery of compiling the *Dictionary*. His sense of the tragic curve of design against perform-ance is repeatedly expounded in essays in the *Rambler*, written in the intervals of that enormous task. Particularly memorable for their gloom are Johnson's meditations upon public libraries. Where others would see the collaborative effort of human learning and the triumph of a minority of timeless classics, Johnson's thoughts turn upon the mediocrity and destined oblivion of the vast majority of literary performances.[1] No doubt such expressions of gloom were emotionally satisfying, but they also had an important rhetori-cal function. The vanity of literary ambition was a recurrent topic well calculated to fill out an argument in solemn and reflective fashion, and it was by such means that, within the brief compass of the periodical essay, Johnson was able (in Boswell's words) to come forth as 'a majestick teacher of moral and religious wisdom'.

The wisdom that he taught was a kind of Christian orthodoxy. Nor was this confined to his work as moral essayist; after all, he wrote the *Lives of the Poets* 'in such a manner, as may tend to the promotion of Piety.'[2] None the less, Johnson's religious beliefs represent something less than the boldest and most original aspects of his mind. It is as if, while so secure in his own culture, he was frightened and appalled by the infinite spaces that that culture did not touch. We miss in his writing both the questing imagination and the cult of the immediately authentic and personal that are found in writers less confidently at home in their own societies. Johnson, with his masterly powers of comparison and generalisa-tion, was well fitted to

> Let Observation with extensive View,
> Survey Mankind, from China to Peru;

but these lines share the complacency which makes *Rasselas*, a profoundly gloomy moral tale, seem stodgy beside the freer and more explosive narratives of Swift and Voltaire. Johnson's self-confinement within the world of reason and nature has important consequences for his critical outlook. He believed that literature could offer very little in the way of religious understanding, and that on the whole it should not try. Devotional poetry was unpleasing because it attempted to express a sacred experience with imperfect and worldly arts. Poetry for Johnson shows nature improved and regularised, but not transcended; its province is the natural and not the supernatural. However, he does not always condemn the material of theology as 'too sacred for fiction', for that would mean condemning *Paradise Lost*. Although there are times in the 'Life of Milton' when he seems about to accuse the poet of *lèse-majesté* – his design involves matters 'too ponderous for the wings of wit' and 'the want of human interest is always felt' – the conclusions that he draws are fulsome and safe. *Paradise Lost* is the noblest of epics, and it illustrates the 'known truths' of scripture so effectively as to be a 'book of universal knowledge'. The key point, however, is that Johnson, almost alone in his age, does not concede that Milton went beyond 'known truths' – the truths of Christian reason and nature – to those of revelation.

At its highest levels, then, poetry is still not transcendental. Poetic truth does not take precedence over the truths of other disciplines such as theology and philosophy. At lower levels, Johnson views fiction as a secular and somewhat licentious activity. Boswell tells of him refusing to take precedence over a Doctor of Divinity, and claiming that he chose tragic poetry as his first métier because he lacked the money to study law. None the less, he did consider authorship in the widest sense as the first of professions in so far as it contributed to the 'intellectual pre-eminence' of the nation.[3] Literary criticism was a different matter, belonging only among the 'subordinate and instrumental arts', and he doubted whether a knowledge of its technicalities could make the lay reader 'more useful, happier or wiser'.[4]

A more general indication of the secularity of poetry may be found in Johnson's concepts of 'labour' and 'genius'. 'Genius' is defined in the 'Life of Cowley': 'The true Genius is a mind of large general powers, accidentally determined to some particular direction.' Thus genius is not a mission or vocation, but an endowment which may lead its possessor into any of the professions, and not merely into poetry or art. Still less is it a guarantee of success, for Johnson's view is that, like Adam and Eve after their expulsion from paradise, poets and others can only achieve this through hard and back-breaking labour. 'Labour', in fact, is one of the key words of the *Lives of the Poets*. Johnson constantly

stresses the hard craftsmanship and toil involved in literary production, and dismisses stories of inspired and instant composition as
credulous fabrications. What this does is to bring poetry closer
to the other skills and occupations which make up economic life.
The breadth of experience that we find in the *Lives* stems from
Johnson's convictions that the conduct of a poet's life may be as
instructive as his art, and that the art itself is not so mysterious
that it cannot be illuminated by common observation. Like Fielding, Johnson is a master of vivid and down-to-earth analogy. There
is nothing very wonderful, he assures us, in the sharp bursts in
which Milton is said to have worked:

> Something of this inequality [of inspiration] happens to every
> man in every mode of exertion, manual or mental. The mecha-
> nick cannot handle his hammer at all times with equal dexterity;
> there are hours, he knows not why, when his hand is out.

Perhaps the iconoclasm is too abrupt in that; but one object of
Johnson's investigations is to locate the ideal steady worker (the
antithesis, perhaps, of himself). This ideal is most conspicuously
found in Pope, who revised his drafts with 'indefatigable diligence'.
Johnson does his best to encourage such punctilio by means of
his niggling examinations of poetic craftsmanship in the final
sections of the *Lives*. He takes an almost perverse pleasure in pic-
king out examples of faulty diction, imagery and versification. Such
technical concerns might be no more than a subordinate aspect
of criticism considered as a humane activity, but they were at least
as important as the rules or skills of any other craft. If poetry
(or 'composition' as he liked to call it) is of a piece with other
crafts, this implies that the great examples of its practice are to
be treated not as museum-pieces but as models to be studied and
imitated by apprentice poets. The result is a practical criticism
of the workbench rather than of the academy or lecture-room.

   And yet, while always inclined to enjoin labour – it was part
of his function as a moral teacher – Johnson reserved his highest
admiration for native genius, for the gift of God rather than the
contrivances of man. There is an eloquent statement of his priorities
in the 'Preface to Shakespeare', couched in terms of 'design' and
'performance' rather than 'labour' and 'genius':

> Every man's performances, to be rightly estimated, must be com-
> pared with the state of the age in which he lived, and with his
> own particular opportunities; and though to the reader a book
> be not worse or better for the circumstances of the author, yet

as there is always a silent reference of human works to human abilities, and as the enquiry, how far man may extend his designs, or how high he may rate his native force, is of far greater dignity than in what rank we shall place any particular performance, curiosity is always busy to discover the instruments, as well as to survey the workmanship, to know how much is to be ascribed to original powers, and how much to casual and adventitious help.

The object of Johnson's historical enquiry into the state of Shakespeare's age – the part of the 'Preface' which this passage introduces – is to assess the poet's 'native force'. He has already lamented Shakespeare's carelessness of fame and moral purpose, and his clumsiness at what required effort and study; but he goes on to suggest that all these defects may, in one way or another, be blamed on the age in which he lived. Even his indifference to his own dramatic texts might be attributed to a 'superiority of mind, which despises its own performances, when it compared them with its own powers'. The purpose of editorial and historical work on Shakespeare's texts, then, is to enable us to glimpse the superlative powers of mind that lay behind his erratic and critically vulnerable performances. But however great those powers, they did not exempt Shakespeare from the doom of man – which is to be subject to other men's criticism and censure.

In February 1767, Johnson had a conversation with George III, his constitutional monarch, who proposed that he should undertake the literary biography of his country. The interview, at once fascinating and richly comic, is recorded at length by Boswell. Afterwards, Johnson described the King as 'the finest gentleman I have ever seen', and told his friends that 'I find it does a man good to be talked to by his Sovereign' (note the passive construction). It is hard to imagine many subsequent English critics in this posture (Eliot, perhaps?). The King's mention of literary biography was not a prelude to royal patronage, however, and Johnson owed his eventual commission to furnish *Prefaces, Biographical and Critical, to the Works of the English Poets* to a consortium of London booksellers in 1777. The booksellers supplied the list of poets to be included; these were almost invariably contemporaries. This must have been the last standard edition of the English poets without a real or feigned educational purpose. Johnson was allowed to add a few poets to the list at his own discretion, and, as Wordsworth was later to remark, his recommendations can scarcely be mentioned without a smile. They were Thomson, Blackmore, Pomfret, Yalden and Watts.

Each of the *Lives* is divided into three parts: a biographical narrative, a general summary of the author's powers of mind, and comments on his individual works. The formula is flexible, and in general none of the three parts takes precedence over the others. These critical and biographical prefaces were originally to be prefixed to the works of each author in the multi-volume edition of the poets, but as Johnson got to work they became lengthy enough to justify publication in separate volumes. They are arranged in a haphazard, vaguely chronological order, like the poets in an Oxford anthology. The result – together with Johnson's disinclination to include poets on historical rather than commercial grounds – is a serial biography defining not a tradition or pantheon but a loose gathering of individuals. (Johnson had already produced a vast anthology of English writing arranged in wholly abstract, serial order in the *Dictionary*.) The scale of the major *Lives* (Cowley, Milton, Waller, Dryden, Addison, Pope) provides some index of the eminence of their subjects, but Johnson also reprints his *Savage* at similar length. And there are certain moments when he sets out to rank individual poems and to place their authors in a formal hierarchy. *Paradise Lost* is allowed 'with respect to design, the first place, and with respect to performance the second' in world literature, while Joseph Warton's question whether Pope was a poet meets the answer that 'if the writer of the *Iliad* were to class his successors, he would assign a very high place to his translator, without requiring any other evidence of Genius.' There is something faintly half-hearted about each of these judgments; the second is only a generous testimonial. On the whole, those who look to the final sections of the *Lives* for penetrating appraisals of the radical unity and uniqueness of individual works, and then of their standing against one another in the mausoleum of Literature, will be acutely disappointed. Johnson's major interests lie elsewhere. The 'General Observations' on individual plays in Johnson's edition of Shakespeare are equally terse; the main purpose of his annotations in general is to establish the sense of the text, and he must have felt little or no temptation to launch into extended critical commentary.

One critical discussion in which he is totally engaged comes in the middle section of the 'Life of Pope'; it is a comparison of the poetic characters of Pope and Dryden, modelled implicitly on Pope's own contrast of Homer and Virgil in his Preface to *The Iliad* (1715). The question at issue is one of 'native force', and not of the ranking of particular performances. In biographical terms, Pope has been revealed as a meticulous labourer, Dryden as a mercurial genius. Johnson crystallises this opposition by means of a contrast of their prose styles, which is remarkable for its power of characterisation:

> The style of Dryden is capricious and varied, that of Pope is cautious and uniform; Dryden obeys the motions of his own mind, Pope constrains his mind to his own rules of composition. Dryden is sometimes vehement and rapid: Pope is always smooth, uniform, and gentle. Dryden's page is a natural field, rising into inequalities, and diversified by the varied exuberance of abundant vegetation; Pope's is a velvet lawn, shaven by the scythe, and levelled by the roller.
>
> Of genius, that power which constitutes a poet; that quality without which judgment is cold and knowledge is inert; that energy which collects, combines, amplifies, and animates; the superiority must, with some hesitation, be allowed to Dryden.

What is it, we might wonder here, that separates neoclassical 'genius' or 'poetical vigour' from romantic imagination? (Pope had earlier written that '*Homer* was the greater Genius, *Virgil* the better artist.') The answer is that Johnson assumes the commensurability of rival geniuses, and in the next paragraph virtually reduces the question to the terms of a mathematical formula ('If the flights of Dryden therefore are higher, Pope continues longer on the wing').

The restraint and self-limitation that Johnson observes in making this comparison (or 'determination', as he calls it) are remarkable. The rules of the contest are known, there is a strictly finite number of possible moves and the protagonists are limited to two. Johnson makes no attempt to connect up this discussion with a total or global view of literature, even though there are powerful implicit connections, for example in the concepts of labour and genius. The shape of the *Lives* in general is episodic and aggregative rather than organic and convergent. Each 'Life' is a succession of separate 'determinations', concluded with summary judgments referring outwards to general moral and aesthetic principles which Johnson lays down *in medias res*. In other words, his concern is less with portraying an individual temperament or an organic life's work, than with setting down the facts of each biography and adjudicating upon these facts in terms of a series of universal rules. These rules, which together make up the framework of reason and nature, are variously derived from the separate disciplines of ethics, theology, psychology, literary criticism and so on. Johnson makes no attempt to overthrow the boundaries between the disciplines or to arrive at a single, transcendent synthesis of 'the poet', nor does he match his poets against a totalised 'society'; the realisation of global abstractions like these was to be the critical achievement of Words-worth. Johnson's criticism makes use of far more empirical categor-ies such as the writer's career, his public image, his native force and his style of labour, and these categories are notably deficient in accounting for the radical uniqueness and emotional impact of individual works on the one hand, and the institutional presence of literature and society on the other.

What sort of public attitude to literature is presupposed by the *Lives of the Poets*? Their form is that of an aggregation, a work of reference; in contemporary terms, they resemble, say, a diction-ary of British Prime Ministers rather than a *Great Tradition* or *Guide to English Literature*. They help one to read the poets but they do not provide preliminary instructions in such reading, either in what to read or in how to read it. One chooses the poet for oneself, and then consults the 'Life'. And Johnson tends to evaluate the poets on strictly equal terms, as if he were writing a reference for them or a publisher's report on their books. That is, he treats them as colleagues working within a general frame of assumptions which does not need to be investigated; he need only define their special concerns (pastoral, devotional poetry and the like) and indi-vidual merits and faults. This implied frame of assumptions is not quite life itself; Johnson's reader will be aware not only of his general adherence to reason and nature but of his dislike of fantasy, of republicanism, of critical sycophancy and of the aristocracy. But these are individual traits, not those of any group that the writing defines. Johnson does not address himself to a minority, nor does he regard the poets he discusses as representatives of a minority. The corollary of his belief in the common reader is that Johnson had no idea that he was serving 'culture'. Not 'literari-ness' but general literacy was the standard he set himself.

It is for these reasons that his criticism belongs to a vanished world. His notions of writing and reading are deeply individualistic. The reader is not a special person; if not *homo sapiens*, he is *homo rationis capax*. The author like any individual is held responsible for his actions and writings, receiving praise or censure accordingly; and his choices are made within a competitive society in which he is obliged, by one means or another, to force himself upon public attention. We may return to Johnson's description of the author as

> a kind of general challenger, whom every one has a right to attack; since he quits the common rank of life, steps forward beyond the lists, and offers his merit to the publick judgment.
>
> (*Rambler* no. 93)

The author, that is, does not contribute to a 'culture' or social totality, but puts himself forward in a market-place or competitive arena. This view shares the individualism of bourgeois economics, and is a celebration of 'equality of opportunity' within a constituted but not a corporate state. In historical terms, Johnson's constitutionalism stands between the absolutism of two critical systems, the early neoclassical and the romantic. His chosen method of critical biography involves an impressive compromise between the permanent hierarchy of the literary academy and the pure democracy of the contemporary market-place. If we are satisfied by the academic consolidation of literary criticism since Johnson's day, it will be the institutional side of his work that we shall wish to emphasise. But its real value, in my view, is now the opposite of this. He shows how criticism may be based on discrimination and assessment (however inadequate his criteria may sometimes be) without congealing into closed and authoritarian forms. And he shows its power to record the drama and confusion of living authorship, as well as sifting and grading the deposits of the dead.

2   William Wordsworth: The Poet as Prophet

Sublimity and transcendence: the later Eighteenth Century

The achievement of the *Lives of the Poets* was from one point of view a rearguard action. Johnson was fighting off the challenge of critical views which, mistaken or half-baked as they may have seemed at the time, are for us loaded with historical pregnancy. These are the – fitfully radical – views which used to be classed as 'pre-romantic'. Among them were Joseph Warton's sceptical question whether Pope was a poet; the theories of 'primitivists' such as Blair and Ferguson who maintained that poetry flourished in barbaric times and was gradually extinguished by the march of civilisation; and the cult of originality prompted by Edward Young's *Conjectures on Original Composition* (1759). Young lamented the subjugation of the creative spirit by the burdensome duty of emulating the past:

> But why are *Originals* so few? not because the writer's harvest is over, the great reapers of antiquity having left nothing to be gleaned after them; not because the human mind's teeming time is past, or because it is incapable of putting forth unprecedented births; but because illustrious examples *engross, prejudice,* and *intimidate.* They *engross* our attention, and so prevent a due inspection of ourselves; they *prejudice* our judgment in favour of their abilities, and so lessen the sense of our own; and they *intimidate* us with the splendour of their renown, and thus under diffidence bury our strength.

Here we have the sense of the age and exhausting fertility of civilisation, and of the contemporary writer's refusal to give up hope. Though he lacked the mildly subversive fervour of Young, Johnson cannot be accused of increasing the burden of the past, and was scrupulously on guard against an attitude to the classics that would engross or intimidate. In fact Young was an Anglican moralist who placed Addison above Dryden and Pope, and placed Addison's behaviour on his death-bed above the greatest of his works; in most ways his outlook is as neoclassical and as profoundly remote from modern taste as Johnson's own. Yet he does express a heightening of the sense of cultural power-struggle involved in creativity that is distinctly modern. Artistic originality involves rejection, revolt and almost superhuman strength; Young is one of the first writers to habitually speak of genius as 'divine'. In a revealing simile, he compares the world of letters to 'some metropolis in flames, where a few incombustible buildings, a fortress, temple, or tower, lift their heads, in melancholy grandeur, amid the mighty ruin'. These incombustible buildings are 'originals' or works of genius. Not only has a trial of strength between works taken the place of Johnson's economic struggle between their authors, but the victorious works are endowed with an innate, mysterious grandeur and indestructibility. It is precisely the enhancement of the grandeur and power of literary achievements that provides the dynamic of romantic criticism.

Johnson was not insensible to the emotive power of literature – his aversion to the last act of *King Lear* is sufficient proof of this – but it is a measure of the extent of the romantic revolution in culture that his accounts of it seem so frigid and stereotyped to us, even at the moments of his greatest critical incisiveness. In the 'Preface to Shakespeare', for example, the psychological arguments with which he so effectively demolishes the doctrine of the Unities are over-intellectualised to a degree. Johnson seems to look upon dramatic performance as an act of recitation rather than a theatrical experience, and regards the members of the audience as judicious individuals who are 'never out of their senses', rather than as a group to some extent submitting themselves to the rhythms of the spectacle. His discussion of theatrical illusion is appropriate to a 'cool', non-involving medium, and it is significant that when he compares the experience of drama to that of another art, he should make the choice of landscape painting.

No doubt this reveals the anaemia of the eighteenth-century sensibility to tragedy, but there is a wider discrepancy, which we might point to by contrasting the measured and public level of Johnson's dealings with Shakespeare with Goethe's comment, as reported by Eckermann:

> had I been born an Englishman, and had all those numerous masterpieces been brought before me in all their power, at my first dawn of youthful consciousness, they would have overpowered me, and I should not have known what to do. I could not have gone on with such fresh light-heartedness; . . .[1]

On the whole the romantics do not compare poetic and dramatic power to landscape painting, but to the impact of actual landscape. Keats likened his reading of Homer to Cortes' discovery of the

Pacific, 'Silent, upon a peak in Darien'. For Goethe and Young, the great classics were natural obstacles to be circumvented, but for Keats they were to become the locked repositories of secret and almost magical powers, available not to the general reader but to the devotee and future poet. Such attitudes must lead either to total subjectivism of response or to a hermeneutic mode of criticism proclaiming the secret and recondite properties of literary works as their artistic essence. This facet of romantic criticism, which may be illustrated by Blake's salutation of Milton ('he was a true Poet & of the Devil's party without knowing it'), is totally opposed to the Johnsonian outlook.[2] Johnson does not engage in interpretation, or the attempt to penetrate to a hidden core of the literary work, at all. The properties which he comments and passes judgment upon are of the surface, and the work itself is no more than a surface.

The growth of the sense of literary power that has been anticipated here was long drawn out. An important, though early stage, was the eighteenth-century cult of sublimity. The term was often used merely to describe a category of poetic excitement – the thrill of vastness, as it were – but it also meant an ideal of elevation, both stylistic and moral. Of particular importance was the connection of sublimity and Christian feeling. Both Miltonic and Hebrew poetry typified the sublime, and since their sublimity expressed man's worship of nature and its Creator, God himself came to be seen as its ultimate source.[3] The 'primitivist' scholars located the origin of poetry in an act of pagan nature-worship, sometimes envisaged as a communal rite but more often as a spontaneous expression of joy and wonder at natural phenomena.[4] The crucial jump here is that which sees poetry as a privileged communication of transcendental experience; not as a literary imitation of the truths of revealed religion (Johnson's conservative view of *Paradise Lost*) but as itself the agent of revelation. In particular, the odes of Gray and Collins show an influential fusion of the pagan legend of the Muses with the Christian sublime. Their presentation of Milton as the blind seer who

> rode sublime
> Upon the seraph-wings of Extasy,
> The secrets of th' Abyss to spy

> (Gray, 'The Progress of Poesy')

was not entirely new; but whereas Marvell had likened him to Tiresias in a poem which for the most part praises a fellow-craftsman for doing a good job, Gray and Collins conjure up the figure of Milton in a context of magical harmony and effortless inspiration. Their poems show a curious mixture of classical (Apollonian) and Hebraic motifs. The image of poetry as natural harmony, symbolised by the wind-harp or Aeolian lyre, is juxtaposed with the sublime and craggy figure of the poet-prophet in his Miltonic, Norse and Celtic manifestations. Collins' elegy on Thomson ('In yonder grave a Druid lies') exemplifies this sort of mixture, while the Hebraic poet-prophet is most melodramatically realised in Gray's 'The Bard', with its shaggy and funereal hero who prophesies the doom of the Plantagenet Kings and then flings himself from a rock.

The form of these poems is that of the Pindaric Ode, a lineal predecessor of the romantic and modern lyric. The eighteenth-century ode, as defined for example by Young in his essay 'On Lyric Poetry' (1728), is a stiflingly literary affair, 'poetical' in the sense of being more rhapsodic and less prosaic than any other form. The stylistic obscurity of Gray's odes is wholly deliberate, and the poet helpfully provides prose summaries at the bottom of each page. Within this form, so clearly intended to overawe the reader, Gray and Collins expressed their own awe at the majestic tradition of which they saw themselves as the feeble and diffident heirs. To claim any nearer kinship to the great bards of antiquity would be little less than poetic blasphemy. And so Collins addressed a long and obsequious poem to Sir Thomas Hanmer, the latest editor of Shakespeare, and Gray – poised between self-pity and democratic guilt – memorialised the 'mute inglorious Milton' of a country churchyard.

The central myth in Gray and Collins is the history of poetry itself.[5] Their contemporary Thomas Warton turned to academic scholarship and wrote the first *History of English Poetry* (1774–81), but his unfinished achievement is of less importance than the general availability of the potted theories of poetic history which the romantics (beginning with Wordsworth's Appendix on poetic diction, 1802) would take over for polemical purposes. The spread of antiquarianism is neatly illustrated by Gray's confession that he 'never sat down to compose poetry without reading Spenser for a considerable time previously'.[6] None the less, the activities of the poets and literary scholars who make up what has been called the 'school of the Wartons' look bumbling and amateurish when set beside the major theoretical investigation of the nature of tradition in the later eighteenth century, that of Sir Joshua Reynolds. Reynolds's *Discourses on Art*, delivered annually from 1769 to 1790 in his capacity as first President of the Royal Academy, were conceived as carrying on the Johnsonian tradition, and Johnson himself regarded Reynolds as one of his school. In fact they embody a crucial departure from Johnson, and were to exercise their own, quite separate influence upon literary criticism.

Johnson detested the idea of a literary academy; Reynolds presided over an Academy of Arts. Its purpose, he decided, was not only to provide good teachers but to act as a 'repository for the great examples of the art', so that the student should be exposed to 'that idea of excellence which is the result of the accumulated experience of past ages'. The art collection, in other words, would be there for pedagogic and not for antiquarian reasons; thus Reynolds represents a new stage of the institutionalisation of the arts, the theory of the educative function of the museum. The students of the Academy would gain technical proficiency by copying particular masterpieces, and they would acquire reason and taste – the elements of artistic maturity – by critical study of the whole range of the art. In the earlier discourses Reynolds, like Johnson, emphasises that success is proportionate to labour; and he also advises the younger students to obey the rules unquestioningly, and asserts that none of the great painters was given to dissipation. All this is very much what a master would say to his pupils. In later discourses, devoted to more advanced instruction, he concentrates upon the spiritual profit to be drawn from the study of the great masters. The highest veneration, he argues, should be reserved for the 'grand style' of historical painting of noble and uplifting subjects, exemplified by the High Renaissance and the work of Michelangelo and Raphael. The grand style is set above the 'ornamental' style of the Venetians and the bourgeois realism of the Dutch. It expresses not only a classical ideal but a highly literary one, since the historical painting is an illustration of events that have found prior expression in imaginative or historical narrative. Reynolds, indeed, considers the physical beauty and dignity portrayed by the painter as somewhat inferior to the moral beauty which is the province of the poet.

The centrepiece of his discussion of the grand style lies in his contrast of the two great masters of painting, Raphael and Michelangelo. Reynolds argues that Raphael has the best all-round combination of excellences, but finally prefers Michelangelo for his greater sublimity and imaginative power. The difference between this contrast and Johnson's contrast of Dryden and Pope (written a few years later) is that Johnson sums up the native endowments of two artistic lives, while Reynolds is debating the seniority of two great monuments in the pantheon of culture. How did this academic approach affect the students – the would-be artists – sitting at his feet? Before the Academy was even founded David Hume had experienced doubts about the wisdom of setting up

an alien cultural achievement as the standard of contemporary perfection. 'So many models of Italian painting brought to England,'
he complained, 'instead of exciting our artists, is the cause of their
small progress in that noble art.'[7] While it would be wrong to
overlook the consideration that Reynolds (himself a great portrai-
tist) gives to forms of arts less exalted than the grand style, the
ideal defined in the *Discourses* is less that of the creator than of
the superbly cultured critic – the man who has mastered and, above
all, compared every branch of the arts. Perhaps the best-known
passage in the *Discourses* is his ceremonious description of that
'sovereign judge and arbiter of art', the Man of Taste – a patrician
and acquisitive figure, 'making the universe tributary towards furnishing his mind' (and presumably his country mansion as well).

Reynolds's main contribution to literary criticism lies in the idea
of the grand style, which was later taken up by Arnold. But it
is an apt symbol of the romantic revolution that the President of
the Academy was confronted by a rebellious student, who wrote
rude words all over his master's textbook. The student was Blake,
and his annotations to the *Discourses* were made in 1808, thirty
years after he had finished his studies, and sixteen years after Reynolds's death. The time-lag says much for the power of Reynolds's
academic teaching, and for the pre-eminence of his reputation.
How was Blake to puncture the prestige of such an opponent?
Not content with marginal interjections ('Nonsense!', 'A lie!',
'Contemptible!') and blunt statements of his own antithetical position ('All Sublimity is founded on Minute Discrimination'), Blake
repeatedly denounces his enemy as a hireling and a toady. Reynolds's admiration for his own master Michelangelo was particularly galling: 'He praises Michel Angelo for Qualities which Michel
Angelo abhorr'd, & He blames Rafael for the only Qualities which
Rafael Valued.' Blake was in fact driven to insist that he talked
a fundamentally different language from Reynolds, even when they
seemed to agree. This is the key fact about the annotations, even
though a historian of ideas could find certain similarities in the
two men's thought.[8] Their basic disagreement is over Reynolds's
conviction that the standard of excellence can be taught. For Blake,
this meant a denial of the innate and intuitive quality of creative
genius:

Reynolds Thinks that Man Learns all that he knows. I say on
the Contrary that Man Brings All that he has or can have Into
the World with him. Man is Born Like a Garden ready Planted
& Sown. This World is too poor to produce one Seed.

Hinted, but never clearly stated, in these annotations is Blake's belief in the transcendental nature of art, as not the imitation of the visible word but the visionary expression of eternal reality. Reynolds, Burke, Bacon, Newton and Locke are the materialistic mockers of 'Inspiration and Vision'. In this light, it was nonsense to talk of Raphael teaching Michelangelo, or Michelangelo teaching Raphael, since one genius had nothing to teach another. On the face of it this ought to demolish the eighteenth-century problem of the 'burden of the past' altogether; the pantheon of Old Masters could simply be ignored. But in fact the romantic worship of transcendent genius was to bring back the problem in a new and severer form, one manifestation of which was Blake's own imperious self-identification with Milton and the prophets.

The preface to *Lyrical Ballads*

Nothing is more widely accepted in literary history than that the publication of *Lyrical Ballads* in 1798 heralded a revolution in English poetry. Some modern scholars have attacked this reading of history, but without much success. However the picture may be complicated by painstaking research into the literature of the 1790s, it is enough for our purposes that the campaign of Wordsworth and Coleridge was eventually to prove such a resounding publicity triumph. Their claim to have overthrown the eighteenth-century canons of taste and to have reconstituted the genuine tradition of English poetry came in time to be universally recognised; and the new paradigm introduced by the romantics lasted, with modifications, throughout the century. One important element of that paradigm was their consciousness of revolution itself. They not only produced the new poetry but the essential commentaries upon it (notably Wordsworth's Preface to *Lyrical Ballads*, Coleridge's *Biographia Literaria* and passages of Hazlitt, de Quincey and Keats). Scholars would later learn to write history in such a way that earlier changes of style in the arts (Renaissance, mannerism, baroque) came to be understood as cultural revolutions, but it is European romanticism which first displays all the features of such a revolution, and bequeaths them to such successors as realism, impressionism and modernism. Among these features – in the English context – are the intensely fruitful collaboration between strongly divergent individuals (the 'Lake school'); a critical vendetta of unrelenting hostility waged by supporters of the poetic 'ancien régime'; the experience of discipleship with which the new writers were able to inspire their followers and even to change their lives (the classic record of this is de Quincey's); the obsessed mixture of awe and debunking displayed by the next generation, Keats, Shelley and Byron, all so acute in their mockery of Wordsworth, and so deeply indebted to him; and finally, the change of sensibility which the innovating poets seem to personify but which is in fact so widespread as to elude causal analysis altogether. This list might be extended, but central to all these phenomena is the impact of *Lyrical Ballads* itself, with its repudiation of the established tradition and its offer to remake society through the agency of poems of deliberate technical experiment.

Hazlitt, in his lecture 'On the Living Poets' (1818), was the first to say that the key to the English romantics lay in their debt to the French Revolution. The relationship is complex and paradoxical. The political verse inspired by their early Jacobin sympathies, such as Wordsworth's 'Salisbury Plain',[1] is raw in the extreme, and their immediate expressions of political disillusionment, such as Coleridge's 'France: An Ode' – originally published as 'Recantation: An Ode' – are not much better. Wordsworth in *The Prelude* tells how, after the onset of the Terror had destroyed his abstract humanitarian faith, his imagination was restored by renewed contact with nature and with the primary affections of English country people. The *Lyrical Ballads* are full of vignettes of such people, humble and inarticulate figures who stand outside the worlds of culture and property; and Wordsworth shows a marked preference for the old, the mad, vagrants, idiots and unmarried mothers over ordinary working people. The poet's role is primarily that of memorialist and *post facto* moralist, pointing out the general truths that are illustrated by the commonplace events of the tale. Wordsworth clearly did see the poetic description of ordinary lives as a way of promoting the democratic growth of social sympathy. He defended 'The Idiot Boy', for example, on the grounds that it was intended to promote the welfare of the mentally handicapped. But there is no question that the more successful of the *Lyrical Ballads*, such as 'Old Man Travelling', are in a reflective, contemplative mode, and the 1798 volume ends with 'Tintern Abbey', a meditative poem whose powerful eloquence is in total contrast to the bare and mawkish diction of the more doctrinaire ballads. This dichotomy between the poetry of description, simple, unpretentious and 'levelling', and the impassioned and prophetic poetry of reflection, runs throughout Wordsworth's career. It is already present in the first of the three prefaces to *Lyrical Ballads*, the 'Advertisement' to the edition of 1798. This is a terse and inconspicuous essay which does little more than explain why the poems in the volume may strike the reader as slightly unusual. There is a single hint of more revolutionary claims:

> It is desirable that . . . readers, for their own sakes, should not suffer the solitary word Poetry, a word of very disputed meaning, to stand in the way of their gratification; but that, while they are perusing this book, they should ask themselves if it contains a natural delineation of human passions, human characters, and human incidents.

The fact is that Wordsworth, who here disavows the word 'Poetry', has already lectured his readers on the 'honourable characteristic' of the art, and goes on to intimidate them by dark references to the authority of 'our elder writers' and to the arduousness of critical judgment, as attested by none other than Reynolds. Thus readers are simultaneously urged to trust their own judgment, and to consider an appreciation of *Lyrical Ballads* as the ultimate reward of a cultivated taste. If it were not prefixed to one of the most famous volumes of poetry ever written, this would long ago have been recognised as a grotesque example of literary blackmail; some of Pope's Dunces were immortalised for less. The two faces of the 'Advertisement', however, represent a duality which is endemic to Wordsworth's critical thought. In Wordsworth as in the National Assembly, revolution was to be the foster-parent of a new authoritarianism.

Wordsworth in later life said that he 'never cared a straw about the theory'; but the volume of criticism that he wrote between 1798 and 1815 is substantial. There is a long-standing problem about the relation of this criticism to his poetry. On the one hand, the doctrines of the 1800 Preface to *Lyrical Ballads* do not always seem to fit the poetry; on the other hand, it is not clear why, to supplement the poetry, a statement of doctrines should be needed. The various impulses at work in the 1798 Advertisement suggest that the prefaces should be read as social gestures rather than as abstract and logical contributions to literary theory – though their influence was no less extensive for that. Wordsworth's social situation was in fact a peculiar one. He and Coleridge did as much as anyone to define the social status of the major nineteenth-century poet (Coleridge, however, was a good deal less successful in enjoying this status). Yet they began their 'Great Decade' as impoverished and isolated Jacobins, ostracised by their country neighbours, their gentility somewhat shabby.[2] Sales of their early work were minimal, and an obscurity like Blake's might have faced them. Coleridge in *Biographia Literaria* was to advise young poets to make sure of another profession; he himself nearly became a Unitarian minister. He was prevented by an annuity from the Wedgwood brothers in 1797, and Wordsworth also was supported by private bequests – £900 from a fellow-student, Raisley Calvert, in 1795, followed by his wife's dowry and legacies from her family – until he secured the Stamp-Distributorship for Westmorland and later for part of Cumberland. A lot of this good fortune followed the poet's public conversion to the cause of Monarchism and reaction, though de Quincey (not necessarily a reliable witness) tells of Wordsworth and Southey expressing republican sentiments and joking about the royal family as late as 1807. Much has been written about the Lake poets' religious and political recantations; less about their adoption of middle-class values and lifestyle. Wordsworth became the bourgeois *paterfamilias*, needing money to run Rydal Mount and raise his growing family. Coleridge's theory of the 'clerisy' portrays intellectuals as a professional élite, recognised as one of the permanent estates of the realm. Their defiance of the public is understandable when we remember that neither depended much upon sales for a living; what they needed was the good opinion of philanthropic middle-class individuals and government officials. Such patronage, bestowed on the poet by his social equals, involved no mercenary obligations (apart, presumably, from distributing stamps), and confirmed his self-esteem and sense of mission.

The Preface to the second edition of *Lyrical Ballads* (1800) is Wordsworth's most far-reaching act of self-justification. The result is a critical document of an entirely new kind: a poetic manifesto offering a trenchant statement of universal principles designed to supersede all existing theory and tradition. This plan was not fully realised until the enlarged Preface of 1802, with its explicit warning that acceptance of the new principles must entail a total revaluation of the reader's judgments of 'the greatest Poets both ancient and modern'. Wordsworth did not succeed in a total rationalisation of his poetic practice, and some of his arguments remained tortuous and muddled. Yet the gap between the Preface and its generic predecessors, such as the prefaces of Dryden and Fielding with their artful assimilation of the new work to existing authority, might be compared to that between earlier constitutions and the great documents of the revolutionary age such as the Declaration of Independence and the Declaration of the Rights of Man. Like these, the Preface to *Lyrical Ballads* makes a 'self-evident' statement of universal principles valid far beyond its particular occasion. It defines poetry and the poet in the abstract rather than by reference to tradition and precedent, and it is written in the confident language of eighteenth-century rationalism (whereas the critical prose of the later romantics is far more unstable, and its relationship to rational thought increasingly problematic). The theory of poetic language that it puts forward seems to promise a complete emancipation of poetry from the tyranny of literature and its conventions.

Hazlitt wrote that the Lake poets 'founded the new school on a principle of sheer humanity, on pure nature void of art', and that poetry for them 'grew like a mushroom out of the ground; or was hidden in it like a truffle, which it required a particular sagacity and industry to find out and dig up'.[3] The 1800 Preface, after announcing the need for a fundamental enquiry into the elements of criticism, psychology and social history, puts forward a series of radical arguments aimed at breaking down the established distinctions of Augustan or any other centralised literary culture. The main force of the attack is directed at the Augustan habits of poetic diction. To say that a whole century's poetry was vitiated by its diction was itself reductive, since diction was the lowest of the strictly poetic elements in the Aristotelian hierarchy. Wordsworth was contemptuously reinterpreting the 'burden of the past' which had weighed down his predecessors as a burden of clichés, a great mass of phrases and figures which 'from father to son have long been regarded as the common inheritance of poets', but were now fit only to be thrown on the scrap-heap – a verdict that he swiftly executed upon all but five lines of a sonnet by Gray. Wordsworth justified his attack on poetic diction with the thesis that there was 'no essential difference between the language of prose and metrical composition': an argument which disposes of any set of conventional distinctions that a society might use to separate literary from other kinds of discourse. He rejected an artificial 'poetic' idiom in order to turn to nature and the twin ideas of natural description and natural inspiration. The first, descriptive or mimetic idea consorts with the stated aim of the *Lyrical Ballads*, which is to trace the 'primary laws of our nature' as they are reflected in the 'incidents of common life'. The language that he will adopt, Wordsworth says, is purified of conventional poeticisms and of anything that does not result from looking 'steadily at my subject'. In addition, it is to be the language of rural life, since this is a more natural and more permanent language than that of the city or the upper classes. The second idea – that of natural inspiration – is also present in 1800, although the transition from a mainly mimetic to a mainly expressive theory of poetry is one of the principal developments that takes place between 1800 and 1802.[4] Already in 1800 we read of poetry as a 'spontaneous overflow of powerful feelings'. Inspiration is a theme of the earliest of the *Lyrical Ballads*, as the poet celebrates the 'impulse from a vernal wood' that replaced any amount of moral philosophy ('The Tables Turned'), and the 'hour of feeling' when

> One moment now may give us more
> Than fifty years of reason;
>> ('Lines written at a small distance from my house . . .')

Atavistic sentiments like these had a powerful attraction for Wordsworth, and yet his theories do not bring about a total dislodgment of the artificial element in poetry. His argument surrounds natural inspiration with a network of moral and rational channels and filters, like the purification plant of a reservoir. Deliberate cultural intervention is needed if the sources of feeling are to be made into a drinkable product. And we shall find that this aspect of the theory, which contradicts some of the bolder affirmations of the poems, is reinforced by the whole context of discourse in the Preface itself.

A central Wordsworthian concern is with language. While there is no doubt about the force of his opposition to stale and stilted poetical idioms, his criterion of natural language – 'the real language of men' – is notoriously ambiguous. It is neither a wholly rhetorical nor a wholly sociological category. Since he describes the language of rustics as 'a more permanent and a far more philosophical language' than that of sophisticated poets, Wordsworth has been seen as defining a permanent poetic rhetoric.[5] If so, it is a rhetoric based on some strong aversions, but without any definite rules. But the 1798 'Advertisement' had claimed that the language of *Lyrical Ballads* had a sociological basis, being chosen from 'the language of conversation in the middle and lower classes of society'. By 1802 Wordsworth had changed this to 'a selection of the language really spoken by men', with the emphasis upon the modifying influence of the selection process. Coleridge was later to scoff at the idea of the poet 'wandering about in search of angry or jealous people in uncultivated society, in order to copy their words'.[6] It was certainly wise to drop the word 'conversation' with its suggestions of everyday exclamations and gossip. Wordsworth had probably meant to indicate the language of folk-tale, reminiscence and popular narrative – 'the real language of men in a state of vivid sensation' (the phrase is common to the texts of 1800 and 1802). The implications of this are ethical rather than sociological; real language is language which expresses the feelings with directness and sincerity, as men are supposed to do in the 'natural state' of rustic life. The adequacy of the language can then be established pragmatically, by examining particular poems and their power to move us, so that the Wordsworthian theory of rustic life is technically a side-issue. For at this point he shifts the focus of the argument from the poem as end-product to the process of composition. If the method of writing can be shown to be 'natural', then the language will be so too.

Whatever he means by 'real language', it is the mainstay of his attack on the poetic tradition. In the Appendix on poetic diction (1802), Wordsworth's target is not simply Augustan diction, but any inherited poetical rhetoric. Borrowing heavily from the primitivist theorists such as Ferguson and Blair, he argues that the earliest poets expressed themselves in figurative language as the natural vehicle of passionate feeling. Later poets lacking in genuine feeling tended to repeat the same rhetorical devices to obtain a heightened emotional effect. The tradition-conscious poet, in other words, is a kind of commercial entertainer well versed in the tricks of his trade. His opposite, the true poet, must cut loose from this 'motley masquerade', and struggle for recognition in the face of a corrupt public taste. If he is to find his poetic identity, he must totally ignore his predecessors. This seems – and for a time it was – a wholly revolutionary position, like Blake's.

How, in fact, was poetry written? Wordsworth's radicalism went further in part of the expanded Preface of 1802, where he decided to strengthen his argument about poetic language by taking the difficult case of dramatic verse. Clearly dramatic speech should sound real and plausible, but how could its origins be anything but willed and artificial? Wordsworth admitted that the poet's task was 'in some degree mechanical, compared with the freedom and power of real and substantial action and suffering'. We might concede this to be true, while feeling that real action and suffering is often unrealised because inarticulate. But Wordsworth assumed that command of language was innate in everyone. All that the poet needed to do, therefore, was to put himself in the situation of his characters, and

> even confound and identify his own feelings with theirs; modifying only the language which is thus suggested to him, by a consideration that he describes for a particular purpose, that of giving pleasure.

The final qualification is larger than it seems at first sight; but it does not alter the striking assertion that once the right state of feeling is attained, the proper language will come automatically. Wordsworth describes another technique for the simulation of feeling in the famous passage where the poet, now apparently an author of meditative lyrics, seeks to recreate the emotion that he has 'recollected in tranquillity'. In each case, the spontaneity of poetry is the outcome of a deliberately induced emotional state.

It is not only the poet's feelings that are deliberately induced. In the 1800 version, Wordsworth went straight on from his denunciation of poetic diction to 'answer an obvious question, namely why, professing these opinions have I written in verse?' His answer was not wholly satisfactory, but the main point is clear: metre must be added to 'natural' language for the purpose of giving pleasure. But why should metre be exempted from the objections he brings against poetic diction? If we compare his theoretical accounts of the two elements which distinguish poetry from prose, there can be no question about his discrimination in favour of metre. Metre tends to 'divest language . . . of its reality', and therefore to make descriptions of harrowing events more palatable (hence Shakespearean tragedy is preferable to *Clarissa*); but poetic diction is condemned precisely because it obscures reality. Metre is said to be regular and uniform, where poetic diction is arbitrary and capricious; but the advocates of poetic diction, such as Johnson in the 'Life of Dryden', had stressed its regularising and controlling function. Wordsworth views metre as a mechanical adornment, and adds that part of the charm is caused by association with the pleasure received from previous metrical works. But when poetic diction aspires to the charm of imitation, he condemns it as false and artificial. (We might add that an insistent metric is the main sign of the 'poetic' status of the experimental poems of *Lyrical Ballads.*) Wordsworth, in effect, treats metre as the positive sign of tradition, where poetic diction is the negative sign. The basic problem is that he is deeply attached to metre, and recognises its primitive emotional power; but at the same time, fearing to leave a gaping anomaly in his system, he denies it an intrinsic creative role. He describes it as ornamental, and then makes the startling observation that, given comparable passages in verse and prose, 'the verse will be read a hundred times where the prose is read once.' Perhaps the reason for all this confusion (and for Coleridge's exhaustive attempts in *Biographia Literaria* to clear it up) is that metre occupies a crucial position in the dialectic of the natural and the cultural idea of poetry. Metre for the modern poet is a social skill, an aspect of the laborious and visible poetic craftsmanship which Johnson scrutinised in the *Lives of the Poets.*

And this is why Wordsworth can only grudgingly admit it to poetics, as a mere process of arrangement, a necessary constraint upon the poet's inspiration. Yet Wordsworth also knew that metre has innate psychological functions. Did he perhaps obscurely sense that metre is a primordial attribute of poetry, which could not be rationalised away however hard he tried; that metre is at once a mechanical skill and the product of organic, instinctive perception, so that its ambivalence is that of poetry itself?

Nothing could be further from Wordsworth's outlook than Johnson's vision of the drudgery of authorship as an allegorical drama of the human condition. The poet whom Wordsworth envisages does not toil over his work, for the crucial operations occur in his mind and not on the manuscript page. This devaluation of literary labour belongs in the general category of romantic idealism. It is associated with the cult of originality and genius, going back to Young,[7] and also with the remarkable semantic shift undergone by the word 'poetry' in later romantic writing; 'poetry' came to be habitually used to mean an essence or spirit, where it had formerly signified a genre. Romantic idealism is not merely a philosophical position, however, and at the same time as the creation of poetry comes to be seen as an internal and invisible affair, the poet himself is elevated to a level far above that of the humble craftsman. The author (a word which Wordsworth tends to avoid, preferring 'Poet' with a capital 'P') has become the quintessential 'authority'.

In Wordsworth's theory, as we have seen, the poet's authority does not derive from his command of language. But while poetry is the natural expression of the ordinary and basic emotions of life, this does not mean that poetic success is open to all. The poet is a man of exceptional gifts, who has rigorously cultivated his mind through a discipline of meditation. Having done this, he can boast, as Wordsworth does, that each of his poems has a 'worthy purpose'. The poetry may have its source in the springs of inspiration, but it has been duly filtered through the poet's conscience and moral sensibility. It is notable what a solitary and internalised picture this gives of poetic creation. The key determinants – the author's mental endowments, his experiences of observation and habits of meditation, and finally the inspiration itself – are all held within the self. Thus the poet is not, as Johnson had said, a 'general challenger' who 'offers his merit to the publick judgment'. There is no challenge or submission or reward; only the eventual recognition of his intrinsic and inalienable merits. I have suggested that Wordsworth's peculiar class position helped him

to take this attitude, the results of which are seen in his lofty eloquence and poetic pride.

It was not only by writing Odes to Liberty that the romantics
participated in the revolutionary 'spirit of the age'. Though the
change in social structure seemed to threaten the very existence
of poets and poetry, men such as the later Wordsworth, Browning
and Tennyson emerged in the Victorian period as revered and
leading members of the bourgeoisie. The early deaths of Byron,
Shelley and Keats left unanswered the question of what other role
– apart from that of Bohemian exile – the major nineteenth-century
poet could adopt. All of these poets, however, claimed to be the
incarnation of higher and more permanent values than those which
the contemporary social world acknowledged. They were much
more than just the spokesmen of these values. Wordsworth's prefaces had pioneered the claim that to accept the authority of a
new volume of poems was to accept a particular social ideology.

There is a distinction to be made between the proud individualism of Wordsworth, his determination to stand on his own two
feet unaided by tradition, and his eventual acknowledgment of
a spiritual kinship with his fellow-poets which differs from his feelings towards ordinary men. 'Resolution and Independence' illustrates all three kinds of feeling: it is a powerfully egotistical poem,
it presents a famous symbol of fellow-man in the Leech-gatherer,
and it also, through the recollections of Chatterton and Burns,
invokes a kind of freemasonry among poets:

> We Poets in our youth begin in gladness;
> But thereof come in the end despondency and madness.

Wordsworth is determined to attribute his loneliness as a poet
to external causes. So much depends on the poet's own efforts
– 'By our own spirits are we deified' – because he has been robbed
of an established tradition. He can no longer write directly and
sincerely in the Augustan mode, but that mode is only the expression of a frivolous and corrupted society. In order to justify
his poetry it is necessary to remind his readers what the foundations
of 'real society' are. When he did this, Wordsworth was using his
poetry as a base from which to launch one of the many competing
ideologies of the revolutionary age. As an abstract and total account
of social relations, the theory of poetry he put forward invites comparison with the other new ideologies such as utilitarianism, republicanism and Burkeian conservatism. Naturally it shares some
elements with its rivals: the rationalistic frame of the 1800 Preface
is taken from republicanism, while the lofty and dignified role that

he assigns to 'pleasure' would align Wordsworth with the utilitarians. But it would be a mistake to reduce his theory to its political constituents and to call it conservative, utilitarian or democratic. The romantic theory of poetry is a distinct ideology, in conflict with those around it. Conceived by Wordsworth and Coleridge as a substitute for their shattered beliefs in republicanism and pantisocracy, it would later become a powerful weapon against the assumptions of utilitarians and nineteenth-century liberals.[8]

Wordsworth's claim for the poet's authority is implicit in the very language of the Preface – a stately and orotund prose that is totally at variance with the 'natural' ideal that it is employed to convey. For genuinely 'natural' and spontaneous prose in the romantic period we may go to the marginalia and graffiti of Blake or to the notebooks of Coleridge, but certainly not to Wordsworth. Within the Preface, however, there is strictly speaking not one style, but two. The first, which dominates the text of 1800, is the style of egotistical self-defence. Its lofty and occasionally provocative arrogance resembles the 1798 'Advertisement', but the manner is now that of a credo, a first-person affirmation. In the 1802 text, however, Wordsworth added a more stately and impersonal section, presenting an abstract sketch of the nature of the poet and his function in society. Here he presents his 'sublime notion of Poetry' in extravagant terms:

> Poetry is the breath and finer spirit of all knowledge; it is the impassioned expression which is in the countenance of all Science. Emphatically may it be said of the Poet, as Shakespeare hath said of man, 'that he looks before and after.' He is the rock of defence of human nature; an upholder and preserver, carrying everywhere with him relationship and love. In spite of difference of soil and climate, of language and manners, of laws and customs: in spite of things gone silently out of mind, and things violently destroyed; the Poet binds together by passion and knowledge the vast empire of human society, as it is spread over the whole earth, and over all time.

The noble idealism of this is only equalled by its abstraction from any tangible social reality. What we respond to is chiefly the religious fervour; it is the prose equivalent of the Miltonic and visionary verse of much of *The Prelude*. To speak of the poet in 'ideal perfection' is to instil a belief in the miracle of incarnation. The realm of permanent values can be made flesh in history; if we can envision the 'vast empire of human society', and feel relationship and love towards it, Wordsworth's work has begun to bear fruit. The religious terms in which he couches his new ideology make him the first of the nineteenth-century literary prophets. His 'vast empire' is a secularised Kingdom of Heaven, in which the poet can assume his full stature as priest and even as god.

The messianic vision came to dominate Wordsworth's verse as he planned his 'great philosophical poem' and began work on *The Prelude*. The opening lines record an occasion when

> poetic numbers came
> Spontaneously, and cloth'd in priestly robe
> My spirit, thus singled out, as it might seem,
> For holy services:

Imagination is the 'vision and the faculty divine', and the poet is its priest. At his loftiest he may aspire to

> breathe in worlds
> To which the heaven of heavens is but a veil[9]

– but at the same time he is fated not to fulfil his designs, and to feel a continuing guilt about his own inadequacy:

> Thus from day to day
> I live, a mockery of the brotherhood
> Of vice and virtue, with no skill to part
> Vague longing that is bred by want of power
> From paramount impulse not to be withstood,
> A timorous capacity from prudence;
> From circumspection, infinite delay.

> (*The Prelude*, Book 1)

There are many varieties of romantic despondency, but Wordsworth's usually has the appearance of a saving ritual, a kind of humility that is the reverse of unproductive. His membership of the 'brotherhood/Of vice and virtue' obliges him to bear witness as a critic in this world as well as aspiring to a higher, and to bring his readers down to the level of common humanity as well as up to the realm of absolute values. Mankind, he wrote in the 'Essay Supplementary', must be 'humbled and humanized, in order that they may be purified and exalted'.

Thus Wordsworth is both the possessor and even apostle of the 'vision and the faculty divine', and the critical revolutionary bringing plain, down-to-earth remedies for the ills of literature and society, confident in his direct grasp of the principles of universal nature. Coleridge would later attack the authority of Wordsworthian natural reason in the name of literary experience and tradition, just as Burke had attacked the French revolutionaries and their doctrines of the Rights of Man. But Wordsworth's assumption of this authority was an essential part of his legacy to literary criticism. Criticism, he suggests, has a task of social hygiene before it, which should be the common pursuit of the right-minded:

> reflecting upon the magnitude of the general evil, I should be oppressed with no dishonourable melancholy, had I not a deep impression of certain inherent and indestructible qualities of the human mind, and likewise of certain powers in the great and permanent objects that act upon it which are equally inherent and indestructible; and did I not further add to this impression a belief that the time is approaching when the evil will be systematically opposed by men of greater powers and with far more distinguished success.

Here was a programme for such successors as Arnold, Eliot and Leavis: critics of culture who share his propagandist instincts, as well as his contempt for frivolities such as 'frantic novels', German tragedies and a taste for sherry. In these lines the defence of a volume of poems gives rise not merely to an ideology but to a crusade.

Poetic power: Wordsworth and de Quincey

> High is our calling, Friend! Creative Art . . .
> Demands the service of a mind and heart,
> Though sensitive, yet, in their weakest part,
> Heroically fashioned . . .

> ('To B. R. Haydon')

One of the remarkable aspects of Wordsworth's later years was his concern for the architecture of his collected works. He began to consider the classification of his shorter poems in 1809,[1] and by 1815 he had devised the complex scheme that was until recently perpetuated by the Oxford editors. At the same time, he planned what was to have been his greatest poem, 'The Recluse', and in the Preface to *The Excursion* (1814) he wrote of his life's work as a vast Gothic cathedral of which *The Prelude* and the minor poems were subsidiary chapels. The nave, in the event, remained uncompleted, but this remarkable simile is enough to show how profoundly his attitude to poetry had changed since he and Coleridge had launched their revolution with a handful of experimental ballads. Much of his later criticism, like the sonnet to Haydon, is concerned with the heroic nature of the artist's vocation. He steadily abandons the mimetic and anti-literary doctrines of 1800 ('I have at all times endeavoured to look steadily at my subject') in favour of a more exalted and mystified version of 'poetic truth'. In the first of the three 'Essays upon Epitaphs' (1810), he stipulates that an epitaph should not be too precise or analytical, but should view the deceased 'through a tender haze or a luminous mist'. The result would not be falsehood, as might be expected, but a higher order of truth – 'truth hallowed by love – the joint offspring of the worth of the Dead and the affections of the Living!'

This higher order of truth is what both he and Coleridge would soon be calling 'imaginative' truth. The term 'imagination' is twice used in the Preface to *Lyrical Ballads*, once in a positive and once in a negative context, but its precise significance remains obscure. In the Preface of 1815, however, Wordsworth rejected the definition of imagination in terms of mimesis (ascribed to a contemporary lexicographer, William Taylor of Norwich) in favour of one reflecting his new sense of the dignity of poetry:

> Imagination, in the sense of the word as giving title to a Class of the following Poems, has no reference to images that are merely a faithful copy, existing in the mind, of absent external objects; but is a word of higher import, denoting operations of the mind upon those objects, and processes of creation or of composition, governed by certain fixed laws.

We have come a long way from the ambition of transcribing natural emotions and common incidents expressed in the 'Advertisement' of 1798. The movement, however, had been anticipated in Wordsworth's poetry. *The Prelude*, for example, begins with a passive invocation of the muse of nature ('Oh there is blessing in this gentle breeze'), and ends with natural objects transformed into the emblems or outward manifestations of mind. The poet climbs Mount Snowdon and interprets the panorama from the summit as 'the type of a majestic intellect'; and he finally closes the poem with a eulogy of the human mind, 'A thousand times more beautiful than the earth / On which he dwells'. The critical counterpart of this movement is the 1815 Preface, written to explain the classification of his shorter poems. Wordsworth's system of classification was a psychological one, avoiding the traditional hierarchy of genres which he had rejected in 1800. Instead, a new and idiosyncratic hierarchy was set up. The main part of the Preface consists of the distinction of fancy and imagination, and then of a review of the 'grand store-house' of lofty imagination present in great literature. Examples are given from the Bible, Milton, Spenser and Shakespeare – to which list, anticipating the judgment of posterity and defying 'these unfavourable times', Wordsworth unashamedly adds himself. He was now relying on a new understanding of the poetic tradition, rather than the principles of abstract reason, to legitimise his authority.

The 1815 Preface was followed by the supplementary 'Essay' which constitutes his most embattled piece of literary propaganda. Here at last he let fly at Jeffrey of the *Edinburgh Review* and at the other critics whose hostility had galled him for years. In the first paragraph, dropped from subsequent editions, little is left of his normally imperturbable stance:

> By what fatality the orb of my genius (for genius none of them seem to deny me) acts upon these men like the moon upon a certain description of patients, it would be irksome to inquire; nor would it consist with the respect which I owe myself to take further notice of opponents whom I internally despise.

What Wordsworth did feel he owed himself was an imposing piece of self-justification. The 'Essay', however, is a complex document, partly a discussion of the act of reading, partly a history of English poetry and partly a rehearsal of his own claims of greatness. The latter aspect may be disposed of first. Wordsworth begins by discussing the qualifications for critical judgment. He asserts that the qualified critic must have devoted the best part of his understanding to literary study (significantly, he has no trust in the common or naive reader). But he then turns furiously on the majority of cultivated readers with their 'palsied imaginations and indurated hearts'. The true critic is distinguished by his reverence for original genius; no doubt, as in the 1798 'Advertisement', there is a strictly contemporary yardstick that he has in mind. He proceeds to give a history of English public taste, angled to prove that genuinely original poets have always been neglected – an important example of the post-revolutionary rewriting of history. Finally he pronounces himself satisfied with his own hostile reception; it is proof that he has not worked in vain. A poet's allegiance, he says, is owed not to the literary public but to the 'People, philosophically characterized' and the 'embodied spirit of their knowledge'.

Maybe such allegiance is easily sworn; and the spectacle of a poet publicly awarding himself the crown of survival is a little undignified. However, we have here the faith which kept Wordsworth going as a poet, and saved him from the defeatism of the late Augustans. The conspicuous satisfactions which he managed to draw from initial public rejection were far from discouraging to later poets. And the 'Essay' has a classic status, not merely on account of the eloquence that genius can bring to the task of self-vindication, but because of its analysis of the concept of taste. Though he stresses the rarity of taste (which may, therefore, be considered the possession of an élite), he also redefines it in such a way as to assert the reality of literary revolutions. Taste, Wordsworth points out, is not a passive response to literary consumption, but the product of 'intellectual acts and operations'. Here he introduces an idea which is of crucial importance throughout romantic theory – the idea of poetic power.

'Every author, as far as he is great and at the same time *original*, has had the task of *creating* the taste by which he is to be enjoyed.' The great author, on this view, does not stand at the bar of public opinion; he has the task of forming that opinion, and need make no concessions to it until he has done so. The act of reading poetry is not one of acquiring knowledge, but involves 'the exertion of a co-operating power' in the reader's mind. This power is a latent sympathy or source of psychic energy. Once the poet has overcome the reader's resistance or inertia and awakened it, it makes a permanent extension of consciousness – 'widening the sphere of human sensibility, for the delight, honour, and benefit of human nature'. Genius – the ability to communicate and excite such power – then appears as an arduous moral and educational responsibility, and the poet as a shaper of civilisation. Wordsworth's discussion presents a curious mixture of psychological analysis and submerged political implications. There is something Napoleonic about the great poet, seen as a wielder of 'power':

> If every great poet with whose writings men are familiar, in the highest exercise of his genius, before he can be thoroughly enjoyed, has to call forth and to communicate power, this service, in a still greater degree, falls upon an original writer, at his first appearance in the world . . . Genius is the introduction of a new element into the intellectual universe: or, if that be not allowed, it is the application of powers to objects on which they had not before been exercised, or the employment of them in such a manner as to produce effects hitherto unknown. What is all this but an advance, or a conquest, made by the soul of the poet?

Political metaphors are never far from the surface of romantic criticism. No doubt this reflects the disappointment of their youthful revolutionary hopes, but the evidence in Wordsworth's writings is that his political energies were thoroughly sublimated. By 'power' he means an emotional charge which takes possession of the reader and moves him to vital and passionate response; an elemental aspect of literary experience which had previously been muffled by such traditional formulae as those of 'sublimity' or 'pity and terror'.

'Power' became a jargon-word among romantic critics and reviewers. It was found particularly useful when dealing with the uneven and unpolished works of Byron, Shelley and Keats. Thus Lamb wrote of Byron that 'I never can make out his great power, which his admirers talk of'.[2] Coleridge offered to demonstrate the 'specific symptoms of poetic power' in Chapter Fifteen of *Biographia Literaria*, and concluded that 'In Shakespeare's poems, the creative power and the intellectual energy wrestle as in a war embrace.' Shelley spoke of the 'electric life' burning in the words of modern poets, while de Quincey wrote unforgettably of the conflict of 'power' and self-repression that he saw in Dorothy Wordsworth's face.[3] It was de Quincey, also, who did his best to preserve the term for serious criticism with his famous distinction of the 'literature of knowledge' and the 'literature of power' – essentially a popularisation of Wordsworth's argument in the 'Essay Supplementary'. De Quincey's 'literature of power' means simply imaginative literature, or literature considered as one of the fine arts, and the communication of power is the awakening of latent emotions and feelings in the reader. In fact, though he speaks of a 'literature of knowledge', de Quincey also suggests that this is not really literature at all: 'All that is literature seeks to communicate power; all that is not literature, to communicate knowledge.'[4] Since this is a crucial moment in the evolution of the term 'literature' as the permanent, imaginative heritage of a people, it is significant that it emerges not only in opposition to eighteenth-century aesthetics, but in opposition to the utilitarian emphasis on useful knowledge.[5] It was de Quincey, a lifelong critic of Benthamism and political economy, who forged the idea of a 'literature of power' as a weapon of Victorian debate.

De Quincey was one of the many writers in whom Wordsworth's seminal influence took effect. That influence, indeed, may be pursued throughout later romantic criticism. Given Wordsworth's combination of profound originality and extreme self-assurance, it is not surprising that he himself should show divided aims, so that very different emphases could be drawn from his work; he could be seen as revolutionary or authoritarian, as nature-worship-per or cultural dictator, as enemy of literature or apostle of the imagination. It remains to be recorded that, in a personal and idiosyncratic way, Wordsworth himself was able to reconcile many of these conflicts. After all, the original source of 'power' for him lay not in the arts but in nature itself. All other sources of the experience of power in his work are eventually compared to the forces of nature. This is true of the experience of the Metropolis in Book Eight of *The Prelude* and of the books that the poet read as a boy in Book Five. It is also true of poetry, including Wordsworth's own, so that our exploration of his poetics must finally go full circle, from nature to art and back to nature again.

A simple example is the genre of the epitaph, to which Wordsworth devoted three consecutive essays in 1810. These neglected essays are the most mature expression of the Wordsworth who revolted against the literary Establishment of 1800. The epitaph as he describes it is a genuine mode of folk-poetry, expressing common feelings in the ordinary language of men. It has a very tangible social function, and yet one which transcends the world of human society, since it is an expression of man's belief in immortality. If for a moment we can be persuaded to think of the epitaph as a central poetic genre, it will not be hard to accept Wordsworth's feeling for the elementality and permanence of rustic life centred upon the village churchyard. Still better, the epitaph is not 'a proud Writing shut up for the studious', but an outdoor object, and part of the permanent landscape: 'it is concerning all, and for all: – in the Church-yard it is open to the day; the sun looks down upon the stone, and the rains of Heaven beat against it.'

The 'Essays upon Epitaphs', then, present an idyllic and somewhat feudal vision. It is no more than an idyll, of course, because whatever their merits epitaphs belong to one of the minor genres, and Wordsworth does not claim otherwise. They may epitomise wisdom and common humanity, but not the energy of 'power'. And yet in his poetry Wordsworth aspired to a vision in which even the most grandiose and heroic of artistic works might appear as natural objects. The aspiration is stated at the beginning of one of the great visionary passages in *The Prelude*:

> forgive me, Friend,
> If I, the meanest of this Band, had hope
> That unto me had also been vouchsafed
> An influx, that in some sort I possess'd
> A privilege, and that a work of mine,
> Proceeding from the depth of untaught things,
> Enduring and creative, might become

A power like one of Nature's.

(Book 12)

Wordsworth goes on to recall the summer of 1793 when he roamed over Salisbury Plain. Amid the prehistoric monuments of the plain, he 'had a reverie and saw the past': lurid visions of battle, of human sacrifice, and then, in calmer moments as he came across the great megaliths of the plain, the worship of the Druids. The 'lines, circles, mounts' left by the Druids are a perfect image of the work of art which has arisen out of culture to merge with the natural landscape. These monuments were 'imitative forms', designed to represent the plan of the heavens. In Wordsworth's imaginative vision, the Druids who made them become unmistakable archetypes of the tribe of the Bard:

> gently was I charmed
> Into a waking dream, a reverie
> That, with believing eyes, where'er I turned,
> Beheld long-bearded teachers, with white wands
> Uplifted, pointing to the starry sky,
> Alternately, and plain below, while breath
> Of music swayed their motions, and the waste
> Rejoiced with them and me in those sweet sounds.

The long-bearded Druids are set over against a bloodthirsty society, with no taint of that society's guilt or toil, though they are its 'teachers'. We see them performing ritual gestures to the sounds of a wind-borne music – a community of poets worshipping in tune with the 'gentle breeze' of natural inspiration. It is an atavistic, arcadian vision, located in a society far removed in time, though continuous with us in its occupation of natural space. Wordsworth's evocation of Stonehenge to exemplify his view of art as a 'natural' power – the poem as megalith – closes the penultimate Book of *The Prelude*, and it is counterbalanced in the final lines of the poem by a Utopian exhortation to the poets of the future. They too will be exempted from the general human condition, and set in authority over men as the prophets and teachers of a Christian revelation. The source of this vision, however, lies not in religious orthodoxy but in the romantic exaltation of the poet and the world of literature:

> Prophets of Nature, we to them will speak
> A lasting inspiration, sanctified
> By reason and by truth; what we have loved,

Others will love; and we may teach them how;
Instruct them how the mind of man becomes
A thousand times more beautiful than the earth
On which he dwells, above this Frame of things
(Which, 'mid all revolutions in the hopes
And fears of men, doth still remain unchanged)
In beauty exalted, as it is itself
Of substance and of fabric more divine.

The perfection that the poet reveals is at two removes from the world in which we live our lives, and make and suffer 'revolutions'. Beyond society and untouched by it lies the 'Frame' of nature, and above that the realm of mind. It is to such an ideal, Platonic world that the romantic poet would conduct us, offering us reason and truth in the form of a sanctified symbol. The symbol is realised in literature. Wordsworth's criticism must be read alternately as symbol and as interpretation of the symbol; that is to say, as the expression of a creative vision seeking to awaken a co-operative 'power' within us, and as a far-reaching but misleading and contradictory poetic theory. No other poet-critic has left so much for his heirs to fight over.

3   The Romantic Critics

Reviewers and Bookmen: from Jeffrey to Lamb

'The language of poetry naturally falls in with the language of power.' So Hazlitt, in his essay on 'Coriolanus', underlined the political analogy which is implied by much of romantic criticism. The poetic imagination aggrandises and dominates; its possessor commands and holds sway over the emotions of his readers. The analogy is double-edged. Though intended as a ringing affirmation of the poet's authority, it frequently expresses his underlying impotence. Coleridge, for example, sounds slightly peevish as he manipulates the concept of power in the following remarks:

> All men in power are jealous of the pre-eminence of men of letters; they feel, as towards them, conscious of inferior power, and a sort of misgiving that they are, indirectly, and against their own will, mere instruments and agents of higher intellects. ... So entirely was Mr. Pitt aware of this, that he would never allow of any intercourse with literary men of eminence; ...[1]

It is not only Pitt's political adherents who might have felt that the boot was on the other foot. Once Wordsworth, Coleridge and Southey had renounced their revolutionary beliefs, they succumbed all too easily to the charms of the men in power. Moreover, their retreat to the Lake District did not protect them from an unparalleled degree of political animosity. There was in fact no position of dignified 'eminence' to which the romantics could escape unscathed. Wordsworth in the Preface to *The Excursion* might challenge comparison with Milton for his high purpose, but, as Byron savagely reminded his readers, Milton was no renegade from the republican cause:

> Would he adore a Sultan? He obey
> The intellectual eunuch Castlereagh?

Wordsworth appears in the notes to *Don Juan* as 'this poetical charlatan and political parasite [who] licks up the crumbs with a hardened alacrity' at the table of Lord Lonsdale (to whom *The Excursion* was dedicated).[2] Such bitterness ran high in the years of the Peninsular War, of Waterloo and the Peterloo Massacre – the years, too, in which Wordsworth's greatness, or at least his influence, came grudgingly to be admitted. While the better critics tried to hold the balance between their aesthetic and political inclinations, much that was written was as crude as a cartoon by Rowlandson. The atmosphere was not improved – though neither, in all probability, was it made any worse – by the emergence of the great reviews. With the founding of the *Edinburgh* in 1802, and the *Quarterly* as its Tory competitor in 1809, literary criticism became more a matter of party lines than at any time since Pope and Swift. The quarterlies were far from indifferent to the major developments in poetry, and Wordsworth at least found that it was far better to be baited than to be ignored.

The quarterlies were a product of the Scottish enlightenment, and played a significant part in the nineteenth-century broadening of culture. The *Edinburgh Review* was founded to promote political and social reform. Hazlitt, writing in 1825, saw it as a great organ of democratisation, spreading the example of informed, rational comment on public and intellectual issues to a wide readership (its rival, by the same token, was dedicated to leading multitudes by the nose).[3] Though articles in the *Edinburgh* and *Quarterly* were by far the longest and best paid, these two journals were not alone in their field. John O. Hayden records that the number of periodicals carrying regular reviews doubled between 1800 and 1810, and reached a peak of at least thirty-one in the early 1820s.[4] This explosion of literary reviewing must be considered as a social phenomenon in its own right.

Probably all of the early reviews were run by small cliques. For breadth of outlook and the sense of the columns being open to all-comers we must wait until the mid-Victorian period. Jeffrey's inveterate habit of rewriting his contributor's copy is symptomatic; the *Edinburgh* and *Quarterly* in their early days were closed shops. None the less, Hazlitt's enthusiasm was not entirely misplaced, and his claims would have been fully justified had they been made on behalf of the institution of reviewing as a whole, and not just in defence of one particular editor. To have a periodical composed entirely of book reviews presupposes a constant stream of new books demanding attention, and a literary or cultivated class anxious to be informed about them. Their anxiety to be informed stems from a consciousness of social change – to consider oneself enlightened one must keep up with events – so that it is no accident that the first of the great reviews was on the side of the Whigs.

The stream of new books is felt as at once a promise and a threat. There is the promise of intellectual progress and cultural improvement; one is bound to widen one's sensibility (in Wordsworth's phrase) by keeping up with the new. But there is also the threat of losing one's bearings, of being carried along in the cultural torrent with no sense of fixed standards or priorities which can be taken for granted. Any review, therefore, is bound to combine up-to-dateness with a sense of stability, providing a source of judgment on which the reader can rely. That the early *Edinburgh* and *Quarterly* have achieved such a bad reputation is partly due to venality and corruption, but more to their overemphasis on this stabilising function. Thus Jeffrey began his review of Southey's *Thalaba* (the first of his onslaughts on the Lake Poets) in volume one of the *Edinburgh* with the following stultifying credo:

> Poetry has this much, at least, in common with religion, that its standards were fixed long ago by certain inspired writers whose authority it is no longer lawful to call in question; and that many profess to be entirely devoted to it who have no good works to produce in support of their pretensions.

Jeffrey was completely sincere in suggesting that Wordsworth and Southey were propounding a dangerous, Rousseauistic heresy, but the very existence of a review casts doubt on this notion of incontestable authority.

Behind the early reviews lay the ideal of Hume's Man of Taste, serenely applying the comparative method to each new book and trying it by the standard of everything that already existed. The critic's stance was judicial and informative, his style was pellucid and his points were lavishly illustrated by quotation. Jeffrey came closest to this ideal, though outside his notorious attacks on the Lake School his lawyer-like displays of trenchant platitudes are often rather dull. Jeffrey was no orthodox neoclassic, and though he detested Wordsworth he admired various romantic traits in Scott, Crabbe, Byron and Burns. Where he seems to take up the burden of Addison and Pope is in striving to defend a literary decorum plainly based on class. The standard of politeness and gentility is fixed, but writers seem increasingly unwilling to conform to it; hence the critic's patience is easily tried, and contempt and ridicule come to his aid. The challenge of simplicity and 'vulgarity' in literature was the main thing that had to be met. Besides the attacks on Wordsworth, Jeffrey's essay on Burns was given over to fine discriminations of what was, and was not, acceptable to a gentleman, while he found Scott's ability to please both informed judges and the general public to be the most provocative feature of 'The Lady of the Lake'. But if the democratic impulse in poetry had to be viewed with intense suspicion, neither was patrician hauteur any more acceptable; hence, perhaps, Brougham's savaging of Byron's *Hours of Idleness* in the *Edinburgh Review* for January 1808: 'The poesy of this young lord belongs to the class which neither gods nor man are said to permit.' The politeness and gentility of the *Edinburgh* was essentially middle-class.

But this, perhaps, is to look at the matter too impersonally. Keats was not alone in being praised by the *Edinburgh* because he was damned by the *Quarterly*; the judicial rhetoric of periodical reviewing was often only a façade. It is nice to see Hazlitt gracefully extricating himself at a tricky moment in *The Spirit of the Age*: 'We had written thus far when news came of the death of Lord Byron, and put an end at once to a strain of somewhat peevish invective, which was intended to meet his eye, not to insult his memory.' All too often reviewing was intended to meet somebody's eye. Poets who had smarted under the lash were inclined, like Coleridge, to sneer at the whole business as a despotism of eunuchs, with broad hints of their own superior potency.[5] The quarterlies had succeeded in demonstrating the existence of a new public eager for literary instruction. In the Victorian period the reviews were destined to reach a level of integrity and seriousness which made them the central organs of literary culture; but that time was not yet. How could the public be offered a less partial and opportunistic version of critical reason and truth?

One answer lay in the literary survey and lecture. In 1804 the Royal Institution in London began to offer public lectures on non-technical subjects, and four years later Coleridge gave there the first of his lecture-courses, and the first important series of public lectures on literature in England. Coleridge's motives for lecturing were mainly financial, and despite his personal magnetism his success was very variable. Sometimes we hear of him holding forth to a fashionable London audience of six or seven hundred, and attracting droppers-in like Byron and Rogers. At other times he disconsolately faced a dozen or so in a hotel at Clifton. In all, he gave ten courses of lectures between 1808 and 1819, and the results must have awakened the rivalry of Hazlitt, whose three courses began in 1818. Hazlitt and Coleridge between them covered the development of English literature from Chaucer onwards; a new mode of criticism had arisen to fulfil a new demand. Coleridge's prospectus for his 1818 course exhibits rather nakedly the lecturer's rueful sense of his audience, earnest for literary instruction so long as they could feel it was useful, not too arduous, and productive of small talk in the presence of ladies. But here he was selling himself short. When the lectures succeeded it was because they were an intellectual event, not a useful social diversion. The young men present were scribbling down their notes for posterity.

The intellectual origin of the romantic lecture-courses lay in Germany. Hazlitt made his acknowledgments to A.W. Schlegel's *Vorlesungen über dramatische Kunst und Litteratur* (1809–11) in the Preface to *The Characters of Shakespeare's Plays*. In his erratic 1811–12 course, the first of which we have detailed records, Coleridge suddenly pulled himself together in the ninth lecture when (perhaps not for the first time) he had managed to procure a copy of Schlegel.[6] In 1813 we find him writing from Bristol to his London hosts, the Morgans, asking them to send his copy of the *Vorlesungen* together with two thick memorandum-books inscribed 'Vorlesungen: Schlegel' which he had taken to his earlier lectures at the Surrey Institution.[7] There is no question that a good proportion of the material in his lecture-courses was plagiarised; scholars argue over whether there is sufficient original material to support his enormous reputation as a Shakespeare critic. Coleridge tended to claim that his thoughts coincided with the Germans, rather than being overwhelmingly influenced by them. Whether or not this can be proved, it can hardly affect our recognition of the greatness and originality of the German romantic critics whose words he liked to borrow.

Basically, their achievement was to view literature as an international cultural heritage to be understood in the light of a philosophy of history. Literary history, that is, if properly interpreted, reflects or embodies the essential history of civilisation. The primitive literary historians of eighteenth-century England had put forward a simple version of this essential history: poetry, they argued, flourishes in a rude and barbarous state of society, and recedes as rationality and decorum advance. This argument was so widely disseminated that few romantic critics could refrain from outlining a potted history of culture. Although the primitivist theory regularly had an anti-Enlightenment thrust, since it focused on the shortcomings of 'rational' civilisation, its crudity was typical of Enlightenment historiography. To the German critics influenced by Kant and Herder, history appeared a more complex process and one that demanded more systematic study. Culture was interpreted in terms of dialectical oppositions such as Schiller's naive and sentimental, and Schlegel's classical and romantic; the nostalgia inherent in the primitivist case was acknowledged, even though its licence was extended. Since different kinds of artistic excellence could be achieved at different times, criticism became a subtle blend of normative and relativistic tendencies.

It was the elder Schlegel who applied the new approach to a methodical survey of European drama from Aeschylus down to Goethe and Schiller. He was disparaged for his professorial approach both in Germany and England, but the *Lectures on Dramatic Art and Literature*, translated into English in 1815, now appear as one of the foundation stones of modern humanistic criticism. Schlegel has the epic sweep, if not quite the depth, of an Auerbach or a Lukács, and his is the first Grand Tour of the European literary museum. Much depends on his ability to get the tone right – to bring a sense of rational, urbane and yet personal appraisal to every work that he studies. English readers were particularly attracted by his treatment of Shakespeare, a majestic expression of the Shakespearean vogue in Germany which had begun with Lessing and Herder. Schlegel's emphasis on fair-minded appreciation might seem thoroughly neoclassical – the ideal expression of Hume's doctrine of universal taste – were it not for his emancipation from the historical parochialism of the Enlightenment (Shakespeare is no longer the 'child of nature'), and his confident recognition of the irrational. For Schlegel was able both to endorse the new values of poetic power and creativity, and to contain them within a framework of rationalistic history. His doctrine of organic form, which was immediately borrowed by Coleridge, is a clear example of such containment. Schlegel was able to write with warmth of the romantic 'expression of the secret attraction to a chaos which lies concealed in the very bosom of the ordered universe'[8] precisely because he felt able to explain it. He is a modern humanist, however, because his rationalism seems something less than inevitable; it is only one of the possible ways of responding to the challenge of the human condition that he expounds (Wordsworth, Coleridge, Hazlitt are among those who represent other ways) and this gives it a willed and precarious quality. The criticism of the other romantics is more far-reaching, but its relation to rationality is much more problematic than his.

One irrational aspect of literature is its connection with national pride. The English response to the fulsome reception of their national poet in Germany was necessarily ambivalent. Coleridge and Hazlitt rushed to supply an 'English' Shakespeare, purloining the best features of Schlegel while going one better and pointing out the German critic's shortcomings. The detachment of Schlegel's comparatist outlook, however, owed much to his nationality. The European dramatic heritage appeared to him as a sequence of foreign literatures; he could survey these impartially (allowing for some bias against the French) while proclaiming that the present and future belonged to his own country. But patriotism was an issue that divided English critics. De Quincey became a champion of the international character of great literature; he saw that poets belong not to the nation-state but to the 'vast empire of human society'. Hazlitt, likewise, wrote of those capable of appreciating the writers of Shakespeare's age as 'true cosmopolites'.[9] But the attitude which has often been uppermost in English studies is the reverse of this – the conservative nationalism represented by Coleridge. Coleridge speaks of 'mock cosmopolitism',[10] and when lecturing on English literature his heart often swells with patriotic pride. At best, he shows that grasp of the inner nature of national institutions to which John Stuart Mill was to pay tribute; but at his worst – as on King Alfred – he gives us Kiplingesque school-history. None the less, Coleridge has an unprecedented intimacy with the historical tradition of literature, above all in his fascination with the seventeenth century. Lamb's influential *Specimens of English Dramatic Poets Who Lived About the Time of Shakespeare* (1808) are precisely what their name implies – specimens gathered on aesthetic grounds by a good antiquarian. Hazlitt's *Lectures on the Age of Elizabeth* are reputed to have been mugged up in six weeks, presumably to satisfy a public demand. Coleridge stands alone in the depth with which he took the imprint of seventeenth-century language and its ways of thought.

Although Hazlitt and Coleridge both attempted the genre of the critical survey, neither embraced it wholeheartedly as Schlegel had done. As had happened a century earlier, a mode of rationalistic criticism imported from the continent was transmuted into a more English form, in which the social attitude conveyed by the critic seems at least as important as his facts and arguments. The study of English literary history in the nineteenth century became the preserve of those whom we may call the 'book-men' – the cosy, antiquarian bibliophiles whose outlook was defined by Lamb and Hazlitt, the essayists of the 1820s. John Gross has shown that the bookish ethos emerged with the *London Magazine* (1820–9) to which Lamb, Hazlitt, de Quincey and Landor all contributed. This was at once a metropolitan phenomenon ('It was less like a magazine than a club', Gross comments)[11] and an attempt to insulate the critic from all those considerations of standards and party politics which ruled in Edinburgh reviewing.

The bookishness of the essayists may be approached by way of the new attitude to drama that was emerging. Johnson's discussion of the Unities of Place and Time in the 'Preface to Shakespeare' had dislodged the neoclassical rules, without putting anything very satisfactory in their place. All the romantics felt that his blunt assertion that 'the spectators are always in their senses' was derogatory to art, and several accepted the challenge to produce a new theory of dramatic illusion. Schlegel and Coleridge both argued that drama makes its appeal to the imaginative faculty, and our experience of it is a kind of voluntary dreaming. Hence, Coleridge says, there is neither complete delusion nor complete detachment, but 'a sort of temporary half-faith' or, in his most famous phrase, a 'willing suspension of disbelief'.[12] This is a psychological account which applies to drama and to the 'perusal of a deeply interesting novel';[13] that is, it will do as well for solitary reading as for the theatre. Schlegel, by contrast, goes on to discuss what he calls the 'theatrical effect' – the communal effect of drama, based on the traditional comparison of drama and oratory. The poet in the theatre, he argues, can 'transport his hearers out of themselves' by evoking the 'power of a visible communion of numbers'.[14] Schlegel reminds his readers of the dangers of mass emotion, and hence of the necessity for censorship and state regulation of theatres. This is all very orthodox and Platonic. Coleridge, however, disregards the effect of the communal audience as completely as Johnson had done. The English romantic critics in general have lost the sense of the essentially public character of drama. Coleridge, Hazlitt and Lamb all express the feeling that Shakespeare's plays are far better when read than on the stage. The case is argued most fully and interestingly in Charles Lamb's essay 'On the Tragedies of Shakespeare, Considered with Reference to their Fitness for Stage Representation' (1811). Lamb does recognise a 'theatrical effect', but he attributes it entirely to the actor rather than the dramatist, and goes so far as to suggest that *Hamlet*, rewritten without the poetry, the intellectual content and the profundity of characterisation, would retain the same degree of theatrical impact. This essay is something of a *jeu d'esprit* – an argument that actors since Garrick have been getting too big for their boots. But it is also an important expression of changing taste. Lamb was not alone in his revolt against the crudely spectacular and melodramatic appeal of theatre in his own day, but the conclusions that he drew show a profound distrust of theatrical performance, which he sees as an inevitable vulgarisation of the written text. (He did not, however, abstain from theatregoing.) The nineteenth century in general came to emphasise those aspects of Shakespeare which seemed to deny performance. It turned his dramas into novels.

Lamb points out that dramatic speech is, like the novel in letters, a non-realistic convention – and in good drama the purpose of the convention is to give us knowledge of the 'inner structure and workings of mind in a character'. But the inner structure of a literary character can only be truly savoured by the solitary reader:

> These profound sorrows, these light-and-noise-abhorring ruminations, which the tongue scarce dares utter to deaf walls and chambers, how can they be represented by a gesticulating actor, who comes and mouths them out before an audience, making four hundred people his confidants at once?

Hamlet, inevitably enough, is the character referred to, and it seems obvious that Lamb is making him into a private *alter ego*, rather than a tragic hero and Prince of Denmark. Lamb is explicit in his belief that Shakespearean characters need 'that vantage-ground of abstraction which reading possesses over seeing', and are properly 'the objects of meditation rather than of interest and curiosity as to their actions'.

'Meditation': the term is Wordsworthian, but it takes on an un-Wordsworthian literariness here. For Lamb is defining a literary or poetic element in drama which can only be profaned in the theatre. The ideal reader of Shakespearean drama, he implies, is the connoisseur savouring his appreciation in the solitude of a book-lined study. The cultivation of older English literature in the nineteenth century can hardly be separated from this image of the bookish life, with its frequentation of forgotten authors and rare editions and its mellow storehouse of anecdotes and 'characters'. Lamb and Hazlitt savour the atmosphere rather than the substance of reading; they delight in melancholy reminiscences, in out-of-the-way quotations, and in confessions of personal likes and dislikes; their world is the world as seen from a comfortable armchair. Yet the leisured bookman of the *Essays of Elia* and Hazlitt's essays was necessarily only a persona, a fiction created by harassed professional men (Hazlitt was a journalist and lecturer, Lamb a civil servant). The bookman represented a spare-time ideal of which all men might become amateurs. As the century continued, the notion of romantic withdrawal to the world of the study became increasingly trivialised. At best, *fin-de-siècle* bookmanship might be represented by a figure such as Saintsbury, relaxed, agreeable and (to the modern reader) intolerably mannered, but none the less a formidable professional scholar. Equally representative, however, was the commercial approach of the *Bookman* magazine (founded in 1891) with its gossip about publishers' autumn lists and its portraits of best-selling lady novelists.

Lamb's essay on Shakespeare argued that the essentially poetic element in drama lay in characterisation. This may suggest that there are broad connections between the rise of bookmanship and the rise of the Victorian novel – both of them reflecting the trend toward the cultivation of private experience. Lamb's essays themselves are indebted to Fielding and Sterne, and look forward to Thackeray and Dickens; the ruminative voice of Elia is not so far from that of the more clubbable Victorian novelists. Both novelists and bookmen may be seen as offering ideals of gentility and spiritual culture to the new middle- and lower-middle-class reading public. Yet the bookish ideal was certainly a meagre one, which insulated its adherent from the pressures of social reality while eliciting none of the ethical and imaginative zeal tapped by the more robust gospels of Dickens, Ruskin or Carlyle.

The Victorian novelist of lower-class origins first had to learn to adopt the social tone of gentility; one can see this in Dickens, and later in the young H.G. Wells. Similarly, the bookman had to pretend to a leisure he did not possess. A title such as Leslie Stephen's *Hours in a Library* suggests, surely, the fruits of idle browsing, not the industry of a prolific historian, intellectual and *D.N.B.* editor. And for all the candour of the self-portrayal of the Regency essayists, what is missing from their work is any sense of themselves as writers. The essayists did not tell the full truth about their reading experiences, since reading for them was part of the work of earning a living. The bookman with time on his hands is made to seem the antithesis of the reviewer and contributor to the *London Magazine*. (A clear illustration of the gulf between 'bookman' and reviewer is provided by the state of Jeffrey's library when it was auctioned off after his death: 'a very poor collection, made up largely of law books and review copies'.[15] Jeffrey was much more interested in his wine cellar, one of the finest in Scotland.) While the reviewer is a metropolitan creature, the bookman often flourishes best in a country home or cottage. Early examples are Southey, who protested that letting Wordsworth into his library at Keswick was 'like letting a bear into a tulip garden'; and de Quincey, who never forgave the same poet for cutting open the pages of a new volume of Burke with the Dove Cottage butter-knife.[16] Hazlitt was proud of his country retreat, Winterslow Hut in Wiltshire, and in 1839 his son published the first selection of his so-called *Winterslow Essays*. Though a coaching inn, Winterslow Hut directly anticipates the writer's cottage of later in the century – peaceful, rustic, but not too far from the railway station. But Winterslow was also the place where Hazlitt mugged up the *Lectures on the Age of Elizabeth* from borrowed volumes in six weeks – a glimpse of the reality underlying the ideal.

If Hazlitt stops short of total candour, the strain of living up to the bookish ideal manifests itself in his outbursts of self-pity. There is his notorious confession that 'Books have in a great measure lost their power over me', and his dejected response to Keats's *Endymion*:

> I know how I should have felt at one time in reading such passages; and that is all. The sharp luscious flavour, the fine aroma is fled, and nothing but the stalk, the bran, the husk of literature is left.
>
> ('On Reading Old Books', 1821)

One might read 'literature' here as the subject of Hazlitt's professional attentions as writer and journalist, while what he aims at and cannot manage is the pure appreciation due to 'poetry'. This is the 'fine aroma' which he, like so many of his successors, saw it as the critic's duty to try to convey. The desultory and impressionistic nature of his and Lamb's criticism is an attempt to realise such a poetic essence of the literature with which they deal. Lamb's preface to his *Extracts from the Garrick Plays* (1827), for example, after dwelling fondly on the 'luxury' of reading through the collection of old plays at Montagu House, outlines his editorial method in these terms:

> You must be content with sometimes a scene, sometimes a song; a speech, or passage, or a poetical image, as they happen to strike me. I read without order of time; I am a poor hand at dates; and for any biography of the Dramatists, I must refer to writers who are more skilful in such matters. My business is with their poetry only.

The critic as bookman soaks himself in an atmosphere of passive literariness, and finally draws out of it a single elixir, poetry alone. This is the decadence of the romantic sense of poetic power – its containment within a cosy and ruminative sphere of the private consciousness which augurs no harm to anyone and can be held up as a spiritual ideal to the new middle classes. But in the best criticism of Hazlitt, as well as of Coleridge, Keats and Shelley, the sense of power which inspired and frustrated the romantics has far more heroic manifestations than this.

Samuel Taylor Coleridge

Biographia Literaria

'The Poet is dead in me', Coleridge told Godwin in 1801. His criticism embodies an attitude to the past very different from the random plundering of old books and fabrication of archaic forms that had been responsible for 'The Ancient Mariner', 'Christabel' and 'Kubla Khan'. In a letter to Sir George and Lady Beaumont in 1804, Coleridge announced that he was now turning to a far more disciplined and methodical form of literary study:

> Each scene of each play I read as if it were the whole of Shakespeare's works – the sole thing extant. I ask myself what are the characteristics, the diction, the cadences, and metre, the character, the passion, the moral or metaphysical inherencies and fitness for theatric effect, and in what sort of theatres. All these I write down with great care and precision of thought and language (and when I have gone through the whole, I then shall collect my papers, and observe how often such and such expressions recur), and thus shall not only know what the characteristics of Shakespeare's plays are, but likewise what proportion they bear to each other.

The voice of the virtuous literary scientist would often be heard in the years leading up to *Biographia Literaria*. The origins of Coleridge's leaning to systematic literary analysis around 1804 might be found in his visit to Germany (1798) and his acquaintance with the trend of German criticism; more immediate considerations, however, were his need to earn money by writing and lecturing, and to distract himself from his personal miseries. Two other main strands led to his emergence as a critic. The first was his discovery that he could use literary theory as a form of disguised self-expression. In October 1800 he had written to Humphry Davy of his plan for an 'Essay on the Elements of Poetry' which would be 'in reality a disguised system of morals and politics'. His political interests at this time were intense; he was discovering a new basis for his beliefs after his repudiation of the republican cause, and was contributing leaders and even parliamentary reports to the *Morning Post*.[1] As he had rejected democracy and the doctrine of abstract rights, it is tempting to suggest that the 'disguised system of morals and politics' was to have been a Burkeian riposte to the arguments from natural reason in the contemporaneous Preface to *Lyrical Ballads*. But we do not know, and Coleridge did not openly dissociate himself from Wordsworth's doctrines until 1802. Three years later, personal confession had become a more urgent necessity than working out a political creed. A new scheme went down in his notebook:

> Seem to have made up my mind to write my metaphysical works

as my Life, and in my Life – intermixed with all the other events
or history of the mind and fortunes of S.T. Coleridge.[2]

This was possibly the crucial moment in the evolution of the form
of the *Biographia*. In adopting the autobiographical form, Coleridge seems to have been making things easier for himself, much
as Wordsworth did in writing a *Prelude* to his 'great philosophical
poem'. Coleridge continued to dream of a metaphysical Treatise
on the 'Logos', though not of an objectively structured treatise
on poetry. But the majority of his published prose consists of
systems of morals and politics: witness *The Friend*, *The Statesman's
Manual*, *Aids to Reflection* and the *Constitution of Church and
State*. Criticism was to prove a vital but not a lasting interest of
his.

The other strand leading to the *Biographia* is that of disagreement with Wordsworth. This was brought into the open by the
revised Preface of 1802. Coleridge responded both by claiming
his share in the original conception of 1800 ('Wordsworth's Preface
is half a child of my own brain')[3] and by taking a very cool look
at the revised version, complaining of its obscurity and over-
elaborate diction. Two letters of July 1802 suggest that the Preface
had been the occasion of a mild quarrel with Wordsworth, in which
he was enlisting his friends' support: 'we have had lately some
little controversy on the subject, and we begin to suspect that there
is somewhere or other a radical difference in our opinions.' The
difference of opinion was over the key question of the nature of
poetic diction. Disagreement with Wordsworth was both now and
later the most important factor which goaded Coleridge into ordering his thoughts about poetry and getting them down on paper.
The main critical chapters of *Biographia Literaria* were eventually
written in the summer of 1815, when he had received a further
prod from Wordsworth's Preface and 'Essay Supplementary',
which had come out in March.[4] Coleridge had sketched out his
distinction between fancy and imagination long before, but it was
only after Wordsworth's discussion of 1815 that it took its final
shape. Yet the disagreement was not a matter of friendly correction
of Wordsworth's statements, despite the show of courtesy in the
Biographia. In writing his critique, Coleridge was announcing his
disaffiliation from the poetic revolution that Wordsworth had advocated and led. Already in 1802, while 'The Ancient Mariner' was
still included in the new edition of *Lyrical Ballads*, he had told
Southey of his intentions of 'acting the arbitrator between the old
school and the new school'. Southey must have found this air of
detachment surprising, to say the least.

What kind of book is the *Biographia*? In the struggle to make sense of it, readers have turned to the programmatic statement at the end of Chapter Four, where Coleridge promises to

> present an intelligible statement of my poetic creed; not as my opinions, which weigh for nothing, but as deductions from established premises conveyed in such a form as is calculated either to effect a fundamental conviction or to receive a fundamental confutation.

The image of Coleridge as the great rationalist among critics survives, although there are few who feel either fundamentally convinced by his deductive arguments, or capable of fundamentally confuting them. In order to achieve either result, we have to reconstruct the arguments, to complete what Coleridge himself left fragmentary and implicit. Theoretical his procedure may have been, but impeccably rational it certainly was not. And in any case, the immediate purpose of the above passage is, characteristically enough, to forestall complaints of obscurity. Moreover, it comes in a book that he was not ashamed to subtitle 'Biographical Sketches of My Literary Life and Opinions'. Considered as literary criticism, the biographical framework is the source of some of its strengths and of most of its weaknesses. *Biographia Literaria* might be seen as the albatross of what Fredric Jameson has called 'dialectical criticism', or criticism which is based on a constant strategy of self-awareness and self-commentary. Coleridge's acute self-consciousness gives even his most daring paragraphs an air of calculation or controlled exhibitionism; yet his impulse to show off is as often checked by that impulse to hide behind turgid qualifications, empty elaborations and professions of good faith which gives to his prose its garrulous, cobwebby quality. Far from being a rational treatise, the *Biographia* is a remarkable product of romantic egotism, in which thought constantly reflecting on itself merges into thought transparently attempting to conceal its own nature.

Fortunately, the book falls into two halves, and the Shandean – and Pecksniffian – aspects are mainly apparent in the first half. The first three chapters are a tedious parade of self-defence against real and imagined enemies. Between digressions, Coleridge tells of his early literary education and tastes, ending with a remarkably fulsome tribute to Southey. Then, in Chapter Four, he recounts the climax of his early development – his meeting with Wordsworth – and at last rises to his subject, passing from garrulousness to one of the finest expressions of the critic's experience in English literature.

There is just one intermediate stage in the transition, for the theme which opens Chapter Four is Coleridge's attempt to dispel 'this fiction of a new school of poetry' and the 'clamors against its supposed founders'. He begins to emerge as the kind of revolutionary who aims to consolidate the change of power by denying that it ever took place. He suggests that the hostility which greeted *Lyrical Ballads* was largely accidental, since the omission of less than a hundred lines would have precluded nine-tenths of the criticism. Moreover, the 1800 Preface was chiefly to blame, as it unnecessarily put people's backs up; the *Lyrical Ballads*, Coleridge feels, should have come into the world more quietly. Despite the venomous attacks on Jeffrey elsewhere in the *Biographia*, this line of argument prepares us for the lengths to which Coleridge was prepared to go in conceding his opponents' case in order to discredit the Preface and Wordsworth's own account of his poetic strengths.

In the 'Essay Supplementary', Wordsworth had written that the great poet must create the taste by which he is to be enjoyed – thus defending his decision to produce a manifesto. Coleridge was now disputing this. His argument makes the reception of a poet not a public and sociological phenomenon, as it was for Wordsworth, but a private and psychological one. Poetry speaks for itself, regardless of the general state of culture, as long as the poet does not needlessly irritate the reader – that is what he seems to be saying. The proof lies in his own experience:

> During the last year of my residence at Cambridge I became acquainted with Mr. Wordsworth's first publication, entitled 'Descriptive Sketches'; and seldom, if ever, was the emergence of an original poetic genius above the literary horizon more evidently announced.

Coleridge proceeds to summarise the essential impact that Wordsworth's poetry made upon him:

> It was the union of deep feeling with profound thought; the fine balance of truth in observing with the imaginative faculty in modifying the objects observed; and above all the original gift of spreading the tone, the atmosphere and with it the depth and height of the ideal world, around forms, incidents and situations of which, for the common view, custom had bedimmed all the lustre, had dried up the sparkle and the dew-drops.

This famous passage draws on the language of poetic 'power' which we have already seen in Wordsworth and de Quincey: consider the adjectives 'deep', 'profound', 'imaginative', 'original'. The poet's power is that of seeing the world in its ideal wonder and novelty, and of communicating his vision to others. Coleridge is concerned with the psychological and ontological status of this power. He 'no sooner felt' Wordsworth's genius, he tells us, than he 'sought to understand' it. He felt that it involved the inter-relationship of feeling and thought, of observation and the 'imagi-native faculty', and of the ideal world and the world of common experience. These were the antinomies from which he would con-struct his theory of imagination. And a theory of imagination, he believed, was a philosopher's stone which would not only 'furnish a torch of guidance to the philosophical critic', but would make the production of great poetry easier and less sporadic than in the past; for 'in energetic minds truth soon changes by domestica-tion into power'.

By the end of Chapter Four, then, we have been made to antici-pate something far more ambitious than just 'Biographical Sketches'. But equally Coleridge can claim that the theoretical programme he is now announcing contains the inner meaning of his literary life. For the skeleton of argument in the book follows the pattern of a 'circuitous journey', which M.H. Abrams has shown to be common to many other romantic confessional works.[5] Quite possibly Coleridge was half-consciously imitating one of these, Wordsworth's *Prelude* (Wordsworth had read the poem to him in 1807). The 'circuitous journey' of romantic autobiography is inaugurated by a natural or instinctive experience of insight into reality; it proceeds by a process of investigation and interrogation of accumulating experiences until the final point is reached at which the initial experience is maturely comprehended in the light of universal reason. In *The Prelude* this path is traversed by the poet who comes to a mature religious understanding of the glimpses of man's connection with nature that he experienced as a child in Book One. In the *Biographia*, the primal experience is that of Coleridge's critical response to the 'union of deep feeling with profound thought'. His task then is to deduce the nature of the imagination in ontological terms, and to apply the result to the psychology of the creative act, to the aesthetic definition of the work of art and finally to the purposes of poetic analysis, culminat-ing in the examination of Wordsworth's achievements in the hope of a full understanding of his imaginative genius. Such, at least, is the foundation on which Coleridge based his reputation as a philosophical critic. Like the vast majority of his literary schemes,

he did not fulfil it, though he made a moderately concerted attempt
to do so.

The structural parallel between the *Biographia* and *The Prelude*
should not, of course, be allowed to obscure the vast contrast
between the mode of discourse of the *Biographia* and any work
of Wordsworth's. In political terms, Coleridge's discussion of the
imagination and of diction in the context of philosophical and literary tradition is a Burkeian reply to the Tom Paine manner of the
1800 Preface. Yet the gossipy and anecdotal parade of learning
in the *Biographia* owes nothing to Burke and is a deliberate rejection of eighteenth-century clarity. Coleridge's thinking proceeds
not through rational and deductive statement, but through ratioci-
native commentary. His feverish sense of intellectual complexity
is conveyed by a chaotic mixture of styles: seventeenth-century
prolixity jostles with German cloudiness, romantic precision and
evocativeness with proto-Victorian humbug. The contents of the
first volume (Chapters One to Thirteen) are equally varied, with
chapters of exhortations and anecdotes sandwiched amid the
philosophy.

Coleridge starts out from Chapter Four with a heavily derivative
account of philosophical history. Eventually we reach the transcendental system enumerated in the Ten Theses of Chapter Twelve,
translated without acknowledgment from Schelling. Among the
intermissions are those in which Coleridge speaks of truth as the
'divine ventriloquist', and accuses Hume (on nebulous grounds)
of plagiarising Aquinas. Yet this section of the *Biographia* has
considerable historical importance for the part it played in disseminating the Kantian revolution in England. Coleridge tells how he
rejected the mechanical account of the operations of mind put
forward by the British empiricists. He traces the theory of association down to the eighteenth century, and attacks the tenets of the
prevailing Hartleian philosophy. He objects to Hartley's theory
on two grounds: first, that it is implicitly materialist and thus anti-
Christian; second, that it denies the active and voluntary nature
of consciousness. What the materialistic philosophers have discovered, Coleridge argues, are not the determining laws of mind
itself but simply some of the conditions of mental activity. The
individual is logically prior to such conditions and is able to mould
them to his own use rather than merely obeying them passively.
The acts of perception and consciousness are not determined but
voluntary; it is only on this view of mental activity that we can
comprehend the creative quality of art and thought. Coleridge's
sense of the mind's creative activity is illustrated by the example
of jumping (in which we initially resist the external force of gravity

in order to make use of it) and by the beautiful analogy of the water-insect in Chapter Seven:

> Most of my readers will have observed a small water-insect on the surface of rivulets which throws a cinque-spotted shadow fringed with prismatic colours on the sunny bottom of the brook; and will have noticed how the little animal wins its way up against the stream, by alternate pulses of active and passive motion, now resisting the current, and now yielding to it in order to gather strength and a momentary fulcrum for a further propulsion. This is no unapt emblem of the mind's self-experience in the act of thinking. There are evidently two powers at work which relatively to each other are active and passive; and this is not possible without an intermediate faculty, which is at once both active and passive. (In philosophical language we must denominate this intermediate faculty in all its degrees and determinations the imagination. But in common language, and especially on the subject of poetry, we appropriate the name to a superior degree of the faculty, joined to a superior voluntary controul over it.)

The mind here is both the stream and the insect – the experience of the self and the self that experiences. The 'intermediate faculty' of mental motion which provides the field of operation for both the active and passive powers of mind is what Coleridge names the imagination; while 'a superior degree of the faculty, joined to a superior voluntary controul over it' constitutes the imagination that is operative in art. Thus the passage is a direct anticipation of the distinction of primary and secondary imagination in Chapter Thirteen, and foreshadows its essential ambiguity. For what precise differences does Coleridge envisage between the act of imagination in general, and that act in respect of poetry, and the 'act of thinking' of which he examines the 'mind's self-experience' here? These questions can only be answered, if at all, from within the cloudy terrain of Coleridgian metaphysics.

Coleridge, who was willing to speak of a 'revolution in philosophy',[6] if not in poetry, found in Kant and the post-Kantians a more adequate correspondence to his own intuitions about the nature of mind as both active and passive. The need was now to adopt a philosophical system which would clarify the distinctions which the water-insect analogy leaves begging. But it was one thing to endorse the Kantian critique of rationalism and empiricism, and quite another to follow the German philosophers in their subsequent quest for the definition of the Noumenon or Absolute Idea.

The religious objections that Coleridge had brought against Hartley raised themselves again; a philosophy which found its starting-point in the creative powers of mind was as likely as one which started from the laws of nature to lead to atheism or pantheism. Coleridge himself had left behind the heterodoxy of the 1790s, and was now a staunch Christian apologist. In his new position he could do without Hartley, but not without the Germans, and he chose to base his aesthetics on the transcendental idealism of F. W. J. von Schelling, even though Schelling's system, expounded in Chapter Twelve of the *Biographia*, is implicitly pantheistic.[7]

Coleridge's theory of imagination offers a metaphysical basis for the fancy-imagination distinction empirically arrived at in Chapter Four. Whereas fancy is an arbitrary rearrangement of conscious material, poetic or secondary imagination is a willed creative act in which the poet moulds and reshapes his experience of the external world to produce an artistic form *sui generis*; an act analogous to the primary imaginative act by which we constitute and perceive reality itself. Such is the distinction that Coleridge seems to intend, and while we might argue that it is only one of degree, he insists that it is one of kind. Besides the task of establishing that there is such a generic difference between imagination and fancy, Coleridge faces at least two other problems. The first is whether the act of primary imagination by which the mind reshapes external reality is to be understood as an everyday psychological phenomenon (that is, as present in ordinary perception) or as a mode of perception of ultimate truth (and so as partaking of religious and philosophical insight). J.R. Jackson has argued, in the face of the prevailing opinion, that the latter alternative was what Coleridge meant.[8] This emphasis, of course, lends support to the philosophical dignity of poetry, since the secondary imagination 'echoes' the primary. But if primary imagination is part of ordinary sense-perception, then the chief characteristics of its 'echo' in poetic creation must be naturalness and spontaneity.

The reason for this ambiguity may be that in Schelling's *System des Transcendental Idealismus* Coleridge had found a way of deriving the imagination from a First Cause secure in the mystified realm of pure logic. The imagination in Schelling was a metaphysical entity serving as the medium of human participation in the creation of the world.[9] Coleridge hoped that such a theory could underpin his own more concrete concerns. But when – having completed his logical argument with the Ten Theses establishing Schelling's 'I AM' principle as basic in Chapter Twelve, and the further argument about the product of the interaction of two forces in Chapter Thirteen – he was faced with the necessity of applying merely logical principles in the realm of psychology, he panicked. The result was the notorious break in the argument, with its spurious letter from a 'friend' advising the postponement of any full discussion until it could take its proper place in the Treatise on the *Logos*, which Coleridge never completed. After these excuses, he offered no more than a page of hasty and cryptic definitions.

The second problem arises from the first one. For regardless of the purely logical tangles in which he found himself, it would seem that Coleridge at the time of the *Biographia* had not made his mind up about the ultimate nature of poetry. In his later prose works, he invariably draws a distinction between the faculties of (mechanical) 'Understanding', and of the (philosophical) 'Reason'. Reason, in *The Statesman's Manual* (1816), *The Friend* (1818) and elsewhere, is presented as the highest of human faculties. If the secondary imagination of the *Biographia* is to be understood as a mode of perceiving ultimate truth, then it is hard to see how it is distinguishable from the Reason. This would make Coleridge's theory one concerned with the psychology of being a good Christian, rather than having anything necessarily to do with art. But if, as has usually been understood, the secondary imagination is a special case of ordinary perception, then it is a specifically poetic faculty indeed, but the relation of that faculty to the philosophical Reason remains forever obscure. Coleridge tells us that a great poet is a 'profound philosopher', but refuses to be more specific.[10] After 1818, however, he gave up writing literary criticism while remaining a Christian apologist, which may well suggest some doctrinal embarrassment. The theory of imagination, then, may be read as his failed attempt to translate his intuitions into the nature of mental activity, as represented by the water-insect analogy, into the language of metaphysics. The cryptic definitions at the end of Chapter Thirteen represent a blurred though impressive affirmation of the creative nature of the mind; but the metaphysics which he has so ceremoniously summoned to his aid in defining the 'imagination or esemplastic power' give us no clear indications about poetry at all.

At this point, the first volume of the *Biographia* ended. The second volume represents a complete break, taking us back at once to the meeting with Wordsworth, the planning of *Lyrical Ballads* and the shortcomings of the 1800 Preface. Coleridge is now preparing for the long-promised statement of his 'poetic creed', and he launches the discussion by defining his notions 'first, of a poem; and secondly, of poetry itself, in kind and in essence'. These definitions are the main business of Chapter Fourteen. The definition of 'poetry', Coleridge tells us at the end, has been anticipated by the preceding discussion of fancy and imagination: this claim is the only evidence of a logical link between the metaphysics of the *Biographia* and the literary criticism. In terms of the rationalistic criteria by which Coleridge has consistently asked to be judged, it is very weak evidence. For the question 'What is poetry?' he says, is virtually the same as the question 'What is a Poet?', and there follows a famous description of the poet 'in ideal perfection' as one who 'brings the whole soul of man into activity', fusing together its various faculties by means of 'that synthetic and magical power to which we have exclusively appropriated the name of imagination'. The prophetic and symbolic quality of the prose invites direct comparison with Wordsworth's 'What is a Poet?' passage of 1802. But we may say of it, as Coleridge himself said of the Wordsworth passage, that it is 'very grand, and of a sort of Verulamian power and majesty, but it is, in parts ... obscure beyond any necessity'.[11] This is Coleridge's tribute, not only to the power of imagination, but to its magic. Yet, just as the poet in him was half-dead, the mode of revelation had been superseded in the *Biographia* by that of commentary. As a whole, the book presupposes the efforts of previous writers and thinkers, the accumulation of traditions of usage and all those other matters which Coleridge refers to as the 'obligations of intellect' as a kind of screen between the author and the reality (whether metaphysical or textual) to be investigated. The final paragraphs of Chapter Fourteen make an incongruous conclusion to one of his more convincing performances in the role of literary scientist. For the description of the poet succeeds his definition of 'a poem', a definition which is comparatively drab, and equally obscure, but in the long run a good deal more important.

Coleridge had worked at his definitions in notes and in lectures for several years, but in *Biographia Literaria* he was distinguishing between the ideas of 'poetry' and 'a poem' for the first time. He even says that 'a poem of any length neither can be, nor ought to be, all poetry'. 'Poetry,' that is, is original creation, the product of the secondary imagination in man. Coleridge cannot explain it except in prophetic and magical terms. 'A poem', however, is an artificial construction serving a limited cultural purpose. It is

> that species of composition which is opposed to works of science by proposing for its immediate object pleasure, not truth; and from all other species (having this object in common with it) it is discriminated by proposing to itself such delight from the

whole as is compatible with a distinct gratification from each component part.

The definition falls into two parts. The first refers us to the neo-classical formula for the poet's purpose (to instruct by pleasing) and to Wordsworth's opposition of poetry and science. The second tells us what kind of pleasure is peculiar to poems, and combines a doctrine of poetic form with a doctrine of the psychology of aesthetic response, both of which Coleridge proceeds, somewhat cryptically, to elaborate. It will be seen how neatly he has separated off the area of purely aesthetic concerns from that of the 'truth' of poetry which may have been proving an embarrassment to him.

Coleridge's formal doctrine is that the criterion of a genuine poem is unity; the parts must cohere to form a whole. This is compatible with, though not the same as, the doctrine of 'organic form' which he expounded in his Shakespeare lectures in words purloined from Schlegel. Organic form, when it goes beyond the level of explicit analogy, becomes an expression of romantic nature-mysticism, in which birds can be described as lyrical composers, and poets affirm that their art is as natural to man as humming to bees, twittering to swallows or mourning to small gnats. Schell-ing, the most rhapsodic of the German post-Kantian philosophers, seriously expounded a mysticism which corresponds to the licensed assertions of the romantic nature lyric.[12] But the notion of organic form which Coleridge took from Schlegel is simply an attractive way of distinguishing internal and intuitive from rigid and external structuring. Organic form appears later in the *Biographia*, but the formal doctrine of Chapter Fourteen is couched in the more tradi-tional aesthetic terms of 'harmony' and 'proportion':

> if the definition sought for be that of a legitimate poem, I answer it must be one the parts of which mutually support and explain each other; all in their proportion harmonizing with, and support-ing the purpose and known influences of metrical arrangement.

The principle of harmony, it is clear from this, decisively affects the question of metre. Metre can only be successfully 'superadded', in Wordsworth's phrase, if all other parts or elements of the poem are made consonant with it; and so metre alone is sufficient ground for the distinction between prose and poetry which Wordsworth had rejected. Thus Coleridge's definition of a poem directly antici-pates his commentary on the 1800 Preface.

The other aspect of Coleridge's definition is his doctrine of the psychology of aesthetic response. The presence of metre, he argues, tends to promote the kind of pleasure which is peculiar to poetry. This specifically poetic pleasure is the result of heightened attention. The importance of metre is that it stimulates our attention to every facet of linguistic communication, producing not a generalised, blurred sense of meaning or message, but 'a distinct gratification from each component part'. Coleridge's concept of aesthetic attention effectively solves the hopeless muddle in which Wordsworth had found himself when he denied that metre made any generic difference to poetry, while admitting that a piece of verse would be read a hundred times where its prose equivalent was read once. The solution is contained in the following statements:

> If metre be superadded, all other parts must be made consonant with it. They must be such as to justify the perpetual and distinct attention to each part which an exact correspondent recurrence of accent and sound are calculated to excite. ... The reader should be carried forward, not merely or chiefly by the mechanical impulse of curiosity, or by a restless desire to arrive at the final solution; but by the pleasurable activity of mind excited by the attractions of the journey itself.

Not least among the 'attractions of the journey itself', it may be suggested, were the pleasures of sound. Coleridge and Wordsworth were noted for the chanting intonation with which they read verse aloud. The concern with pleasure and the perfection of form in these passages foreshadows the musical qualities of later romantic and symbolist poetry; the same qualities were enthusiastically advocated by Hazlitt in his *Lectures on the English Poets*. When we think of poetry as harmonious and pleasurable we are very likely to see it as a kind of music. But Coleridge's concept of aesthetic attention leaves something to be accounted for – the sense of poetic power. This is the quality that thrills through his own response to Wordsworth's *Prelude* (1807):

> An Orphic song indeed,
> A song divine of high and passionate thoughts
> To their own music chaunted!
>
> ('To William Wordsworth')

Coleridge's definition of a poem is a formalist definition, and what it does is to give a more dynamic and analytic understanding of the poem as aesthetic object. To see the poem in terms of power, however, is to see it as the product of a creative activity of mind in the poet – of 'high and passionate thoughts' – and as capable of exciting a similar creativity in the mind of the reader. Though it was this discovery, prompted by Wordsworth's poetry, that had inaugurated his 'circuitous journey' in Chapter Four, he was unable to bring it wholly within the province of rationalised aesthetics. That is why he adopted the expedient of distinguishing 'poetry' from 'a poem', and why when it came to defining 'poetry' – where power was involved – he launched into the rhapsody on the 'poet, described in ideal perfection', with which Chapter Fourteen ends.

If aesthetics could not cope rationally with the power of poetry, what about practical criticism? It was to this that he turned in the next chapter claiming to elucidate the 'specific symptoms of poetic power' in an analysis of 'Venus and Adonis'. Though he discussed the use of imagery in some particular passages of Shakespeare's poem, these discussions are rather desultory, and follow what Wordsworth had done in the 1815 Preface. Coleridge's main concern is not with the linguistic energy of the poem, but the moral energy and 'genial and productive nature' of the mind that produced it. Coleridge lists four main symptoms of power in Shakespeare's poems – sweetness of versification, powers of dramatic creation, handling of imagery and 'depth and energy of thought' – and the chapter culminates with a brilliant but very general appreciation of the 'protean' quality of Shakespeare's genius. Shakespeare, who 'darts himself forth, and passes into all forms of human character and passion', is contrasted with Milton who draws all things to himself, 'into the unity of his own ideal'. Shakespeare and Milton are seated upon 'the two glory-smitten summits of the poetic mountain'; the question from here on is whether there is to be a third summit, occupied by Wordsworth. But first, a good deal of the critical view is still blocked by a jerry-built edifice called the Preface to *Lyrical Ballads*.

Coleridge on Wordsworth

Coleridge's reply to Wordsworth is one of the most dramatic documents of English criticism. Here, in the clash of two strongly idiosyncratic minds, is a telling realisation of that conflict between author and critical authority which is implicit throughout literary history. The fact that Coleridge was Wordsworth's friend and admirer should not disguise the magnitude of the conflict. Wordsworth's sense of mission and his sternly egotistic genius stand, even today, as awkward obstacles to our sense of English poetry as a continuous tradition. Coleridge's purpose was to show how the best of Wordsworth could and must be assimilated within that corporate tradition. The price of such assimilation was high, since not only Wordsworth's theories but the whole idea of a poetic language – and, by extension, of creative genius – independent of literary education and cultural precedent was at stake. Coleridge won the argument, but his was in part a victory of the intellectual or one-man academy over the unsophisticated, visionary poet. His detached and judicial air is particularly notable when he exposes Wordsworth's weaknesses in expounding his own point of view. The issue is, of course, greatly complicated by the personal relationship between the two men. Their close association during the writing of the 1800 Preface makes some of Coleridge's later misunderstandings seem wilful and perverse. At the same time, he is still Wordsworth's warmest advocate, though the 'GENUINE PHILOSOPHIC POEM' that he envisages as the poet's crowning achievement is partly a product of his own over-intellectual expectations of genius. If he read between the lines of the *Biographia*, Wordsworth could hardly have found its argument welcome. Coleridge claims, it is true, that the excision of the Preface and a few dozen lines of *Lyrical Ballads* would be enough to satisfy the poet's most stringent critic; but the damage his arguments seem calculated to cause is more far-reaching than this. What they do, in effect, is to cut the poet off from what he believed were his external sources of creativity, undermining that sense of confident oneness with the world of nature which irradiates the *Lyrical Ballads* and the 1805 *Prelude*. Where Wordsworth himself felt cut off from the Platonic essence of nature (as we know from the 'Immortality Ode'), Coleridge suggested that his grasp of what was left behind, the human and material world, was imperfect and unrepresentative. Poetic powers like his rested wholly on inner resources and intuitions. In inviting his friend to look still more into himself, and to cultivate his solipsistic bent, Coleridge was condemning some of the best things (as well as the worst things) Wordsworth had written by the standards of poetry that he was still expected to write. The demise of the 'genuine philosophic poem' shows how misguided these expectations were.

'Language', Coleridge wrote, 'is the armoury of the human mind; and at once contains the trophies of its past, and the weapons of its future conquests.'[13] Wordsworth's criticism was the work of a poet who saw his responsibility as necessarily extending to questions of culture, but Coleridge in the *Biographia* speaks with the voice of a philologist, not of a poet of nature. Such a voice can command the past and the future but may feel threatened by a poet who writes as if in an eternal present. In fact, Coleridge launched a two-pronged attack on the Preface, aiming to save Wordsworth's poetry as literature while countering its cultural effects. The underlying motive of Wordsworth's theory of diction seems a very simple one: it was to expose the sterility of Augustan verse and to state the case for a revolutionary plainness of style and subject-matter as trenchantly as possible. But the argument had implications which Coleridge recognised and fought against for all he was worth. That is why he attacks the Preface as a philologist, linguist, sociologist, aesthetician and philosopher, but never as a fellow-poet. The author of 'Frost at Midnight', 'The Ancient Mariner' and 'This Lime-Tree Bower My Prison' – poems as radical and as free of intellectualism as any of Wordsworth's – has given way to a brilliant dialectician exposing the absurdity of the left-wing views he had held in his own youth. He is not interested in Wordsworth's immediate objects, only in the conformity of his views with tradition and precedent; thus there is 'no poet whose writings would safelier stand the test of Mr. Wordsworth's theory than Spenser'.[14] He plays down the revolutionary aspects of Wordsworth's poetry, and he pronounces the experiments of *Lyrical Ballads* an unmitigated failure.[15] Some of his arguments, as Hazlitt and others noticed, were taken from Wordsworth's bitterest opponents; and the *Biographia* was seen as an act of apostasy by the *Monthly Review*, which rated Wordsworth as a 'very moderate writer', but greeted his critic as an 'unintentional defender of good taste and good sense in poetry'.[16]

The argument commences with a diversion: Chapter Sixteen, a charming little essay on the Renaissance lyric. The key to it is perhaps found in a footnote referring to Sir Joshua Reynolds and his belief that good taste is acquired from 'submissive study of the best models'. Similar references had appeared in the 1798 'Advertisement' and the 1800 Preface. Coleridge asserts that the fifteenth- and sixteenth-century lyrics and madrigals are among the best models, but the simplicity and purity of diction which he admires in them are the reverse of Wordsworthian simplicity. Their writers used a highly polished diction, and 'placed the essence of poetry in the *art*', or, as we should say, in perfection of form. This is a tacit rebuke to Wordsworth, and establishes the context of philosophy and literary history within which the Preface is to be discussed. Coleridge admits that there is a more ambitious kind of poetry than this, and from here on he tends to divide good poetry into two sorts: first, a simple (though preferably polished and musical) mode written not in the 'real language of men' but in a purified and public traditional style which he christens the 'lingua communis'; and second, a more impassioned and imaginative mode in which style becomes more personal and idiosyncratic. The first is found in the madrigalists and in Chaucer and Herbert, and is opposed to the false simplicity or 'matter-of-factness' of the experimental *Lyrical Ballads*. The second is Miltonic, and also Wordsworthian. Coleridge looks to a combination of the two modes for the perfection of English poetry; it seems a prophecy less of what Wordsworth would do than of the 'musical' imagination of Keats and Tennyson.

In Chapter Seventeen he at last reaches the discussion of the Preface, and outlines an alternative theory of language. Language is not the natural expression of man, but the bearer of culture and civilisation; it is what the human race laboriously creates, and each individual has to learn. Wordsworth had stressed the spontaneity of the individual's use of language, finding in rustics the virtues that we would now find in children. Coleridge replies that a language is created and sustained by the educated classes of a society; its best parts are the products of philosophers and not of shepherds. The sociological bearing of his defence of the values of education leads to the theory of the clerisy or intellectual class that he was to develop in *Church and State* (1830). In relation to poetry, it leads to concurrence with Johnson's and Reynolds's view of literary language. The headnote 'Poetry essentially ideal and generic' could have been written by either of them, and his substitution of the literary concept of a *lingua communis* for Wordsworth's 'real language of men' clearly harmonises with Johnson's ideas about poetic diction. But in Coleridge's case, the neoclassical ideas are underwritten by Kantian transcendentalism, in the shape of his commitment to the 'Science of Method'.

Coleridge's essays on Method dominate the otherwise haphazard material of *The Friend* (1818). Like his metaphysics, his interest in method is logically prior to literary criticism, though he turns to criticism for its application and illustration. Essentially these essays are an analysis of the operations of the perfect or 'philosophic' mind; they elaborate Coleridge's ideal of intellectuality. The truly educated man, Coleridge writes, is accustomed to contemplate, not things on their own, but the relations between things. He possesses a 'prospectiveness of mind' or 'surview' which enables him to express his thoughts with the maximum of discipline and organisation. It may well be argued that poets work through quite other faculties than the methodical intellect, and perhaps this was why Coleridge became half-ashamed of 'The Ancient Mariner' and 'Kubla Khan'. None the less, the *Biographia* is based on the assumption that the principles of Method must be applied in the sphere of poetry.

The language of rustics is lacking in Method on two counts. The rustic is poor in linguistic resources; Coleridge does not share

Wordsworth's faith in the natural articulateness of men under the stress of passion. Moreover, being uneducated, he has nothing to express save 'insulated facts'; he has not learned to contemplate the relations between things. In arguing this, Coleridge not only seems blind to any non-intellectual mode of human awareness, but rejects the particularism of detail which is the essence of much romantic poetry and poetic theory. He is far more pertinent when he comes to the formal aspect of the choice of diction and metre. When Wordsworth spoke of selecting from the real language of men, what he mainly had in mind was a selection of its vocabulary. But Coleridge points out that the essence of style lies in 'ordonnance', or the syntax and arrangement of thought. Thus in order to adopt the 'language of a class', we must imitate not merely its vocabulary, but its word-order as well. This argument leaves Wordsworth in a cleft stick. The *Lyrical Ballads* use the word-order appropriate to verse rather than prose; hence they are not in the real language of men. Since the presence of metre forces the poet to use a different word-order, poetic diction, defined as the form of linguistic ordonnance appropriate to metre, is something that he cannot avoid. A choice of different styles or 'languages' is inevitable in any culture which can distinguish between verse, prose and conversational forms.

Presumably there is no logical necessity for these alternative styles to form a hierarchy, but Coleridge evidently believes that this is and ought to be the case. Verse, he argues, ought to command a heightened style; this follows both from the principles of harmony and aesthetic attention introduced in Chapter Fourteen, and from the authority of the poetic tradition. The final objection he deals with is Wordsworth's argument that once the 'arbitrariness' of poetic diction was allowed, no limits could be set to it. On the contrary, Coleridge replies, the limits are set by 'the principles of grammar, logic, psychology!' These would not have sufficed as revolutionary slogans in 1800, but then neither could Wordsworth have written, as Coleridge does, of Gray's sonnet 'That the "Phoebus" is hackneyed, and a schoolboy image, is an accidental fault, dependent on the age in which the author wrote and not deduced from the nature of the thing.' The abuses of Augustan style which bulked so large in 1800 are now shrugged off as trifling matters which do nothing to disturb Coleridge's sense of literary precedent broadening down from age to age. And though he is famous for his emphasis that the principles of logic and grammar must be organically and intuitively applied by the poet, this is balanced by his insistence on their objective, canonical status. Thus Wordsworth's theory of diction is incapable of furnishing either rule, guidance or precaution that might not, more easily and more safely, as well as more naturally, have been deduced in the author's own mind from considerations of grammar, logic and the truth and nature of things, confirmed by the authority of words whose fame is not of one country nor of one age.

In these closing words of Chapter Eighteen, the 'author' is firmly put down by the consensus of literary authority. The time is now ripe for Coleridge to examine Wordsworth's claims as a poet to enter the pantheon of literature.

The formal balance-sheet is presented in Chapter Twenty-Two, but Coleridge has long before this made some damaging points about the *Lyrical Ballads*. Most importantly, he uncovers a failure of realism, a failure on Wordsworth's part to disclose the world as it really is. We may go back to Chapter Fifteen, where he praised Shakespeare's prodigious dramatic powers and unerring treatment of 'subjects very remote from the private interests and circumstances of the writer himself'. It is precisely this power that, in Coleridge's view, Wordsworth lacks. We might, indeed, wonder whether a poet whose gift was so fundamentally solipsistic would be well equipped to become the 'profound philosopher' of whom Coleridge speaks. Yet Coleridge was no empiricist, and saw no contradiction in boosting Wordsworth's philosophic powers at the very same time as he denigrated his grip on reality. The principal example here is 'The Thorn'. Coleridge ridicules the device of the sea-captain as narrator, pointing out that the poem veers uncertainly between the dullness and garrulity attributed to the captain, and a degree of imaginative intensity which appears to belong to the poet's own character, and cannot be taken from the 'language of ordinary men'. This might seem a trivial failure, but Coleridge brings the same objection against *The Excursion*, a far graver matter. 'Is there one word, for instance, attributed to the pedlar in the *Excursion* characteristic of a pedlar?'[17] This is a very harsh exposure of the solipsistic tendency of Wordsworth's imagination. Wrapped in his own life, Coleridge seems to be saying, Wordsworth understands neither society, nor rustics, nor the 'language of men' that he professes to write. He struggles to cover this up with 'matter-of-factness', 'a laborious minuteness and fidelity' in the representation of objects, together with the 'insertion of accidental circumstances' such as those of the Wanderer and the sea-captain.[18] Coleridge's strictures on 'The Thorn' thus turn out to be aimed at much more than a single, mawkish ballad. They are but pallidly counteracted by a page or so of praise for Wordsworth's 'truth

of nature', mainly in his nature-lyrics. The social realism of Wordsworth's poetry is something to which Coleridge does no justice
at all.

In Chapters Nineteen and Twenty he distinguishes between the
legitimate mode of poetic simplicity – here the 'neutral style' of
Chaucer and Herbert, based on a literary *lingua communis* or purified diction – and the style ordained for the higher and more philosophical powers of Wordsworth. The advocate of the real language
of men is revealed as 'a poet whose diction, next to that of Shakespeare and Milton, appears to me of all others the most individu-
alized and characteristic'. Coleridge relies largely on quotations
to convey his sense of this idiosyncrasy; so much so that, in the
final chapters of the *Biographia*, the deductive, rationalistic ideal
of criticism he had aspired to earlier seems to give way to a new
and more empirical procedure like that which was later to be championed by Matthew Arnold. Arnold quotes in order to avoid
abstract definitions which he feels inappropriate to poetry, but Coleridge's use of extensive quotation to redress the balance of his
critique and reveal the 'positive' side of Wordsworth suggests that
he has run out of steam. None the less, these last chapters are
a decisive rejection of the 'simple Wordsworth' in favour of the
lofty and Miltonic poet-prophet, whose strengths, Coleridge
argues, come from his internal powers of meditation and imagination rather than from a direct grasp of the real world. The Preface
to *Lyrical Ballads* had expressed Wordsworth's strong conviction
that his poetry was the spontaneous vehicle of natural emotions
and of natural responses to external objects. In the 1815 Preface,
despite his stress on the modifying role of imagination, he had
not altogether abandoned this conviction. Coleridge, however,
argues that his diction depends for its success on 'striking passages'
that come from within – passages which belong quintessentially
to poetry rather than to prose and which reflect the full idiosyncrasy
of his genius. The faults which he assiduously notes down in
Chapter Twenty-Two are of two main kinds: the matter-of-factness
and abuse of the dramatic form which result from Wordsworth's
mistaken attempts to write on subjects remote from his private
interests, and, as the converse of this, a self-indulgent idiosyncrasy
of style which fails to 'satisfy a cultivated taste'. All of which emphasises the solipsism of Wordsworth's imagination. When he moves
from the poet's defects to the beauties, Coleridge in effect lists
those qualities of mind which make such solipsism heroic: Wordsworth's precision of language, the weightiness of his thoughts, his
'meditative pathos', and finally, the 'gift of imagination in the
highest and strictest sense of the word'. These qualities which dis-

tinguish Wordsworth and qualify him for that 'FIRST GENUINE PHILOSOPHIC POEM' which Coleridge believes may be the summit of his work. The implication is that it is precisely by following the ideal of the self-reflecting philosopher which Coleridge had inherited from the post-Kantians that Wordsworth would achieve this. But Coleridge's ideal of sceptical self-consciousness was at variance both with the prophetic confidence and the humble fidelity with which Wordsworth alternately approaches the world of nature.

Though their background is Kantian, Coleridge's list of Wordsworth's virtues seems on the face of it rather academic. The issues raised by the *Biographia* strike deep, but the depth does not extend to establishing the 'strictest sense of the word' imagination. His final tribute to Wordsworth's imaginative power is paid by means of quotations, and, characteristically, Coleridge reserves the full articulation of his meaning for a further work:

> I shall select a few examples as most obviously manifesting this faculty; but if I should ever be fortunate enough to render my analysis of imagination, its origin and characters, thoroughly intelligible to the reader, he will scarcely open on a page of this poet's works without recognizing, more or less, the presence and the influence of this faculty.

It is with a declaration of faith rather than a *quod erat demonstrandum* that the long critique ends.

The *Biographia* is a product of the revolution it condemns; so much must be obvious. It is a work of intellectual commentary, creating a field of brilliantly ingenious discussion and hard-hitting debate, out-flanking the positive, abstract rationalism of the Preface and all but overwhelming it. Coleridge's critical performance is almost impossible to sum up, magnificently far-sighted as he is in some directions, and unable to see what is in front of his nose in others. If we subtract that part of the book which grew out of Wordsworth's poetic impact and the outspoken radicalism of his prefaces, we are left with little but a Shandean façade, some desultory reminiscences, and some borrowed metaphysics. For if the apotheosis of the poetic imagination seems to be prompted by Wordsworth, so is Coleridge's theory of language and his doctrine of aesthetic attention. The second half of the *Biographia* is dominated by his obsession with contradicting Wordsworth, correcting his views and stating the terms on which he may be accepted as a great writer. What kind of personal and creative symbiosis had gone on between Wordsworth and Coleridge, we can only guess. Whatever view we take of the outcome, there could be no more graphic demonstration of the clash of interests in criticism and the power-struggle that ensues when poet and critic meet, to use Coleridge's phrase, 'in a war embrace'.

Shakespearean Criticism

Apart from the *Biographia,* Coleridge's criticism consists almost entirely of scattered lecture-notes and marginalia, and of reports of his lectures and conversation. Very high claims have been made for this material. T. M. Raysor introduced his edition of the Shakespeare criticism in 1930 with the statement that 'In the history of English literary criticism there is no work which surpasses in interest Coleridge's lectures upon Shakespeare.' Yet the lectures do not really live up to their reputation, especially when one is familiar with the works of Schlegel and Schiller from which many of their most famous ideas are drawn. Coleridge, in general, inherits the comparative and historicist outlook of German thought, adding to it a more detailed interest in poetic texture and an explicitly patriotic concern with the English literary heritage. To his Shakespeare lectures Coleridge brought a genuine sense of mission, feeling that he was the first English critic capable of appreciating the Bard's true powers. The eighteenth-century critics, he complained, were in the habit of treating him like an errant schoolboy; he devoted two lectures (now lost) in the 1811–12 course to a savage analysis of Johnson's Preface. Coleridge was the first major English critic to idolise Shakespeare, and he saw in him not only a great genius, but a genius of diametrically opposite type to Wordsworth. It seems almost commonplace to describe Shakespeare's as a protean imagination, darting forth and passing into all the forms of human character and passion, and it was in any case what Schlegel had said. But Coleridge's characterisation of Shakespeare's genius both contrasts with and complements his description of Wordsworth. Both the great extrovert genius and the great solipsist owe their preeminence, he suggests, to their intellectual and meditative powers. Shakespeare was not a child of nature but a philosophical poet whose greatness was the result of reflection and of 'knowledge become habitual and intuitive'.[19] And it was not in knowledge of the world so much as in knowledge of himself – but of his 'representative' self – that he excelled.

It is in this way that Coleridge adapts his post-Kantian view of genius to fit the case of the great dramatic poet, and we need not be surprised that as a practical critic he stresses the novelistic, at the expense of the theatrical, side of his achievement. Coleridge's favourite role as a Shakespeare critic is precisely that which John-

son, in his 'Preface' and notes on the plays, refused to fill. It is
the role of omniscient narrator, explaining and commenting on
the action in such a way that nothing is lost and verisimilitude
is enhanced to the utmost degree. The narrator of a nineteenth-
century novel has privileged access to the secret motives of his
characters; so it is with Coleridge and Shakespeare's heroes. His
imagination responds most strongly to the enigmas of character
in the plays, and to the creation of realism and 'atmosphere' in
Shakespeare's opening scenes. His analysis of the beginning of
Hamlet is unforgettably evocative, but it is the fruit of lavish concentration on speeches and actions which the theatrical audience must
take in very quickly. Opening scenes in novels tend to be far more
amply presented than in Shakespeare, even where the material
is 'dramatic' – consider *Middlemarch* – and though Coleridge's
discussion will enrich the experience of anyone who has studied
the text of *Hamlet*, we are often disconcerted by the relentless
pace at which productions of plays we have studied (and still more,
dramatisations of novels) seem to get under way.

A good example of Coleridge's procedure in discussing Shakespeare is his commentary on the opening of *The Tempest*, in the
ninth lecture of 1811–12. This is the first lecture in which Schlegel's
influence is acknowledged and beyond dispute, and Coleridge
approaches *The Tempest* by way of Schlegel's distinction between
mechanical and organic form. He then illustrates this by analysing
the altercation between Gonzalo and the Boatswain in the brief
scene of the storm. As he tries frantically to organise the crew,
the Boatswain forgets the deference due to rank and rudely challenges Gonzalo either to silence the elements with his authority,
since he is a Counsellor, or to get out of the way. Gonzalo fails
to answer the taunt directly, however:

An ordinary dramatist would, after this speech, have represented
Gonzalo as moralizing, or saying something connected with the
Boatswain's language; for ordinary dramatists are not men of
genius: they combine their ideas by association, or by logical
affinity; but the vital writer, who makes men on the stage what
they are in nature, in a moment transports himself into the very
being of each personage, and, instead of cutting out artificial
puppets, he brings before us the men themselves. Therefore,
Gonzalo soliloquises, – 'I have great comfort from this fellow:
methinks, he hath no drowning mark upon him; his complexion
is perfect gallows'.[20]

The fact is that this is not a soliloquy. The whole royal party are on stage when it is spoken, and it is obviously meant to cheer them up. Coleridge's 'ordinary dramatist' is a short-sighted theatrical technician for whom each speech must be a response to the one before. Gonzalo's speech is certainly different in that it emerges from a whole imaginative conception, but its function, surely, is to reassure the audience by a momentary nonchalance hinting that the bangs and rumbles in the wings are not to be taken seriously. It does not give us insight into the unique individuality of Gonzalo, which is the last thing we want in the middle of a storm. Coleridge's concern, however, is to show the rounded conception of Shakespeare's characters and the philosophical powers revealed in his mastery of an inexhaustible range of mental types.

The theme of Coleridge's Shakespeare criticism is that of 'Shakespeare's Judgment Equal to his Genius'. His analyses are punctuated by exclamations ('But observe the matchless judgment of Shakespeare!'), and the tone is almost invariably hagiographic. One of his marginalia records his bafflement over a passage in *Coriolanus* (IV.vii.28–): 'I cherish the hope that I am mistaken and, becoming wiser, shall discover some profound excellence in what I now appear to myself to detect an imperfection. S.T.C.'[21] Coleridge affirmed that criticism of Shakespeare should be 'reverential', and we might say that in his hands it becomes a kind of spilt natural theology. Paley sought for evidences of design in the natural universe, arguing back from the watch to the watch-maker. The belief that the hand of God was discoverable in every aspect of Nature sanctioned the minutest study of natural history in the eighteenth century; this was the heyday of the botanising and bird-watching parson. Criticism of Shakespeare, too, could produce proofs of design and Authorship where careless eyes had seen nothing but accident: such was the justification to be advanced by de Quincey for his essay 'On the Knocking at the Gate in *Macbeth*' (1823), and it is implicit in Coleridge's attempts to make the smallest details of the texts yield evidence of Shakespeare's conscious control, and hence of his creative omnipotence. Like a parson examining the geological vestiges of the Flood, he feels vaguely threatened when something in the text proves recalcitrant.

Coleridge on Shakespeare, then, is a commentator who tends to translate drama into fiction at the behest of a quasi-theological piety. It is not surprising that his reverence should sometimes seem personal or ideological rather than purely aesthetic. If he confessed to having a smack of Hamlet himself, he also compared Macbeth to Napoleon and Caliban to the Jacobins, and praised Shakespeare for his patriotism, his conservatism and his habit of 'never introducing a professional character, as such, otherwise than as respectable'.[22] Shakespeare's political and patriotic merits, however, were subordinate to his highest excellence as a manifestation of 'divine' genius. We have traced Coleridge's concern with judgment and genius as a theme of his criticism, but it led him in the end to abandon criticism for Christian apologetics. As early as *The States-man's Manual* (1816) he described the reason, the organ of the immediate spiritual consciousness of God, as a higher faculty than the imagination.[23] When criticism comes to be recognised as a mediated form of theology, its scope must be very limited. Coleridge finally came to such a recognition; so much is suggested by his marginal note on a volume of Milton (c. 1823?):

> Of criticism we may perhaps say, that those divine poets, Homer, Eschylus, and the two compeers, Dante, Shakespeare, Spenser, Milton, who deserve to have Critics, κριταί, are placed above criticism in the vulgar sense, and move in the sphere of religion, while those who are not such scarcely deserve criticism in any sense.[24]

Before reaching this slough of critical Despond, he had a last fling at aesthetic theory in the lecture 'On Poesy or Art' (1818). Though a fine source for rapt Coleridgian utterances, this lecture is little more than a translation of Schelling, and in any case it offers a theory of the visual arts rather than of literature. His later years produced only some desultory critical table-talk, and some hints about the place of literature in society. In *The Friend* (1818), he somewhat economically divided human social activity into the 'two main directions' of Trade and Literature – forces which both sustain the national identity of a society, and seek to transcend it.[25] But what is the social function of the imaginative element in Literature? We would naturally look for an answer to this in *On the Constitution of the Church and State* (1830), where Coleridge outlines his theory of the national culture. Here he argues for the recognition of the 'clerisy' – the class of intellectuals and educators – as one of the permanent estates of the realm. The task of the clerisy is to exercise the faculty of Vision (that is, imagination), as well as those of Reason and Understanding. Yet apart from a dutiful quotation or two from Wordsworth, the figure of the poet plays no part in Coleridge's description of the clerisy, whose culture consists of the traditional hierarchy of *literae humaniores*, crowned by theology. There is no Coleridgian equivalent to Words-worth's 'rock of defence for human nature', or to Shelley's 'un-acknowledged legislator'. *Church and State* really confirms the academic and intellectualising tendencies that were present throughout his earlier career in literary criticism. It leaves us, however, with the baffling paradox of Coleridge, a brilliantly intelligent literary critic by any standards, and for many the undisputed master of the discipline in England, yet who fails so many of the tests we put to critics, including in the end the test of commitment to the creative spirit itself. Coleridge, it seems, can admit of poetic genius only as a means to more intellectual and spiritual ends. Whatever the personal struggles that marked his thought, there is a logical link between his criticism of Shakespeare and Wordsworth, and the later years in which the evidence of his disillusionment with criticism and even with literature is so strong.

Shelley, Hazlitt and Keats

In his famous dictum about 'negative capability', Keats chooses Coleridge as his example of the non-poet irritably reaching after fact and reason. Coleridge had managed to convince himself that the poetic spirit, while deeply hostile to British empirical philosophy, could be subsumed under the higher reason of Kantian transcendentalism. Others did not agree. None the less, the theme of opposition to utilitarian doctrine is very widespread in the period, from Coleridge's *Church and State* to de Quincey, Hazlitt, and Shelley's 'Defence of Poetry'. The ancient quarrel between philosophy and poetry took on an urgency quite unknown in Johnson's time, for the ideological upheavals of the 'age of revolutions' had shaken customary beliefs about the nature and demarcations of culture. The metaphysics of Coleridge and the literary witch-hunting of the quarterlies suggest the variety of possible conservative responses to this situation. The revolution in literary values instigated by Wordsworth was, however, carried on by Keats, Shelley and their circle. Like many of their predecessors, they show signs of a deep frustration and insecurity about the position of the poet, but for them the frustration is a source of energy and a guarantee that they can only benefit from living in a revolutionary age. They respond with militant assertions of the ideals of literary culture, and with poetry fervently embodying those ideals. Shelley, in particular, is a prophet of humanism denouncing the tyranny of aristocratic government and bourgeois materialism. We have to distinguish here between the broad humanism of the romantics and the effect of their beliefs within the narrower sphere of poetry and criticism. After his death Shelley came to personify the charisma and magic of poethood for generations of Victorians who had no time for his political views. Though he failed in his revolutionary aims, the attitude of poetic absolutism which he asserted against Peacock's rational and 'enlightened' view of history found a much wider echo. It was symptomatic of the romantic revolt that the language of criticism became unpredictable, and its relation to rational thought problematic.

One of the ways in which romantic militancy and the breakdown of the eighteenth-century cultural consensus are reflected in language is in the redefinition of the word 'poetry'. 'Literature', as we have seen, was redefined concurrently as an existing tradition or heritage of imaginative works, and this sense was established as normal. The mutations undergone by the word 'poetry' were more exotic and temporary. Essentially what took place was a species of linguistic imperialism, which was able to claim the sanction of Plato since a passage in the *Symposium* describes poetry as originally a generic term for the processes of creation and invention. Wordsworth declared that the philosophical opposite of poetry was 'Matter of Fact, or Science', and Coleridge stipulated that 'All the fine arts are different species of poetry.'[1] Elsewhere he suggested 'poesy' as the generic term and 'poetry' for the metrical art alone, but this distinction failed to stick. Once poetry came to denote a common quality of all the arts, a new importance was given in literary criticism to the problems of the relationship between the arts, and of the place of the poetic faculty in human nature as a whole. Hazlitt memorably tackles the former question, and Shelley the latter. The poets, in the meantime, found that the words 'poetry' and 'poesy' could be used with an easy evocativeness that was unprecedented. Hence the title 'Sleep and Poetry'; lines like 'Perhaps on wing of Poesy upsoar', and 'Framed in the silent poesy of form'; the kiss in Keats's 'Isabella' where Lorenzo's lips 'poesied with hers in dewy rhyme'; and, at rock-bottom, Coleridge's grisly lines to his future daughter-in-law:

My Derwent hath found realiz'd in thee, . . .
The fair fulfilment of his poesy,
When his young heart first yearn'd for sympathy!

('To Mary Pridham', 1827)

'Poesy' seems to have been the more 'poetical' form and rapidly became trivialised to mean fantasy, yearning or love-play. Apart from its wilder excesses, however, the extended definition of poetry implied a heightened sense of the poet's responsibility and mission. This in turn led to the romantic instability; messianic conviction alternated with failure and despondency.

Keats, for example, can sound very down to earth when it is

a question of what he is actually writing: 'I must make 4000 Lines of one bare circumstance and fill them with Poetry', he says of *Endymion*. Yet a sentence earlier he writes that 'the high Idea I have of poetical fame makes me think I see it towering to [*sic?*] high above me.'[2] The classic statements in his letters are meditations on what it is to be a poet (the 'poetical Character') rather than on poetic technique. Keats was both ambitious and fearful of becoming a poet; in his description of the poet as 'the most unpoetical of any thing in existence' and in the initiation scene of 'The Fall of Hyperion' he seems alarmed by the prospect of losing his identity and submitting to an alien power. He often had to tell himself to keep his head, even if that meant renouncing poetic aspirations. 'There is no greater Sin after the 7 deadly than to flatter oneself into an idea of being a great Poet – ... how comfortable a feel it is that such a Crime must bring its heavy Penalty?' he wrote priggishly of Leigh Hunt.[3] This is a reminder that the intensely literary pretensions to which Keats gives classic expression were almost commonplace among his fellow-writers. It was necessary to be a great poet; simply to be a poet was not enough. In an 1817 letter to Haydon, another artistic pretender, Keats announced his choice of Shakespeare as his presiding genius. Shakespeare came to seem his special good fairy in the struggle between his reverence for the literary past and his search for authentic self-expression. As a romantic literary poet, Keats felt his relation to his predecessors not as a public but as a peculiarly private relation. When he announced his rejection of the Miltonic mode of the first 'Hyperion' ('Miltonic verse can not be written but in an artful or rather artist's humour'), he said bluntly that 'I wish to give myself up to other sensations.'[4]

The contradiction between the poet's sense of high calling and public responsibility and the private and unique character of his struggle to develop, is surely what accounts for the difficulties the romantics experienced in handling the traditional literary genres. Wordsworth, despite the influence of Milton, created new models for the long poem in *The Excursion* and (far more radically) in *The Prelude*. But Keats and Shelley sought poetic fame in forms far closer to traditional tragedy and epic, though their real concerns lay elsewhere. Shelley's Preface to *Prometheus Unbound* expresses the literary alienation that is central to their work:

This Poem was chiefly written upon the mountainous ruins of the Baths of Caracalla, among the flowery glades, and thickets of odoriferous blossoming trees, which are extended in ever winding labyrinths upon its immense platforms and dizzy arches suspended in the air. The bright blue sky of Rome, and the effect of the vigorous awakening spring in that divinest climate, and the new life with which it drenches the spirits even to intoxication, were the inspiration of this drama.

In traditional terms the inspiration should have produced an ode, not an epic verse drama. *Prometheus Unbound* strives after a consciously revolutionary, symbolic form to accommodate its author's visionary humanism. Keats's 'Fall of Hyperion' seems to me a more successful poem, though Keats was less aware of the problem of generic alienation and so left the poem unfinished and, surely, unfinishable. The personal inspiration which he brought to the classical fable seems exhausted by the scene with Moneta, and in telling the story of Apollo he would simply be covering the theme of poetic initiation twice over. Both poems are expressions of their authors' belief in the public and monumental status of great literature. Yet in the lyrics of Keats and Shelley, and in some of the criticism of their contemporaries, a new evaluation of the poetic art quite independent of the public, classical genres was emerging.

Shelley's 'Defence of Poetry'

Shelley's 'Defence of Poetry' (1821) is the most outspoken of the romantic assertions of the public function of poetry. It was written, so he told Peacock, in a 'sacred rage' to vindicate the 'insulted Muses' against his friend's challenge in 'The Four Ages of Poetry' (1820).[5] Peacock's essay is a satire on his contemporaries (Wordsworth, Coleridge, Southey, Scott, Byron, Moore and Campbell are all named targets) written in the form of a pastiche of Enlightenment historiography. He sees poetry as a product of man's earliest civilisations and posits an iron age followed by a golden age (the classical flowering of tragedy and epic) followed by a silver age and, finally, an age of brass. There is little in his outline of cultural history that was not anticipated by the Scottish primitivists of the eighteenth century. But Peacock presents it with great verve and dash, and adds an extra turn of cynicism, as when he attributes the rise of poetry entirely to the savage's need to flatter his chieftain. His attack on the modern age is a *reductio ad absurdum* of arguments that had already been brought against Wordsworth and Coleridge. Wordsworth's return to nature, he asserts, is the second childhood of the art, a hopeless and puerile raking over of the past which serves as a prelude to poetry's final extinction. The backward-looking, semi-barbarous modern poet has been left stranded by the progress of the mechanical and social sciences, and has nothing to contribute to social utility: 'The march of his intellect is like that of a crab, backward.' Even the pleasure that he gives is not enough to ensure his survival, since there are enough good poems already, and anything still to be produced must be worse than what already exists.

Peacock is in no doubt about who are the real revolutionaries of contemporary poetry, but he writes off their movement as a predestined failure. The shallow determinism of the position he adopts can only really be refuted by an unanswerable demonstration of the power and creativeness of the present generation. This explains Shelley's anxiety to destroy his friend's position, and the impotence of mere arguments to do so. Moreover, Peacock's espousal of utilitarian values – however much this has a merely debunking intention – challenges his antagonist to declare his own attitude to utilitarianism. Shelley, as poet and political revolutionary, mounts his defence from the left, and argues that poetry belongs in the van and not in the rearguard of social progress; hence his arguments do not ultimately conflict with a rational and enlightened utilitarian standpoint.[6] What these arguments lack he tries to make up with the rapt and imperious utterance of a 'sacred rage'.

The 'Defence' opens with the contrast of reason and imagination. Peacock had said that poetry, once the 'all-in-all of intellectual progression', had been left behind by the development of reason and science. Shelley replies that as the 'expression of the imagination', poetry is 'connate with the origin of man'. Its origins are found in the pleasure we take in imitation, whether in dancing, singing or creating a language. Thus Shelley replaces Peacock's debunking historical account of poetry's genesis with an anthropological explanation grounded in the universal nature of man. If he is right, either poetry must retain its original centrality in modern society, or we have ceased to be fully men. For Peacock, such centrality belonged to 'semi-civilized society', whereas Shelley summons all his faith, ingenuity and power of persuasion to the task of asserting that it still persists and that poets are the 'unacknowledged legislators'. He does so by adopting the extended neoplatonic definition of poetry and writing a panegyric on human creativity throughout history, giving all the credit to poets as they come highest in the hierarchy of creative spirits. The difficulties in the way of such an argument are airily disposed of. Shelley asserts, for example, that the superiority of poetry in the restricted sense over other modes of social activity is proved by the fame of the poets, which is only exceeded by that of 'legislators and founders of religion, so long as their institutions last'. The latter, however, are artificially bolstered up by the flattery of the vulgar, and by the fame which is rightfully theirs 'in their higher character of poets'! Very soon, in fact, the distinction between reason and imagination becomes of use only as a weapon against 'mere reasoners'; Shelley describes Shakespeare, Dante and Milton as 'philosophers of the very loftiest power', and claims that poets excel all others in political, social, ethical and religious insight. Reason and imagination are certainly merged in the 'Defence' itself, which opens with a parade of distinctions and definitions, but ends in pages of impressionistic rant. Poets, we discover, may be not only the rulers of society but autocrats who justifiably present a watered-down version of the truth for popular consumption ('Few poets of the highest class have chosen to exhibit the beauty of their conceptions in its naked truth and splendour'). And Shelley himself is a super-autocrat who can award or withhold the title of poet at will (Rousseau was a poet, but Locke, Hume, Gibbon and Voltaire were 'mere reasoners'). If we read it, as we must, as special pleading, the 'Defence' is unconvincing and somewhat repellent.

There is more to be said than this, since the 'Defence' at best – as in the section on Milton – is an eloquent affirmation of human freedom. Peacock sees poets as slaves to history, and Shelley reacts by airlifting them into the permanent world of the human spirit. The historical narrative in the 'Defence' is devoted to showing that poetry is immanent in history without ever being fundamentally corrupted by it. The poets unveil the essential morality of their societies, rather than having to abide by that morality as the Augustans thought. They teach love and mutual sympathy to their fellow-men, with measurable effects: 'the presence or absence of poetry in its most perfect or universal form, has been found to be connected with good and evil in conduct or habit.' The spirit of poetry, as is evident here, can withdraw from a world unsympathetic to it, and Shelley's history of culture is a narrative of the fluctuating presence of the poetic spirit. He dismisses the usual historical and religious explanations of the Dark Ages, for example, since it was the 'extinction of the poetical principle' that really counted. After the eleventh century, things began to improve as the 'poetry of the Christian and chivalric systems' began to manifest itself. But the historical role of poetry, though something of which Shelley is proud, is not quite the essence of the art as he sees it. 'Let us not be betrayed from a defence into a critical history of poetry and its influence on society': 'betrayed', because the primary reality of poetry is its permanence and eternality; only secondarily is it manifested in history. Thus Shelley can speak of 'that great poem, which all poets, like the co-operating thoughts of one great mind, have built up since the beginning of the world'. His outlook is fundamentally idealist and anti-historical, however useful as a corrective to Peacock's vulgar brand of historicism. And his veneration of poetry as something at once above history and decisively engaged in history is evidently of a religious kind; it is no accident that he describes poets as 'hierophants of an unapprehended inspiration'. The 'Defence' is, in T.E. Hulme's term, 'spilt religion', but it is also a bold attempt to expropriate what is worth keeping in actual religions, especially Christianity, in the name of poetry. Shelley both discredits Christian transcendentalism and borrows metaphors from it freely for his eulogistic rhapsodies. Thus he can be misread as saying that poetry is spiritual and other-worldly, whereas these are never more than the metaphors of his evangelical humanism. For all this, the 'Defence' must be read more as a hymn to the ideal unity of humanist values, than as any kind of poetic analysis or programme. It might have served as a rallying-call to contemporary poets, but it remained unpublished until 1840, eighteen years after his death.

Hazlitt and Keats

Shelley's criticism rests on the conviction that poetry and philosophy are essentially at one; the poet, in his view, is virtually omnipotent. Keats was more cautious and hesitant in assuming the prophetic stance. 'An eagle', he wrote, 'is not so fine a thing as a truth.' Keats's sense of the rival claims of poetical justice and social justice is paralleled by the frank acknowledgment of such a conflict in the criticism of William Hazlitt. Hazlitt's work is distinctly uneven, but he was an original critic, not merely an indefatigable literary politician and a populariser of stock romantic attitudes. The complexity of his response to poetry is evident from his contrast of poetic and political values in his essay on *Coriolanus* in *The Characters of Shakespeare's Plays* (1817). It was a passage which achieved some notoriety: Gifford derided it in the *Quarterly*, Hazlitt hit back in his *Letter to William Gifford* (1819), and Keats was sufficiently moved by the reply to copy out a long extract in his journal-letter to his brother and sister-in-law (February–May 1819). Hazlitt had originally argued that in portraying the conflict of leaders and led in ancient Rome, Shakespeare 'seems to have had a leaning to the arbitrary side of the question', and 'spared no occasion of baiting the rabble':

What he says of them is very true: what he says of their betters is also very true, though he dwells less upon it. The cause of the people is indeed but little calculated as a subject for poetry: ... The language of poetry naturally falls in with the language of power. The imagination is an exaggerating and exclusive faculty: it takes from one thing to add to another: it accumulates circumstances together to give the greatest possible effect to a favourite object. The understanding is a dividing and measuring faculty: it judges of things, not according to their immediate impression on the mind, but according to their relations to one another. The one is a monopolizing faculty, which seeks the greatest quantity of present excitement by inequality and disproportion; the other is a distributive faculty, which seeks the greatest quantity of ultimate good, by justice and proportion. The one is an aristocratical, the other a republican faculty. The principle of poetry is a very anti-levelling principle.

The antitheses are suspiciously neat but none the less effective. Hazlitt was a republican, proud of his political consistency and a merciless critic of the apostasy of Coleridge and Wordsworth. He was also an advocate of the romantic imagination in poetry. In writing of the interests of poetry as essentially opposed to democracy he was giving hostages to the enemy, but he was able to turn this weakness into a strength – partly by habitually separating literary from political criticism, and partly by the vigour of his polemics against the Lake school, who from his point of view had the worst of both worlds by adopting the 'arbitrary side of the question' in politics, and the levelling principle in poetry. Hazlitt's is a parliamentary mind, conscious of his allegiances and capable of switching between cross-bench negotiation and vitriolic abuse of the other side. He is prepared to concede the Tory affiliations of *Coriolanus* if that will aid a romantic interpretation of the play. While recognising and revering the imperiousness of the poetic imagination, he later made it clear that the imagination was not a party-political weapon, but belonged in a higher sphere: 'When it lights upon the earth, it loses some of its dignity and its use.'[7] This suggests the essential ambiguity of his position. Though he was habitually and often pungently aware of the ideological tendencies of art, his criticism played an influential part in the nineteenth-century retreat into an aesthetic kingdom separate from everyday life.

Hazlitt attacked poets like Coleridge who meddled in politics; they lived 'in an ideal world of their own', and could only bring confusion into public affairs.[8] He attacked Shelley, a fellow republican, for his intellectual unreliability and extremism.[9] But he also attacked the utilitarians, Shelley's 'reasoners', for the inhumanity and self-interestedness of their abstract rationalism. His dissection of the Lake school in the lecture 'On the Living Poets' is done with a brilliance and perversity which puts it in a class by itself. The true motive of 'these sweeping reformers and dictators in the republic of letters', he asserts, is the madness of egotism:

> They took the same method in their new-fangled 'metre ballad-mongering' scheme, which Rousseau did in his prose paradoxes – of exciting attention by reversing the established standards of opinion and estimation in the world. They were for bringing poetry back to its primitive simplicity and state of nature, as he was for bringing society back to the savage state: so that the only thing remarkable left in the world by this change, would be the persons who had produced it. A thorough adept in this school of poetry and philanthropy is jealous of all excellence but his own ... He tolerates only what he himself creates; he sympathizes only with what can enter into no competition with him, with 'the bare trees and mountains bare, and grass in the green field.' He sees nothing but himself and the universe.

This surely is the sort of line that Burke, whom Hazlitt much admired, might have taken. Analysis reveals an extraordinary mixture of motives in it. Though personal animus is undoubtedly present, the attack on Wordsworth's egotism is consistent with his analysis of the 'intellectual egotism' of *The Excursion* in *The Examiner* four years earlier – an analysis which stands behind Keats's phrase for Wordsworth's style, the 'egotistical sublime'. But it may be argued that the imperiousness of Wordsworth's poetic attitude is precisely what is to be expected of that 'exaggerating and exclusive faculty', the imagination. Though a political radical, Hazlitt seems to prefer the status quo in literature to a new initiative such as Wordsworth's. There is a brooding pessimism in his outlook, which sometimes becomes the bitter pride of the last adherent of a lost cause.

Hazlitt as a cultural critic too often seems to be writing from a position of self-defence. He distinguished between the diffusion of taste, the object of the periodical press of his own time, and its improvement – there was no principle of universal suffrage in matters of taste. As an art critic, he attacked public patronage of artists and the institution of the academy – genius would make its own way in the world, and there was no point in encouraging the second-rate – but supported the setting up of a national gallery. Public taste might be improved by 'a collection of standing works of established reputation, and which are capable by the sanctity of their name of overawing the petulance of public opinion'.[10] Late in life he became still more outspoken against the philistinism of public taste:

> I would rather endure the most blind and bigotted respect for great and illustrious names, than that pitiful, grovelling humour which has no pride in intellectual excellence, and no pleasure but in decrying those who have given proofs of it, and reducing them to its own level.
>
> ('On Reading New Books', 1827)

In the matter of culture, then, Hazlitt himself leant towards the 'arbitrary side of the question'. And he was essentially a man of letters: the choice is like a confession. Political passions infused his writing (his final work was the *Life of Napoleon*) but they do not seem to have moved him to political action. There is a certain realism about the literary democrat who turns against the mob in these circumstances. It costs him more than other people to do so, so that the result is a heartfelt and not a supercilious response. None the less, the alternatives painted by Hazlitt are so rigid that the passage seems little more than a cry of frustration. We must conclude that for all his intelligence and mastery of the telling phrase and the cutting polemic, Hazlitt lacked the pertinacity of a genuine social thinker.

As a strictly literary critic his claims are stronger, though he is at his best in discussing two areas of writing which do not involve the conflict of poetry and philosophy at its sharpest. The first of these is realistic fiction, and the second the meditative or musical lyric. Hazlitt's *Lectures on the English Comic Writers* contain a superb discussion of the eighteenth-century novel, which he warms to as a more human and democratic art form than poetry. Best of all is his appraisal of Hogarth (a curious inclusion, in some ways) whom he sees as the culmination of English realism. Hogarth, however, is a representative of the 'familiar style' in painting, falling short of the 'grand style' because he lacks an imaginative and ideal dimension. Hazlitt finds the same falling-short in a 'painterly' poet like Crabbe, and in the art of painting in general. Though an excellent art critic and a fine judge of the realistic mode, he looked upon realism as firmly subordinated to the mode of imagination.

His fullest statement of the imaginative nature of poetry comes in the essay 'On Poetry in General', the first of the *Lectures on the English Poets* (1818). Read superficially, this essay seems no more than a vague romantic rhapsody; it is an oration rather than a treatise, presenting an impassioned list of the attributes of poetry in an appropriately florid and extravagant prose. But though his method is metonymic rather than definitive, Hazlitt intended his statements to be rationally defensible (he defended them vigorously against the legalism of Gifford), and at times they are effective and precise. The 'general notion' of poetry with which he opens sounds Shelleyan in its expansiveness, though it actually says a good deal less than at first appears:

> Many people suppose that poetry is something to be found only in books, contained in lines of ten syllables, with like endings: but wherever there is a sense of beauty, or power, or harmony, as in a motion of a wave of the sea, in the growth of a flower that 'spreads its sweet leaves to the air, and dedicates its beauty to the sun,' – there is poetry, in its birth.

It is not that poetry subsists in the wave of the sea or the growth of the flower; rather, these can inspire us with a poetic 'sense of beauty, or power, or harmony'. Hazlitt opposes poetic power to the mere representation or description of an object. Poetry is the result of internal processes of apprehension and contemplation:

> It is strictly the language of the imagination; and the imagination is that faculty which represents objects, not as they are themselves, but as they are moulded by other thoughts and feelings, into an infinite variety of shapes and combinations of power.

The difference from Wordsworth's and Coleridge's accounts of imagination is that they tended to stress its cognitive and visionary nature, while Hazlitt presents it as a wholly aesthetic process, appealing to a particular (and, of course, particularly desirable) kind of sensibility. His distinction between imagination and description is strongly reminiscent of Schlegel's and Schiller's contrasts of the ancient and modern spirit; Hazlitt, in their terms, is claiming poetry as an essentially modern or romantic art-form.[11] He goes on to discuss the differences in aesthetic potential among the fine arts. Poetry is more imaginative than painting: 'Painting gives the object itself; poetry what it implies.' Here again is the distinction between the expression of the reflective mind and the mere pictorial representation of objects. Poetry is further enriched, however, by its possession of the quality of harmony, which is associated with the third of the fine arts, that of music. Hazlitt calls poetry the 'music of language':

> Wherever any object takes such a hold of the mind as to make

us dwell upon it, and brood over it, melting the heart in tender-
ness, or kindling it to a sentiment of enthusiasm; – wherever
a movement of imagination or passion is impressed on the mind,
by which it seeks to prolong and repeat the emotion, to bring
all other objects into accord with it, and to give the same movement of harmony, sustained and continuous, or gradually varied
according to the occasion, to the sounds that express it – this
is poetry. The musical in sound is the sustained and continuous;
the musical in thought is the sustained and continuous also.

If this is peculiarly evocative, it is surely not because it is generally
applicable to poetry, but because it is an uncanny prediction of
the concentrated lyric poetry of the nineteenth century. The passage virtually provides the formula of Keats's Odes.

Modern scholars are agreed that most of Keats's theories were
developed from Hazlitt, and that his poetry was in some respects
a deeply theoretical endeavour, but I am not sure that all the connections have yet been made.[12] In general, Hazlitt may have
prompted Keats to discover how natural objects could be treated
in a poetry of refined and synaesthetic, rather than directly moral
or sensual, appeal; the 'Odes' avoid both the stolidness of Wordsworth and the cloying richness of *Endymion*.

There is a more precise point of connection between 'On Poetry
in General' and Keats's 'Odes'. It springs from a passage discussing
the Elgin Marbles, which were of such consuming interest to Hazlitt, Keats and their circle:

It is for want of some such resting place for the imagination
that the Greek statues are little else than specious forms. They
are marble to the touch and to the heart ... By their beauty
they are raised above the frailties of passion or suffering. By
their beauty they are deified. But they are not objects of religious
faith to us, and their forms are a reproach to common humanity.
They seem to have no sympathy with us, and not to want our
admiration.

Ian Jack has written that 'It would be curious to have the comment
of Keats on this passage.'[13] I would argue that in effect we have
that comment: it is the 'Ode on a Grecian Urn'. The difficulty
that Keats appears to have missed the first of Hazlitt's lectures,
though he became a regular attender later on in the course, may
be overcome by supposing either that he read it in manuscript
or book form (the *Lectures* were published several months before
the 'Ode' was written), or that he knew Hazlitt's earlier and more

diffuse discussion of the Marbles in his *Encyclopaedia Britannica* article on the 'Fine Arts' (1817). As for the difference between a vase and a sculptured frieze, this is a complication, but no more. Ian Jack identifies the heifer led to sacrifice in Stanza IV as that in the South Frieze of the Elgin Marbles. Keats's 'Attic shape' surely stands for the whole of Greek plastic art, as does Hazlitt's account of the 'Greek statues', written in the tradition of German analyses of the Hellenistic spirit.

The 'Ode on a Grecian Urn' is a poem about the relations between the arts, which comes directly out of the aesthetic debate of its time. Keats calls the Urn a 'Cold Pastoral'; that is his concession to Hazlitt's viewpoint, but it is belied by the very choice of the Urn as subject for a poem. The poem reveals the nature of the Urn's 'sympathy with us', and yet Keats is, so to speak, cheating by weaving around the Urn the expressive harmonies of another medium. Finally the 'silent form' speaks:

> Cold Pastoral!
> When old age shall this generation waste,
>   Thou shalt remain, in midst of other woe
> Than ours, a friend to man, to whom thou say'st,
>   'Beauty is truth, truth beauty,' – that is all
>   Ye know on earth, and all ye need to know.

Hazlitt had described the forms of the Elgin Marbles as a 'reproach to common humanity', but the Urn is a friend to man and does not reproach. Far from rejecting our admiration, it holds it spellbound. None the less, the Urn's message reveals its own self-sufficiency and aloofness from human considerations, since no mundane 'philosophical' sense can be attached to the words '"Beauty is truth, truth beauty"'. We should, of course, notice the wonderful contextual subtlety with which Keats has hedged around the Urn's flat statement, which could be seen as at once a rebuke to Hazlitt's brash impatience with the Greek statues, and as a tacit confirmation of his general principle that the values of the imagination are paramount only within the 'aesthetic' realm. What Keats conveys is not an *objet d'art* speaking to us directly, but a poetic statement put in the mouth of another art and then translated back into the art of language; the statement is not didactic but oracular, a direct 'expression of the imagination' reported to us by an admirer rather than authored by Keats himself.

Keats's poem expresses the full allure of aestheticism, without quite taking the leap into vulgar commitment. Similarly, Hazlitt's essay steeps itself in the literary emotions and in less sensitive hands than Keats's could be made into a thoroughgoing aesthete's charter. The essay can offer some general guidelines to the other Odes, directing us to their more symbolistic features. The idea of poetry as the 'music of language' is present in the third stanza of 'To Autumn', where the first two lines invite us to number the poem itself among the songs of autumn:

> Where are the songs of Spring? Ay, where are they?
> Think not of them, thou hast thy music too, –

The list of autumnal sounds that follows is introduced by two lines of landscape-painting describing the sunset; once again, the three art-forms are fused. In the 'Ode to Psyche', the poet offers himself as choir, priest and builder of a temple for the goddess of his choice. Psyche is forgotten and unworshipped, the 'latest born and loveliest vision far/Of all Olympus' faded hierarchy'. The poet, and he alone, can commemorate her and restore the 'faded hierarchy'; but the music, painting and architecture of the temple subsist in 'some untrodden region of my mind', so that this revival, so typical of the solipsistic use of classical motifs by the romantic poets, can be an imaginative achievement only. The 'Nightingale' Ode is, again, a poetic brooding and dwelling upon its subject, weaving together visual beauty, musical harmony and the 'magic casements' of literary tradition in its striving for the maximum intensity. These are all intensely literary poems, not in the simple name-dropping sense (though literary names are dropped throughout Keats's minor verse), but in their presentation of nearly all experience in terms evocative of literature and the other arts. This process of aesthetic mediation involves a new poetic diction which deliberately transmutes life into art, sensation into dream and message into oracle. Hazlitt's view of the opposition between imagination and social concern helps to illuminate the secular other-worldliness of Keats's poetry, his fascination with the Immortals and with a supremely sensual initiation into mysteries that transcend the world of the ordinary senses. In a few great poems, Keats was able to choose the ground on which to reconcile the warring poles of critical dialectic. In life, however, he, like Hazlitt, remained struggling irresolutely between poetry and philosophy.

Hazlitt and de Quincey

Hazlitt's influence on Keats was the last and most fortuitous of the interactions between criticism and original creation which so profoundly mark the romantic period. The points of similarity between them initiate the line of development from romanticism to aestheticism, which emerged as a conscious movement in England in the second half of the nineteenth century. Keats was undoubtedly able to overlook the journalistic flaccidity and the amount of borrowed finery that creep into Hazlitt's writing. For Hazlitt's critical personality is evidently that of the bookman rather than of the more refined and fastidious aesthete. He may have been the first to describe critics as 'middlemen', and he plays at least four roles with varying success in his criticism – those of polemical reviewer, aesthetician, literary connoisseur and public educator. His literary surveys are probably most read today, although they were composed in a great hurry to meet a public demand. *The Characters of Shakespeare's Plays* and all three lecture-courses came out between 1817 and 1820. These lectures contain some splendid passages, but they also tend to lapse into the superficiality of literary history without tears.

In his comments on the task of criticism, Hazlitt invariably speaks for the impressionistic method of the connoisseurs and bookmen whose ethos was sketched at the beginning of this chapter. He believed that the appreciation of poetry was a matter of 'instantaneous sympathy', and that the literary imagination delighted in 'power, in strong excitement' at the expense of humanity and principle.[14] The critic's task was to express the joys of poetic excitement and passion, when taken under licence and in moderate draughts. Hazlitt deplored Johnson's incapacity for 'following the flights of a truly poetic imagination',[15] and attacked the analytic methods of Dryden and the French:

> A genuine criticism should, as I take it, reflect the colours, the light and shade, the soul and body of a work: here we have nothing but its superficial plan and elevation, as if a poem were a piece of formal architecture ... That is, we are left quite in the dark as to the feelings of pleasure or pain to be derived from the genius of the performance or the manner in which it appeals to the imagination.[16]

It is only one step further to the Pavlovian responses of Lamb, when confronted by a passage from *The Revenger's Tragedy*: 'I never read it but my ears tingle, and I feel a hot flush spread my cheeks.'[17] This is a translation of the ecstatic response of the romantic poet to literary experience into the domestic language of bookish sensibility. Hazlitt usually works on a more intellectual or comparative level than this; he praises writers for their 'poetic-ality', their 'gusto'. He describes his aim in his lectures as being to 'read over a set of authors with the audience, as I would do with a friend, to point out a favourite passage, to explain an objection; or if a remark or a theory occurs, to state it in illustration of the subject, but neither to tire him nor to puzzle myself with pedantic rules.'[18] This combines Lamb's desire to make his private experience public (his remark on *The Revenger's Tragedy* is the kind of intimate confidence that carries no risk) with a lightly pedagogic concern. A great deal of nineteenth-century criticism exists somewhere between these two alternatives, and Hazlitt's own work is weaker and more patchy where – as in *The Characters of Shakespeare's Plays,* which were not delivered as lectures – the pedagogic motive is lacking.

A different blend of cognitive and affective elements is found in his collection of 'Contemporary Portraits', *The Spirit of the Age* (1825). These essays combine vivid portraiture with an intellectual apparatus of concepts – such as mechanism and impulse, method and imagination, authority and democracy – which serve to relate the individual sitter to the *Zeitgeist* or 'Spirit of the Age'. At his best, on Bentham, Malthus, Jeffrey or Sir James Mackintosh, Hazlitt clearly anticipates the cultural criticism of Carlyle and Mill. But he never gets down to a precise exposition of the 'Spirit of the Age', or straightforwardly declares his own attitude to it. He is very much the reporter, hedging his bets. Wordsworth's levelling genius is a 'pure emanation of the Spirit of the Age', but then so is the *Edinburgh Review.* Hazlitt may be dissociating himself from both, but just where he stands is uncertain – why, except as his patron, should Jeffrey be so much more favourably treated than Wordsworth? The volume was published anonymously, and it may be that Hazlitt took pleasure in intriguing his readers while exploiting the idea of the *Zeitgeist* for all it was worth. Where his own preferences do emerge, they suggest an impulse towards literary escapism. The carriers of the *Zeitgeist* such as Wordsworth and Jeffrey are portents to be wondered at, but they cannot exactly be liked; and old enemies such as Coleridge and Gifford are treated as harshly as ever. The tart edge to Hazlitt's commentary on his times is only forgotten in his final essay on Charles Lamb and Washington Irving ('Elia, and Geoffrey Crayon'). He affectionately portrays Lamb as an antiquarian who prefers 'byeways to highways', a poetic soul who is untainted by the 'Spirit of the Age' and stands aloof from its animosities. Hazlitt, too, seems to be hinting that life is best when one can take flight on the wings of imagination. His gallery of 'contemporary portraits' ends with two sentences (they refer to the dramatist Sheridan Knowles, another friend of Hazlitt's) which conjure us out of the contemporary world altogether:

> We have known him almost from a child, and we must say he appears to us the same boy-poet that he ever was. He has been cradled in song, and rocked in it as in a dream, forgetful of himself and of the world!

Long disappointed in his political hopes, and embittered by a series of desertions from the republican cause, Hazlitt in *The Spirit of the Age* seems emotionally incapable of feeling at home in the contemporary world. Intellectually he responds to it; but finally he can only gesture towards a resting-place in the cult of childhood and literary reverie. Once again he was putting his weight behind that withdrawal of the poetic sensibility from social concerns which constitutes romantic decadence.

As a contrast to Hazlitt's escapism, we may look finally at Thomas de Quincey – famous for his opium reveries, and yet a very practical and socially committed literary critic. De Quincey's most famous essay, 'On the Knocking at the Gate in *Macbeth*' (1823), seems at first to be an ordinary product of bookish impressionism. 'From my boyish days I had always felt a great perplexity on one point in *Macbeth*'; this is how it opens. But what follows is not an exercise in buttonholing intimacy, but a meditation of Wordsworthian discipline and austerity. De Quincey goes on to outline the solution of a critical problem that has puzzled him for twenty years. He shows how the knocking at the gate intensifies our sympathy with the complex feelings of the murderers, and distracts us from simple horror at their crime. This is a superb empirical demonstration of the 'manner in which it appeals to the imagination' – the kind of criticism which Hazlitt recommends, but can never achieve with such force. Nearly two decades later, when Coleridge, Hazlitt and Lamb were dead, de Quincey re-emerged as a critic of far broader literary and cultural interests. His *Reminiscences* of the Lake Poets, his remarks on the poetic diction controversy and his distinction of knowledge and power show him as the critical heir of Wordsworth and Coleridge, reinterpreting in rational terms the prophetic insights of romantic poetry. In an essay on 'Goldsmith' (1848), de Quincey reasserted the international character of great literature and its embodiment of a kind of power which is a challenge and an alternative to the social power wielded by the state. Literature, he argued, was a force tending towards international brotherhood and cultural unity, and this was why poets were so often slighted in their own homeland. This idea owes much to Wordsworth, and clearly anticipates Arnold; it represents a critical approach in complete contrast to Hazlitt's disillusionment and solacing aestheticism. Thus de Quincey, unlike Hazlitt, proved able to respond to the new energy of social thought and the revival of liberal hopes in the 1820s and 1830s, so that his final incarnation was as a minor Victorian sage and not as a romantic critic. The mixture of public educator and private daydreamer in both Hazlitt and de Quincey sums up the essence of the nineteenth-century literary culture which their generation had done so much to create.

4   Victorian Criticism: The Republic of Letters

The Definition of Literary Culture

In Shelley's poem 'Julian and Maddalo', the poet's friendship with Byron is recaptured at certain moments with supreme naturalness. Arriving before Maddalo is up one morning, Julian observes the Count's baby daughter, whose eyes gleam

> With such deep meaning, as we never see
> But in the human countenance:

He then starts to play with the child, and so

>   after her first shyness was worn out
> We sate there, rolling billiard balls about,
> When the Count entered . . .

In romantic criticism, as well as poetry, we are able to meet the creative genius face to face. Romantic egotism, even while it exalts the poet and puts him on a pedestal, can include this interest in personality and in the everyday life of oneself and one's friends. Hazlitt, Lamb and de Quincey were the intimates of great poets; but they also felt themselves their equals, and cherished their own experience as Shelley does in these lines. The early Victorian critics inherited the romantic beliefs about genius, but these beliefs had now solidified; they were becoming a teaching, a body of doctrine.

'Julian and Maddalo' is set in Venice. Whether in Italy or the Lakes, the community of poets was best able to flourish far from the metropolitan centre of culture. Meanwhile, Londoners such as Hazlitt and Lamb resorted to bookmanship, a deliberate, make-believe isolation of the self from the sense of a present cultural context. To be immured in the library was to be taken out of time and into permanence. The early Victorian generation of intellectuals – Carlyle, Newman, Macaulay, Lewes, J. S. Mill – had no time for such escapism. Instead, when they looked at poetry at all they were concerned with locating it within a cultural framework. The notion of romantic genius had to find its place amid the institutions of society and the general body of concepts ordering intellectual life. One thing that happened was that the intellectuals themselves became 'sages', taking it as their mission to pronounce upon the totality of social life in the prophetic manner exemplified by Wordsworth.

The sages were opposed to many features of nineteenth-century society, yet they arose in response to a demand which that society had created. The industrial revolution brought about the spread of literacy and education, and the dissemination of more intellectual modes of consciousness, in many areas of life. George Eliot records such a process, the 'bringing to consciousness' of a small market town, in *Felix Holt*. This is an elusive concept, but is clearly related to the disturbance of settled religious faith and political quiescence. 'Consciousness', then, means receptivity to new ideas propagated from the metropolis; the most certain evidence for it lies in the spread of reading-rooms and libraries and in the existence, popularity and influence of the sages themselves. The mode in which the sages write is that of the lay sermon, an instructive and edifying discourse which, however dogmatic in content, must exploit the questionable authority of the book rather than the customary authority of the pulpit. The nineteenth-century reader of the sages could not but be aware of disagreement and the necessity of choice among them, and he turned increasingly to this choice as a substitute for, or at least a supplement to, religious orthodoxy.

The sages wrote for a mass audience, not for their peers; for this reason they used a far more strident rhetoric than their predecessors, even those with propagandist aims such as Burke. They were writing to be heard at a time of social change, and they combined an appeal to traditional sanctities or absolute values with an expression of the new historical awareness that came in with the romantics. Change was visibly taking place, but it was frequently attributed to unthinking forces – the machinery in the factories, the iron laws of supply and demand, or the unpredictable risings of the people. The sages unanimously insisted that the decisions of men determined their own history. Carlyle's idea of 'Hero-worship' and Mill's concept of the 'collective mind' are attempts to determine the agency through which historical development is made. This agency could be seen in terms of politics, but the sages tended to locate it outside the directly political realm, in the field of what Arnold was to call 'culture'. It was in defining culture that they took over the prophetic mantle of the romantic poets.

When Mill discusses Bentham, and when Carlyle and Marx denounce the 'cash-nexus', they are insisting that men and not the machine must be the measure of social relationships. In their attacks on rival ideologies, the sages upheld the ideal of a balanced culture in which society's general spiritual welfare was held to over-rule all merely sectional interests. Carlyle's attacks on utilitaria-nism, Ruskin's denunciation of political economy, and Arnold's defences of culture against the nonconformists, the working-class activists and the natural scientists, may all be read as protests against the attempts of the champions of particular sectors of cul-ture to dictate to the whole. The idea of a general culture in which all social and intellectual institutions have their appointed place became an increasingly conscious one; and this idea formed the basis of a critique of the materialism and spiritual anarchy of current society. In one tradition of thought carried forward into the twen-tieth century, literary criticism came to dominate the ideal of cul-ture. The early Victorian prophets were not primarily literary critics, however, and they did not follow the romantics in looking upon poetry as a source of the highest wisdom or an end in itself. None the less, literature in the broad sense was felt by most writers to be central to the cultural ideal. The older associations of the word remained important in this context: 'literature' could be used to indicate the humane education imparted at Oxford and Cam-bridge, as well as the reviews and other media of contemporary debate.

Looking back, it seems clear that the Victorian intellectual world was far more 'literary' in its bias than the intellectual world of today. One of the signs of this is the extent to which literary interests and values were taken for granted. After the deaths of Byron, Keats and Shelley, poetry virtually dropped out of public contro-versy. Carlyle argued in 'Signs of the Times' (1829) that the way in which thought was now propagated was by 'machinery', by the formation of societies and the holding of public dinners. In fact, the range of Victorian learned societies and pressure-groups pro-vides an excellent indication of the broadening of culture, and the discovery of controversial new matters of social and intellectual concern. Very few of these societies were literary. They were pre-dominantly concerned with new scientific and social–scientific fields, religion, ethics and politics, and architecture and the visual arts. In the field of imaginative literature the societies were con-cerned with writers' conditions (the Society of Authors was founded in 1884), with Old English (the Early English Text Society, 1864) and with the study of single authors. The single-author societies suggest that in literature it was a writer's 'oeuvre' which constituted a field of study equivalent to one of the new disciplines such as sociology or anthropology. As it happens, they were almost entirely the creations of one man, F. J. Furnivall, who founded the Chaucer, Wycliffe, New Shakspere, Browning and Shelley societies, all within a period of twenty years. General literary societies were not needed, except on an urban and regional basis. Literature – outside the new industrial towns – was still held to be the preserve of all educated men.

There was one group of nineteenth-century intellectuals, however, who did wish to see literature deprived of its privileged status. These were the utilitarians of the *Westminster Review*. Various writers in the early volumes of the *Westminster* (founded in 1824) set out to unmask literature as part of the façade of social reaction. Literature, they argued, was the preserve of the aristocracy, the occupation of a leisure class. Its benefits for the individual were greatly exaggerated, and its privileged place in education served to bolster conservatism and repression. Literary ability was the gateway to posts in the civil service and the Excise (even a poet could be made a Distributor of Stamps). The study of the humanities was the one indispensable qualification for political advancement. No wonder that reform was so slow and industrial progress so hampered, for, as one writer put it, 'woe be to the state whose statesmen write verses, and whose lawyers read more in Tom Moore than in Bracton.'[1]

The immediate target of these attacks was the classical curriculum. The reviewers were prepared to countenance the study of English and modern languages for utilitarian purposes. (It is notable that Mill, Arnold and Newman all went out of their way to defend classical studies in the university. Training in classical literature was essential to their conception of culture; the status of modern literature was not so clear.) The early Benthamite reviewers seem also to have encountered the ideology of the romantic movement, and show hostility and prejudice against literature as such. 'Literature, we have said it before, is a cant word of the age; and, to be literary, to be a *litterateur* (we want a word), a *bel esprit*, or a blue stocking, is the disease of the age. The world is to be stormed by poetry, and to be occupied by reviews and albums', proclaimed the *Westminster Review* in 1825. The reviewers' identification of literature with aristocratic values was at best a half-truth (though one not lost on Arnold); yet it was to be through the classical education provided by the public schools, and the study of the humanities in the universities, that the merger between the old aristocracy and the new industrial plutocracy in nineteenth-century England was cemented. The late Victorian statesman or administrator did not merely know Greek, he had probably passed numerous examinations in it. But when the *West-*

minster reviewer spoke of literature as the preserve of gentlemen of leisure, he seems to have mistaken the image for the reality. I have argued that the idle, unworldly bookman of the 1820s was the fiction of busy and harassed literary journalists. Byron apart, the romantics are not notable for their aristocratic connections. In the next generation, the image of the bookman virtually disappeared; the new intellectuals were missionary and restless. A dilettante like Leigh Hunt, whose *Imagination and Fancy* was published in 1844, was an anachronistic survival in the Victorian world. It was only much later, in the wake of the Aesthetic Movement, that the languid bookman came back. Pater spoke of Lamb's *Specimens* as the 'quintessence of criticism', and their author was belatedly canonised as the choicest spirit of the early nineteenth century.

The hostility of the utilitarians raises the question, what were the class affiliations of Victorian literary culture? There can of course be no simple answer to this. Not only were there differences between writers, but the leading writers, above all Dickens, were divided in themselves. Frequently Dickens reflects the values of the commercial bourgeoisie. Acquiring culture and becoming a writer are portrayed in his works as among the means of self-help. Mr Brownlow with his book-lined study represents the ideal of the good life in *Oliver Twist*, but when Oliver, asked if he would like to be an author, replies that it would be a much better thing to be a bookseller, he is felt to have said something preternaturally smart. Authorship for Dickens was a fundamentally entrepreneurial activity. In this he was at the opposite pole from Matthew Arnold, whose advocacy of literary values is inseparable from his advocacy of a corporate ideology which would take the place of *laissez-faire*. Despite the aristocratic associations of Arnold's 'grand style', he was really the prophet of the new ethic of service to the state, which was elicited by the growth of the middle-class professions and of the civil service both at home and in the colonies. Arnold envisages an international culture which, however, seeks to ratify rather than to deny the unique characteristics and individual spheres of interest of its constituent nation-states. And though they lacked Arnold's far-sightedness, many other Victorian critics saw themselves as middlemen in an essentially corporate process of production and consumption. Critics discussed such 'administrative' questions as those of anonymity, the relation between specialist and general reviewing, and the right choice of manner and tone. Men of letters such as Macaulay, Bagehot; Lewes and Stephen were superlatively competent reviewers, able to give a trenchant and searching account of almost any book that came to hand. The pace of Victorian reviewing at its most frenetic may be seen in one of George Eliot's surveys of 'Arts and Belles Lettres', which appeared in the *Westminster Review* for April 1856. The article begins with a review of volume three of Ruskin's *Modern Painters* – a crucial influence on Eliot's theory of literary realism. It continues with notices of fiction including Meredith, Wilkie Collins and Kingsley, foreign-language books by Stendhal, de Nerval and some German writers, Francis Newman's version of the *Iliad*, four volumes of Bohn's classics, and a batch of new poetry concluding with *Leaves of Grass* – a total of twenty-nine volumes in all.

The reviews themselves in the mid-nineteenth century – the *Fortnightly*, the *Cornhill*, the *Saturday*, the *Nineteenth Century* – were far more professional, open and objective than the old *Edinburgh* and *Quarterly*. The increasingly complex mechanism of publishing and reviewing itself affected the attitude of the critics. At least one anonymous mid-century reviewer felt that the machine had taken over:

> The manufacture of novels goes on with increasing activity. For the last two months novelists have been at work 'full blast.' We have, in consequence, some thirty volumes before us. Now, as each volume contains on the average about three hundred pages, and as we cannot possibly read more than one page a minute, especially when we have to cut the pages, it would take us, reading and cutting for five hours a day, a month to get through the pile. If, however, novelists write their tales by machinery, critics must review them by the same means.[2]

Mill's essay on 'Civilization' (1836) is a classic study of the process of 'massification' in advanced societies; and in it he denounces the commercialisation of literary values and suggests the formation of an authors' 'collective guild' to bypass the apparatus of booksellers and publishers. The apotheosis of the middleman is satirised in Gissing's *New Grub Street* (1891), where the prosperous journalist and literary agent are contrasted with the starving novelist and scholar.

What has become of literature, in this mechanised, corporate world of letters? The early Victorian critics were in two minds about the industrialisation of the press. On the one hand, it gave the literary journalist a feeling of power, importance and cultural centrality. On the other hand its characteristic products seemed ephemeral, meretricious and crude. One way of expressing this ambivalent feeling was to have two alternating definitions of the term 'literature'. Carlyle is the main exponent of the idea of literary culture before Arnold, and he supplies his readers with such definitions. There is the expansive definition, by which Carlyle conjures up the whole empire of the written word:

> Could ambition always choose its own path, and were will in human undertakings synonymous with faculty, all truly ambitious men would be men of letters...all other arenas of ambition, compared with this rich and boundless one of Literature, meaning thereby whatever respects the promulgation of Thought, are poor, limited and ineffectual. (1829)[3]

The alternative is the evaluative definition, strongly resembling de Quincey's 'literature of power':

> for that finer portion of our nature, that portion of it which belongs essentially to Literature strictly so called, where our highest feelings, our best joys and keenest sorrows, our Doubt, our Love, our Religion reside, [Johnson] has no word to utter; (1828)[4]

Keeping a refined and intensified definition of literature in reserve is a typical strategy of the literary apologist; what it does is to insist that literature has its appointed place in the realm of values, while not for a moment relinquishing its control over culture as a whole. In the work of Newman and Mill, as well as Carlyle, there are proposals for repairing the division between fact and value, by bringing the conditions of intellectual and spiritual debate closer to the desired ideal. Yet these two critics, though deeply sensitive to the power of poetry, differ from Carlyle in the equivocal value they assign to literature.

Mill's early Benthamism was modified by the spiritual crisis in which he discovered Wordsworth and the place of the poetic 'culture of the feelings' in human life. A by-product of the crisis was his attempt (which will be discussed below) to take the romantic view of poetry to its logical extremes. Yet even in those of Mill's essays which stress the importance of poetry for men of intellectual culture, there is an undercurrent stressing what intellectual culture can do for poets. An entry in the diary he kept for 1854 rejects Carlyle's use of the term 'Artist' to express 'the highest order of moral and intellectual greatness'; this honour, Mill says, belongs to the philosopher.[5] It is unlikely that he had ever thought otherwise. His public views on literary culture and education are expounded in the essay on 'Civilization' and in his 'Inaugural Address', delivered at St Andrew's University in 1867. In 'Civilization' he is concerned with the threat to 'individual character' posed by the trend towards a corporate society in which power is in the hands of masses. The erosion of literary values by 'quackery' and 'puffing' makes a graphic illustration of the pressures of the age. But Mill's assertions about falling standards are backed up by very little evidence. The causes of his anxiety seem to be the growth of the periodical press and the adverse terms of the market for serious publishing. Mill, in fact, was the first post-romantic critic to write in defence of literary culture in the urgent, prophetic tone we now associate with F. R. Leavis. He had two concrete proposals to make: the first was to change the economic basis of publishing, while the second – far more significantly – was for the reform of the universities. In universities, freed from religious tests and thrown open to competitive entry, the pursuit of truth could continue untouched by commercial pressures, and so the moral and intellectual character of the middle classes would be restored. Events were to show this as a highly practical vision; Mill's fears were unfounded, and his 'higher classes' emerged from the first century of mass advance with all their privileges intact.

Mill sketched a curriculum that would include classics, history, philosophy and the sciences. Although modern literature is granted a place, it appears as part of history. He enlarged upon the content of school and university education much later, in the three-hour 'Inaugural Address' that he delivered as Rector of St Andrew's. Here he distinguishes between the two main branches of education – those of intellectual and moral instruction – and adds almost as an afterthought that there is a third branch, the aesthetic, which deserves to be regarded far more seriously than it is. The arts serve to 'keep up the tone of our minds'.[6] Clearly this was only lip-service; Mill would seem to have thought that the 'culture of the feelings' was too private an affair to be assigned any more definite a place in academic studies. Classical languages and literature continued to occupy the central place in Mill's educational ideas, but then he himself had been taught Greek from the age of three.

John Henry Newman also paid his tribute to the imagination in the form of a youthful essay, 'Poetry with reference to Aristotle's Poetics' (1829), which expresses romantic and aesthetic sympathies while never quite contradicting the beliefs of the author's maturity. There are important parallels between the two men's discussions of university education, as well. Newman's starting-point, once again, was that the universities had largely lost their intellectual authority to the new institutions of periodical literature. His defence of liberal education was an attempt to restore the position. Both he and Mill see the branches of knowledge as related to one another by considerations of intellectual utility, and ask for liberal education to be judged by the effect it produces on the student. Thus, for Newman

> A habit of mind is formed which lasts through life, of which the attributes are freedom, equitableness, calmness, moderation, and wisdom; or what in a former discourse I have ventured to call a philosophical habit.[7]

Here he is defining culture in intellectual terms, and in a way that is calculated to favour classical studies. 'Wisdom' is almost inevitably that of the ancients, 'moderation' is in all things Greek and 'calmness' is all too easily attained in the study of dead civilisations. Newman uses the term 'literature' to mean the humanities as a whole, as opposed to the faculties of science and theology. Each branch of study in his idea of a university has to justify itself as an intellectual discipline. The central discipline in his view is theology. Poetry does not constitute an authentic discipline, though a place is reserved for philological study. A strict follower of Newman could, no doubt, find a place for literature by seeing it as the heir of the classics; Arnold, with more temerity, was to suggest it as the heir of theology.

Both Mill and Newman foresaw something like the modern division of intellectual life. Their direct influence has counted against the university study of literature, rather than in its favour. They are prophets of specialisation, lamenting the decline of learning in the face of the periodical press with its continuous diet of instruction and commentary. Newman became a university Rector in Dublin, and a Cardinal of the Church of Rome; but Mill, notwithstanding his brief term at St Andrew's, remained an independent man of letters. At the time when 'Civilization' appeared, he was editing the *London and Westminster Review*. His early career, as much as any Victorian's, evinces the literary bias of the reviews and periodicals which became the focus of Victorian intellectual life. The seat of culture, as Arnold later saw, lay not in the universities but in the metropolitan world of letters. While Mill and Newman viewed this with distaste, their contemporary Thomas Carlyle wrote of it with unabashed enthusiasm. The man of letters, he announced, was the modern Hero.

Thomas Carlyle

Like so much else, Carlyle's view of literary heroism can be traced back to German romanticism. In a discussion of the 'State of German Literature' (1827), he cited Fichte's view of the artist as the interpreter of the Divine Idea to mankind:

> Literary Men are the appointed interpreters of this Divine Idea; a perpetual priesthood, we might say, standing forth, generation after generation, as the dispensers and living types of God's everlasting wisdom, to show it in their writings and actions, in such particular form as their own particular times require it in.

The elevation of the artist was also the elevation of the critic, who stood 'like an interpreter between the inspired and the uninspired'. Carlyle's essay might have been entitled 'State of German Criticism'; he reports that criticism has taken a new form in Germany, concerning itself not with externals such as biography and craftsmanship, but with the 'essence and peculiar life of the poetry itself'. Its method, moreover, is not impressionistic, but scientific and systematic, appealing to principles deduced from the 'highest and calmest regions of philosophy'. And it is into those regions, and not into the peculiar life of poetry, that Carlyle, like the later Coleridge, is ultimately anxious to lead us. However, the heroes of his early essays – Burns, Novalis, Jean Paul and above all Goethe – belong to that romantic notion of literature in which poetry and philosophy are as one.

Or is it that all forms of human greatness are ultimately as one? This is the underlying proposition of the lectures *On Heroes, Hero-Worship and the Heroic in History* (1840). Though perhaps his most influential performance, they are something of a mixed bag. Carlyle tells the stories of his heroes superbly, especially when they are slightly unfamiliar; he is much more memorable on Thor and Odin, Mahomet, Dante, Knox and Cromwell than on Shakespeare, Johnson and Burns. It is easy to enjoy his narrative gifts without taking the underlying mystical belief in the Hero as participator in the 'open secret' of the universe too seriously. Moreover, Carlyle was expounding an evolutionary history of human society, as well as a redemptive saga of the universe. Each form of society, he argued, generates its own particular mode of heroism. Hence the historical series: God, Prophet, Poet, Priest, Man of Letters and King or Dictator. Such a series, which ends up with Johnson, Burns and Napoleon as legitimate successors of Odin and Mahomet (Carlyle tactfully does not mention Jesus), might well suggest a historical decline, but Carlyle argues that the case is not so simple. Instead of our reverence for the hero diminishing, it is that the standards we exact of our gods and heroes are constantly rising. The result is that the story of modern heroism is invariably a story of failure. This lesson is seen in the histories of Cromwell and Napoleon, who laid claim to the divine rights of kingship, and also in the modern Men of Letters who are the successors of the great poets such as Dante and Shakespeare.

The view of history in *On Heroes* was not particularly new, and in many ways the book is a culmination of the romantic age. The idea of the modern author overshadowed by the burden of the past had been familiar at least since Gray and Collins. Carlyle's selection of heroes must have struck some as archaic and literary in the 1840s, since he failed to celebrate such new types as the scientist, the statesman and the captain of industry. His view of literature as a power in the state echoes the truculence of the romantic poets:

> 'Literature will take care of itself,' answered Mr Pitt, when applied-to for some help for Burns. 'Yes,' adds Mr Southey, 'it will take care of itself; and of you too, if you do not look to it!'
>
> ('The Hero as Man of Letters')

Yet the conclusion that Carlyle draws from this anecdote is a new one:

> The result to individual Men of Letters is not the momentous one; they are but individuals, an infinitesimal fraction of the great body; they can struggle on, and live or else die, as they have been wont. But it deeply concerns the whole society, . . . I call this anomaly of a disorganic Literary Class the heart of all other anomalies, at once product and parent; some good arrangement for that would be as the *punctum saliens* of a new vitality and just arrangement for all.

This is a crucial modification of romantic individualism. Carlyle is not concerned with the rights and privileges of 'mighty poets', but with a whole literary class and its place in the social organism. He is looking towards the organisation of that class in the corporate state at the very moment of celebrating the role of individual genius in history. Carlyle believes that 'it is the spiritual always that determines the material',[8] and that it is men of genius who originate social developments, acting as interpreters of the 'sacred mystery of the Universe' for ordinary mortals. Modern society has generated in the Men of Letters a whole class of such seekers after the light. The Man of Letters, in effect, is a phenomenon for the cultural critic rather than for the epic storyteller, and it is as a cultural critic that Carlyle speaks in his lecture on Johnson, Rousseau and Burns.

Books, says Carlyle – 'that huge froth-ocean of Printed Speech we loosely call Literature' – are the university, church and parliament of the modern spirit. The literary world is the central cultural institution. But the man of letters is not recognised in the state, at least in the British state; he is an 'unrecognised unregulated Ishmaelite', living in a garret, ruling 'from his grave, after death' whole generations who would not have given him bread while living. This 'curious spectacle' is symptomatic of a wider cultural disability, reflected in the fate of the other modern hero, the political revolutionary adulated during his lifetime only to have his reputation blackened for posterity. Such a disability is reflected, too, in the shortcomings that Carlyle discovers in Johnson, Rousseau and Burns, the products of an enlightened and sceptical age who never found the spiritual truths they sought. This essay, like all Carlyle's work, is a programme for the moral regeneration of society. But it is also a defence of his own class, expounding at once a vision of a time when the failing and unrecognised Man of Letters will exude 'palpably articulated, universally visible power', and a view of history which makes him the legitimate heir of the ages.

Carlyle, then, is the representative literary prophet before Arnold, and the romantic idealism and archaism of his view of society are representative too. Yet, it might be asked, has any writer talked more about literature, and given us less literary criticism? He is concerned with the state of soul revealed by his men of letters, but hardly at all with their prose and verse. In his essay on Burns in the *Edinburgh Review*, he says somewhat breezily that 'True and genial as his poetry must appear, it is not chiefly as a poet, but as a man, that he interests and affects us';[9] and for criticism in the modern sense on Burns we turn straight to Matthew Arnold. This is evidence more of a difference of interest, however, than of any more fundamental incompatibility. Arnold and the other Victorian critics may have had more respect for the literary text, but they all regard the task of criticism as being to arrive at a series of responses to individual authors. Invariably the author was seen 'as a man' and the response was framed in moral terms. Carlyle as well as Johnson stood behind the monumental *English Men of Letters* series of critical monographs, founded by John Morley in 1877. While Johnson pioneered the brief critical Life, Carlyle's influence suggested that those so honoured should be a carefully chosen gallery of writers from the past whose personalities stood out against their times. The contri-

butors to the *English Men of Letters* included R. H. Hutton, Leslie
Stephen, Henry James, Mark Pattison, T. H. Huxley, George
Saintsbury and Frederick Harrison. Perhaps it is not too much
to claim that Carlyle's discovery of the identity of the modern hero
indicated the course of critical work for the next two generations.
His conclusions about particular authors, too, have often been
echoed by more determinedly 'literary' critics.

Tennyson and Mill

Nevertheless, it is one thing to proclaim the poet as a great man,
and another to show an informed interest in his poetry. The major
irony of the Carlylean view of culture, half exultation over the
'huge froth-ocean of Printed Speech' and half celebration of the
poetic heroes of the past, is that it may be the contemporary poet
who feels most excluded from it. The private, daydream world
of the romantics and the bookmen was a more natural habitat
for poets than for the energetic Victorian critics, and it was the
poets, after all, who were closer to the realities of Carlyle's garret.
There is a fine expression of the poet's helplessness in the new
literary world in one of the lyrics of *In Memoriam*:

> What hope is here for modern rhyme
>   To him, who turns a musing eye
>   On songs, and deeds, and lives, that lie
> Foreshorten'd in the tract of time?
>
> These mortal lullabies of pain
>   May bind a book, may line a box,
>   May serve to curl a maiden's locks;. . .
>
> But what of that? My darken'd ways
>   Shall ring with music all the same;
>   To breathe my loss is more than fame,
> To utter love more sweet than praise.

> (LXXVI)

The 'mortal lullabies of pain' are materialised as an artefact and
set adrift in the public world where they become waste paper or
at best something idly glanced at on a secondhand bookstall. We
remember Johnson's contemplation of the futility of human effort
as enshrined in libraries. It would not suit Tennyson's case to admit
that he can be in any way affected by neglect and oblivion, however;

as a modern lyric poet, it was his fate and duty to go on ringing with music regardless of whether anyone heard him. The 'darken'd ways' are at once ways unillumined by heavenly light (the contrast is with the beatified Hallam of the preceding poem) and the pages of an unopened book. A sturdy private faith is invoked to bolster the poet against neglect. We may suspect a certain posturing in this, when we remember the enormous success of *In Memoriam*, and the public standing it gave its author. Tennyson inherited the romantic duality of public exhortation and private daydream, but the emotions of his poetry are so generalised that any number of people besides poets could draw sustenance from its pious resolutions and inward sorrows.

Tennyson's poetry was felt to epitomise 'modern rhyme' by its earliest admirers. The lesson in 'pure poetry' which critics such as A. H. Hallam and Mill found in 'Mariana' and 'The Lady of Shalott' forms a convincing link between the aims of the romantics and those of the aesthetes and symbolists later in the century. Yeats, for example, acknowledged a debt to Hallam's review of Tennyson's *Poems, Chiefly Lyrical* (1830), and this review, though necessarily immature, is one of the most important attempts to establish and clarify the definition of poetry inherited from the romantics. Hallam distinguishes between pure poetry, which is unpopular because it demands an active response, and fashionable verse which beguiles the reader with 'mere rhetoric'. Poetry is losing ground in the present age, since its 'subjective power' is overshadowed by the increase in social activity with its 'continual absorption of the higher feelings into the palpable interests of ordinary life'.[10] Modern poetry must expect to become, not a popular art-form, but an affair of votaries and sects. So far Hallam is giving a highly intelligent restatement of themes from Wordsworth's prefaces. But he accuses Wordsworth's poetry of too often resorting to mere rhetoric, and argues that the highest poetic mode is not that of reflectiveness but of sensation, as represented by Keats and Shelley. Tennyson, clearly, is in the Keatsian tradition.

Hallam did not live to elaborate a complete theory of 'pure poetry', but such a theory is to be found in Mill's two essays 'What is Poetry?' and 'The Two Kinds of Poetry' (1833). These essays are, in effect, an attempt to give philosophical substance to the romantic use of the word 'poetry' to denote a quality common to all the arts. Thus Mill is committed to 'pure poetry', though he does not seem interested in 'poetry for poetry's sake'. He investigates it as a psychological phenomenon (it was, of course, as a psychological phenomenon or anti-depressant that he had first taken up poetry). The questions he asks are, what kind of mind produces poetry, what sort of communication does it constitute, and how do we respond to it? The discursive content of the communication is of little moment.

Mill's view of poetry appears when he asks the question, how does a poet describe a lion? The answer is that he does so by imagery. He must try to suggest the likenesses and contrasts which belong to the emotional state which the spectacle of the lion would excite. What is described, then, is the state of excitement in the spectator, and the description must be judged not by its representation of the lion itself, but by its truth to the emotion aroused. Thus Mill distinguishes between poetry, a purely subjective utterance, and narrative fiction, which he speaks of somewhat contemptuously. Poetry is a higher form than narrative, a 'delineation of the deeper and more secret workings of the human heart.' But it is also a more esoteric form, appealing only to those whose imagination is more highly developed. And just as poetry is more subjective than narrative, it is more private than 'eloquence' or rhetoric, so that all poetry is of the nature of soliloquy:

> eloquence is heard, poetry is overheard. Eloquence supposes an audience; the peculiarity of poetry appears to us to lie in the poet's utter unconsciousness of a listener. Poetry is feeling confessing itself to itself, in moments of solitude, and bodying itself forth in symbols which are the nearest possible representations of the feeling in the exact shape in which it exists in the poet's mind.[11]

This translation of feeling into symbols and imagery is reversed in the process of poetic response.

In 'What is Poetry!' Mill outlines the definition of poetry and suggests how it may be applied to the arts of music, painting and architecture. In 'The Two Kinds of Poetry' he distinguishes pure from didactic poetry, and argues that pure poetry issues from a specifically poetic cast of mind. The born poet is the 'poet of nature'; his counterpart, who uses verse as a vehicle for thoughts which could have been expressed in prose, is the 'poet of culture'. Shelley is the example of the first. Wordsworth of the second. Shelley's lyricism is a spontaneous product, an inspired and exuberant stream of images controlled only by the poet's dominant state of feeling and his natural 'fineness of organization'. The result is poetry 'in a far higher sense than any other'. Wordsworth's attempts in the lyrical mode are 'cold and spiritless', however, and he remains distressingly earth-bound:

Wordsworth's poetry is never bounding, never ebullient; has little even of the appearance of spontaneousness: the well is never so full that it overflows. There is an air of calm deliberateness about all he writes, which is not characteristic of the poetic temperament; his poetry seems one thing, himself another; he seems to be poetical because he wills to be so, not because he cannot help it: did he will to dismiss poetry, he need never again, it might almost seem, have a poetical thought.[12]

Written at the age of twenty-seven, 'The Two Kinds of Poetry' is a brilliantly precocious theoretical exercise. If it falls short of total clarity, this is probably because Mill remains tied to the Wordsworthian psychological vocabulary of 'feelings', 'associations', 'states of excitement' and so on. Yet the essay is also a notable example of biting the hand that has fed one. Mill's determination to expose the contradictions of Wordsworth's theory and practice seems coldly wilful in the passage quoted above. In view of the admiring tone in which he reported his first meeting with Wordsworth in 1831, and the role later ascribed to Wordsworth's influence in his *Autobiography*, it is impossible not to suspect him of unconscious dishonesty in the 1833 essays. In any case, though he denies Wordsworth a place among the born poets, he never suggests that Shelley attained creative maturity. A philosopher may not be able to become a poet, he writes, but 'a poet may always, by culture, make himself a philosopher'. Poets, providing that they are indeed poets, can only benefit by acquiring some intellectual culture. Here Mill betrays his underlying concern with education and the constitution of the well-balanced mind. He mentions two poets who possessed a 'logical and scientific culture', Milton and Coleridge; and thence we may trace the line leading to his later work through the magnificent essays on Coleridge and Bentham. There are two other pieces closely linked to the essays of 1833, those on Tennyson (1835) and Alfred de Vigny (1838). In his review of Tennyson's first two collections, Mill shows how the theory of pure poetry as the expression of subjective emotions may be applied to poems such as 'Mariana'. But he also speaks of Tennyson's growing 'maturity of intellect', the advancing 'intellectual culture' that was enabling him to ripen into a true artist. A poem such as 'The Palace of Art' was not merely a rendering of sensations but a symbolic representation of spiritual truths. In welcoming this aspect of Tennyson's work, Mill does not seem at all far from Victorian orthodoxy.

Mill's theoretical insight is great, but his critical judgments are not quite to be trusted. A wider question poses itself. What are we to make of a utilitarian philosopher whose poetic theory comes so close to that of the aesthetes? Mill is a psychologist adapting the theory of 'pure poetry' to his own uses, very much as I. A. Richards, ninety years later, was to construct a psychological theory of poetic communication under the influence of Clive Bell's notion of 'significant form'. Both *Principles of Literary Criticism* and Mill's early essays reveal a hidden compatibility between apparently opposing doctrines. Aesthete and utilitarian are united by their opposition to the belief that poetry has a rational content and must therefore be treated on a level with other forms of discourse. The aesthete's religion of art serves to disguise a retreat from the romantic poet's claims for the moral and cognitive value of the poetic activity. Poetry for the aesthete is largely self-validating; too proud to compete in the intellectual market-place, he claims privileged access to a mode of reality which can only be embodied in poetical forms. The utilitarian is only too glad to assign to the poet a unique psychological function, so long as this esoteric, purely emotive function disqualifies any claims he might have as a philosopher and social reformer. Both Mill and Richards write eloquently about the pure poet whom they confine, in effect, to uttering 'pseudo-statements'.[13] Poetry for the aesthete is a solipsistic, for the utilitarian simply a specialist, pursuit. Either emphasis is a denial of the romantic ideal of the poet as a man speaking to men – speaking to our whole being, with as much claim to our full and general attention as any other man can have. Nothing in Mill's work contradicts the idea that the highest offices of art are, first, to give moving expression to pre-existent truths, and second, to act as a therapy or cure for depression.

Although the doctrine of art for art's sake was familiar from the time of Gautier's preface to *Mademoiselle de Maupin* (1835), it was not until the time of Pater and Swinburne that aestheticism emerged as a coherent force in England. The particular forms of English aestheticism will thus be dealt with in the final section of this chapter. The debate between romantic and utilitarian views of art is, however, one which has cropped up in varying forms since its inception in the 1820s. It is surprising, perhaps, that it was not taken further by the early Victorians, and that there is not more to refute George Saintsbury's observation of the 'general critical poverty' of the period 1830–60.[14] The advocates of 'pure poetry' were virtually unread in their own time. At the other extreme, Victorian positivism did not address itself to the development of a science of criticism; the nearest approach to this comes in two books by E. S. Dallas, *Poetics* (1852) and *The Gay Science* (1866). *The Gay Science* undertakes a psychological analysis of the faculty of imagination, but Dallas, a journalist on the London

Times, completed only the first two volumes, which were not well received.[15] The better-known mid-Victorian reviewers such as Bagehot, G. H. Lewes and R. H. Hutton were all opposed to the idea of criticism as science; they failed, however, to put anything very much in its place. The reason why literature was felt to elude scientific codification was, broadly, that it was a medium of individual, idiosyncratic expression. This suggests that the true alternative to the aesthetic and the utilitarian positions would be found in the moralistic doctrine of art which received its most decisive critical formulation in the work of Arnold in the 1860s. Arnold's immediate predecessors here were Carlyle, Emerson and Ruskin.

The Birth of American Criticism: Emerson, Whitman and Poe

'A breath as of the green country, – all the welcomer that it is *New*-England country, not second-hand but first-hand country, – meets us wholesomely everywhere in these *Essays*': these are the words of Carlyle, introducing the first collection of Ralph Waldo Emerson's writings to the English public in 1841. Throughout the nineteenth century, American authors could be very successfully incorporated into Victorian literary culture in terms such as these. Later in the century, what Santayana was to call the genteel tradition gave rise to a criticism that was avowedly provincial and to the migration of writers of the stature of Henry James and T. S. Eliot from Boston to London. The first generation of American critics, however, laid stress on the fact of American difference. Emerson and Whitman drew on the revolutionary inheritance in American life to present a bardic vision which is fundamentally opposed to Mill's etiolated notions of poetry.

Emerson's essay 'The Poet' (1844) describes its subject in 'ideal perfection' much as Wordsworth's Preface had done. The American poet does not yet exist, though (Emerson adds) 'neither could I aid myself to fix the idea of the poet by reading now and then in Chalmers's collection of five centuries of English poets.' America like England is affected by the 'diffidence of mankind in the soul' and by the assumption that 'all thought is already long ago adequately set down in books';[16] but the truly American poet is simply charged with writing down what is in front of him, since 'America is a poem in our eyes'. By 'America' Emerson, like many other nineteenth-century writers, means to signify a combination of virgin nature awaiting exploitation, and the challenge of political democracy. The poet's mission is to attend to the inspiration of nature and to become an oracle giving voice to the 'divine *aura* which breathes through forms.' Emerson is Wordsworthian in affirming that 'All men are poets at heart,' while nevertheless reserving a special mission for the poet.[17]

The oracular poet needs interpretation, however. This is the source of the intellectual vocation celebrated in 'The American Scholar' (1857), written five years after Emerson had resigned from the Unitarian ministry. The scholar, a representative of 'Man Thinking', is a secular priest whose function is to receive and impart both the works of nature and the authentic utterances of visionary poets, rejecting whatever is secondhand and inauthentic. The scholar-priest must follow an arduous and solitary discipline, though writers of genius, Emerson argues in 'The Poet', can short-circuit the activity of scholarly interpretation by acting directly as 'liberating gods' for the people at large: 'An imaginative book renders us much more service at first, by stimulating us through its tropes, than afterward, when we arrive at the precise sense of the author.' Scholarship, according to Emerson, should not be concerned so much with establishing the precise sense of the author as with pointing to whatever is 'transcendental and extraordinary' in books.

The poet's relationship to the people and to virgin nature is, of course, mediated through language. For Emerson language itself is 'fossil poetry', a petrified structure of images and tropes each of which 'was at first a stroke of genius, and obtained currency, because for the moment it symbolised the world to the first speaker and to the first hearer'. A new world demands a new or at least a renovated language. In 'Literary Ethics' (1838), considering the intellectual tasks that face the American scholar, Emerson turns to the 'noonday darkness of the American forest', to the 'aboriginal woods' where 'you shall find all new and undescribed', and 'the eagle and the crow see no intruder'. Needless to say, he is silent about the native American population of these woods. Emerson's vision is of an unoccupied and unnamed continent, where 'tropes, fables, oracles, and all other poetic forms' lie dormant in the very geography. In such a world the exercise of poetic imagination is a collective, not merely an individual, responsibility, and the critic as Transcendentalist can affirm that 'all literature is yet to be written'.

Walt Whitman, disavowing merely literary aims, set out to write it. *Leaves of Grass*, he claimed retrospectively in 'A Backward Glance o'er Travel'd Roads' (1888), was not to be seen as a 'literary performance' but as the 'autochthonous song' of a new nation rejecting any literary authority derived from the Old World. Even Shakespeare belonged to the buried past, and would be displaced by the poems of 'realities and science and of the democratic average

and basic equality' to be produced in the New World. Whitman
to some extent replaces the Transcendentalists' backwoodsmanship
with a commitment to intellectual and artistic modernisation, looking forward to the critical rhetoric of Ezra Pound. Nevertheless,
he celebrated the pioneering spirit of rural America and, in 'A
Backward Glance', he had to admit that he had suffered the common fate of pioneers. His almost shamanistic 1855 preface to *Leaves
of Grass* had compared the poet to the President of the United
States – not only a 'common referee', but first among equals. The
poet was a spokesman for liberty and equality and was himself
answerable to democratic interrogation; his popularity was, apparently, the index of his power. 'The proof of a poet is that his country
absorbs him as affectionately as he has absorbed it', Whitman had
optimistically written. In the long run he would be proved right,
but in 1888 he was forced to confess that 'from a worldly and
business point of view *Leaves of Grass* has been worse than a
failure'.

Poetry for Whitman should be 'answerable' to the nation and
its politics:

> Of the great poems receiv'd from abroad and from the ages,
> and to-day enveloping and penetrating America, is there one
> that is consistent with these United States, or essentially appli-
> cable to them as they are and are to be? Is there one whose
> underlying basis is not a denial and insult to democracy? ('A
> Backward Glance')

Among other nineteenth-century poets, Emily Dickinson has no
truck with questions such as these, while Edgar Allan Poe's indifference to them gave rise to the most influential American critical
theory of the century. Poe was by no means an unpatriotic writer,
but in his eyes Whitman's prescriptions would doubtless have exemplified the 'heresy of *The Didactic*' which was one of the major
legacies of New England Puritanism. Poe's essays 'The Philosophy
of Composition' (1846) and 'The Poetic Principle' (1850) put forward an ideal of 'pure poetry' which deeply impressed Baudelaire
and the French Symbolist movement, and which therefore contributed (at least indirectly) to virtually all subsequent formalist
theories.

Poe – 'Three fifths of him genius and two fifths sheer fudge,'
according to James Russell Lowell's 'A Fable for Critics' (1848)
– was one of the great opportunists of criticism. His views on poetry
lay claim to universal validity but in the end, it might be said,
they are not much more than Poe-try. His doctrine that the only

authentic work of literary art is one which can be taken in at a single sitting stands, for example, as a justification of the short-windedness of Poe's own verse and of the best of his prose. He took from Coleridge the notion of organic unity and its idiosyncratic corollary that 'A poem of any length neither can be, nor ought to be, all poetry'; for Poe (though, of course, not for Coleridge) this was sufficient to dispose of the poetic claims of an epic such as *Paradise Lost*. Since the 'unity of effect or impression' sought by the true poet would be dissipated once the reader's concentration was disturbed, a long poem was a contradiction in terms. The effect of 'totality' could only be achieved by the brief lyric or – as he argued in a review of Hawthorne's *Twice-Told Tales* – the prose narrative requiring 'from a half-hour to one or two hours in its perusal'. There is a curious mixture in this of a dogma perhaps analogous to the neoclassical Unities, and of the empirical psychologist consulting his stopwatch.

'The Philosophy of Composition', purportedly a sober examination of Poe's own methods, explains that he designed his poem 'The Raven' as a kind of emotional machine to achieve the maximum intensity of artistic effect. In form, length, subject-matter, atmosphere and diction 'The Raven' was intended to provide the most beautiful and melancholy reading experience possible. Our suspicions with regard to Poe's essay should be aroused, however, by the fact that 'The Raven' manifestly does not produce the effect predicted. If it provides a rather different experience, this may be best accounted for by the element of the grotesque, so characteristic of its author, which 'The Philosophy of Composition' passes over in silence. The grotesque element in 'The Raven' most evidently appears in the raven itself, and the effects of its speech. Poe's theory (like those of the twentieth-century structuralists), reduces the raven's speech to a merely linguistic event, the repetition of the magic word 'Nevermore'. Why 'Nevermore'? His explanation seems at first sight to be a masterpiece of deductive logic:

Having made up my mind to a *refrain*, the division of the poem into stanzas was, or course, a corollary: the *refrain* forming the close of each stanza. That such a close, to have force, must be sonorous and susceptible of protracted emphasis, admitted no doubt: and these considerations inevitably led me to the long *o* as the most sonorous vowel, in connection with *r* as the most producible consonant.

The sound of the *refrain* being thus determined, it became necessary to select a word embodying this sound, and at the same time in the fullest possible keeping with that melancholy which I had predetermined as the tone of the poem. In such a search it would have been absolutely impossible to overlook the word 'Nevermore.' In fact, it was the very first which presented itself.

Pretty clearly, the final two sentences here reveal that the actual process followed was rather more inductive than deductive; and this is what we conventionally expect of poets. But there is more to be said, since – if poems aiming at the maximum intensity of effect *were* to be constructed by the methods Poe describes – then he himself was apparently not the first to attempt it.

Among the matters on which Poe's 'Philosophy of Composition' remains silent is his debt to Tennyson. (In 'The Poetic Principle', however, he was to quote 'Tears, idle tears' in full and to describe his English contemporary as 'the noblest poet that ever lived'.) Tennyson's 'Mariana' (1830) uses the words 'dreary' and 'aweary' in a monotonous refrain, with more or less the results that Poe describes; Mill, for example, wrote of the poem that 'Words surely never excited a more vivid feeling of physical and spiritual dreariness.'[18] Poe's choice of 'Nevermore', and of the long *o* as the most melancholy vowel, is better understood when we remember that Tennyson had already pre-empted one of the alternatives. Similarly, 'The Philosophy of Composition' lays down one hundred lines as the optimum length for a poem. 'Mariana', at eighty-four lines, had somewhat undershot this, but this helps to excuse Poe's otherwise inexplicable error in allowing 'The Raven' to run on to a hundred and eight.

The Poe–Tennyson connection was remarked by another mid-century American critic, Henry Timrod, who wrote that if Poe's theory led to the conclusion that Tennyson was the noblest of poets, it implied that Poe himself came a close second.[19] The more we examine Poe's somewhat repetitious essays, the more we are likely to agree with Whitman that they 'belong among the electric lights of imaginative literature, brilliant and dazzling, but with no heat'.[20] Nevertheless, he formalised and made explicit the shift to the short poem which was already implicit in romantic theory, and which in turn would come to dominate the classroom methods of textual analysis associated with the New Critics.

Poe's review of Hawthorne boldly asserts the aesthetic claims of prose fiction, and another of his legacies (for better and worse) is his assertion that both creative and critical writing are rational, indeed clinical, procedures. In literary composition, he argues, every word should contribute to the fulfilment of the initial design. The critic – or, as in 'The Philosophy of Composition', the self-critic

– may then demonstrate with inexorable logic how the design was fulfilled. Poe's project in this was that of the archetypal rational literary theorist, but once we attend to the flaws in his argument, and then put it beside such extraordinary works as *Eureka*, 'The Unparalleled Adventure of One Hans Pfaall', 'The Balloon-Hoax' and so on, 'The Philosophy of Composition' asks to be read as an almost Swiftian satire on the human susceptibility to rational persuasion. If we are prepared to admit that an orang-utan must have carried out the murders in the Rue Morgue, then why should not 'The Raven' have been constructed by a computer program? The poem itself, however, preserves its uniqueness – gawky, oddly distinguished and not over-impressed by its author's retrospective analysis. A systematic criticism on the lines adumbrated in 'The Philosophy of Composition' would be an absurdity, as I believe Poe intended. The nearest that we come to a genuinely systematic criticism among the nineteenth-century successors of Coleridge is in the writings of another formidably idiosyncratic figure, John Ruskin.

Ruskin and Morris

Mill, Carlyle, Emerson and even Poe provide us with critical texts which are clearly distinct from the rest of their intellectual enterprise. In Ruskin's case there is no such convenience, and anthologies of the *Literary Criticism of John Ruskin*, like other selections from his works, have a somewhat haphazard air. A prophetic conviction of the unity of culture is fundamental in his thought; yet the place of literature in this, though a central one, is never that assigned to it by Victorian cultural orthodoxy. He is nearest to orthodoxy in the concern with the morality of great art and with the ranking of geniuses that he shares with Arnold. Poetry for Ruskin is an evaluative term, applying to all the arts and defined as 'the suggestion, by the imagination, of noble grounds for the noble emotions'.[21] The best poetry, this seems to imply, is that which most closely expresses the divine plan of the universe. But any idea that he is returning to the eighteenth-century Sublime is undercut by his sharp disagreement with Reynolds over the nature of the grand style. Ruskin's text in his discussion 'Of the received Opinions touching the "Grand Style"' is a quatrain from Byron's 'Prisoner of Chillon'. Great poetry, he argues, inheres not in generalities but in the vivid presentation of minute particulars. Ruskin's conception of genius, however, is brought out in his discussions of Turner and Tintoretto rather than of his literary heroes, and it is the minute particulars of visual representation that he hunts out and dissects throughout the five volumes of *Modern Painters*. None the less, the literary sections of the book involve a kind of direct dealing with poetic imagery and statement, exemplified in his analyses of Byron, Wordsworth and Scott, which is exceedingly rare in Victorian criticism. Only Arnold, among the merely literary critics, even began to take the object to pieces and to look at the parts as they really were. Ruskin did this time and again. His inspiration, as with his exhaustive analyses of natural forms, was, like Coleridge's, a kind of natural theology. *Modern Painters* ends on an apocalyptic note, as Ruskin affirms his ever-growing reverence for Turner's genius and portrays the act of criticism as a frail human counterpart to God's task on the Day of Judgment. In his later work his mode of analysis became an excessively literal iconography, based on the interpretation of sacred texts. The 'objective' interpretation of 'Lycidas' that he offers in *Sesame and Lilies*, for instance, has what Joyce's Buck Mulligan would call the true scholastic stink. Ruskin's evolution from a Wordsworthian concern with natural representation to a mode of myth or archetypal criticism has found an outspoken modern defender, however, in Harold Bloom.[22]

Ruskin could be a more forthright critic of contemporary literature than almost any of his rivals, though his power of harnessing contemporary criticism to cultural diagnosis was best exercised in architecture and the visual arts. Throughout his criticism he is concerned with art as the expression of man's history, which he traces in its social, psychological, religious and topographical aspects. His overall design is so grand that it is only too easily misrepresented in isolated (and frequently eccentric or dogmatic) extracts. What are we to make of the astonishing discussion of Shakespeare, for example, in the 'Mountain Glory' chapter of *Modern Painters* Volume Four? Bred on the 'plains of Stratford', Shakespeare, Ruskin tells us, was on a level with his race; yet this is cited as proof, not as negation, of his thesis of the 'mountain power over human intellect'. May it not be that certain hills around Stratford, or even a fleeting glimpse of the white cliffs of Dover, were essential to the development of the Shakespearean genius? And in any case, he lacks the 'ascending sight' of a great visionary such as Dante, who could look up in the mornings towards Fiesole! Taken in isolation, this mode of argument seems weirdly ramshackle, but the conclusion does bring into focus an aspect of Shakespeare's sensibility which had not often been seen so sharply. And set in the whole context of *Modern Painters*, such a confrontation with Shakespeare is an almost inevitable product of Ruskin's systematic exploration of the nature and principles of creative imagination, and of his fervent, Wordsworthian awareness of the influence on mankind of the beautiful and permanent forms of nature.

Ruskin, in fact, was the one Victorian who inherited the ambitions of the major romantic critics. The conclusion of *Modern Painters* is an elegy for the romantic genius of Scott, Keats, Byron, Shelley and Turner, condemned by a godless society to 'die without hope'. Homer, Dante and Milton, as well as the romantics, were among his formative influences; but his deep understanding of poetry usually comes across in passing references, instead of being explored for its own sake. The literary text is just one of the subjects of his massive project of cultural analysis. This is why Ruskin seems distinct from the merely literary world of so much Victorian criticism, with its restricted discussions of individual works in relation to the author's personality, his literary milieu and the reader's responses. The effect of Ruskin's criticism was to set up alternatives to Victorian bookishness, rather than to broaden its scope. In later books like *Sesame and Lilies*, he expresses a view of culture which is essentially religious and constitutes a subordination of the imaginative spirit to doctrinal and iconological concerns. (He had, however, abandoned the sectarian Evangelicalism of his youth.) In the earlier work his vision is of a culture centred not upon literature but upon man's relation to nature as expressed in the visual arts, especially painting and architecture. At all times, however, he was moving away from the individuality of literary expression to more communal notions of culture. He was anticipated in his stress on the visual arts by Pugin, whose condemnation of modern building in *Contrasts* (1836) was part of an explicit programme to restore the Catholic faith. Ruskin in turn decisively influenced William Morris, who became the propagandist of a radically socialist idea of culture in which literature as the nineteenth century knew it would cease to exist.

Ruskin describes his basic approach to art criticism in the 'Nature of Gothic' chapter in *The Stones of Venice*. He speaks of the necessity of 'reading a building as we would read Milton or Dante'. His own method of 'reading', however, was almost unprecedented; it involved relating architectural style, not merely to the spirit of a culture, but to its material base. Gothic architecture for Ruskin is the direct expression of the religious beliefs and the social and economic organisation of the medieval community. It is also an expression of the eternal romantic spirit, engaged, as the German romantics had suggested, in a perpetual conflict with the principles of classicism. Ruskin ranges dialectically from level to level of sociological, technological, cultural and religious discussion, at the same time as he lays down rules for restoring freedom of expression to the contemporary arts and crafts. Architecture and the decorative arts, he implies, have a more genuinely communal basis in the skills and traditions of the people than literary culture has ever had. At the same time, architecture no less than poetry is illuminated by the 'Seven Lamps' of Sacrifice, Truth, Power, Beauty, Life, Memory and Obedience. It has – or should have – no deficiency in expressive power.

The implications of this were drawn by Morris, whose vision of a civilisation based on the practice of the handicrafts was a deliberate rejection of literary culture. Morris believed that worthwhile art was the expression of a whole people, and not of the individual or of a coterie. As a poet, he stood for the revival of the primitive, oral forms of legend and saga, but in his lectures and essays he expounded a definition of culture as based on the arts of building and ornamentation, and not of literary expression. It was here that he combined the stress on architecture as the truly communal art, inherited from Ruskin and Pugin, with a socialist critique of the distortions of culture under capitalism. Marx and Engels had described the exclusive concentration of artistic talent in particular individuals as a 'consequence of division of labour'.[23] Morris in *Hopes and Fears for Art* denounced the 'hierarchy of intellect in the arts'.[24] He was attacking the individualism of the artist, the cultural snobbery which placed the artist above the craftsman, and the coterie attitude of aestheticism. To speak of the 'hierarchy of intellect' was to link high art, with its academic standards and traditions of exclusion, to the whole existence of intellectuals as a class and the prevalence of 'ranking' and 'grading' attitudes in society. (George Eliot's novels, for example, are full of processes of assessment of the characters by the author and by one another, and show how the critical attitudes of high culture reflected the habits of ordinary life.) Morris's view of art was an openly revolutionary one; he was prepared to see art die, if it was not already dead, to compel the birth of a new tradition.

Morris, as has often been pointed out, was a prophet of desirable rather than of possible worlds. His conception of a new art seems to have been dogged by triviality; we can find this in his own very diffuse creative work, in the 'epoch of rest' portrayed in *News from Nowhere* and in the sense that his lectures give of ignoring the highest potentialities of art (Beethoven, Rembrandt, Tolstoy), not to mention its capacity to revolutionise itself from within.[25] The Nowherians are penetrating critics of nineteenth-century fiction, although they have no impulse or need to construct artistic works which go beyond the texture of their everyday lives.[26] Morris's value for criticism, in fact, lies in the light he can shed on an inherited literary ideology. The idea of the man of letters as hero was an attempt to assert the cultural authority of the intellectual class. Morris links this to the privileged status of intellectuals and the need for an army of workers to process their ideas for transmission to the public. In his exposure of the luxury status of contemporary art he anticipates the doctrine of 'commodity fetishism' in a twentieth-century Marxist such as Christopher Caudwell. As for the actual cultural policies of socialist states, these have been far closer to the letter of Matthew Arnold than to the spirit of William Morris.

Matthew Arnold

It was Morris who denounced the 'hierarchy of intellect in the arts'; but Morris was a gentleman of leisure, with an unearned income that he was free to devote to aesthetic or to socialist ends as he chose. He, and not Matthew Arnold, was in that sense the 'literary man'. A speech that Arnold made at a Royal Academy banquet in 1875 serves to underline the point. Called upon to reply to the toast of 'Literature', in a company which included Gladstone, Disraeli, the Prince of Wales and a large section of the British establishment, Arnold began as follows:

> Literature, no doubt, is a great and splendid art, allied to that great and splendid art of which we see around us the handiwork. But, Sir, you do me an undeserved honour, when, as President of the Royal Academy, you desire me to speak in the name of Literature. Whatever I may have once wished or intended, my life is not that of a man of letters, but of an Inspector of Schools (a laugh), and it is with embarrassment that I now stand up in the dreaded presence of my own official chiefs (a laugh), who have lately been turning upon their Inspectors an eye of some suspicion. (A laugh.) (*The Times*, 3 May 1875)[1]

The audience, of course, found this hilarious fun; they knew their man, and knew he would not embarrass them, and punctuated with their laughs it all sounds dashing in the *Times* report. We need not stress the irony that Arnold, the champion of literary culture, felt driven beyond that culture to make a living. He took up school-inspecting, it seems, partly to provide himself with an income and partly as a 'philosophic gesture' to establish his social identity.[2] The problem of social identity is central to a consideration of his literary criticism, as well as of his failure as a poet. Arnold was the classic Victorian exponent of culture because he saw with an unrivalled clarity the path that literature must take to remain free from the encroachments of positivism and political ideology on the one hand, and from a trivialising aestheticism on the other. And Arnold taught that integrity in the literary sphere was above all a question of style and tone. The literary critic, therefore, could unmask the moral and intellectual habits of his contemporaries in a way that other commentators could not. But who was the literary critic, and what was revealed in his tone? Arnold has a vivacious, an unmistakable personality, but he has no settled voice, as Wordsworth and Johnson have in their prose; he has a remarkable range of rhetorical inflections, and even in a performance as integral in conception as *Culture and Anarchy*, he proves astonishingly difficult to pin down. The immediate cause of this, it would seem, is histrionic; it arises from his attempt to command an ever-increasing audience.

Arnold's early prefaces are examples of prose with a purely intellectual appeal. They must have made a frigid impression on some of the small band of admirers of his early poetry. His Oxford lectures on Homer and his study of *Popular Education in France* (1861) show him addressing a wider, but still a specialist readership. His sense of the general and acute relevance of culture and literary criticism emerged in the 1860s. By 1863 he was conscious of seizing his 'chance of getting at the English public', writing to his mother that 'everything turns upon one's exercising the power of persuasion, of charm'.[3] So he developed into a licensed performer, dazzling the public with inspiring rhetoric, withering irony and disarming self-display. He is the most exhibitionist of the Victorian prophets. Mill trusted in cold reason, and Carlyle in stump-oratory, to reach in time their natural audiences. Arnold, however, feels compelled to advertise himself, to put on an act in front of the footlights. When the charm fails to work he seems less substantial and more of a pretender than any of his rivals.

Arnold's poetry is intensely melancholic. The theme of loss of self occurs in relation to the melancholia. Empedocles, who is true to his own nature, throws himself into the crater of Etna; Arnold, in suppressing morbid and suicidal impulses, perhaps also suppressed himself. His poem 'The Buried Life' (1852) expresses the dichotomy of public and private selves. The buried self exists at a 'subterranean depth', and can only come to the surface in certain hours of private fulfilment 'When a beloved hand is laid in ours'. For Arnold, the public adult is a 'baby man':

How he would pour himself in every strife,
And well-nigh change his own identity;
That it might keep from his capricious play
His genuine self . . . .

The extent of worldliness in this may be judged if we compare
it with the Tennyson poem quoted above; Arnold's darkened ways
on the whole do not 'ring with music all the same'. It may have
been precisely the indirectness involved in essays in criticism which
proved so attractive to him. There is no necessary incompatibility
between criticism and self-definition, as the examples of Johnson
and Wordsworth show. Yet Arnold is far more of an interpreter
and 'appreciator' than they are. Many of his essays, especially in
the first *Essays in Criticism* (1865), are contributions to a gallery
of minor culture-heroes, and many are expressions of his admiration for the French critics Scherer and Sainte-Beuve. Arnold
is alone among major critics in the space he gives to reporting
the judgments of others. Is there a 'genuine self' in such work?
What is certain is that, even when his manner seems earnest and
passionate, he is frequently engaged in 'capricious play'. And it
is the capriciousness that justifies Geoffrey Tillotson's description
of him as the 'clever salesman' of criticism.[4]

Arnold's worldliness exploits a kind of play which had originated
in his youth, as the wayward son of Thomas Arnold of Rugby
– the pose of the dandy, or aesthetic man about town. Arnold's
relation to the aesthetic movement is a puzzling one, since his
urbanity is a more complex thing than the swashbuckling brilliance
of Whistler and Wilde. Aestheticism as a fashion involves the cultivation of the arts as a species of social imposture. The aesthete
disdains to meet the supporters of utility at the level of rational
argument, relying, instead, on associating culture with elegance,
snobbery and hauteur. By outraging the bourgeoisie, they sought
to strengthen their claim to recognition as an élite. (Theirs was
thus a spiritual imposture, very different from the economic expedients of the Grub Street writers celebrated by Pope and Johnson.)
Arnold, however, avoided the transparent cliquishness of the aesthetes, and spoke for 'Oxford', for 'criticism' and the 'republic
of letters'. But it was no longer enough to state that literature
was more solid and permanent than any alternative value-system.
Arnold intended to make it seem more attractive and glittering,
too. His appeal was to the sensibility as much as to the intellect.
The brittle and self-validating assertions that he sometimes let pass
as cultural propaganda go beyond mere affectation; yet, in a non-
pejorative sense, imposture is a feature not merely of Arnold at

his worst, but at his most characteristic. Poet and charmer, preacher, polemicist, sage and school-inspector – they were all roles which he played with equal facility. His 'high seriousness' is serious enough, but such things as the 'theory of the three classes' in *Culture and Anarchy* are pasted together for the occasion. Arnold was well aware that the values he was struggling to assert were precarious and almost undemonstrable. He set out to charm the reader because plain statement was not enough. Perhaps it was that his life's work was to preach the importance of a culture which, in certain senses, 'wasn't there' – he was not a 'man of letters', he turned down university posts, and literature could not provide him with a comfortable living. Thus Arnold devoted far more time than any previous critic to identifying and attacking the enemies of literature, and made himself into a master-rhetorician, inventing many of the watchwords and strategies which have been used in a continuing (and continuously over-dramatised) struggle. But on the intrinsic nature of literature he sometimes seems rather blank. The essence of culture, like the genuine self, almost remains unrealised; this is the Arnold problem.

Homer and the Grand Style

One word which suggests many sides of Arnold's achievement is 'Hellenism'. His classicising tastes were evident in his first volume of poems (1849), and especially in 'Empedocles on Etna' (1852), a poem which recalls Keats in its mixture of classical setting and romantic self-expression. His career as a critic began with the Preface to the 1853 volume, from which 'Empedocles' was omitted. Citing the authority of Aristotle and Schiller, Arnold maintained that passive suffering was unsuitable for poetry, since morbidity must not be confused with genuine tragedy. 'Empedocles', with its thinly disguised expression of a modern poet's anguish, was condemned on the score of self-indulgence. Arnold's search for an austerer version of classicism led him to Aristotle's doctrine that poetry imitates human actions, and that the actions should have a permanent appeal. Hence the poet should avoid both modern settings and peculiarly modern emotions. In fact, Arnold continued to use modern settings; 'The Scholar-Gipsy', 'Thyrsis' and 'Dover Beach' were all written after 1853. His critical conscience, however, led him to supplant 'Empedocles' with the neo-classical tragedy 'Merope' (1858), a frigid performance which he hoped to endow with the 'character of Fixity, that true sign of the Law'.[5] (Lionel Trilling has commented that 'perhaps no poet ever hoped a more inauspicious thing for his work'.) Fortunately, it was not only the writing of 'Merope' that came out of the 1853 Preface. After discussing the Aristotelian doctrine of tragedy, he went on to attack the romantic poets for their idolatry of Shakespeare at the expense of the Greeks. Too much study of Shakespeare, he wrote, encourages the modern vice of concentrating on the value of 'separate thoughts and images', at the expense of overall construction. Keats was typical of the modern poets who lack the power of producing a 'total-impression', at which the Greeks had excelled. Arnold's attitude to Shakespeare was always a little uneasy; the 1849 volume contains his well-known sonnet ('Others abide our question; thou art free. . .'), but it was long before he included the dramatist among his exemplars of the 'grand style'. What is shown in the Preface, however, is Arnold's concern with the literary culture available to the poet and the models he is likely to turn to for imitation. It is the waywardness of Shakespeare's genius that makes him a doubtful influence for modern poets. The implications of this would be drawn in the *Essays in Criticism* in 1865.

Arnold's 'anti-romanticism' of 1853 was in fact founded upon an idealisation of the Greek at the expense of the modern spirit. To this extent, he was the heir of the German Enlightenment. His declared allegiance was to Goethe, and he was influential in the movement that separates Carlyle's Teutonic mysticism in the 1820s from Pater's celebration of the classicising Germany in his essay on Winckelmann fifty years later. Arnold's idealisation of the Greeks has both a poetic and a broadly cultural aspect. His endorsement of Greek poetry is characteristically vague. The qualities he finds in it are first the 'grand style', and second 'Architectonicè'or the power of construction in order to produce a unified 'total-impression'. The 'grand style', at this stage, seems little more than a tag Arnold has picked up from Reynolds, while 'Architectonicè', so much more impressive-sounding than 'design' or 'construction', is from Goethe. These are terms that we shall meet again, but the Preface is also notable for its expression of a theme that Arnold would leave behind in his mature years, the nostalgia of the modern intellectual. The present is an 'age wanting in moral grandeur', an 'age of spiritual discomfort', an age when poetic excellence is unattainable. The phrases pile up, and suggest the same effect of melancholy that is so pervasive in Arnold's poetry. In his 'Memorial Verses' on Wordsworth, for example, he had suggested that modern anxiety could be counteracted by the example of a prophet and teacher:

He too upon a wintry clime
Had fallen – on this iron time

Of doubts, disputes, distractions, fears . . ..
He spoke, and loos'd our heart in tears.

Despite this act of public homage, Arnold's lasting cure for the times was not to be found in Victorian sentiment. The 1853 Preface is a plea on behalf of the young poet. What he needs, it declares, is 'a hand to guide him through the confusion, a voice to prescribe to him the aim which he should keep in view, and to explain to him that the value of the literary works which offer themselves to his attention is relative to their power of helping him forward on his road towards this aim'.[6] The need, in effect, is for a source of cultural standards, and it is to be provided in the form of literary criticism.

Here Arnold is giving to criticism a new importance. What he wants is not a return to neoclassicism – the critic as provincial magistrate applying the laws – because literary value is now (in a sense) relative and not absolute. The critic has a historical role: he is crucially concerned in a major enterprise of civilisation, the production of new art. He is at the centre of culture, and responsible for its progress. Arnold, consciously or not, was reversing the balance of relationship between critic and poet, and calling upon the critic to mediate the influence of the past in the way most relevant to the contemporary scene. This is an essentially nine-teenth-century notion, based on the idealisation of the reviewer whose job was to apply a standard of 'permanent' value to the shifting directions of the contemporary intellect. Hence, as John Holloway has pointed out, 'criticism' and 'culture' became virtually interchangeable terms in Arnold's system.[7] Arnoldian criticism constructs a tradition, or global view of the literary hierarchy, and is characteristically preoccupied with assigning authors to their rightful places within that hierarchy. Arnold alternates between the pretence that such judgments are *sub specie aeternitatis* and the open admission that they are made from the point of view of the present.

The impact of Arnold's poetry was responsible for his election to the Chair of Poetry at Oxford in 1857. His inaugural lecture was entitled 'On the Modern Element in Literature'. Any hopes that he was about to pass judgment on his contemporaries must have been quickly dashed, for he defines a 'modern' literature as one which is the product of an advanced civilisation and which has adequately come to terms with its own age. Hence the literature of Periclean Athens is as modern – no, it is more modern – than that of Victorian England. Though paradoxical, Arnold's definition is important on account of its implicit relativism. 'Adequate' writers, he strongly suggests, are those best able to help us comprehend our own times. Lionel Trilling has pointed to the novelty of this criterion in literary criticism;[8] its closest precedents seem to lie in the cultural criticism of the 1830s. One thinks of Mill's exposure of the inadequacies of Bentham, and Carlyle's of *laissez-faire*. Arnold uses the language of the Victorian prophets when he speaks at the beginning of his lecture of the need for a moral and intellectual 'deliverance'. Intellectual deliverance, however, is to be sought exclusively in the study of literature. It is only through literature that we can relate the nineteenth century to certain earlier periods 'founded upon a rich past and upon an instructive fulness of experience': the Periclean, Macedonian and Augustan periods of classical civilisation, and the Elizabethan period in England. Of these, the age which manifested the fullest literary maturity was the Periclean. Arnold plays off Greece against Rome, and when he comes to discuss the period of Augustus his criticism takes on an inquisitorial note. Lucretius was 'morbid', Virgil was not 'dramatic' enough and Horace was insufficiently serious; all three failed to measure up to the highest demands of civilisation. Perhaps for Augustan Rome we are intended to read Victorian England, since in fact all three charges could be levelled at Arnold and other contemporary poets. It is as if he were able to rationalise and survive his own sense of poetic failure by projecting his problems onto a whole age. His conclusions in this lecture, however, are much less important than the kind of critical exercise in which he had engaged. Arnold later used the broad term 'criticism of life' to define the function of poetry; this implies that great poetry is of permanent value for its comments upon unchanging human nature. 'On the Modern Element in Literature', however, shows him evaluating the poets' criticisms of life in a much more particular sense. Ostensibly a broad review of cultural history, its method is to judge everything by its relevance to the present day.

Arnold continued his indirect diagnosis of Victorian culture in his lectures *On Translating Homer* (1861–2). These begin with deceptive simplicity. His name has been put forward as a translator of Homer, but he has 'neither the time nor the courage'; in any case, two versions have just appeared. All that he can do is to offer some practical hints to future translators. The practical hints take the form of a major essay on poetic style, while the two hapless recent translators are the occasion of Arnold's first polemic against what he would soon call Philistinism. The result is the first work of his critical maturity, and in some ways his most unqualified success.

Arnold's analysis of Homeric translation is concerned entirely with style, not with 'Architectonicè'. He argues that existing translations utterly fail to convey the Homeric manner, and that this manner is compounded of four qualities: rapidity, plainness of diction, plainness of thought and nobility. His main thesis, as we might expect, is concerned with nobility. This is an elusive quality, demonstrated by means of subtle and penetrating poetic analysis; but it is also a metaphor, leading inescapably into the realm of ideology. Arnold exploited this duality, first positing that Homer was 'eminently noble', and then going on to formulate a broad philosophy of culture.

For a start, Homer's status affected the whole literary tradition. G. H. Lewes had argued in 1846 that, far from being the foundation stone of the tradition, he was essentially a primitive author:

> it seems to us impossible for any dispassionate reader of Homer not to be struck with the excessive rudeness and artlessness of his style – with the absence of any great o'ermastering individuality, which, were it there, would set its stamp upon every line, as in Dante, Milton, or Shakespeare – with the absence, in short, of everything that can, properly speaking, be called art.[9]

Such a view had been taken to heart by Homer's latest translator, Francis Newman, brother of Cardinal Newman and Professor of Latin at University College London. Newman, an eccentric rationalist, had reproduced the *Iliad* in a ballad metre reminiscent of Scott. Still worse, he had studded his text with deliberate archaisms, in order to suggest the primitive sound of Homer's language for the Greeks of the classical period. But Arnold saw the *Iliad* and *Odyssey* as major monuments of culture, which it was imperative to rescue from the whims of scholars and charlatans. 'Mr Newman' became the butt of the lectures, and Arnold treated him mercilessly. The translator managed a lengthy and sometimes spirited reply; Arnold responded with the decisive 'Last Words'.

For all its clumsiness, Newman's use of archaisms had been an attempt to recapture the strangeness of Homeric poetry and its remoteness to modern ears. He thought Homer should be rendered in a language analogous to Chaucerian English. But though Arnold rejected the primitivist view of Homer, he believed as strongly as Newman that translation ought to convey a conscious view of literary history. The question was, which was the appropriate 'revival' style for the *Iliad* to be done in? Arnold opted for a translation in hexameters (an idea as eccentric as any of Newman's), and the aura of an established classic. The sensitivity of his argument should not blind us to the nature of the Homeric specimens that he himself offers:

'Xanthus and Balius both, ye far-famed seed of Podarga!
See that ye bring your master home to the host of the Argives
In some other sort than your last, when the battle is ended;
And not leave him behind, a corpse on the plain, like Patroc-
lus.' . . .
So he spake, and drove with a cry his steeds into battle.

Arnold here has achieved the goal of 'rapidity', but he has done
it at the cost of some fussy and crowded diction and some flat-footed
syntax. Even to the Victorians, accustomed to oral recitation, the
bouncing hexameters would soon become wearily monotonous.
Newman complained that Arnold's translations would eliminate
any sense of singularity or surprise in the Homeric style; 'no one
could learn anything' from such a translation.[10] Perhaps this was
what Arnold intended. One does not get the impression that translation was for him, as it would be for an Augustan or a modern
poet, in any sense a creative exercise. Despite the shrillness with
which Newman defends himself, he does manage to suggest that
Arnold viewed the *Iliad* as a piece of official literature.

The Homeric controversy was exemplary from another point
of view. Newman argues as a scientific scholar, pedantically blind-
ing the reader with his professorial command of facts. Arnold's
approach is a forensic one; where Newman repeatedly demands
proofs from his antagonist, Arnold uses every method except scientific demonstration to produce a strong conviction in the reader.
The result is an object-lesson in at least one branch of literary
argument, the art of teaching the scholars a lesson. Scholarship
is exposed as a blunt, crude instrument, where what is needed
is the 'poise', 'tact' and fine discrimination of an exquisite sensibility. Criticism must display 'the finest tact, the nicest moderation,
the most free, flexible, and elastic spirit imaginable', since the perceptions with which it has to deal are 'the most volatile, elusive,
and evanescent'. In the Homer lectures we can see Arnold creating
a reservoir of critical vocabulary which almost every subsequent
English critic has dipped into. Here was a mode of discourse
(indebted, as he acknowledged, to his French master Sainte-Beuve)
which seemed for the first time to convey the distinctive – the
'adequate' – expression of literary as opposed to scientific culture.

In sharp contrast to his earlier prose, the Homer lectures were
couched in a highly emphatic and informal style, well suited to
the Oxford lecture-hall and, by extension, to the public stage which
Arnold now aspired to occupy. While it is cultivated writing in
the traditional sense, the range of reference is there for comparative
purposes and not for elaboration merely. George Saintsbury later

paid tribute to the originality of the synoptic, evaluative method of *On Translating Homer*.[11] In addition, Arnold combines an assertive and truculent laying-down of principles with a sustained procedure of arguing by example. The following is typical (he has just referred to Horace's *bonus dormitat Homerus*):

> Instead, however, of either discussing what Horace meant, or discussing Homer's garrulity as a general question, I prefer to bring to my mind some style which is garrulous, and to ask myself, to ask you, whether anything at all of the impression made by that style is ever made by the style of Homer. The mediaeval romancers, for instance, are garrulous; . . .

Very brief examples usually suffice for him. 'Last Words', for instance, contains a succinct page or two on Tennyson, which goes far to remedy the absence from Arnold's work of any extended consideration of the Victorian poets. A few brief quotations serve to relate Tennyson to the wayward fancifulness of the Elizabethans, and to the themes of modern self-consciousness and the lack of critical standards. Arnold's boldness, his essential literary arrogance, lay in applying this glancing method to the statement of critical principles and definitions. Most provocative of all is his definition of the 'grand style'.

The grand style is Homer's style; it is the style of nobility. Moreover, it is a style that in its very essence defies adequate definition:

> Nothing has raised more questioning among my critics than these words, – 'noble', 'the grand style'. People complain that I do not define these words sufficiently, that I do not tell them enough about them. 'The grand style, – but what is the grand style?' – they cry; some with an inclination to believe in it, but puzzled; others mockingly and with incredulity. Alas! the grand style is the last matter in the world for verbal definition to deal with adequately. One may say of it as is said of faith: 'One must feel it in order to know what it is.' But, as of faith, so too one may say of nobleness, of the grand style: 'Woe to those who know it not!'
>
> ('Last Words')

'Arrogant'; 'evasive'; 'hypocritical'; there are any number of ways of being provoked by this, and Arnold would like nothing better than for us to rise to the bait, thereby suggesting that our real place is among the crying, parrot-like masses. The terminology of faith is very deliberate here; culture is a kind of faith, and like faith, it has its pontiffs. But the peculiar weapon of the man of culture, such a passage insists, is his charm. The possession of charm is a licence to the critic to throw the normal conventions of rational discourse out of the window.

Just what kind of licence Arnold is taking in these sentences is not immediately clear. 'Nothing has raised more questioning among my critics. . .'; the implication of this is that the terms 'noble' and 'the grand style' are in some sense Arnold's own possession. But the derivation of the terms, both in Arnold's work and outside it, is complex. Arnold, as has been said, uses 'nobility' to describe a social as well as a literary manner. The term 'the grand style' plays a major role in another essay he wrote in 1861 besides *On Translating Homer*. This is the preface to his study of *The Popular Education of France*, later published separately in *Mixed Essays* (1879). Here he speaks of the 'grand style' as the chief cultural legacy of the aristocracy which had been swept away by the French Revolution. A successful aristocratic class – such as those of Rome and eighteenth-century England – was able to foster the 'grand style' in the people over which it ruled. Arnold believed that some other body must be found to perform this function in modern democratic society, if anarchy and 'Americanization' were to be avoided; hence the rule of the aristocracy must be superseded by the authority of the state. Arnold's evasiveness about the 'grand style' in poetry, however congenial to the 'flexible and elastic' literary sensibility, was directly linked to his somewhat mystical use of the term in politics.

Arnold, then, does not use these words as an innocent critic of poetry. The 'critics' to whom he is replying may be civil servants or educationalists as well as students of Homer, and he nowhere tells us for certain to what category of concepts, political, ethical or poetical, the 'grand style' belongs. Had a reader of the early 1860s been asked with whom he associated the two terms under discussion, however, he would have been as likely to mention Ruskin as Matthew Arnold. Arnold had read and admired Sir Joshua Reynolds, but he had also read the third volume of *Modern Painters* (1856), which opens with a famous chapter on the 'Received Opinions touching the "Grand Style"'. Ruskin takes up Reynolds's description of Michelangelo as the 'Homer of painting', and glosses this with the statement that 'Great Art is like the writing of Homer'. In the same chapter, he defines poetry, with 'some embarrassment', as 'the suggestion, by the imagination, of noble grounds for the noble emotions'. Arnold had originally dismissed Ruskin's remarks on Homer with some asperity;[12] how much greater must his embarrassment have been when it became apparent that he could not

do better in defining the 'grand style' than to invent a woolly varia-
tion on the Ruskinian formula. Hence – after the diversion caused
by his assertion that definition is superfluous – we read that 'I
think it will be found that the grand style arises in poetry, when
a noble nature, poetically gifted, treats with simplicity or with severity a serious subject.'

At least both Ruskin and Arnold were embarrassed by such
definitions, which in themselves are as nugatory as Hazlitt's or
Shelley's definitions of poetry. How, it might be asked, could the
idea of the 'grand style' be seriously intended as an analytical tool?
The answer is that Arnold distinguishes between levels of style
by a systematic discussion of examples, and by a method of elimination. In particular he is at great pains to distinguish the ballad
manner, from Chapman to Newman and Scott, from the epic. He
is a master at exposing the jerkiness and bathos of the ballads,
as in Scott's

> Edmund is down, – my life is reft, –
> The Admiral alone is left.

But how to demonstrate its alternative? Here he approaches the
core of the difficulty, and discovers an empirical solution to it:

> I may discuss what, in the abstract, constitutes the grand style;
> but that sort of general discussion never much helps our judgment
> of particular instances. I may say that the presence or absence
> of the grand style can only be spiritually discerned; and this
> is true, but to plead this looks like evading the difficulty. My
> best way is to take eminent specimens of the grand style, and
> to put them side by side with this of Scott.

The 'eminent specimens' are from Homer, Virgil, Dante and Milton (not Shakespeare), and they are the direct forerunners of the
'touchstones' in 'The Study of Poetry' (1880). Arnold is like Ruskin
in insisting that artistic value inheres in particulars; the two-to-four-
line specimens of style are as simplified and portable as Ruskin's
sketches of Gothic windows or cornices, or his 'true' and 'false'
griffins.[13] Where Arnold is original is in his deliberate flouting
of the conventions of rational logic. He is like a matador dazzling
us with his graceful, taunting passes before the bull of positivism.
His lethal weapon is the precise particularity and not the blunt
generalisation. Yet this is a spectator-sport with a dubious, emotive
appeal. The qualities of the touchstones are declared to be self-
evident, and nothing is easier than to persuade the suggestible

reader that he sees what Arnold tells him, particularly when to do so is the mark of sensibility and taste. Argument from touch-stones is a subtly didactic procedure, relying as much on the appeal to cultural snobbery as to imaginative intuition. Arnold's intention is to subject literary value to a direct, empirical test, and to highlight the inability of rationalistic method to cope with poetry's delicate nuances. Yet neither the polemical context of *On Translating Homer*, nor the idea of the 'grand style' with its associations of vague sublimity, are well calculated to bring this out. The 'grand style' passages commemorate fallen greatness, from Homer's war-rior-heroes to the 'noble simplicity' of Wordsworth's 'Michael'. Are they talismanic symbols of a vanished aristocracy, or simply specimens of a certain sort of literary style? Arnold does not dis-avow the link between poetry and social ideology, though he is anxious that it should not be too overt. After *On Translating Homer*, however, his campaigns as a social and as a strictly literary critic part company enough to invite a degree of separate analysis.

Essays in Criticism and *Culture and Anarchy*

> About the year 1629, seven or eight persons in Paris, fond of literature, formed themselves into a sort of little club to meet at one another's houses and discuss literary matters. Their meet-ings got talked of, and Cardinal Richelieu, then minister and all-powerful, heard of them . . . Himself a man in the grand style, if ever man was, he had the insight to perceive what a potent instrument of the grand style was here to his hand.

So Arnold introduces his examination of 'The Literary Influence of Academies' in *Essays in Criticism*. He saw the literary academy as a 'potent instrument' to counterbalance the pluralistic (or, as he put it, the anarchistic) effects of democracy. Arnold utterly rejected a Johnsonian sturdy complacency towards the individuality of the English. Where Richelieu had founded an actual social insti-tution, however, he was content to posit the mental analogues of such institutions. The habit was a pervasive one, but the major social institutions of the spirit in Arnold's writings are 'criticism' and 'culture', as defined in *Essays in Criticism* and later in *Culture and Anarchy* (1869).

The theme of the contrast between real and spiritual institutions is introduced in the Preface to *Essays in Criticism*. On the one hand are the *Saturday Review* and the Woodford branch of the Great Eastern Railway – bastions of the Philistine middle class – and on the other hand Oxford, 'queen of romance', the beautiful city 'so unravaged by the fierce intellectual life of our century'. Arnold is playing to the gallery throughout the Preface, but he is certainly in earnest when he disavows any professorial authority in what he has written. He is not an 'office-bearer in a hierarchy' – an actual hierarchy, that is – but a 'plain citizen of the republic of letters'. The two essays which introduce the volume, 'The Function of Criticism at the Present Time' and 'The Literary Influence of Academies', are studies in the constitution of the 'republic of letters'. Arnold's criticism of the literary world has none of the abstractness of Wordsworth, or the venom of Coleridge. He writes not as a romantic outsider but as a periodical essayist, providing the expected combination of hard-hitting topicality and the confident assertion of permanent standards. But (and it is one of the many paradoxes of the two essays) his is at the same time a prophetic voice, unmasking the shoddiness of the whole gamut of contemporary debate. Most of what passes for criticism at the present time is false, he asserts – but true critics are the unacknowledged legislators of the national life. That these essays have remained classics is a tribute to their clarity of purpose and to Arnold's eloquent championship of the literary intelligence.

His starting-point in 'The Function of Criticism' is where he left off in the 1853 Preface – the education of the poet. This is a cultural problem, rather than a psychological one as it was for Mill. Arnold sees the poet as essentially a communicator of ideas. The critic's job is to see that the best ideas are available to him. This might seem a largely utilitarian task, but Arnold's enthusiasm for it, together with his vagueness about the creative power, implies that criticism is a good in itself. 'Literary criticism' for him is something close to Carlyle's 'Literature', the current of ideas in society as a whole. The poet may either have a naturally flourishing culture to draw upon, as Sophocles and Shakespeare had, or, like Goethe, he may be an intellectual Titan able to reconstruct such a culture by his individual efforts. Either way, the poet exists in a distinct relation to the spirit of the age, but the critic forms that spirit. When Arnold says, '1789 asked of a thing, Is it rational? 1642 asked of a thing, Is it legal?', it is of the critical activity that he is speaking. He does not bother to say what relevance these questions had for poetry.

Arnold's reversal of the relations between poetry and intellectual life lies behind his comments on the romantic age. Goethe, he insists, was alone in combining a creative with a heroic critical effort; English romanticism, by contrast, was a 'premature' outburst unsustained by the critical spirit. This was his most influential formulation of a theme which can be traced back to his early letters to Clough, which are full of outbursts against the English romantics. Nevertheless, there is a large element of romantic idealism in the quality Arnold names as the quintessence of the critical spirit – disinterestedness. It has often been pointed out that he himself was not disinterested. T. S. Eliot spoke of him as 'rather a propagandist for criticism than a critic'.[14] Yet the full implications of this have rarely been examined. If the critic is not disinterested, what is the nature of the privileged, central status which Arnold claims for him?

The aim of criticism is 'to see the object as in itself it really is'. To do this, it must follow the rule of disinterestedness,

> By keeping aloof from practice; by resolutely following the law of its own nature, which is to be a free play of the mind on all subjects which it touches; by steadily refusing to lend itself to any of those ulterior, political, practical considerations about ideas which plenty of people will be sure to attach to them, which perhaps ought often to be attached to them, which in this country at any rate are certain to be attached to them quite sufficiently, but which criticism has really nothing to do with. Its business is, as I have said, simply to know the best that is known and thought in the world, and by in its turn making this known, to create a current of true and fresh ideas.

This, surely, is one of Arnold's pseudo-definitions; a mixture of woolliness and polemic. The concept of disinterestedness represents him at his most suggestive and most elusive. As a critical concept it has taken on an independent life, which goes far beyond Arnold's specific usage. His own understanding of the term emerges from the series of polemical passages which make up 'The Function of Criticism'. Pursuing a definition by opposites, he cites the complacent chauvinism of Mr Roebuck and other spokesmen of the middle class. His devastating response to these is to quote the newspaper report about a child-murderer – 'Wragg is in custody'. Arnold clearly feels some sympathy for Wragg (he would hardly have been a school-inspector if he did not), but he also invites Mr Roebuck to reflect on the grossness of her Anglo-Saxon name. So nobody could accuse him of raising a case of child-murder in order to get involved in the 'rush and roar of practical life'. If disinterestedness partly means the ability to take a whole and unblinkered view of society, it also refers to an aloof, indirect and reflective mode of thought. The state of being free from prejudice is more important to Arnold than any humanitarian kindness toward Wragg herself.

It is admirable that he raises the case of Wragg, but not that
he uses her to enforce an attitude of contempt for political practice.
He goes on to rebuke his predecessors in social criticism, Cobbett,
Carlyle and Ruskin, who failed to remain *au-dessus de la mêlée*
in the Arnoldian manner. They are too 'blackened ... with the
smoke of a lifelong conflict in the field of political practice' to
succeed in their aim of puncturing British self-esteem. The praise
of disinterestedness belongs not to them but to Burke, who set
intellectual truth above party and was ready to follow the free
play of the mind even when it undermined his own case. The quotation Arnold uses to show Burke in this light is a highly untypical
one, as he admits. But Burke's concession that the French Revolution was a 'mighty current in human affairs', to oppose which might
come to appear 'perverse and obstinate', does indeed show a
remarkable ability to see the object as it really is. Arnold's perception of this is curiously reminiscent of another great moment of
nineteenth-century criticism: Engels's letter to Margaret Harkness
(1888), in which he speaks of the 'triumph of Realism' which compelled Balzac to go beyond his own class sympathies and political
prejudices in his portrayal of France under the Restoration.[15]
Burke admittedly was a political writer, Balzac a novelist. But
perhaps a similar critical act is involved in pointing such instances
out. And what both Arnold and Engels possessed was an 'interested' intelligence of a high order; something that gave them the
advantage, perhaps, over their disinterested exhibits. In each case
an act of cultural appropriation is involved. Part of Arnold's work
is concerned with the acceptance of and adjustment to the new
democratic age; the other part with criticism of it. Burke's denunciation of the French Revolution returns again and again to the
evil of ideological politics – that is, of putting ideas into practice.
Arnold dissociates himself from the conservatism of Burke by calling him a product of an 'epoch of concentration', where the present
time is an 'epoch of expansion'. But he also was a counter-revol-
utionary. Culture, he believed, should refine the tone of the political establishment rather than attacking its substance as Cobbett,
Carlyle and Ruskin had done.

Arnold often sounds supercilious toward the earlier Victorian
sages. It is as if he had to clear a space for himself, to wean the
public from them in order to fulfil his own mission as a critic.
Though he could not surpass them in moral passion, he could do
so in urbanity. In 'The Function of Criticism' he tries to subsume
their message in his own – they are all enemies of the Philistines
– and then claims that he alone has the tact needed to get this
message across. It is a bold, opportunist gesture, calculated to strike

a chord with the more sophisticated part of the reading public. But what he offers in place of the sages' bluntness can seem like a 'parliamentary language', a suave and decorous process of phrase-making:

> Where shall we find language innocent enough, how shall we make the spotless purity of our intentions evident enough, to enable us to say to the political Englishman that the British Constitution itself, which, seen from the practical side, looks such a magnificent organ of progress and virtue, seen from the speculative side, – with its compromises, its love of facts, its horror of theory, its studied avoidance of clear thoughts, – that, seen from this side, our august Constitution sometimes looks, – forgive me, shade of Lord Somers! – a colossal machine for the manufacture of Philistines?

Any explosion, evidently, is going to be as muffled as Arnold can make it. The muffling is to be achieved by the critical virtues of 'flexibility' and 'tact', transposed into hesitations and modes of politeness. The final phrase is not the thunderous bellow we should have had from Carlyle or Ruskin, but a little damp squib of 'vivacity'.

Later in the essay, Arnold returns to the attack on the liberal theologian, Bishop Colenso, which he had commenced in his essay 'The Bishop and the Philosopher' (1863). The earlier essay is notable for its statement of the centrality of criticism among the humanities. The critic is not a specialist like the philosopher or theologian, but the 'appointed guardian' of general culture. It is he who is most fitted to assess the broad intellectual standing of specialist contributions. Once again, this depends on the judgment of tone. Colenso's demonstration of the literal falsity of certain Biblical passages might be true, Arnold wrote, but it was 'unedifying', lacking the 'unction' which might have conveyed reassurance to religious believers.[16] This concern with cushioning religious faith against the impact of the dissolution of church dogmas was to become a major theme in Arnold's work. In *Literature and Dogma* (1873) and *God and the Bible* (1875), he set out to repair the damage wrought by scientific theologians like Colenso by means of a 'literary–critical' reading of the Bible, stressing imaginative rather than literal truth. Whatever their value as theology, these books show Arnold anxious at all costs to preserve the reconciling and cohesive functions of faith.

They also remind us of the potency of criticism for him, since one of its tasks was to redress the balance of Victorian Christianity.

The critic owes his authority, in Arnold's view, to his command of tone. This is said to be the result of 'disinterestedness'. Now disinterestedness, as we have seen, may indeed be demonstrated in the individual cases of a Balzac or a Burke. But Arnold is suggesting that it should become the ethic of a social group – the cultural élite. When disinterestedness becomes a conscious, group ethic it must inevitably refer to some wider 'interest'. Arnold hardly makes this explicit; his strategy is to evoke the notion of criticism as a pure activity informed by romantic idealism. The underlying interest of the disinterested critic is, however, quite clear from Arnold's other work. He sees the critic as an intellectual civil servant, with a vested interest in social cohesiveness. He works for cohesiveness by confining fundamental antagonisms to the intellectual sphere and by prescribing norms of polite discourse which presuppose a mutually agreed social identity. Hence the justification that Arnold offers for criticism is that, however tactfully and flexibly, it represents the 'higher' interests of the state. Where those interests conflict with the demands of rationality, Arnold unhesitatingly chooses the interests of the state. This is the message of the companion-piece to 'The Function of Criticism', 'The Literary Influence of Academies', and also of the later *Culture and Anarchy*. Yet he remains conscious of being a lone voice, the prophet of a minority, and his view of the state is far in advance of the conventional Philistine one. At the end of 'The Function of Criticism' he contrasts the provinciality of English thought and institutions with the 'great confederation' of which, 'for intellectual and spiritual purposes', Europe consists. Through this vision of the critical mind we can attain to the 'promised land' of a new creative era. The final sentence, though measured and urbane, shows Arnold deliberately taking his place among the Victorian prophets:

> That promised land it will not be ours to enter, and we shall die in the wilderness: but to have desired to enter it, to have saluted it from afar, is already, perhaps, the best distinction among contemporaries; it will certainly be the best title to esteem with posterity.

In themselves, Arnold's attacks on English complacency, and his slogans for the critical activity – 'a free play of the mind on all subjects', 'a disinterested endeavour to learn and propagate the best that is known and thought in the world' – are unexceptionable. The problem arises from the social doctrines which Arnold makes these phrases carry. Much of the underlying rhetorical drama of *Essays in Criticism* results from his oscillation between the two poles of intellectual freedom and constraint. One set of constraints that must be put on the free play of the mind are what we call rationality. But in *On Translating Homer* we saw his rejection of conventional rationality in favour of an alternative approach. In 'The Literary Influence of Academies', he turns away from the exploratory deployment of critical method towards a view of criticism as submission to established authority.

Arnold is not proposing the formation of an English academy; it is the model or idea of the function of an academy in the republic of letters that counts. The Academy, he says after Renan, 'represents a kind of *maîtrise en fait de bon ton* – the authority of a recognised master in matters of tone and taste'. No doubt this is so, though many would deny that the presence of an academy favours the critical spirit – that it fosters 'an open and clear mind', or 'a quick and flexible intelligence'. But Arnold's belief is that criticism flourishes most freely where there are recognised social and intellectual standards – a *bon ton* that must not be offended against. In a libertarian, anarchic culture like that of England, it languishes.

This, then, is an essay on the differences between the French and the English. It shows Arnold at his finest and most vivacious as the gadfly of the English intelligentsia. The crotchetiness of vigorous English prose and the brutality of Victorian critical invective are tellingly juxtaposed with examples of French clarity and finesse. Shakespeare and the English poetic tradition are made to seem liabilities rather than assets. An abundance of individual genius, Arnold implies, is a poor complement to a deficiency in intelligence; it is not enough to blunder haphazardly into greatness. Within its own terms, Arnold's essay is a triumphant demonstration of how an 'estranged' view of English culture can shake the familiar picture, and shock us out of our provinciality. Yet the issue of the Academy itself and its supposed influence is clearly something of a red herring. The sociological proposition contained in the title of the essay is completely circular ('French culture is subjected to the discipline of the Academy, therefore it is more disciplined'), and Arnold gives no hint that there might be representatives of the French spirit who consider the Academy a controversial, or an irrelevant institution. Arnold's own view of contemporary French literature has found few defenders, from his day to ours, though the vivacity of this particular essay can still blind readers to the essential stuffiness and – yes – provinciality of the picture he gives. For example, his point about the virtues of literary consolidation and the foundation of a tradition could have been made perfectly by reference to the line of major novelists in nineteenth-century France. But Arnold wrote essays on a series of dismally minor contemporaries: Joubert, Amiel, the de Guérins and (the nearest he came to celebrating a great contemporary French writer) George Sand. Seven years after *Madame Bovary*, he endorsed the ineffable Joubert's condemnation of realist works, declaring that 'they have no place in literature, and those who produce them are not really men of letters'[17] – a pronouncement of academic anathema *par excellence*. His taste, as far as France was concerned, was entirely dictated by a small group of poets and critics around Sainte-Beuve and the *Revue des Deux Mondes*, and his essays are inspired by the wish to pass on the work of this group to the English.[18] Thus Arnold might be held not to have promoted but to have actually delayed the reception of the best nineteenth-century French literature in England. Although Swinburne had written on Baudelaire in 1862, the major achievements of French realism and symbolism were not a serious influence until the 1880s.

If Arnold's view of France is untrustworthy, he does suggest how a writer's very style and tone betray deference to, or independence of, a centralised cultural authority. There is only the mildest admission in 'The Literary Influence of Academies' that such an authority might not be wholly desirable: 'There is also another side to the whole question, – as to the limiting and prejudicial operation which academies may have; but this side of the question it rather behoves the French, not us, to study.' One may, of course, find confirmation in this that the whole essay is a tactical exercise, and even perhaps an example of devil's advocacy. Certainly the dialectic of authority and the free play of the mind is maintained throughout the *Essays in Criticism*. Arnold is at his most impressive as a champion of freedom in his essay on Heinrich Heine. The battle-lines drawn up here would have been recognised by any nineteenth-century radical liberal. On the one side are the French Revolution, Goethe, Shelley, Byron and the 'liberation' of the modern spirit; on the other side are 'accredited dogmas', 'routine thinking' and the 'Philistinism', Heine's *ächtbrittische Beschränktheit*, of the British middle classes. Perhaps the real point for Arnold lay in his depreciation of the English romantic achievement, which is here at its most outspoken. Despite Shelley and Byron, he writes, the English poets of the revolutionary era were inward- or backward-looking; Scott became the 'historiographer royal of feudalism', Wordsworth retired into a spiritual monastery and Coleridge 'took to opium'. English poetry is outside the 'master-current' of the nineteenth century because, like the German mystics championed by Carlyle, it has failed to keep abreast of modern ideas. Arnold here was fulfilling the unfulfilled promise of 'On the Modern

Element in Literature', in language which at times echoes the earlier essay. In depicting Heine, the Jewish successor of Goethe, as a 'soldier in the war of liberation of humanity', joining the forces of Hebraism and Hellenism in battle against middle-class Philistinism, he had at last specified the nature of the 'modern spirit', and traced its embodiment in the work of a major, if flawed, contemporary poet.

The Arnoldian pendulum, however, swung only briefly toward 'liberation'. After *Essays in Criticism*, he turned to still more popular modes of communication. *Friendship's Garland* (1871), a series of newspaper columns, was a knockabout farce in which his message to British Philistia was put in the mouth of the German Baron Arminius von Thunder-Ten-Tronckh. Having tried the roles of cultural critic and cultural ambassador, Arnold then put himself forward in *Culture and Anarchy* as its lay preacher. The book has a playful resemblance to a sermon in its repetition of key phrases, in its overt appeal to faith at certain points and its expansion of a text from Bishop Wilson – 'To make reason and the will of God prevail!' Culture has substantially taken the place of the will of God in this essay, but Arnold is as coy about defining Culture as most Victorian churchmen were about the deity. Like his ecclesiastical contemporaries, too, Arnold immediately found himself under attack from a stubborn rationalist, Frederic Harrison, whose 'Culture: A Dialogue' (1867) set out to ridicule the blithely unphilosophical approach of his opening chapter. Arnold was delighted at this confirmation of the success of the role he was playing, and it may even have led him on to the further extravagancies of, for example, the class-analysis in Chapter Three. (Harrison, for his part, consoled himself in later years with the idea that Arnold's gospel of culture was only a restatement of the doctrines of his own master, Auguste Comte.[19])

The dazzling surface of parts of *Culture and Anarchy* does not disguise its seriousness of purpose. Like 'The Literary Influence of Academies', it is an examination of the nature of social authority. Arnold begins by summoning up the spirit of the Academy, defining its purpose as to bring into the 'main current' all the vital elements in the national life. He develops a crucial analogy here between a cultural establishment – whatever form it might take – and the Established Church. Both institutions ought to serve the Hegelian concept of social 'totality', which is one of the key terms of the book. The Established Church, however, is weakened by the political indifference revealed in the debate over Irish Church Disestablishment, and, more fundamentally, by the strength of Nonconformity. Arnold exposes the puffed-up provinciality of the

Nonconformists so relentlessly that the book might well have been named 'Culture and Bigotry'.[20] His underlying case is that Puritanism, the religion of the middle classes, has never been openly absorbed into the national life, so that British culture, which should be unified, is distorted by sectarian conflict. The existence of sects whose values and customs challenge the dominant culture is thus a violation of the principle of totality. But there is one crucial exception to this general rule that Arnold makes – that of Culture with a capital C. No sooner has he finished denouncing the Nonconformists for preserving their own separate identity, than he extols the role of the intellectual as a conscious alien standing outside the three classes of Barbarians, Philistines and Populace. The difference is that where the Puritan tradition stands for 'Doing As One Likes', intellectuals, in Arnold's view, are the apostles of 'right reason' and hence of a centralised spiritual authority. He then suggests that this authority may be identified with the interests of the state.

In *Culture and Anarchy* the political analogy underlying the *Essays in Criticism* is brought out into the open. The result is clearly explosive, since some of his statements now seem authoritarian and reactionary. On the other hand, it may be argued that he is attacking *laissez-faire* and that his support of the state interest is simply prophetic of the commonplace assumptions of twentieth-century social democracy. It would, however, be whitewashing Arnold to accept him as a social democrat *tout court*, and even Lionel Trilling, his most sympathetic modern interpreter, who discusses this whole problem very fully, speaks of the 'reactionary possibilities of Arnold's vagueness'.[21] The important question, in my view, is whether and to what extent he abandons his own ideals of Hellenism – defined in *Culture and Anarchy* as 'spontaneity of consciousness' – and the free play of the mind.

Arnold distinguishes between a realm of pure speculation and a realm of applied or cultural thought, and he invariably suggests that what is to be said in the latter realm should be governed by tactical considerations, by what he calls 'flexibility':

> For the days of Israel are innumerable; and in its blame of Hebraising too, and in its praise of Hellenising, culture must not fail to keep its flexibility, and to give to its judgments that passing and provisional character which we have seen it impose on its preferences and rejections of machinery. Now, and for us, it is a time to Hellenise, and to praise knowing; for we have Hebraised too much, and have overvalued doing.

Following the dictates of 'flexibility' is sharply distinguished from

'Doing As One Likes', since 'flexibility' acknowledges a principle of authority outside the self. This principle lies in the objective needs of Culture. But Arnold is never concerned to admit that there could be deep and fundamental disagreement as to what those needs are. He writes of Culture as if it were a tangible institution invested with actual, not with merely hypothetical power; thus Culture for him is a 'religious' tenet. And he himself, of course, is the prophet of Culture, speaking with its inspired voice. Here it might be said that Arnold, who had failed in his career as a romantic poet, had discovered his own source of romantic power.

What did Arnold mean by the injunction to 'Hellenise' in 1869? The concept is deliberately vague and can refer to anything from compulsory state education to the cultivation of art for art's sake. In part the book is a response to Disraeli's Reform Act, and it may imply that the teaching of the working classes is more important than whether they are given the vote. Arnold's own background and profession are important here. He constantly addresses himself to the middle classes, but does not feel himself to be one of them. The son of Arnold of Rugby – a school for the sons of the aristocracy – he saw himself as a public servant, obliged to work for his living but separated by origin and ethos from the commercial bourgeoisie. His idea of loyalty to the state was first advanced in educational writings such as 'Democracy' and *A French Eton* (1864). Between these essays and *Culture and Anarchy* there intervened the extension of the suffrage and the renewed stirrings of the working class. The Reformist demonstration of 1867, London's largest mass-meeting since 1848, had a violent effect upon Arnold, as also upon some Hyde Park railings. The first edition of *Culture and Anarchy* carried a quotation from Thomas Arnold which was applied to these events:

> As for rioting, the old Roman way of dealing with that is always the right one; flog the rank and file, and fling the ringleaders from the Tarpeian rock.[22]

Social change, he argues in all editions, must never be allowed to disturb 'that profound sense of settled order and security, without which a society like ours cannot live and grow at all'. The servility of this is quite different from his earlier 'statist' arguments, and it makes the claim that the men of culture are the 'true apostles of equality' ring somewhat hollow. The tactical reading of *Culture and Anarchy* that Arnold invites might conclude that for the sake of urging the principle of state control, he had accepted the conventional, establishment notion of law and order. His assertions about loyalty in the book are suspiciously 'Hebraistic'.

Culture teaches us to follow the authority of right reason, but to whom can that authority be entrusted? Arnold poses this question with an air of gleefully stepping into the lion's den:

> And here I think I see my enemies waiting for me with a hungry joy in their eyes. But I shall elude them.

The answer, given at the end of a long cat-and-mouse game with his enemies, is that right reason is to be found in the idea of the state. The argument seems a deliberate reply to Mill's *On Liberty*.[23] Mill had located ultimate authority in the self, subject to certain constraints; Arnold rejects individualism and class politics as merely selfish ideals, and puts his faith in the state without any constraint. He distinguishes between the 'ordinary self', self-interested and class-bound, and the altruistic and reasonable 'best self' which culture develops in us. By our best self, we are 'united, impersonal, at harmony'. But whereas Mill's 'self' had the sanction of a whole philosophical and cultural tradition, Arnold's 'best self' is no more than a chimera. We may ask how we are to know if it is the 'best' or the 'worst' (because most timid and self-interested) self which supports particular law-and-order policies? Arnold replies that our best self 'enjoins us to encourage and uphold the occupants of the executive power, whoever they may be, in firmly prohibiting' political demonstrations. Moreover, the 'best self', being independent of class interest, does so with a 'free conscience'. Thus a free conscience would submit to the authorities 'whoever they may be'! What evidence is there in Arnold's own writing of a 'best self' restraining his vivacity, and preventing him from 'writing as he likes'? The question takes us back to the 1853 Preface and the dropping of 'Empedocles'; the 'best self', it would seem, is a deliberately constructed public identity, an antidote to the 'genuine self' of the poetry. Yet Arnold's social writings tend towards uncontrolled rhetoric, not towards restraint. Though *Culture and Anarchy* has its roots in Arnold's whole social experience, it does not offer a satisfactory or even a consistent cultural ethic.

Essays in Criticism: Second Series and other later writings

'The end and aim of all literature', Arnold wrote in his essay on Joubert, is 'a criticism of life'. *Culture and Anarchy* shows the conservative leanings of Arnold's own criticism of life, and its indications are confirmed, up to a point, by his strictly literary essays. The 'criticism of life' formula does not stress the variousness and conflict of values in literature so much as its adherence to a standard of right reason. Arnold's belief in authoritative and normative standards extends to the content as well as the social role of culture. Ephemeral and 'anarchic' elements must be stamped out in literature, as in society.[24] When he claims to speak *ex officio* for literary culture, Arnold tends to present it as a staid, established institution, even as a mausoleum.

An example in which many of the paradoxes of his work are contained is his essay 'Literature and Science' in *Discourses in America* (1889). This was a reply to T. H. Huxley's Birmingham lecture on 'Science and Culture' (1880). Huxley had named Arnold as 'our chief apostle of culture' and had accepted his doctrine as to the end and aim of literature, adding, however, that science was as essential as literature to a criticism of life. This has been regarded as the opening shot in the 'Two Cultures' debate. Certainly both Huxley and Arnold are distinguished by the complacency with which they speak of their respective disciplines. Arnold could not 'really think that humane letters are in much actual danger of being thrust out from their leading place in education'; in any case, only the humanities could relate the results of science to the broader aspects of life, which he defined as 'the sense in us for conduct' and 'the sense in us for beauty'. How would the humanities achieve this? Partly, Arnold implies, by a critical scrutiny of the weaknesses of the scientific approach; but beyond this, he could only evoke their effect with some weary protestations of faith:

> we shall find, as a matter of experience, if we know the best that has been thought and uttered in the world, we shall find that the art and poetry and eloquence of men who lived, perhaps, long ago, who had the most limited natural knowledge, who had the most erroneous conceptions about many important matters, . . . have in fact not only the power of refreshing and delighting us, they have also the power, . . . of wonderfully helping us to relate the results of modern science to our need for conduct, our need for beauty.

The archaic shift from 'the humanities' to 'art and poetry and eloquence' helps to underline that Arnold is not claiming something for the contemporary intelligence, but for men who lived long ago (he goes on to cite Homer). He specifically denies that modern poets and moralists should relate the results of modern scientific research to life. Their lot, presumably, is to go on repeating the wisdom of antiquity. This is desperately inadequate. A large number of Victorian thinkers were concerned with relating the results of modern science to life; one thinks not only of Huxley but of Ruskin, Tennyson, Pater, Hardy and Leslie Stephen. It may be, since he is so vague, that Arnold intended only to deplore the work of rigid social scientists such as Herbert Spencer. But his description of the 'fortifying and elevating, and quickening, and suggestive power' of literature is merely obscurantist. Naturally he appeals to the inert authority of the tradition rather than to its living representatives. It is hard to distinguish between what he says about literature in relation to science, and what a devout believer might be expected to say about religion.

'Literature and Science', then, is a feeble reply to Huxley. But perhaps it is fair to see it less in these terms than as an expression of the changing interests of Arnold's later criticism. The idea that poetry is taking the place of religion is present in the famous open-ing passage of 'The Study of Poetry' (1880): 'More and more man-kind will discover that we have to turn to poetry to interpret life for us, to console us, to sustain us.' Arnold in his later years ceased to stress the intellectual function of literary criticism, and dwelt instead upon the creative and therapeutic power of poetry. He saw criticism more as a mode of creative writing than as an indis-pensable prelude to it. The second volume of *Essays in Criticism* (1888), with its stress on the individual genius of the English poets, is in some ways directly opposed to its predecessor and to the intervening cultural polemics. But we are not dealing with a simple 'volte-face' since these late essays direct attention to some perma-nent aspects of Arnold's sensibility.

In a sense, he was returning to his own career as a poet and to its bases in the romantic movement. Heine was the only poet treated at length in the first *Essays in Criticism*, but the second volume discusses English poetry systematically. Arnold even intro-duces some new items of critical apparatus, such as the distinction between the 'real', the 'historic' and the 'personal' estimates of poetry. This should serve as a reminder that critical objectivity did not come easily to him; the 'historic estimate' seems to prompt his hostility to the English romantics, and the 'personal estimate' accounts for his over-praising such minor French writers as the de Guérins and Amiel. Indeed, the unevenness of some of his critical essays may be accounted for by the tension between his instinctive responses and his striving towards an ideal of objective judgment, appealing to semi-official and authoritative values, which he only rarely convincingly attains.

The essays on Falkland, Amiel, George Sand and the de Guérins are portraits of writers for whom Arnold has a personal affection. These essays are a mixture of biography, lavish quotation, and brief and extravagant critical comparisons, striking a somewhat elegiac note. The name of Maurice de Guérin, he writes, is 'beginning to be well known to all lovers of literature', and his talent has 'more distinction and power' than that of Keats. He and his sister belong 'to the circle of spirits marked by this rare quality' of distinction, a quality which 'at last inexorably corrects the world's blunders, and fixes the world's ideals'. No earlier critic had translated romantic idealism into quite this language of culture-snobbery. Yet the writings of the de Guérins are slender in the extreme, and their story has a conventional romantic pathos. Maurice de Guérin, like Empedocles and like Sénancour's Obermann (who served as the subject of two of Arnold's poems) was a spiritual exile haunted by depression and passive suffering whose only solace is his intense feeling for nature. This feeling, 'an extraordinary delicacy of organization and susceptibility to impressions' from nature, is said to be one of the perennial sources of poetry; de Guérin has it, though more in his prose journals than his poems. Arnold calls such responsiveness to nature 'natural magic', in contrast to the other source of poetry, 'moral profundity'. The distinction may owe something to Mill's essay on 'The Two Kinds of Poetry', but where Mill's example of the pure poet was Shelley, Arnold finds 'natural magic' more characteristic of Wordsworth and Keats. In the form in which we shall discover it in the later series of *Essays in Criticism*, the dichotomy of natural magic and moral profundity took the place of his earlier, more academic and classicising distinction of style and 'architectonicè'.

Where in most respects 'Maurice de Guérin' shows Arnold dutifully following Sainte-Beuve, the essays on Milton, Goethe, and Amiel are indebted to another of the *Revue des Deux Mondes* circle, Edmond Scherer. In the Milton essay, Arnold turns to France for an objective view of a poet whom the English are unable to see disinterestedly. He accuses Johnson of narrow-mindedness, Macaulay of rhetoric and Addison of neoclassical conventionality. This part of the essay is vintage Arnold (he detects in Macaulay 'the inconsistency of a born rhetorician'), but his own efforts as a critic of Milton are less satisfactory. The passages from Scherer that he quotes are outspoken about the deficiencies of the plan of *Paradise Lost* and of the poet's Puritan temper. But if *Paradise Lost* fails in 'architectonicè' it remains an exemplar of the Arnoldian grand style. His concluding remarks on Milton's style are bland generalisations which do not resolve the ambiguities of his attitude. He plays one of the ranking-games of which, in his later years, he became increasingly fond. Wordsworth is pilloried for a single line:

> And at the 'Hoop' alighted, famous inn,

and Thomson, Cowper, Shakespeare himself, are denied the mastery of 'perfect sureness of hand':

> Alone of English poets, alone in English art, Milton has it; he is our great artist in style, our one first-rate master in the grand style ... The number of such masters is so limited that a man acquires a world-rank in poetry and art, instead of a mere local rank, by being counted among them.

Scherer had described *Paradise Lost* as 'a false poem, a grotesque poem, a tiresome poem'. Perhaps Arnold did not give himself space to fully elaborate his own attitude; or maybe he was concealing a Johnsonian boredom. But it is doubtful if his praise of Milton as Grand Stylist would win back many readers who took the 'French Critic' to heart.

A far less calculated comment on Milton comes in one of the lectures *On the Study of Celtic Literature* (1867). Here Satan in *Paradise Lost* is used to illustrate the passionate, Titanic melancholy of the 'Celtic fibre' in the English genius. Arnold was greatly attracted to Celtic melancholy and natural magic, and his rehabilitation of 'Ossian' and its influence pointed the way for the Celtic twilight of the late nineteenth century. In discussing Celtic literature, however, Arnold once again felt the need to bring his subject before the European tribunal. He chose to discuss the contribution of the Celtic poets to European literature in specifically racial terms, analysing literature as the expression of a national spirit which is determined more by heredity than by strictly literary influences. Thus English literature stemmed from the mingling of the Teutonic, Norman and Celtic strains. The Celts possessed sensibility and intuitive tact, the Mediterranean races excelled in style and 'architectonicè', while Philistinism came from the Saxons. The racial mythology here parallels that of the nineteenth-century nationalistic historians and is Arnold's most direct endorsement of imperialist ideology. His tone is at times frankly chauvinistic, in contrast to his usual internationalism. The reader is left with the impression that the study of Celtic literature has an ultimately political purpose. The scattered remnants of the Celts belong within the 'English Empire' and should be given a recognised status in British culture. Arnold's concern with defining an intelligent imperial policy was manifested in a whole series of commentaries on Irish affairs, including his *Irish Essays* (1882). Yet there is an odd mixture of scholarly enthusiasm and political opportunism in a literary-critical essay which ends by calling for the foundation of a Chair of Celtic at Oxford, on the grounds that it would be a 'message of peace to Ireland'.

Arnold's strictly literary criticism up to the mid-1870s gives the sense of an impasse. He was committed to authoritative, academic judgments of literature by European standards which would make no concessions to the insularity and local prejudice of the English. He was committed also to the ideal of classical decorum at the expense of romantic expressiveness; 'Merope' was preferable to 'Empedocles'. Yet it is his arguments for disinterestedness, the academy and the grand style which hold our attention, and hardly ever his 'disinterested' and 'academic' literary judgments themselves. He seems to have adopted the views and methods of classicism, of cultural nationalism and of the Sainte-Beuvian study of individual temperament without ever finding his métier, except in his lectures on Homer. In fact, without the essays collected in the second *Essays in Criticism*, Arnold might now be remembered in literary criticism solely as a polemicist for cultural standards. But his criticism took on new life with the essays on 'Wordsworth' (1879) and 'The Study of Poetry' (1880).

As with Johnson's *Lives of the Poets*, the immediate cause was a commission, involving him in the preparation of an anthology of English poetry. This was the Macmillan 'Golden Treasury' series of *The English Poets*, edited by T. H. Ward. Arnold edited Byron and Wordsworth, wrote introductions to selections from Gray and Keats, and published 'The Study of Poetry' as the general introduction to the series. For the first time he was writing for posterity, or at least for the instruction of the young, and not to satisfy the topical formula of the intellectual reviews.

'The Study of Poetry' begins with the statement that 'the future of poetry is immense'. Arnold is at once setting poetry in the centre of the intellectual world, and stressing its individual and therapeutic power, as something that can 'console' and 'sustain' the reader for whom religious dogmas have failed. He then invokes Wordsworth as the prophet of the centrality of poetry, something that he had only previously done in verse. Poetry, and not criticism, is now his panacea for the dilemmas of modernism and the crisis of faith. The high destiny of poetry, however, necessitates high standards. Poetry is at once a 'consolation and stay' and a 'criticism of life under the conditions fixed for such a criticism by the laws of poetic truth and poetic beauty'. But these laws are not scientifically ascertainable, nor in this essay does Arnold suggest that they can be laid down by an academy. They must be the personal discovery of every reader. Arnold continues to see literary criticism as a process of ranking the poets against one another, but stresses that the comparative process must be applied internally, in the reader's mind. The procedure that he suggests is that of the 'touchstones', foreshadowed, as we have seen, by the specimens of the grand style in *On Translating Homer*. Arnold's specimens in 'The Study of Poetry' ('Short passages, even single lines, will serve our turn quite sufficiently', he says) are from Homer, Dante, Shakespeare and Milton:

> Critics give themselves great labour to draw out what in the abstract constitutes the characters of a high quality of poetry. It is much better simply to have recourse to concrete examples; – to take specimens of poetry of the high, the very highest quality, and to say: The characters of a high quality of poetry are what is expressed *there*.

This is a classic statement, with none of the truculence of his earlier refusal to define the grand style. Arnold now emphasises the tact with which the touchstones must be used, and not the crassness of those unable to apply them. There is a new note of humility in the procedure he recommends, as well as a concrete empiricism which was to be echoed by the twentieth-century New Critics.

Nevertheless, this has been and remains a highly controversial passage. Partly this is because of the nature of the proffered touchstones themselves, taken as they are from the 'grand style' poets plus Shakespeare. Arnold's name for what they have in common is 'high seriousness'; this is a development of his earlier, largely unexplored concept of moral profundity, and signifies his abandonment of the classical categories of style and 'architectonicè'. Lionel Trilling points out that his examples express not seriousness in the broad sense, but solemnity and even a specifically Arnoldian melancholy.[25] Also, as brief passages torn out of context, they can only assume knowledge of the whole poem from which they are derived if they are to be effective. All this is to say that we need to use Arnold's own method with exceptional tact, but given that tact, I think it can be defended. Though the comparative method is the staple of criticism, this is one of the rare attempts to define an empirical procedure for such comparisons, in order that they should combine the necessary breadth of vision with sharpness of focus. And it might be seen as a positive gain that the touchstones are reflections of Arnold's personal taste, and not of the official values of the grand style or the European academy. He emphasises that the touchstones must be 'lodged ... well in our minds', and that he 'could wish every student of poetry to make the application of them for himself'. All that one might wish to add would be that the choice would be made for himself as well. Be that as it may, Arnold's method acknowledges the combination of conscious decision and intuitive response in criticism, and is a far truer account of the process of evaluation than the eighteenth-century ideal of the Man of Taste who must have read everything before he can judge of anything. The danger, which he is certainly prone to, is to make 'high poetical quality' a fetish independent of authentic personal response. Here the criterion of 'high seriousness' is undoubtedly limiting. Yet Arnold gave notably flexible examples of its use in his praise of the 'Shakespearean' quality of Keats, the natural magic of Wordsworth and the poetic personality of Byron.

In the second half of 'The Study of Poetry', he applies the touchstone method to a review of English poetry from Chaucer to Burns. The classic status of Milton and Shakespeare is taken for granted, so that the main discussion centres on Chaucer and the poets of the eighteenth century. Arnold's dismissal of Dryden and Pope as 'classics of our prose' is notorious and somewhat casuistical, but the true test-cases are Chaucer and Burns. Chaucer's historical importance, he argues, is to have founded the tradition of 'liquid diction' and 'fluid movement' in English poetry; a tradition which Arnold had previously overlooked in his search for the grand and elevated style. Chaucer, however, and later Burns, are found wanting in the earnestness and depth of feeling which inform Arnold's touchstones. The argument leading to this conclusion is a genuinely critical one, provocative in its discriminations and explicit in its use of evidence; and it is a demonstration of method, not an *ex cathedra* pronouncement, being intended 'to put any one who likes in a way of applying it for himself' in the anthology which follows.

Essays in Criticism: Second Series consists of the introductions to the 'Golden Treasury' volumes together with a ceremonial address on Milton, a review of Dowden's *Life of Shelley* and essays on Tolstoy and Amiel. The Tolstoy essay is an important, pioneering work in which *Anna Karenina* is sharply contrasted with *Madame Bovary*. Apart from this, however, it is the 'Golden Treasury' essays which form a strong and distinctive group. They show Arnold arriving at his mature assessment of the romantic poets, and particularly of Wordsworth, who becomes the yardstick for the others. Arnold's criticism here is essentially judicial, being not a matter of close or brilliant insights but of sober, general evaluation of the relative standing of the poets with whom he deals. These essays come out of his long process of personal reckoning, but they also stand forth as examples of a genre looking back to the *Lives of the Poets*.

The finest essay in the group, that on Wordsworth, is the least biographical. It contains both a restatement of the theme of the academy, and a further movement away from neoclassical principles. For while in 'The Study of Poetry' he effectively adopted the criterion of moral profundity, in 'Wordsworth' he at last makes his peace with natural magic. The essay has been criticised by A. C. Bradley and, more recently, by Harold Bloom for its stress on the nature-poet in Wordsworth at the expense of the Miltonic visionary.[26] Arnold, indeed, says that Wordsworth 'has no assured poetic style of his own like Milton'; his truest and most characteristic expression is to be found not in his ponderous blank verse but in lines of unstudied simplicity, such as the most elemental of all 'touchstone' lines:

And never lifted up a single stone.

As for his philosophical and visionary aspect, Arnold's 'Golden Treasury' selections reveal how little he felt that either Wordsworth's or Byron's greatness depended on the long poem. In the *Wordsworth*, the only passages from 'The Prelude' are those which Wordsworth himself published independently. The fragment of 'The Recluse' is one of the very few specimens of the poet's Miltonic manner. And in his *Byron*, Arnold is still more ruthless, restricting even his extract from the 'Vision of Judgment' to a few stanzas. So much for 'architectonicè'.

The essay on Wordsworth begins with a history of the poet's reputation, and a restatement of the Goethean ideal of the spiritual confederation of Europe. Shakespeare and Milton have been admitted to the European academy, but how will Wordsworth find a place there? Arnold's argument is that Wordsworth is a major classic, for reasons quite independent of the canons of construction and style. His greatness is not a question of philosophical eminence; here Arnold attacks the 'Wordsworthians', and especially Leslie Stephen, who credit him with a 'scientific system of thought' displayed to advantage in the 'Immortality Ode' and *The Excursion*. Wordsworth's greatness can only be realised when a mass of verbiage is cut away, above all the work done before and after the great decade of 1798–1808. This greatness, however, is a moral greatness, providing that a wide sense is given to the term 'moral' (this is another of Arnold's contributions to critical terminology). For it lies simply in his sense of natural magic, or the joy that sensibility to nature brings into life. 'Joy', unprecedentedly for Arnold, is a keyword of the essay, and the central statement is here:

Wordsworth's poetry is great because of the extraordinary power with which Wordsworth feels the joy offered to us in the simple primary affections and duties; and because of the extraordinary power with which, in case after case, he shows us this joy, and renders it so as to make us share it.

After this we cannot be surprised when Arnold finally drops the mask of disinterestedness, and avows that 'I am a Wordsworthian myself'. The real and the personal estimate are at one.

Though it is a triumph, it should not be forgotten that Arnold's exaltation of Wordsworth still depends on playing the ranking-game, dismissing scores of rival poets, many of them because they are quantitatively inferior; it is 'in his ampler body of powerful work' that Wordsworth scores. In reading Arnold we never for long lose the sense of literary criticism as an endless round of European diplomacy, in which the tactics of the Quai d'Orsay are singled out for particular admiration and suspicion. Arnold takes up an internationalist position – few critics are on balance less chauvinist than he – yet he does so in order to preside over competing great powers and to assess the export potential of their cultural products. In its awareness of race and nationality as a primary fact about literature, Arnold's is criticism for the age of imperialism. It is also criticism which constantly looks to a supra-national, judicial authority:

> The world is forwarded by having its attention fixed on the best things; and here is a tribunal, free from all suspicion of national and provincial partiality, putting a stamp on the best things, and recommending them for general honour and acceptance.
>
> ('Wordsworth')

The 'tribunal', however, is an institution of the spirit only. Arnold sees literature, for the most part, as an institution; he often seems to deny the value of creativity for its own sake, and he abhors anarchy in all its forms. His attempt to fuse the notions of criticism as the free play of the mind and as an impartial tribunal surveying the literary empire displays a Roman as well as a Hellenistic spirit. Yet it would be quite wrong to confuse him with the bland neoclassicism of a figure such as Hume. The urgency and bite of his best writing are generated by frustration and self-doubt, and among his many guises is that of Arminius, the German whose namesake led a revolt against the Roman Empire. The forces of Philistinism have displaced Arnold's empire of literary values from its rightful hegemony over the real, political empire. His object is to reinstate literary culture by assuring his readers that the essential balance of cultural power has not changed. Where such an assurance can be given, it is largely an achievement of tone; an achievement, in fact, of 'religious' assertion which uses the weapons of rationality to affirm a conviction which can neither be falsified nor proved.

Arnold, then, is a critical propagandist. In many ways he appears as one of Carlyle's Men of Letters, an embattled victim of his age who is forever groping towards prophetic detachment and a spiritual vision. He is a failed great writer, like Carlyle's heroes, but unlike them in that his failure brought him popularity, a captive audience and a series of roles to perform on a public stage. No doubt this is what nourished his tendency to pontificate and dictate. But he was alone among the Victorian prophets in the forcefulness of his advocacy of literature and the critical spirit. The choice made him a seminal figure, and provides the explanation of his 'modernity'; professional literary critics from Saintsbury to F. R. Leavis have striven to disentangle the element of 'true criticism' in his prolix and varied work. When we consider his prestige as a forerunner of modern English studies, it might be supposed that his main act of 'true criticism' was his discovery and propagation of the idea of the critical spirit as an institution of unrivalled virtue and power. Yet only the devotees of state control of the arts or of the mystique of the critical expert ought to accept the idea of a 'tribunal'. Criticism in its public aspect may be seen as a parliament perhaps – or a party conference – or even, without T. S. Eliot's distaste, as a 'Sunday park of contending orators'.[27] It is an ongoing process, and one in which real authority is frequently, but never finally, the property of individuals and small groups whose judgments and perceptions command the critical attention we give to an 'author'. In this sense Arnold's own 'tribunal', where it is persuasive, is only a mask for the self. Moreover, the desire to give his judgments institutional weight was only one side of the Arnoldian dialectic. The doctrine of the academy seems to leave little room for the creative sensibility in criticism; its sphere is reduced to that of providing 'flexibility' and 'tact'. The rhetorical brilliance of so much of his writing clearly goes beyond that, but it is only in the late essays, with their mellow empiricism, that the role of personal response in criticism is really acknowledged. (Even here, of course, Arnold warns against a merely personal estimate.) It might be said that the result, as in his selections of Wordsworth and Byron, was to bring him closer to conventional Victorian taste. Such a *rapprochement* was necessary because Arnold's roots, like those of the taste of his period lay among the English romantics. In the late criticism these buried roots receive a little water. The social apparatus of criticism is combined with a romantic naturalism which allows him to distinguish the 'characters of a high quality of poetry' with unprecedented directness.

The later Nineteenth Century

Matthew Arnold bore the brunt of propagandising for literary culture in the Victorian age. He saw literature as embodying the spiritual life of modern society and taking over the edifying and consoling functions of religion. Whether or not his contemporaries agreed with this, he expressed for them the idea of literature as an institution seeking to elevate their society and to legitimise it at the spiritual level; through literature a people could become vicarious participants in a power and perfection absent from their everyday lives. Literature and criticism might be the central source of spiritual authority, as Arnold himself maintained, or merely one such source; but his writings did much to reclaim for them the dignity and social respect whose loss had been lamented by poets and critics since Wordsworth. How deeply was his influence felt? The actual social effect of a writer like Arnold is almost impossible to determine. Perhaps all that we can say is that he wrote with a new urgency, that he found his audience and that his impact was widely acknowledged. His writings decisively named the enemy – middle-class Philistinism – but were aimed to uncover latent disaffection with it as well as preaching to the already converted. A fellow-critic like Leslie Stephen might wonder ruefully whether he was not one of the 'Philistines', but the majority of Arnold's readers must have found the label an apt one for their neighbours rather than themselves. The gospel of culture made a subtle appeal to the emotions of self-esteem, desire for self-improvement, and snobbery.

There were other, quite unconnected factors working to give the 'republic of letters' a semblance of reality: the growth of the Press, the rise of the novel (for so long cold-shouldered by criticism) and its public, and the spread of literacy and elementary education. Before the development of television and radio it must indeed have seemed that literature, and not just literacy, was becoming the staple of mass communication. Of more lasting relevance to criticism, however, was the growth of education. Arnold became a school inspector, and in a later age he would probably have become far more deeply engrossed in educational reform. His emphasis on literary awareness as a 'pursuit of perfection' adds the moral concern that is missing from Mill's, Newman's and Huxley's more purely intellectualist views of the curriculum. And Arnold's view of culture as part of the apparatus of the state coincided with the first of the Education Acts which asserted governmental control and responsibility over the schools. Since the teaching of linguistic skills was the most essential task of elementary education, this necessitated a supply of English teachers who were trained by the colleges and, increasingly, by the universities. In England, the emergence of university English studies must be traced back to the 1820s and to the debate between the utilitarians and their opponents; the first Chairs of English were founded at University College, London in 1828, and at King's College, its Anglican rival, in 1835. The civic universities that were founded in the last quarter of the nineteenth century included English literature on the syllabus from the beginning. By the end of the century, English was being taught at the four Scottish universities and at Oxford, London, Birmingham, Leeds, Liverpool, Manchester, Newcastle, Nottingham and Sheffield. Outside Great Britain, the study of English literature was dictated by the needs of teacher training throughout the English-speaking world. The foundations of the modern literary-critical institution in the United States were already being laid, and – to take merely one milestone – in 1895 what is claimed to have been the world's first course in contemporary English fiction was offered at Yale.[1]

The late nineteenth century, unlike the early Victorian period, has often been seen as an age of criticism. Partly this was due to the growing educational demand for reprints, editions, scholarly surveys, school textbooks and school prizes. The English Men of Letters and other series piled up, and the high level of criticism continued in the intellectual reviews, the finest practitioners being Leslie Stephen and Henry James. But the most conspicuous new source of critical writing was the aesthetic movement, from Swinburne and Pater through to Symons and Yeats. The aesthetes, as much as the professors and the reviewers, were the beneficiaries of Arnold's work and the inhabitants of the area of culture that he had defined. At the same time, all three groups look back past Arnold toward the bookish and world-renouncing attitudes of the later romantics such as Hazlitt and Lamb. The aesthetes in particular tended to deny that culture had any edifying or instructive function for the middle class. Culture was not for society's sake, but a mode of enriching the self.

Walter Pater

Walter Pater is the major intellectual representative of English aestheticism, and the most closely connected to Arnold. T. S. Eliot, in his essay on 'Arnold and Pater', spoke of the 'direction from Arnold, through Pater, to the "nineties"'. The two had earlier been less flatteringly linked by W. H. Mallock in his country-house dialogue, *The New Republic* (1877). Here Mr Luke (Arnold) and Mr Rose (Pater) are somewhat reluctant allies as spokesmen for culture against Huxley, Spencer, Jowett, Ruskin and other contemporary figures. The names indicate the difference between them; Mr Luke is more Hebraic, and – in aesthetic matters – lukewarm. Mallock credits Pater with all the languor and exoticism of the aesthete, which Arnold conspicuously lacks. Public suspicions about the morality of aestheticism had been aroused by the poet Robert Buchanan's attack on the 'Fleshly School' of Rossetti and Swinburne in the *Contemporary Review* in 1871. Mr Rose, though outwardly a gentleman, has a way of making the ladies feel as if they had no clothes on, and he is last seen bargaining with his host over a pornographic volume of the *Cultes secrets des Dames Romaines*. This caricature goes some way to explain why Pater felt it necessary to delete the Conclusion from the second edition of *The Renaissance* in 1877, though it seems very far from the real Pater, with his military moustache (one of his pupils was General Haig) and his withdrawn and fastidious life in Brasenose, his Oxford college.

Pater, indeed, could more fairly be seen as the apotheosis of the 'disinterested' critic; though his sort of disinterestedness undeniably leads to narcissism. He is a much more subtle and fastidious writer than Arnold, but his subtleties tend to seem calculated and self-protective. His debt to his predecessor may be judged from the Preface to *The Renaissance* (1873). He begins by stating the uselessness of abstract definitions, endorsing Arnold's view of the aim of criticism as being 'to see the object as in itself it really is'. But he adds that 'in aesthetic criticism the first step towards seeing one's object as it really is, is to know one's impression as it really is.' It is not clear whether this is a refinement or a travesty of Arnold's position; what it does, however, is to separate the critical act itself from all the considerations of cultural responsibility on which Arnold had insisted. These considerations are not necessarily denied; they are merely indefinitely postponed. Pater's concern is with the subjective impression or effect produced on the critic himself. His terminology, however, is scientific; he speaks not of 'concern' but of 'primary data', and adds that the critic must isolate the particular virtue of a work of art and note it 'as a chemist notes some natural element'. But the critic as Pater sees him is not only a chemist but a connoisseur, the possessor of a 'certain kind of temperament' which enables him to realise the virtues of 'the picture, the landscape, the engaging personality in life or in a book' as he would of a herb, a wine or a gem. Here we meet the idea, so fundamental in aesthetic criticism, of the work of art as a luxury product, demanding prolonged and leisurely tasting. In the mass of Wordsworth's poetry, for instance, the critic has to discover 'the action of his unique, incommunicable faculty, that strange, mystical sense of a life in natural things'; in other words, his natural magic. To do so, Pater writes, is to distinguish the 'virtue' in a body of poetry; the scientific imagery of the Preface culminates in a metaphor taken (like Arnold's 'touchstone') from alchemy. *The Renaissance*, however, is a series of historical studies, based on the Arnoldian themes of Hellenism and modernity. The famous Conclusion states the dilemma of the modern, 'relative' spirit, giving it a far more abstract and philosophical formulation than Arnold had done. Pater's answer to relativism is that you must 'give nothing but the highest quality to your moments as they pass, and simply for those moments' sake'. And the 'moments' he celebrates are moments in the art or thought of Europe, from the middle ages to the time of Goethe, when the Greek spirit was most amply recaptured and reinterpreted. His purpose is not to draw didactic parallels with Victorian culture in the Arnoldian manner. Instead, his interest centres on the creative act of interpretation itself both in the artist and the reader or spectator.

Pater discussed the nature of artistic creation in his fine early essay on 'Coleridge's Writings' (1866; a much abridged version was later included in *Appreciations*). He sees Coleridge as a metaphysical system-builder, struggling forlornly to give a fixed account of the laws of art in the face of the sceptical and relativistic attitude of modern scientific thought. Art, according to Pater, emerges from a gradual, intellectual process, and not from any single, all-embracing act of imagination. His account of the artist at work is intended to challenge the 'blind' and 'mechanical' picture that Coleridge had given of the secondary imagination:

By exquisite analysis the artist attains clearness of idea, then, by many stages of refining, clearness of expression. He moves slowly over his work, calculating the tenderest tone, and restraining the subtlest curve, never letting his hand or fancy move at large, gradually refining flaccid spaces to the higher degree of expressiveness. Culture, at least, values even in transcendent works of art the power of the understanding in them, their logical process of construction, the spectacle of supreme intellectual dexterity which they afford.

We might say that Pater is no longer afraid to acknowledge the 'work' involved in artistic creation, because that work is so specialised that none could confuse it with ordinary social processes of labour. It is the latter which are mechanical; the artist's technique is clearly a craft, and as a result of industrialism the handicrafts themselves have come to seem distinguished and unusual, the repositories of a lost mode of consciousness. There is a parallel between Pater's attitude and that of his contemporaries who spoke of the 'Arts and Crafts'. Moreover, Pater's language is calculated to suggest the particular crafts of sculptor and painter, whose practice, he implies, is at once intensely physical and intensely intellectual. As so often, he is deepening the mystique of poetic creation by subtle analogies with the visual arts and with science.

Further analogies between writing and the visual arts are found in his essays on 'The School of Giorgione', where he compares the effect of lyrical poetry to that of music, and on 'Style' where he compares the creation of prose to architecture. Whether it is a harmony or a logical structure that the writer produces, such analogies inevitably suggest that his task is one of working in a material rather than of working on a meaning. Pater's prose as a whole notoriously possesses the air of being rather than meaning. The explicit material is language. Beneath this, however, is the material of personality. Most critics of Pater have noticed that the critical essay in his hands becomes a mode of self-portrayal. He himself provided an indirect commentary on this when he discussed the dialectical method ('this continuous discourse with one's self') in *Plato and Platonism* (1893). When the air of solipsistic intensity is lacking, his writing becomes slack and belle-lettristic. Several of the essays in *Appreciations* (1889) do nothing to redeem their conventionally bookish choice of subject; Shakespeare, Wordsworth, Lamb and Sir Thomas Browne all induce much the same level of pious reverence.

It is true that Pater distinguishes between mere style, that in which writing resembles music or painting or architecture, and 'great art'. Great art, he says in the final paragraph of the essay on 'Style', depends upon subject-matter; he might almost have defined it as a criticism of life. But perhaps his most influential criticism was that which insists on the ideal harmony of content and form. This harmony could be achieved in prose and in drama, but it was most characteristically found in lyrical poetry where there was 'a certain suppression or vagueness of mere subject, so that the meaning reached us through ways not distinctly traceable by the understanding'. This prescription, from the essay on Giorgione in *The Renaissance*, is backed up by the account that Pater gives of the historical sequence of the arts in his essay on Winckel-mann. The progress of art, he argues, is toward increasing com-plexity and individuality of expression; hence architecture, the first of the arts, was succeeded by sculpture, and later by painting, poetry and music. The idea that painting, poetry and music are more adequate vehicles of modern expression is close to Hazlitt:

> painting, music, and poetry, with their endless power of com-plexity, are the special arts of the romantic and modern ages. Into these, with the utmost attenuation of detail, may be trans-lated every delicacy of thought and feeling, incidental to a con-sciousness brooding with delight over itself. Through their gradations of shade, their exquisite intervals, they project in an external form that which is most inward in humour, passion, sentiment.

Does the difference lie in an increased narcissism? In a tone that is self-congratulatory rather than merely wistful? Certainly there is a touch of Mr Rose in this, as there is when Pater speaks of du Bellay as the poet of a 'refined and comely decadence'.[3] Like every major critic after Hazlitt, Pater had to struggle with the prob-lem of classical and romantic. Perhaps he did not intend the formula for 'musical' poetry in 'The School of Giorgione' to be construed, together with other features of *The Renaissance*, as an aesthete's charter for a poetry of private associations or 'pure' and meaning-less sounds. There are various signs that he came to regret the anti-intellectualism of this essay. *Marius the Epicurean* (1885) is the story of its hero's growing realisation that the luxuriant religion of art must be absorbed in a wider and more mature philosophy. In *Plato and Platonism*, the poetic language of Wordsworth and Tennyson is praised for its philosophical power, and Pater names the essay, the vehicle of sceptical rationalism, as the characteristic modern literary form. The solipsism of this last point is particularly striking, giving his own unique combination of prose–poetry and rational dialectic. But there is a single theme underlying Pater's enthusiasms for lyrical poetry in *The Renaissance*, for a vaguely Christian humanism in *Marius* and for the dialectical method in *Plato and Platonism*. Each is a plausible mode of response to the modern, 'relative' predicament.[4]

Pater's first definition of modernity comes in his review of 'Poems by William Morris' (1868). He is defending the escapist impulses of Morris's poetry. Modern empirical philosophy, Pater argues, leads us to an all-embracing sense of relativism and flux (this argu-ment later became the Conclusion to *The Renaissance*). The necessary response to a world in transition is to cultivate the passing moment, burning with a hard, gem-like flame. This is the justification of the poetry of the earthly paradise, which turns away from contemporary experience toward a beauty which embodies the real fulfilment of our needs. Pater takes Morris as the acme of the 'aesthetic' poet, describing his achievement both as a decadence and a thirst for the exotic:

> Greek poetry, mediaeval or modern poetry, projects above the realities of its time a world in which the forms of things are transfigured. Of that world this new poetry takes possession, and sublimates beyond it another still fainter and more spectral, which is literally an artificial or 'earthly paradise'. It is a finer ideal, extracted from what in relation to any actual world is already an ideal. Like some strange second flowering after date, it renews on a more delicate type the poetry of a past age, but must not be confounded with it.[5]

This is a statement about historicism in poetry: Morris, as the author of 'Guenevere' and 'Jason', has captured the essence of Greek and medieval poetry, producing a sublimation of a sublimation. It is also, it seems to me, a statement about nostalgia. The earthly paradise glimpsed beyond and through an earlier period of history is another Eden – though an artificial, poetic one. The process that Pater discovers in Morris does much to illuminate his own intentions in *The Renaissance*.

'Renaissance' itself means for Pater not so much a rebirth as a successive recapturing of the Greek spirit. Thus the nostalgia for Greece is his subject, and this gives to his view of the historical Renaissance a plangent and unfulfilled cast. The grandeur, sensual satisfaction and cruelty of Renaissance life and art are wholly absent from his book. The process of turning away from contemporary life to the Greek ideal, which is Pater's theme, in fact confesses the modernity of the Renaissance. Pater himself is, like Morris, producing a sublimation of a sublimation; he is nostalgically grasping the nostalgia of the Renaissance at a higher degree of consciousness. He was in close contact with the Oxford Hegelians, and his book embodies a deeply Hegelian view of the relation of history and the intellect.[6] It is the boldness of this embodiment which is Pater's originality as critic and cultural historian. The tradition that he surveys is both internal and external, subjective and objective. It is internal in the sense of being a sequence of spiritual epiphanies, of engaging personalities and exquisite works of art chosen idiosyncratically by a critic who was so little committed to the necessity of their historical existence that he could follow up *The Renaissance* with the *Imaginary Portraits*, which are fictional vignettes on precisely the same themes.[7] But Pater's tradition has an external existence, both symbolic and real. The symbolic existence is present, above all, in the passage on La Gioconda.

Pater's impression of Mona Lisa is certainly fanciful, but given the enigmatic quality of the work itself, it does not seem an ill-judged or inappropriate fancy. His description has simply added itself to the complex of meanings that Leonardo's picture today possesses. But this passage also testifies more directly to the reality of the cultural tradition that Pater is surveying. His theme is the modernity of Mona Lisa, a modernity which in her is unconscious and 'but as the sound of lyres and flutes':

> The fancy of a perpetual life, sweeping together ten thousand experiences, is an old one; and modern philosophy has conceived the ideal of humanity as wrought upon by, and summing up in itself, all modes of thought and life. Certainly Lady Lisa might stand as the embodiment of the old fancy, the symbol of the modern idea.

Whether or not we can credit Mona Lisa's knowledge of the whole of history, such knowledge is presupposed by the relativism and universalism of modern culture. We can and do respond to 'art' from all times and places, ranging it in a *Musée Imaginaire*. Pater is one of the earliest writers to celebrate this phenomenon,[8] which is fundamental in twentieth-century aesthetics and may even be seen as the essence of 'modernity' as it relates specifically to the arts. In twentieth-century criticism there is a crucial division (say that between I. A. Richards and F. R. Leavis) between those who accept a total relativism among modes and styles of art, and those who erect a standard of values derived from a specific, and limited, tradition. It is in keeping with his dialectical evasiveness that Pater's sanction can be found for either point of view. If in the Gioconda passage he is the spokesman of relativism, in the essay on Winckelmann he defines the European tradition in terms which, because they are more specific than Arnold's, again look forward to Eliot. What he says here of the standard of taste and its derivation in classical Greece is not precisely new. But *The Renaissance* gives to the tradition of 'conscious Hellenism' a peculiar stress on the element of consciousness, and this is taken up by the image of a series of beacons passing on the light:

> There is thus an element of change in art; criticism must never

for a moment forget that 'the artist is the child of his time.'
But besides these conditions of time and place, and independent
of them, there is also an element of permanence, a standard
of taste, which genius confesses. This standard is maintained
in a purely intellectual tradition . . . The supreme artistic products
of succeeding generations thus form a series of elevated points,
taking each from each the reflexion of a strange light, the source
of which is not in the atmosphere around and above them, but
in a stage of society remote from ours. The standard of taste,
then, was fixed in Greece, at a definite historical period.

Pater's purpose is to suggest how a society can support a tradition
of art which is autonomous; above it, beyond it and irradiating
it. He does so in tones combining romantic idealism with classical
serenity. But the tradition defined here, it ought to be remembered,
is not so much a fixed 'standard of taste' as the idiosyncratic
sequence of artists commemorated in Pater's book. It is the individual critic rather than a remote 'stage of society' who is the source
of the 'strange light'.

The Preface to *The Renaissance* puts forward the ideal of a 'unity
of spirit' occurring only in certain fortunate periods of culture.
Such unity is composed of individual thinkers and artists coming
together. Whatever the ambiguities of his notion of culture, Pater
never came near to the outlook of Pugin, Ruskin and William
Morris. History for him was the setting from which individuals
emerged, and the tradition, seen as a 'series of elevated points',
had a metaphorical rather than a real existence. For Morris, tradition was the literal process of handing-down, mediated through
the systems of apprenticeship in the various arts and crafts; modern
high art was necessarily sundered from this. But Pater's approach
to cultural history is one that barely distinguishes between the
results of the Renaissance studio-system, and the spiritual elective
affinities that brought Winckelmann to Rome or Goethe to Winckelmann. The sense of deepening nostalgia obscures any perception
of real discontinuity. Pater was never more himself than in his
serene acceptance – which was thereby also a deflection – of the
burden of 'modernity'.

Swinburne's Criticism

Swinburne, beside Pater, is aestheticism vulgarised. His output
as a critic was enormous. Some of it was undoubtedly influential
in its time, and his work on the Jacobean dramatists also made
its mark on Eliot. Swinburne's early essays complement his poetry;

the 'fleshly school of poetry', as Buchanan called it, goes with the romantic school of criticism. Later on, he produced a series of critical books as part of his rather frantic bid for social and academic respectability; the best known is his *Study of Shakespeare* (1879). But none of these do anything to justify his recent editor's contention that 'Swinburne belongs among the great critics'.[9] The most notable aspect of the early criticism up to *Essays and Studies* (1875) is the style, yet this is not charismatic, like Pater's, but merely ostentatious. Swinburne makes deliberate use of ornate metaphor to insist on the unity of the literary work with the other arts and with the natural world. 'Appreciation' thus consists in building up the thickest set of analogies for the work that the critic can muster. Such a critical language quickly runs to cliché. Among Swinburne's specialities are 'painterly' terms ('brilliance of point and sharpness of stroke', 'delicacy and affluence of colour') and musical terms ('weighty and sonorous harmony'). Another constant resource in his work is sea imagery. Shakespeare, predictably enough, is oceanic in his inexhaustibility and profundity, but Swinburne is also reminded of the sea by the rhythms of *Don Juan* and of Blake's 'Songs of Experience', while to enter the 'Prophetic Books' is to 'take a blind header into the midst of the whirling foam and rolling weed of this sea of words'.[10] In the midst of such whirling metalanguage it is not surprising that Swinburne cannot define anything properly. Beside his attempts to explain Arnold's 'clearness' as a poet, for example, Arnold's own definition of the grand style appears a model of precision:

> I have used this word already more than once or twice; it comes nearest of all I can find to the thing I desire to express; that natural light of mind, that power of reception and reflection of things and thoughts, which I most admire in so much of Mr Arnold's work. I mean by it much more than mere facility or transparency; more than brilliance, more than ease or excellence of style. It is a quality begotten by instinct upon culture; one which all artists of equal rank possess in equal measure.[11]

In the last sentence he is relying on the reader's snobbishness or sheepishness to give him a hearing; it is meaningless but is meant to sound impressive. The tendency of his impressionism is to suggest that art is at once the product of ineffable skills, and a cherishable, luxury possession. Rossetti's 'Blessed Damozel' is a 'mystic rose', 'a pure first sunrise', 'a thing too dear and fair for promise or price'.[12] This is no longer something which compensates us for worldly poverty and drudgery as it would have been for Hazlitt and Keats; it is the refined luxury of the aesthete who shares the wealth of the bourgeoisie, has probably been to Oxford and lives on a private income. With Swinburne, commodity-fetishism, as Christopher Caudwell and others would later define it, makes its most tangible entry into criticism.

It would be unfair to judge his review of 'Matthew Arnold's New Poems' solely by its more dandified aspects, however. Swinburne uses the device of a fictitious 'French critic' to say the sharp and abrasive things about Arnold which he does not wish to say in his own person. None the less, he does permit himself a telling assault on Arnold's view of France. The idea that you can take the Academy and the *Revue des Deux Mondes* at their own valuation, Swinburne asserts, is 'nothing short of pathetic'. He was the only one of Arnold's contemporaries who had earned the right to say this. Unhappily, Swinburne's invective became increasingly violent as he grew older, and it was rarely employed as accurately as it was here. He seems to have taken his poetic achievement as a licence to set up as a one-man academy, handing down judgments far more bluntly and pompously than Arnold himself had done. The literary league-table became Swinburne's obsession. Of the Jacobeans, for example, we learn that Marston is to Webster as Webster is to Shakespeare, while Tourneur stands halfway between Marston and Webster, but is no closer to Webster than Webster is to Shakespeare.[13] It is all very prep-schoolish.

The essay from which this is taken, 'John Webster' (1886), contains a typically paranoid attack on critics who accuse Webster of horror-mongering. Swinburne delights in the cruelties of Iago, Flamineo, Bosola and their like, and anyone who objects to the sadism of these characters comes in for a good critical caning. He accomplished some important revaluations, such as his championship of Blake, Dickens and Emily Brontë; he also persistently overrates second-rank writers such as Herrick and Lamb. But the way in which he goes about it is almost uniformly off-putting. Once he had discarded the raptures of aestheticism, Swinburne settled for a neurotic literary pomposity. 'The very greatest poets' ... 'Webster's crowning masterpiece' ... 'his other and wellnigh co-equally consummate poem' ... 'Here again, and finally and supremely here, the purifying and exalting power of Webster's noble and magnanimous imagination is gloriously unmistakable by all and any who have eyes to read and hearts to recognise.'[14] So the phrases roll off – in this case, all within the same brief paragraph. The *Study of Shakespeare* has pages of turgid and muscle-bound rhetoric like this. Swinburne's pretence to authority as a critic, in fact, is usually the worst kind of imposture. As for his relation to earlier nineteenth-century criticism, his own sense of this is summed up in his final 'consecration' ('The time is wellnigh come . . .') of his book on Shakespeare to the memory of the 'three who have written of Shakespeare as never man wrote, nor ever man may write again': Coleridge, Landor and Lamb. The three, after all the flummery, are named in the same breath, but for Swinburne himself, as is seen in his dedication of *The Age of Shakespeare* (1908), the greatest of the three was Lamb.

Swinburne, then, began as an idolater of romantic genius and ended as the Ancient Pistol of Victorian bookmanship. If there was a school of aesthetic criticism, it took on new life at the end of the 1890s in the work of Symons and Yeats, which will be discussed below. In the meantime, the dialectics of aesthetic criticism were converted into neatly turned paradoxes by Oscar Wilde in his dialogue 'The Critic as Artist' (1891). This is a manifesto for a catholic, hedonistic attitude of seeking for beauty 'in every age and in each school', 'ever curious of new sensations and fresh points of view'.[15] Such a critic will avoid the narrow-mindedness that Wilde attributes to creative genius, but is likely to be defenceless against the unending changes of fashion. Wilde's blithe assertions that it is the manner not the matter which counts in aesthetic criticism are quite close to the mark, however:

> Who cares whether Mr Ruskin's views on Turner are sound or not? . . . Who, again, cares whether Mr Pater has put into the portrait of Monna Lisa something that Leonardo never dreamed of?

The logical outcome of this was realised by Yeats, when he chopped up Pater's passage on the Mona Lisa and put it at the beginning of the *Oxford Book of Modern Verse* (1936). But perhaps the result was no more than a companion-piece to Rossetti's 'Sonnets for Pictures', which date from the foundation of the Pre-Raphaelite Brotherhood in 1848, and look back in turn to Keats. Throughout the romantic tradition, in fact, we can find examples of criticism taking possession of works of art and exploiting them as objective symbolisations of the mysterious something in the critic's own soul. When Wilde pointed out the limited scope of creation in his own day, declaring that 'it is to criticism that the future belongs',[16] he was indicating the process of literature feeding on itself that is fundamental to aestheticism. Despite their stress on the esoteric and non-intellectual nature of poetry, the aesthetes' religion of art in fact committed them to criticism as never before. Critical impressionism was their basic mode of experience. It is often surprising how literary this was; how Pater, for instance, shows his visual artists as individual personalities seeking self-expression rather than craftsmen working in a common discipline, and to what extent he puts them in the verbal context provided by thought like that of Pico and poetry like that of Michelangelo and du Bellay. It is this literary cherishing of experience that links *The Renaissance* to the conventional belle-lettrism of *Appreciations*, and even to the frenetic academicism of late Swinburne. The aesthetes continued to pursue the duality initiated by the early romantics, of criticism as public discourse and private daydream.

Harrison and Saintsbury

In *The Renaissance*, Pater presents the neoclassical tradition of rediscovery of the 'ancients', and especially of Greek civilisation, in an explicitly romantic light. In *Appreciations*, he even gives qualified approval to Stendhal's opinion that all good art was romantic in its day.[17] Thus he continued the process of assimilation of the achievements and doctrines of the romantic movement into the literary tradition, which had preoccupied Arnold, Carlyle and Mill. This labour of incorporation went on into the late nineteenth century, but alongside it there was a consolidation of work on Augustan literature, culminating in the criticism of Leslie Stephen and the scholarship of Saintsbury and Birkbeck Hill. With the rise of English studies, criticism and scholarship were becoming a professional routine, and no century could expect to remain uncovered; but there were other reasons for the rehabilitation of the eighteenth century. It was the period which the conservative bookman found most congenial. Nearly half of the volumes in the original *English Men of Letters* series were devoted to Augustan authors. This movement, typified by the apotheosis of Boswell and of Boswell's Johnson (which had begun with Carlyle and Macaulay), was one outlet for hostility to the fashionable aesthetic attitudes of the 1870s. Another outlet lay in the criticism of the novel, which at last began on a more than occasional basis.

Among the more extreme of the anti-aesthetes was Arnold's antagonist Frederic Harrison. The leader of the English Positivists, his artistic heroes were Ruskin and George Eliot. His essay 'The Choice of Books' (1879) is an attack on the frivolity and dandyism of the literary world. Choosing a book was a heavy and weighty responsibility; better that it should be Hume, Gibbon or Adam Smith than a 'kind-hearted play-book' of the kind rescued from the dung-heap by Lamb.[18] For a writer such as George Eliot, he wrote in 1885, science, philosophy and social ideals were the 'substance' of culture, while the 'graceful form and the critical judgment' were merely the 'instrument by which it speaks'.[19] Harrison, however, remained within literary culture (as George Eliot and Lewes had done), mingling historical and philosophical studies with collections of critical essays with titles like *Among my Books* (1912). A less austere kind of bookmanship is exemplified by George Saintsbury, the most prolific of the new professors of English. Saintsbury's only diversions from literary scholarship were in the direction of wine and food. Though remembered for his breadth of learning and his synoptic literary histories, he was also a spokesman for scholarly minuteness, defending the study of the 'variations of the position of a pronoun' against both the Arnoldian 'criticism of life' and the impressionism of the aesthetes.[20] His study of *Dryden* (1881) attempts to restore the idea of literature as a craft, hard work for the writer and still harder work for the critic, who is obliged to toil through everything, regardless of its established reputation, in order to develop a sufficiently catholic view of poetry. Once he had that, however, he could rest on his intellectual laurels, and feel obliged to go no further. It is all summed up in the title of his last, elegiac critical book, *The Peace of the Augustans: A Study of Eighteenth-Century Literature as a Place of Rest and Retirement* (1916). Saintsbury's notion of catholic taste is so clearly aimed at the academic with time on his hands that he became the symbol of the relaxed, traditionalist attitude of early twentieth-century English studies; English as a soft option, a place of sporting refreshment in which the student, though he might be threatened by a surfeit of books, would at least never have to think. Though it is not true that Saintsbury never thought, he was a bookman of the old school in that he made the thinking look fatally easy.

The Genteel Tradition and Henry James

Bookmanship took root in America through the writings of James Russell Lowell, the poet and Harvard professor of Belles Lettres who belongs to the generation of Matthew Arnold rather than that of Harrison and Saintsbury. Lowell is best known as a critic for his essays collected in the two volumes of *Among My Books* (1870, 1876) – the same title was later to be used by Harrison and the books were mostly review copies – and in *My Study Windows* (1871); there were also wide-ranging lectures on English literary history, written for general audiences and not merely for the literature students at Harvard. Lowell's critical ideal was one of 'intellectual hospitality', though he could also be astringent in his attitudes, using his dogged reading habits as a warning to others of feebler constitution. 'Every generation is sure of its own share of bores without borrowing from the past', he said in an essay on 'Spenser': among the writers who could be safely skipped were Dunbar, Robert Greene, George Peele, and the Drayton of *Polyolbion*, which Lowell condemned as the 'plesiosaurus of verse'. In his search for the 'sense of Wonder' to which great literature must appeal, dullness of subject-matter and 'commonness' of style was the enemy. Of Sidney's line 'The baiting-place of wit, the balm of woe' (from *Astrophel and Stella*), he wrote that '*baiting-place* is common, it smacks of the hostler and postilion'.[21] When he tried to sum up the value of poetry, however, he produced a colourless sentiment which reminds us of one of Sidney's oxymorons. 'Poetry', he wrote in *The Old English Dramatists* (1893), 'is a criticism of life only in the sense that it furnishes us with the standard of a more ideal felicity, of calmer pleasures and more majestic pains'.

Lowell's ethos is that so brilliantly portrayed in 'The Genteel Tradition in American Philosophy' (1911) by George Santayana, who (though born in Spain) was also a Harvard professor. The genteel tradition resulted from the failure of the revolutionary perspectives of early nineteenth-century American thought, and the atrophy of the 'hereditary philosophy' of Puritanism brought over from Europe. Poe, Hawthorne and Emerson stood outside the genteel tradition but had a 'starved and abstract quality', according to Santayana, while even Whitman could manage no more than a Bohemian revolt. Santayana's settled classicism, which influenced T. S. Eliot, wrote off most nineteenth-century cultural phenomena as either decadent or innocently childlike. Browning, as well as Whitman, was dismissed as a representative of 'The Poetry of Barbarism' (1900), while Dickens received the tribute of warm but patronising appreciation; he was 'one of the best friends mankind has ever had'.[22] At its highest level, the 'substance, sanity, and ...pervasive wisdom' that Santayana sought in poetry demanded the rarefied atmosphere celebrated in his study of Lucretius, Dante and Goethe, *Three Philosophical Poets* (1910). Here each of the three poets was shown to represent a historical epoch and also to possess permanent, unassailable greatness; together they summed up all European philosophy.

Beside Santayana's rigorous intellectualism, an essayist such as Lowell must seem self-indulgent and flabby. The critic's 'most earnest function', Lowell wrote in 'Swinburne's Tragedies', is to demolish the 'high places where the unclean rites of Baal and Ashtaroth usurp on the worship of the one only True and Pure'. The moral passion here is short lived and synthetic, whatever it may owe to Lowell's Calvinist ancestry. (In any case, the 'pseudo-classicism' of 'Atalanta in Calydon' and Arnold's 'Merope' presented an easy target.) *My Study Windows*, in which this appeared, begins with a relaxed discussion of White's *Natural History of Selborne* and of the birds to be seen in a Massachusetts garden. Lowell also gave expression to a set of beliefs about literature and nationality which, a century later, have come to be pilloried as the supposed ideological basis of conventional 'lit. crit.' Though a patriotic American, he urged European standards of taste on his Bostonian audiences, attributing the excellence of Abraham Lincoln's use of English (for example) to his grounding in Shakespeare, Milton and the Authorised Version rather than to his upbringing in Illinois. Lowell illustrates the national quality of great literature by reference to English rather than to American writing. His essay 'Shakespeare Once More' defends the playwright's characteristic style and vocabulary against the aspersions of Arnold's 1853 Preface, presenting Shakespeare as a 'great national poet' and a 'representative Englishman' possessing a 'perfectly Anglican breadth of character and solidity of understanding'. Fittingly, Lowell was eventually chosen to serve as United States minister to Great Britain, occasioning Henry James's remark that 'the true reward of an English style was to be sent to England'.[23]

James as a critic also began in the genteel tradition. He wrote in 1867 of his desire 'to do for our dear old English letters' something of what Sainte-Beuve had done for the French.[24] He became a regular contributor to the *Atlantic Monthly* and *North American Review*, both of which Lowell had edited, and the style of the intellectual reviews is reflected in the spacious, biographical studies collected in *French Poets and Novelists* (1878) and *Partial Portraits* (1888). James's development as a novelist, however, increasingly moulded his criticism, culminating in the New York prefaces to his own works (1907–9) which transmitted the 'lesson of the master' to posterity. Our concern here is not with the specialist attractions of the New York prefaces, but with the body of general criticism in which James speaks both as reader and practitioner. His achievement lies almost entirely in the discussion of fiction, especially of French fiction. Consideration of James as a practitioner-critic might well start from his polemical manifesto on 'The Art of Fiction' (1884), a reply to a lecture on the same topic by the popular novelist Walter Besant. James's essay is written quite explicitly from the 'producer's point of view', and argues for an imaginative and organic, rather than a merely commercial attitude to fiction. Criticism must confine itself to the artist's execution, not his choice of subject-matter (a rule that James himself seldom followed); nor must it stand in the way of greater realism.

James hardly associated himself with the propaganda for realism and naturalism which in England is represented by some of George Eliot's essays, and in America by William Dean Howells's *Criticism and Fiction* (1891). For James a novel is not a photographic record but a personal impression of life, so that the novelist aims at the 'air of reality (solidity of specification)', not at the concreteness of the thing itself. James's famous reply to Besant's golden rule for beginners – 'a young lady brought up in a quiet country village should avoid descriptions of garrison life' – is that 'Greater miracles have been seen than that, imagination assisting, she should speak the truth about some of these gentlemen'. She must, however, be a 'damsel upon whom nothing is lost'. James's plea for realism coincided with an increased emphasis on the distinction between life and art, of which Besant's common-sense rules had taken little account. Arguing against convention and for open-mindedness, James declares that the novelist's task is to catch 'the very note and trick, the strange irregular rhythm of life'. Even this phrase is not quite what it seems; the 'life' suggested by its fluttering rhythm is that of consciousness, or of external events as they might be felt by a contemplative and introspective observer. From the internal perception or 'impression' to the transmuting artistic vision is not, it turns out, such a great step. The rhetoric of 'life itself' in this essay may well have been useful to later psychological novelists such as Virginia Woolf. But it all leads back to the 'fine intelligence' of the writer himself:

> There is one point at which the moral sense and the artistic sense lie very near together; that is in the light of the very obvious truth that the deepest quality of a work of art will always be the quality of the mind of the producer. In proportion as that intelligence is fine will the novel, the picture, the statue partake of the substance of beauty and truth.

'Fine intelligence' is a complex and qualified Jamesian idea. The writer's intelligence must be nurtured in a rich soil; hence the importance of the trip to Europe for the American writer. James's distrust of a purely American literature was expressed in his study of *Hawthorne* (1879), where he wrote of the immense accumulation of tradition and culture that was needed to 'produce a little literature'.[25] In addition, the novelist's need to translate his moral sense into artistic terms (James wrote to H. G. Wells that 'It is art that makes life, makes interest, makes importance . . .')[26] may be met by the representation within the novel of the viewpoint of the 'fine intelligence' observing and commenting on life. James's 'fine consciences' are, of course, partially naive figures, shown up by the surrounding characters and the narrator's irony. Their presence in his fiction, however, testifies to his convictions that objective realism is not enough, and that adequate feeling or realisation is the prerogative of the subtle intelligence. James met his greatest challenge as a critic where, as in the case of Balzac, he was forced to acknowledge an artistic power that seemed independent of subtlety or moral delicacy.

James's criticism of other writers is largely concerned with the 'quality of the mind of the producer'. When we have digested the expansive, fulsome urbanity of a James critical essay, it often comes down to a study of the defects of the subject's sensibility. These are revealed as exemplary, or (in Jamesian jargon) as constituting a 'case'; his criticism becomes a series of case-histories enquiring into the peculiarities of his rivals and peers. Thus Maupassant, for example, is unmasked as a wholly sensual writer, barely getting beyond the visual, sensual and olfactory aspects of life. The Preface to *Pierre et Jean*, with its rejection of psychological analysis in favour of a purely objective record of events, is diagnosed by James as a rationalisation of the demands of the author's limited sensibility. There was little evidence of 'fine intelligence' to be found in Maupassant, or, for that matter, in Dickens. In his early review of *Our Mutual Friend* (1865), James laid down that a story based upon the elemental passions 'must be told in a spirit of intellectual superiority to those passions'.[27]

He is at his most involved and rewarding as a critic of writers who, if not intellectuals, were at least systematisers like Zola and Balzac. Though he speaks with admiration of Zola's massive architecture in *Les Rougon-Macquart*, we soon realise that he regards this as a merely mechanical achievement, a wonder of the nineteenth century on a par with the Eiffel Tower, the steamship and the railway. Zola, like Maupassant, excelled at the coarser side of life, and he had also made the mistake of confiding to James his ambition of writing *Rome* on the basis of 'a month or two with "introductions" and a Baedeker'. Zola, in fact, wallowed in his material 'quite, if I may allow myself the image, as we zoologically see some mighty animal, a beast of a corrugated hide and a portentous snout, soaking with joy in the warm ooze of an African riverside'.[28] Despite the human qualities revealed by the Dreyfus affair, James finds something disreputable in Zola as an artist, which is brought out in the contrast with Balzac. Where Zola deliberately sought out 'life', Balzac was overtaken by it. He stands in James's work as the Shakespearean artist, the primal creator whose fervid imagination projects a whole world which can stand as a historical representation of the totality of France in his time. Yet this is still not enough for James, who believes in a degree of 'art' or conscious control which Balzac, for all his fascination, lacks. He wrote a total of five essays on Balzac, and the finest of them concludes with a note that is almost wistful:

> Art is for the mass of us who have only the process of art, comparatively so stiff. The thing amounts with him to a kind of shameless, personal, physical, not merely intellectual, duality – the very spirit and secret of transmigration.[29]

Against the intellectual process of art is put a naked and shameless kind of witchcraft.

Art, for James, is life covered up and held at arm's length. The very expansiveness and rhetorical skill of his critical essays suggest that he is really portraying himself, sustaining the bubble of his own creative persona, which is never, it goes without saying, shameless and physical. Much of his later criticism suffers from a lack of any precise and explicit method of analysis; at worst, it seems to express an intelligence bombinating in a near-vacuum. Yet this criticism is only partially applicable, and least of all to his remarkable essays on Flaubert. Flaubert presents the 'intellectual case' – a case which James's essays on him crystallise both in biographical and structural terms. Though Flaubert is the conscious artist *par excellence*, the antithesis of the instinctive, unbuttoned English novelists, James in his 1902 essay accuses *Madame Bovary* and *L'Education Sentimentale* of possessing a crucial formal defect, in the poverty of consciousness of their central characters. Neither Emma nor Frédéric is sufficiently dignified to bear the leading part in a major novel. Flaubert's intellectual superiority over them is not in doubt, but James strongly implies that the 'smallness' of the characters proceeds from a meanness of spirit in their creator – a meanness which he had found abundantly confirmed in reviewing Flaubert's correspondence nine years earlier. So, like all the writers James discusses, Flaubert becomes an object lesson to be rejected by the moral conscience. James delivers the verdict in his most ingratiating way, paying his respects to Flaubert as the 'novelist's novelist' and flattering his audience with 'Are we not moreover ... pretty well all novelists now?' The essay exhibits a fascinating combination of the seductive literary aura that James creates, and the fastidious intelligence operating within it.

Leslie Stephen and A. C. Bradley

All James's best criticism is concerned with his own artistic mentors, who are either his contemporaries or the recently dead. This is why he needs to present them as a series of 'cases'. His essays on French novelists remain valuable for the completeness of their survey of what has become a classical tradition. As the major Victorian sages, poets and novelists died, it became possible to see Victorianism as a tradition too; but there is no equivalent to James's achievement here, let alone a *Lives of the Poets* or a *Spirit of the Age*. Perhaps the sheer exhaustiveness of public discussion to which writers were subjected precluded the magisterial overview. Besides, the nineteenth-century critic had other, and newer obligations: to express his century's historical consciousness, and to display his qualifications as scholar and antiquarian. The literary public were not all novelists, but all bookmen now. The greatest of late Victorian historical critics was Leslie Stephen, philosopher, agnostic, editor of the *Dictionary of National Biography* and author of the monumental series of critical essays collected in *Hours in a Library*. The title speaks of bookishness as surely as does Harrison's and Lowell's *Among my Books*, and Stephen in fact was torn between cosy antiquarianism and a bracingly judicial mode of criticism. He prefaces *Hours in a Library* with a selection of 'Opinions of Authors', voicing the consoling solitariness of library pleasures. He confesses that he loves a book 'pretty much in proportion as it makes me love the author',[30] and writes evocatively of hours spent savouring 'a page of Sir Thomas'. Yet Stephen never indulges the emotions of bookmanship without quietly deflating them as well:

> One should often stop to appreciate the full flavour of some quaint allusion, or lay down the book to follow out some diverging line of thought. So read in a retired study, or beneath the dusty shelves of an ancient library, a page of Sir Thomas seems to revive the echoes as of ancient chants in college chapels, strangely blended with the sonorous perorations of professors in the neighbouring schools, so that the interferences sometimes produce a note of gentle mockery and sometimes heighten solemnity by quaintness.
>   That, however, is not the spirit in which books are often read in these days.[31]

One is reminded that Stephen gave up his Cambridge fellowship for London, agnosticism and the republic of letters. A passage like this is remarkable not for self-indulgence but for its 'gentle mockery' and unobtrusive wit. There are limits to his geniality, often quite narrow ones, so that it was possible for Q. D. Leavis to portray him as a stern Cambridge moralist and ancestor of *Scrutiny*.[32] Stephen himself seems to have been divided in his aims. He was able to contradict himself over Lamb, for example, speaking in 1876 of his 'singular excellence' as a critic who 'only spoke of what he really loved', but then accusing him five years later of having 'helped to start the nuisance of "appreciative criticism"'.[33] A man of letters in the Johnsonian sense, Stephen had no wish to be confused with the aesthetes who had taken Lamb to themselves in the 1870s. The rise of aestheticism may have intensified his own considerable doubt about the value of literary criticism, to which he gave up so much of his time and talents. His biographer, Noel Annan, goes so far as to say that he 'despised the whole business' as trifling beside the concerns of ethics and religion.[34]

Hours in a Library, nevertheless, manifests the 'scientific spirit' that he practised in all three of these fields. The four volumes (with, to a lesser extent, the volumes of *Studies of a Biographer*) are the nearest thing to a canonical series of evaluations across the range of English literature that the Victorian age produced. Their form is that of the periodical essay devoted to a single author. Though Stephen is less ingratiating and pyrotechnic than most of his contemporaries, his essays are finely judged for their audience, relaxed, slightly sardonic and modulating from gossipy biography to scrupulous moral analysis. There is nothing prophetic or eccentric about his writing; nothing calculated to give the reader a jolt. The evenness of tone in essay after essay is the result of a deliberate balancing act. Quite often, we feel, the final verdict could be reversed, but the method and ethical intelligence glimpsed behind it would be precisely the same. Stephen's formal sense of the critic's role is set out in his essay 'Thoughts on Criticism, by a Critic' (1876), which is mainly concerned with the ethics of reviewing. Criticism cannot be a science, though it should aim at a scientific spirit; hence the writing of criticism is a moral act. Stephen's view differs from Johnson's mainly in being couched in more ideological terms. The problem for him is to define 'the sense in which a critic should be liberal'. Liberalism requires a deliberate effort to look from strange points of view, and also 'a certain modesty in expression and diffidence in forming opinions', a non-authoritarian tone. Getting the tone right, and elaborating a sensibility which is catholic enough to respond to varying forms of literature, while maintaining a consistent moral standpoint, is his overriding concern.

The sense in which Stephen himself is liberal lies in devising a mode of moral criticism which is applied to the individual alone. His hours in the library are spent in scrupulous neutrality towards doctrinal and social questions. Virtually the only nexus between art and belief that he allows is that constituted by individual morality – by judgments of the writer's personal integrity, his 'manliness' and his sensitivity to the world outside him. Stephen writes on 'Pope as a Moralist', and on 'Wordsworth's Ethics'. His method, coupled with his relative insensibility to poetry and to literary form, seems to reduce literary criticism to the level of common-sense morality. Thus his virtues of reasonableness and moderation are themselves the manifestations of an ideology, which is closely connected with his religious agnosticism. The analogy between criticism and religious belief is drawn at the start of his essay on Charlotte Brontë in *Hours in a Library*:

> though criticism cannot boast of being a science, it ought to aim at something like a scientific basis, or at least to proceed in a scientific spirit. The critic, therefore, before abandoning himself to the oratorical impulse, should endeavour to classify the phenomena with which he is dealing as calmly as if he were ticketing a fossil in a museum. The most glowing eulogy, the most bitter denunciation, have their proper place; but they belong to the art of persuasion, and form no part of scientific method. Our literary, like our religious, creed should rest upon a purely rational ground, and be exposed to logical tests. Our faith in an author must, in the first instance, be the product of instinctive sympathy, instead of deliberate reason. It may be propagated by the contagion of enthusiasm, and preached with all the fervour of proselytism. But when we are seeking to justify our emotions, we must endeavour to get for the time into the position of an independent spectator, applying with rigid impartiality such methods as are best calculated to free us from the influence of personal bias.

In many ways this is an admirable statement. However ardent our feelings for a writer, their justification should be a matter of rational argument. Stephen here is directly confronting aesthetic criticism, since his target is Swinburne's extravagant enthusiasm for Charlotte Brontë. He goes on to demonstrate in memorable fashion the provinciality of her art, and the failure of her male characters in particular; the Brontë gospel has fallen on deaf ears. However, if such phrases as 'rigid impartiality' are more than polemical devices they sound somewhat chilling, and invite the retort that *Jane Eyre* is not – or should not be – a fossil in a museum. 'Rigid impartiality' is a less humane and less plausible quality to aim for than 'disinterestedness'; it is the kind of thing Arnold would have associated with Bishop Colenso.

Stephen's criticism is not merely judicial, however. His 'scientific' liberal outlook led him in his later work to consider literature as the expression of particular social groups, and not simply of the moral individual. *English Literature and Society in the Eighteenth Century* (1904) was, as Noel Annan says, a 'new kind of literary study',[35] which inaugurated the 'literature and society' approach in twentieth-century criticism. In this he perhaps looks back to Macaulay, whose famous essay on Johnson (1831) contained a brilliant general sketch of Augustan culture. Macaulay both portrays Johnson the man with a Dickensian vividness, and shows his character as the necessary product of his environment and early struggles. Stephen lacks both Macaulay's literary powers and his forensic obsession, but his best historical essays (that on Pope, for example) are concerned with how the individual of genius is shaped by a particular milieu. The heroism of the individual man of letters is surrounded with qualifications in his essays, much as the heroes and heroines are given qualified, muted roles in major Victorian novels. Stephen's gallery of individuals in *Hours in a Library* sums up the tendency of most of the more pedagogic Victorian criticism. On the one hand, Carlyle's analysis and prophecy had been vindicated; the men of letters had indeed become cultural heroes. But though Stephen holds up his subjects for our admiration, he also shows them as typical products of their society, manifesting its spiritual failings and possible mode of redemption. Their historical environment forms their identity, rather than subjecting it to the general constraints of human nature, as was the case in Johnson's *Lives of the Poets*. In this respect the portrayal of 'character' in Victorian criticism parallels the achievements of the Victorian novel, though the one is concerned with the past and the other with contemporary life. The biographies of the men of letters might be set against the stories of Pickwick and Little Dorrit, Lydgate and Adam Bede; none of these strikes us as an isolated moral agent. The task of the critic, as Stephen interprets it, is to show how the gallery of classic authors emerges from social history.

Stephen reflects the ideology of literary culture, but he does not invariably endorse it. In *English Literature and Society* he speaks of literature as 'a kind of by-product', which is not alone an adequate representation of the moral temper of the society in which it occurs. His criticism seems to me to fall short of classical status because of such hesitancies, which also help to produce his remarkable evenness and consistency of tone. His indifference to poetry, coupled with his contempt for anything smacking of literary 'effeminacy', is another severe limitation. Stephen perhaps did not take literature seriously enough. But he is an entertaining, shrewd and reflective writer who stands out in his age for his sociological interests, his Cambridge dryness and precision and the explicitness with which he moulds his criticism to a liberal and rational ethic.

If Stephen's criticism is the product of Cambridge and London, Oxford and the provinces at the turn of the century are represented by A. C. Bradley. Bradley left Balliol in 1882, but returned to Oxford in 1901 as Professor of Poetry after holding chairs at Liverpool and Glasgow. His *Shakespearean Tragedy* (1904) is dedicated 'To My Students' and is the one work of its period to survive as a student textbook. Largely this is a tribute to the centrality and meticulous sensitivity of his readings of Shakespeare's major plays. Bradley's procedure is one of highly detailed, eclectic analysis, bringing textual scholarship and aesthetic, moral, and psychological approaches to bear on the text before him. Overarching it all, however, is the Hegelian outlook he imbibed from his elder brother F. H. Bradley and from Oxford. His synthesis of aestheticism and moral analysis is put forward in the lecture 'Poetry for Poetry's Sake' (1901) and in the postscript to *Oxford Lectures on Poetry* (1909). The opposites are reconciled in a sort of kindly haziness. Though attracted to grand theories of poetry, Bradley treats these as imaginative metaphors rather than as intellectual statements demanding systematic confrontation and refutation. He grants poetry an autonomy of means, but claims that its ends are the same as those of philosophy and religion. Hence we can each stay in our separate departments: 'the pursuit of poetry for its own sake is the pursuit both of truth and goodness'.[36] It seems a recipe for academic quietism.

That this is an unfair (though hardly an unprecedented) interpretation of Bradley is suggested by certain aspects of *Shakespearean Tragedy* and by the essay on Wordsworth in *Oxford Lectures*, which stresses the parallels between the visionary imagination of 'The Prelude' and German idealist philosophy – an insight which remained unpursued until the 1960s. L. C. Knights's attack on Bradley's Shakespearean criticism in 'How Many Children Had Lady Macbeth?' (1933) is partly aimed at a man of straw. Bradley, after all, had explicitly described the question of the Macbeths' fecundity as 'quite immaterial'.[37] The unifying theme of his book is not one of character-biography but of concern with the nature of the 'tragic' experience and Shakespeare's response to it. In tragedy, men are brought up against the universe as a blind and waste-ful process; effectively this is the chaos of meaningless flux as revealed by Huxley, Hardy and Pater. An attitude of resignation would be the simplest response to the tragic facts, but after long and earnest consideration of the problem Bradley suggests that it is to be rejected. The Shakespearean hero is as much part of the universal process as are the forces that he confronts. Hence the nobility of the hero and the survival of goodness must reconcile us to the tragic suffering. This conclusion is a faintly consoling one, reflecting the Victorian ethos of masculine duty. Nevertheless, Bradley suggests that in tragedy we contemplate an ultimate mys-tery in life, meriting much deeper consideration than the 'moral profundity' and 'natural magic' of Arnold or the health and manli-ness of Stephen. His essay on *Lear* in particular testifies to the visionary nature of art and its power to overwhelm conventional social and intellectual categories. It is as if Bradley is hesitantly offering in tragedy an alternative to the orthodox religious view of life. *Shakespearean Tragedy*, in its contemplative way, contains evidence of the survival of the high romantic attitudes to art which the Victorian republic of letters had progressively excluded.

W. B. Yeats

'I cannot get it out of my mind that this age of criticism is about to pass, and an age of imagination, of emotion, of moods, of revela-tion, about to come in its place.' The dissenting voice belongs to W. B. Yeats, writing in 1895.[38] Yeats is the one critic of the late nineteenth century who stands out in opposition to Arnold, inherit-ing a different aspect of the romantic revolution. For where Arnold claimed to speak for the authority of culture, of literature in its relation to the social establishment, we can now see that Yeats spoke, as nobody since Wordsworth had done, with the singular and more absolute authority of the major poet. His prophetic stance is reflected in every aspect of his remarkable series of critical essays. With his habit of reminiscence and informal, circumstantial detail, Yeats often seems to be half talking to himself, setting it down for the record no matter who hears. But now and then comes a *Diktat*, and this is also for the record. He does not waste energy in blandishments and persuasions, as Arnold does; his poetry will carry conviction, or nothing will. Yeats's prose is solipsistic, but (unlike Pater's) it is the extrovert solipsism of a man secure in his identity and proud of gifts that he knows must be reckoned with. At his best, the result is prophecy, and at worst merely eccen-tricity – the eccentricity that later twentieth-century poets such as Auden would find it necessary to adopt as a social retreat. But Yeats's Cassandra role is something with which he seems thoroughly content.

In criticism, as in his poetry, he emerged out of Pre-Raphaelitism, the aesthetic movement and the 1890s. One point of emergence is perhaps indicated by a famous passage from the critical book that he did much to inspire, Arthur Symons's *The Symbolist Movement in Literature* (1899):

> Here, then, in this revolt against exteriority, against rhetoric, against a materialistic tradition; in this endeavour to disengage the ultimate essence, the soul, of whatever exists and can be realised by the consciousness; in this dutiful waiting upon every symbol by which the soul of things can be made visible; literature, bowed down by so many burdens, may at last attain liberty, and its authentic speech. In attaining this liberty, it accepts a heavier burden; for in speaking to us so intimately, so solemnly, as only religion had hitherto spoken to us, it becomes itself a kind of religion, with all the duties and responsibilities of the sacred ritual.[39]

The theme of revolt, the magic word 'symbol' and the suggestion that literature is as yet unliberated are new, as is the sequence of poets, de Nerval, de L'Isle-Adam, Rimbaud, Verlaine, Laforgue and Mallarmé, whom Symons introduced to English readers. When all this is preparatory to the notion of art as 'sacred ritual', however, we may feel that we have been here before. Arnold, after all, had called on literature to take over the responsibilities of religion. But one thing both Symons and (more pertinaciously) Yeats try to do is to redeem poetry from the conventions of the established tradition. Their incense, at least, will be burnt on different altars. Yeats as a critic is far less tied by the established reputations than, say, Swinburne. Nor is he bounded by the slightly unctuous tones of Symons.

Yeats had been influenced not only by the decadents but by William Morris; in addition, he was an Irish poet at a time of national reawakening. Morris had championed and translated the 'folk-bibles' such as the sagas, and it was Yeats's originality as a critic to draw connections between these and the 'sacred books' of the modern symbolists. In his lecture 'Art under Plutocracy' (1883), Morris defined tradition as 'that wonderful, almost miraculous accumulation of the skill of ages, which men find themselves partakers in without effort on their part'.[40] The idea of popular art suggested by this is derived from the Gothic Revivalists, and especially Ruskin. For Yeats, too, tradition was an 'effortless' acquisition, but its essence lay in folk-tales and occult beliefs, rather than in the techniques of crafts such as stonemasonry. The modern poet who studied mythology and magic could bring himself back into contact with his forebears. In 'What is "Popular Poetry"?' (1901), Yeats argued that true poetry originates in the unwritten tradition of the peasantry, and is carried on in a developed culture by a few coterie poets who resist the temptation to make a rhetorical appeal to the educated public. Such poetry is not direct and simple, as Wordsworth thought, but 'strange and obscure', though immediately comprehensible to those who have retained the folk 'mother-wit'. It is at the furthest possible extreme from the 'Kitsch' served out to the disinherited middle classes. Though a palpable rationalisation, like most such theories, this goes beyond Wordsworth and Morris to stress that poetic origins lie in the once universal faculty of visionary, magical understanding. Yeats believed that criticism should be instinctive and 'hieratic', and that the modern artist must be aware that 'it is what is old and far off that stirs us the most deeply.'[41] His aim was to write a 'sacred book' tapping these ancient sources, as previous poets of educated culture had done. Thus he found the essence of literature in a mythopoeic, rather than a lyrical or a moral tradition.

Belief in a mythopoeic tradition implies that poetry is more deeply rooted than modern society, standing over it with a prophetic, demonic power. Yet Yeats's examination of the tradition in his essays on Shelley, Spenser and Blake is undeniably rather bland. He follows Rossetti and Swinburne in recognising the importance of Blake, the one English romantic poet who remained unassimilated by Arnoldian 'culture'. But it is the fact of Blake's being a visionary, rather than the particular details of the vision, which seem to move him. If he had paid more attention to the details, Yeats could not have presented Blake as an ancestral mage, lifted above place and time. As it is, he can speak calmly of 'Blake's anger against causes and purposes he but half-understood' as the necessary madness of one who 'half lives in eternity'.[42] It seems more important to use him as the occasion of a mystic thrill than to understand, or even to sympathise with, Blake's anger. There is little that is alarming or subversive about Blake in Yeats's account; progression, in fact, without contraries. Yet in his early essays he was seeking to enlist Blake and the other visionary poets in a crusade to reassert the place of imagination in life, and to arrest the 'slow dying of men's hearts'.[43]

'We are but critics, or but half create', he wrote in 'Ego Dominus Tuus'. It might have been expected that, when the social mission to which he dedicated himself in Ireland was overtaken by events, criticism would lose its importance for him. Once he had developed his own mythological system, what need could he have for it? In fact, Yeats's continuing output of prose suggests that his system was more of an intellectual construct than he liked to admit; but only a small proportion of the later prose is criticism in any normal sense. An important exception should be made for his speculations on tragedy. Tragedy, he wrote, is a 'drowner of dykes', a 'confounder of understanding' and in watching it 'we feel our minds expand convulsively or spread out slowly like some moon-brightened image-crowded sea.'[44] But tragedy for Yeats was a lesser thing than for Bradley because it had its appointed place in the cycles of history. He could fit his own colleagues of the 1890s into that scheme as the 'Tragic Generation' – the title of a brilliant autobiographical essay (1922), exploiting a framework which is altogether too neat and deterministic. Ireland's bitter road to independence was also fitted into the tragic scheme, but the sense of tradition to which the later Yeats appealed was not one in which the Irish peasantry figured very prominently. It may be that the last stanza of 'Coole Park and Ballylee, 1931' constitutes his farewell to the ideal of the 'book of the people' –

> We were the last romantics – chose for theme
> Traditional sanctity and loveliness;
> Whatever's written in what poets name
> The book of the people; . . .

– even though 'mounted in that saddle Homer rode'. From his eclectic later references to the art of Japan, of Byzantium, of 'ancestral houses' and the Quattrocento one could perhaps draw a new theory of art as the by-product of aristocratic energy and violence; but these are the subject-matter of his major poetry, and not of a body of criticism.

Yeats loved to represent himself and his friends as a doomed generation, the last romantics, which they were not. One of his successors was Joyce; the romantic myth of the artist as priest of the eternal imagination is recaptured in all its fervour by Stephen Dedalus. Joyce deserves mention here for another reason; there are times when his fiction turns into a final wake over the corpse of Victorian criticism. His early work is a culmination of aestheticism. The presentation of Stephen's aesthetic theory fulfils Wilde's notion of the critic as artist, while every one of Joyce's works meets Yeats's prescription for a 'sacred book', becoming at once more strange and obscure, and more destructive of the other-worldly aesthetic ideal as we move through *Ulysses* to *Finnegans Wake*. In the Library chapter of *Ulysses*, however, Stephen abandons aesthetic abstractions for the world of the bookmen, steeping himself in the Shakespeare-biography that was one of the main literary industries of the late nineteenth century. Based on details cribbed from Dowden, Brandes, Sidney Lee and others, Stephen's interpretation of *Hamlet* seems to repeat all the worst excesses of the biographical approach. Yet what it does, in the relentless process of Joycean parody, is to repeat them to the point of philosophical absurdity. The simple pattern that Stephen traces (the pattern of cuckoldry) turns up in so many features of Shakespeare's works that it must lead to a view of artistic creation, not so much as 'myriad-minded' but as anonymous and automatic. It cannot have been Shakespeare, but some psychic urge or cosmic trickster working through him, which produced an *oeuvre* that was so transparently obsessive. As a theory of Shakespeare this is absurd, and is meant to be, but as a theory of Joyce's own writing it both hits the target and destroys that target, since the author is both on exhibition throughout his works, and laughing mockingly at his own manifestations. Thus the comfortable Victorian assumptions about the author's personality hidden behind the work are frustrated, and perhaps untenable. Individual human responsibility was concealed or evaded, and the literary values which had rested upon it now had to be reinterpreted. In modern criticism, the poem and not its author becomes the guarantor of culture and source of its power of prophecy.

Yeats spent a good deal of his life in public libraries, while the literature on Joyce's literary borrowings itself fills a good number of library shelves. Both authors lived the life of the bookman, and both inherited the romantic tradition of the artist. They are great writers partly because they took that tradition out of the Victorian world, and remade it for the twentieth century. The remaking was also a destruction. Yeats's poem 'The Circus Animals' Desertion' might be read as, among other things, an allegory of the end of Victorian art. The 'old songs', the images and 'painted stage' to which he has given his life represent the world of literature, enchanted, 'disinterested' and cut off from life; but it is all an artifice, a lie which the poet can no longer sustain:

> Now that my ladder's gone,
> I must lie down where all the ladders start,
> In the foul rag-and-bone shop of the heart.

The idea that that might make supreme poetry is one for which we might look in vain in the Victorian age. Joyce's dismissal of

Victorian culture, in the Library chapter of *Ulysses*, could not be on a more different plane. But here, quite explicitly, it is a whole literary ethos which is rejected when Stephen, after the fiasco of his Shakespeare lecture, redeems himself in the company of a man whose visit to the Library was spent in checking an advertisement and peering up the backsides of Greek statues. Stephen's audience of 'AE', John Eglinton, Buck Mulligan and the Quaker librarian might indeed have been intended as the last gathering of nineteenth-century literary intellectuals: 1904 seen through the eyes of 1919.

5   Modernists and New Critics

The Children of the New Epoch: Lewis, Pound and Hulme

'We are at the beginning of a new epoch, fresh to it, the first babes of a new, and certainly a better, day', wrote Wyndham Lewis in launching *The Tyro* (1921), a little magazine to which T. S. Eliot was among the most prominent contributors. The 'new state of human life', according to Lewis, was 'as different from Nine-teenth Century England, say, as the Renaissance was from the Middle Ages'.[1] In 1921 Lewis was already a veteran of newness. It was mainly his use of Great War imagery (the gap between past and future being figured as a 'No Man's Land', for example) which distinguished his 1921 pronouncements from those issued in the magazine *Blast*, the 'Review of the Great English Vortex', in 1914. By any standards, *Blast* was a major event in literary modernism, but when it appeared the Tradition of the New already had a considerable history. Virginia Woolf was to claim that human character had changed in December 1910; the (somewhat paro-chial) events she seems to have had in mind were the death of King Edward VII and the London Post-Impressionist Exhibition. Three years earlier A. R. Orage had founded his influential weekly the *New Age*, and the concepts of the 'New Woman' and the 'new journalism' (the latter referring to the sensationalist popular press) were already well-established at the death of Queen Victoria. A good case has been made for the Decadence of the English 1890s as an inherently modernistic artistic movement,[2] and the Nineties resound with such phrases as Hardy's 'the ache of modernism' and Symons' 'the restlessness of modern life'. Havelock Ellis, the friend of Yeats and Symons, had published his essays on Nietzsche, Tolstoy and Whitman as *The New Spirit* (1890). What we now call literary modernism, with its major monuments such as *The Waste Land*, *Ulysses* and the *Cantos*, was preceded by three decades of fitful avant-garde initiatives and a growing appetite for the 'new'.

The 'new spirit' in twentieth-century thought is characterised by its adherence to what Friedrich Nietzsche had called 'critical history.' 'Man must have strength to break up the past, and apply it, too, in order to live. He must bring the past to the bar of judgment, interrogate it remorselessly and finally condemn it', Nietzsche had written in *The Use and Abuse of History* (1874).[3] The condemnation of *a* past, however, invariably led to its substitution by an alternative view of the past. For the early twentieth century, the alternative view was usually a more primitive view, a return to a supposedly aboriginal past. The Victorian period saw the unfolding of geological time, of prehistory, and of anthropology; at the same time as European imperialism extended its rule to the last corner of the earth, works such as E. B. Tylor's *Primitive Culture* (1871) and Sir J. G. Frazer's *The Golden Bough* (1890–1915) helped to popularise a universal view of the primitive as the background to civilised society. Nietzsche in *The Birth of Tragedy* (1871) contrasted the unity of a primitive culture bound together by its myths with modern humanity's alienation and homelessness. Stripped of myth, Nietzsche's 'abstract man' digs frantically for roots, turning to countless other cultures in the vain hope of satisfying his 'great historical hunger'.[4] David S. Thatcher in *Nietzsche in England 1890–1914* (1970) has charted the pervasive impact of Nietzsche's thought on A. R. Orage, T. E. Hulme and their associates including Eliot, Lewis and Ezra Pound. Literary modernism as a whole is Nietzschean to the extent that it addresses a crisis of civilisation and the dissolution of inherited categories of thought, and that it claims to reject the present in the name both of a commitment to the future and a return to primitive origins.

Although the early twentieth century was a period of startling technological innovation, literary modernism was thus very much more than a simple response to the 'Machine Age'. The revolutionary rhetoric of the modernists is itself beset with paradox.[5] Did they see themselves as inaugurating a 'new epoch', or as responding to changes that were already taking place? Was theirs a period of full-blooded innovation, or of remaking connections with aspects of the past that had been overlooked? Was it necessary to go forward or to go back to create the new art? Did modernism bring about as decisive a change in the direction of English literature as romanticism had done a hundred years earlier? Wyndham Lewis's testimony on these questions is valuable, for he came to see himself as an uncompromising revolutionary who, nevertheless, had presided over a revolution which failed to take place. Much of the blame, he thought, attached to Eliot and Pound, his fellow 'men of 1914' (that is, contributors to *Blast*), who had never overcome their incorrigible poetic antiquarianism. Lewis was a modernist painter as well as the author of modernist fictions such as *Tarr* (1918), and the argument between the revolutionary and the 'neo-classical' elements in the modernist outlook in some ways reflects the split between the visual arts and the verbal arts in the twentieth century: avant-garde writers could never manage more than rather feeble imitations of the abstract, non-representational tendencies in Cubism, Vorticism and Constructivism.[6] But Lewis's sense of Pound and Eliot as backsliders and reactionaries in their public assertions ('He doesn't come *in here* disguised as Westminster Abbey', he is said to have remarked of the later Eliot'[7]), is much too simple. As a critic, Lewis is strident, incisive, and a man who like Bernard Shaw 'could be depended on to disagree'.[8] Unfortunately, his disagreements and browbeatings have rarely outlived the occasions that provoked them. Though Lewis was a personality of great force who still has his admirers, Ezra Pound was in the long run a far more effective propagandist for literary modernism. Eliot, meanwhile, established himself as at once the leading revolutionary poet and the 'classical' critic of the epoch.

If Eliot was not disguised as Westminster Abbey when he went to see Lewis, what disguise, one wonders, did he adopt? Born in St. Louis and educated at Harvard, he had studied in Europe and, like Pound, had effectively abandoned the United States even before he decided to settle in England. Democracy was the aspect of American life most abhorrent to these two poets. Their English allies, Lewis and T. E. Hulme, shared their 'European' outlook and predilection towards the radical Right. In the New Epoch that they envisaged cultural health would not depend on the play of market forces, and still less on educational missionary-work in the Matthew Arnold mode. Instead, it would be imposed on the inert majority by the conviction and superior organisation of a vanguard party composed of the intellectual élite. In England, the placid Georgian literary scene was ripe for the sort of explosive confrontation pioneered, in the years after 1910, by another right-wing group, the Italian Futurists. *Blast*, with its strident manifestos, mocking polemics, and its pose of superior intelligence towards everything else in sight, brought together Lewis, Pound and Eliot (whose poems were published in the second number). T. E. Hulme was not involved in *Blast*, but his 'Complete Poetical Works' (all five of them) were printed by Pound in 1915. Pound, always a more 'American' poet than Eliot, left England in disgust soon after the Great War in which Hulme had been killed; meanwhile Lewis embarked on his lonely role as spokesman for a permanent artistic opposition.

When *Blast* first appeared, Pound was at the crest of a wave in literary London. The friend of Yeats, Ford Madox Ford and H. G. Wells, the proponent of Imagism and Vorticism, and the editor who had discovered James Joyce, he was showing himself to be the most gifted literary impresario of the twentieth century. Critical journalism played a large part in this achievement, though Eliot, who benefited enormously from Pound's encouragement, was also unstinting in his acknowledgement of his poetic example. Introducing Pound's literary essays in 1954, Eliot wrote that his fellow-American had been 'more responsible for the XXth century revolution in poetry than any other individual'.[9] Eliot did not, of course, add that one of Pound's principal contributions was the remarkable editorial job that he performed on *The Waste Land*, which its author then dedicated to Pound as *il miglior fabbro*, 'the better artist'. Much more disputable, however, is Eliot's comparison of his poetic mentor with Dryden, Johnson, Wordsworth and Coleridge as poet-critics. Pound's 'criticism and his poetry, his precept and his practice' do not quite compose a 'single *oeuvre*' as Eliot maintains, for much of the criticism is hastily written, repetitive and didactic. Pound is less the philosopher of modernist poetry than its tireless propagandist. In retrospect he is deficient both as a theorist and a practical critic, and his chief value lies in the bluntness and timeliness of his message.

Unlike Eliot, Pound was enough of an American populist to embark on a project of mass education through his writings. This can be seen in the titles of his later works, *How to Read* (1931), *The ABC of Reading* (1934) and *Guide to Kulchur* (1938), but it is also implicit in his earlier journalism with its untiring restatement of the lessons of nineteenth-century aestheticism. In his contributions to the *Little Review*, the *Egoist* and other avant-garde magazines Pound often sounded like an evangelist preacher, with the aesthetic tradition of Gautier, Flaubert, the Goncourts, Whistler and Henry James as his Bible. Pound is the most prominent of those critics who set out, in the words of one literary historian, to reaffirm the aesthetic doctrines of the autonomy of art 'in the new hard and assertive language of early twentieth-century expressionism'.[10] This new stridency did not preclude a generous recognition of his predecessors.

Pound during his English years was a poet with an intense lyrical gift who spent much time advocating the 'prose' virtues of verbal economy, scientific precision and mental hygiene. Under his influence, Eliot (in Lewis's words) was to be 'lifted out of his lunar alleyways and *fin de siècle* nocturnes',[11] but Pound had first to perform this rescue mission on his own verse, and on those of his contemporaries who would rally to his banner. The 'hard and assertive language' of his criticism was influenced by T. E. Hulme, by A. R. Orage, and by Ford Madox Ford.[12] Pound's gift was to translate the demand for unsentimental and intellectually serious verse into an instantly graspable programme for poetry; this was the 'Imagist manifesto', with its famous lists of 'do's' and 'don'ts'. It is difficult not to conclude that the 'image' at the centre of Imagist propaganda is the nineteenth-century 'symbol' rechristened and stripped of its occultist resonances; what matters, however, is the setting in which the image is to be presented. Pound's Imagist manifesto is a declaration of war on the merely ornamental in poetry, much as Wordsworth's Preface to *Lyrical Ballads* had attacked the fading flowers of Augustan poetic diction. The poem is to be cut back to a simple, direct statement, with all inessential words removed. The measure of good verse is the exactitude of good prose: 'no man can now write really good verse unless he knows Stendhal and Flaubert',[13] states Pound in his customary *ex cathedra* manner.

Unlike a number of the protagonists of the 'new epoch', Pound did not suggest that modernity of subject-matter is essential to modern poetry. Instead, he turned to distant and neglected areas of the literary tradition, notably to Provençal and Chinese poetry and to the classical epigram. In the troubador poets he claimed to find the 'precision' and 'explicit rendering' that were lacking in the Victorians.[14] His essay on Cavalcanti (begun in 1910) parallels Eliot's concern with the physicality of poetic language, with the word as a 'perfect instrument', in which the intellectual and the sensual are united. Similarly, Pound's (mis)conception of the Chinese ideogram was as an image embodying what Eliot was to call the 'intellect . . . at the tips of the senses' – and thus as a far more 'poetic' medium than the abstract signifiers used in Western writing. Pound's language can be mystifying when he describes the sort of poetic diction that he prefers, but the rhetorical values he invests in it are clear and consistent: they are those of energy, physical motion, scientific precision and a clean cutting-edge. A poem for Pound is less an incantation than something carved out with a chisel or razor-blade.

These metaphors are not accidental, since Pound in 1913–14 found himself among sculptors and made common cause with them. He took a strong interest in painters such as Picasso, Kandinsky and Lewis, but it was the Vorticist sculptors, Epstein and Gaudier-Brzeska, who awakened his sense of form and taught him to see the poet's work with image and metaphor as akin to the artist's work with 'planes in relation'.[15] His memoir of *Gaudier-Brzeska* (1916) reveals the emotional impact of modernist sculpture on Pound, and its value in energising his sense of belonging to a revolutionary artistic movement. On the other hand, a fascination with sculpture could not provide him with a vocabulary of criticism.

It is, above all, an adequate terminology that Pound as a literary critic lacks. Eliot's impact owes much to his development of such a terminology, burnished by a handful of isolated, gnomic phrases such as 'dissociation of sensibility', 'objective correlative' and 'the mind of Europe', which themselves seem to embody the radiant qualities of the Image, Pound's 'intellectual and emotional complex in an instant of time'.[16] Pound's critical prose, for all its forceful sloganising, does not aspire to this level of subtlety. Its virtues, which are not inconsiderable, are those of the revolutionary simpleton (to use another expression of Lewis's).

T. E. Hulme was another revolutionary simpleton. The legend of Hulme as, potentially, a major philosopher is no longer sustainable. But he was more closely in touch with European philosophical developments than any of his contemporaries, and played an intimate part in the development of modernist criticism through his influence on T. S. Eliot. Eliot is known to have taught both Hulme's 'classicist' ideas and his poem 'The Embankment' in the university extension lectures that he gave in 1916.[17] He quotes 'The Embankment' again, without naming its author, in 'Reflections on *Vers Libre*', an essay published in the following year. Hulme was killed in action in 1917, leaving a mass of unpublished notebooks and papers from which Herbert Read (Eliot's assistant editor on the *Criterion*) compiled the influential *Speculations* (1924). In a foreword to *Speculations*, the sculptor Jacob Epstein compares its author to Plato and Socrates as a mentor for the intellectual youth of his time. Hulme's essays, however, are still more dogmatic and pugnacious than Pound's. There is no attempt to reconcile the author's own conflicting positions. During his studies in Germany and Italy he had been deeply influenced by Bergson, Worringer and other contemporary aestheticians. Before the outbreak of war he contributed art criticism to the *New Age* and become an advocate of 'geometrical' art modelled on the structures of machinery rather than the lines of the human body. Epstein later wrote that 'Abstract art had an extraordinary attraction for him: his own brain worked in that way'.[18] Hulme's interest in poetry can be traced back at least to 1909 when he attended meetings of F. S. Flint's 'forgotten school' (a precursor of the Imagist movement) at the Eiffel Tower restaurant. In *Speculations*, a lecture on 'Modern Art and its Philosophy' (1914) is immediately followed by 'Romanticism and Classicism', his most influential statement on poetry. A point-by-point comparison of these two posthumous essays, however unfair it might be, would leave the impression of Hulme as a deeply muddled thinker.

In 'Modern Art and Its Philosophy' and 'Humanism and the

Religious Attitude', Hulme interprets artistic form, seen in its broadest terms, as the expression of a *Weltanschauung* or world-view. He distinguishes between the 'humanist' art of the Renaissance, based upon the accurate representation of the human figure, and the 'geometric' forms of ancient Egyptian, early Greek and Byzantine art. Geometric art, which for Hulme is the product of a 'religious attitude', is in fact characteristic of archaic and 'primitive' civilisations all over the world. Until the end of the nineteenth century, this sort of art had hardly been considered as art at all. But now, Hulme prophetically asserted, the humanist tradition was breaking up, and modern artists were once again turning to geometrical forms. Modern art involves a determined and conscious break with the past: 'the new forms are deliberately introduced by people who detest the old ones'.[19] Hulme's commitment to artistic and cultural revolution is equally evident in his comments on poetry, not least when he states that 'Personally I am of course in favour of the complete destruction of all verse more than twenty years old'.[20] But, in his writings on poetry, it is romanticism (a much more short-term phenomenon than the 'humanist attitude') which has to be overthrown. Hulme's classicist prescriptions for poetry come oddly from a writer who sets so little store by the classical canons of representation in the visual arts.

In writing of modern poetry, Hulme is far from advocating any conception of 'geometrical' form. Instead, following Bergson and paralleling Pound's notion of the Image,[21] his concern is with the concreteness and '*life-communicating* quality'[22] of poetic language. Bergson's view of art, which Hulme expounds, values poetic language as an embodiment of precision and 'felt life'; these qualities, which were to become central to the New Criticism, are the very opposite of the abstraction which Hulme praised in archaic art. The 'dry hardness' which he praises in Horace and Pope has nothing in common with the 'mechanical line' favoured by modernist painters and sculptors. In 'Romanticism and Classicism' Hulme looks forward to a sort of verse which will be 'cheerful, dry and sophisticated', the vehicle of fancy rather than of imagination. It was this Hulme – a Hulme in retreat, to some extent, from the avant-garde positions taken up in 'Modern Art and Its Philosophy' – who most deeply influenced Eliot.

What critics from Eliot to Raymond Williams were to take from Hulme's writings on the visual arts, however, was his theory of the sociology of artistic change. According to Hulme a new, experimental form of art comes into existence as the reflection of a broader 'change of sensibility'. In 1930 Eliot put forward the same idea, in much the same words: 'Sensibility alters from generation to generation in everybody, whether we will or no; but expression is only altered by a man of genius'. The connection between sensibility and expression is that 'change of sensibility demand[s] a change of idiom'.[23] Hulme's own indebtedness here was to the German art-historical tradition, with its influential periodization of artistic styles since the Renaissance. The keyword 'sensibility' is used by Hulme and Eliot in a much broader and vaguer context than had earlier been customary in English. Hulme at least is quite clear that significant changes of sensibility are few and far between and that they always betoken a change in the underlying *Weltanschauung* or philosophical 'attitude' that a culture expresses. In his introduction to Georges Sorel's *Reflexions on Violence* (1916), Hulme uses the term 'ideology' to cover much the same range as 'attitude' and *Weltanschauung*. It may be objected that ideology is a more political concept, but Hulme's endorsements of classicism in opposition to romanticism and of the religious attitude in opposition to humanism have an inescapable political dimension. What he calls the classical view that 'Man is an extraordinarily fixed and limited animal whose nature is absolutely constant' is, as his next sentence shows, a transparent justification of conservative and authoritarian attitudes: 'It is only by tradition and organisation that anything decent can be got out of him'.[24]

The right-wing and proto-Fascist tendencies of many of the most prominent modernist writers are well known.[25] Hulme's lasting contribution lay in his sociological view of art, with its connections between ideology, sensibility and mode of expression. But it was his mixture of intellectual pugnacity and conservative, militaristic faith which made him such a charismatic figure among the 'children of the new epoch'. Superficially, his whole life seemed of a piece with his praise of 'verse strictly confined to the earthly and the definite', of art with the 'hard clean surface of a piston rod'.[26] The confused and fragmented state of the writings he left behind was unimportant, since in him the modernists had found their terrorist-philosopher.

T. S. Eliot

That intellectual revolutions cannot be made without at least a show of violence was a fact that Hulme, Lewis and Pound were very willing to acknowledge. T. S. Eliot was rather different. An early, humorous letter from Ezra Pound seems to dictate their respective critical roles: 'You let *me* throw the bricks through the front window. You go in at the back door and take out the swag.'[1]

Pound soon tired of smashing windows in literary London, but Eliot stayed on until he came to personify the critical Establishment he had once wished to attack. By 1965, the year of his death, his impressive haul of booty included the Nobel Prize for Literature and the Order of Merit as well as innumerable testimonies to his influence as a poet, critic, dramatist, moralist and arbiter of literary reputations.

Though Eliot stands out as the modernist poet-critic *par excellence* the relations between poetry and criticism in his work are not easy to unravel. In 'The Function of Criticism' (1923) he warned against a hard-and-fast separation between the two activities, stressing the amount of 'critical labour' involved in the 'frightful toil' of composition itself. Other comments, however, suggest that the ultimate source of creative writing is wholly distinct from the conscious and rational level on which criticism operates. His criticism is as notable for its dark and pregnant hints about the mystery of inspiration as it is for demanding that the study of poetry should become an intellectually rigorous pursuit.[2]

The rigour of Eliot's criticism, in any case, is deceptive and sometimes verges on self-parody. The titles of his later books – *The Use of Poetry and the Use of Criticism, Poetry and Drama, The Idea of a Christian Society, On Poetry and Poets* – are often much more magisterial than their contents. Like Coleridge, Eliot in mid-career put his name to a grand and unfinished critical project, *The Disintegration of the Intellect*, which was to have been composed of three volumes, *The School of Donne, The Outline of Royalism* and *The Principles of Modern Heresy*.[3] The prose of his later essays and lectures, pontifical, evasive, self-contradictory and liable to relapse into what Henry James called the 'twaddle of graciousness', has been frequently derided. Nor has the critical procedure of the early Eliot been left unscathed. Stanley Edgar Hyman has commented on its 'emeritus quality',[4] while Hugh Kenner described it as 'a parody of official British literary discussion: its asperities, its pontification, its distinctions that do not distinguish, its vacuous ritual of familiar quotations and bathetic solemnities'. (However, Kenner added, 'the argument, and the tone derived from an extreme economy of phrase, are steadily subversive'.)[5] F. R. Leavis, a former disciple, bitterly attacked 'Tradition and the Individual Talent', Eliot's most famous critical essay, for 'its ambiguities, its logical inconsequences, its psuedo-precisions, its fallaciousness, and the aplomb of its equivocations and its specious cogency'.[6] Eliot's critical achievement is notoriously hard to pin down.

Does his true quality, perhaps, lie in his subversiveness – in his ability to use the critical essay, without appearing to do so, to advance the modernist outlook manifested in his poetry? Did his criticism lose its sense of purpose once the modernist literary revolution was completed? These are tempting hypotheses. It has long been supposed that the publication in 1928 of *For Lancelot Andrewes: Essays on Style and Order*, with a preface in which he declared himself a classicist in literature, an Anglo-catholic in religion and a royalist in politics, marked a decisive turning point in Eliot's *oeuvre*. The *Times Literary Supplement* reviewer of *For Lancelot Andrewes* lamented Eliot's desertion of literary modernity.[7] In considering his criticism the search for the (pre-1928) 'modernist' Eliot is almost irresistible, though its object is something of a will o' the wisp. Ezra Pound did not christen him 'Old Possum' for nothing.

Eliot as modernist

Revolutionary modernism is not a quality attached, at first sight, either to Eliot's *Selected Essays* (1932) or to his earlier collection *The Sacred Wood* (1920). In part – though only in part – this is due to what Hyman in a pioneering study referred to as his 'resolute refusal to print in book form . . . his criticism of contemporaries'.[8] In his final volume *To Criticize the Critic* (1965) Eliot at last reprinted his 1917 essays on Pound and on *vers libre*, and one other article championing a modernist contemporary – his 1923 essay '*Ulysses*, Order and Myth' – has subsequently entered the canon.[9] Eliot's essay on *Ulysses* sounded a note of modernist triumphalism which will scarcely be found elsewhere in his writing. Joyce's abandonment of the 'narrative method' for the 'mythical method', he wrote, had 'the importance of a scientific discovery'. It was a 'method which others must pursue after him', but the only writers capable of doing so were 'those who had won their own discipline in secret and without aid, in a world which offers very little assistance to that end'. Joyce in 1923 was the leader of a small band of the Elect, a secret avant-garde.

The rhetoric of this essay repays study. Much of it amounts to a diatribe against a fellow 'modernist', the Imagist poet Richard Aldington. Aldington had attacked the author of *Ulysses*, 'wailing' (as Eliot puts it) 'at the blood of Dadaism which his prescient eye saw bursting forth at the tap of the magician's rod'. Here is a three-stage argument which might be summarised as follows: 'Aldington and I are against the Dadaists; Aldington, unfortunately, is too vulgar to be able to distinguish between Dadaism and Joyce; only I and a few kindred spirits' – Eliot mentions Yeats and Wyndham Lewis at this point – 'belong to the true modernist brotherhood'. Eliot had written slightingly of the Dadaists on two earlier occasions. In an article in the *Egoist* (July 1919) he mocked at a volume by Tristan Tzara, while in the 'The Lesson of Baude-laire' (1921) he described Dadaism as a 'diagnosis of a disease of the French mind' – 'whatever lesson we extract from it will not be directly applicable in London'.[10] That there were lessons of modernity directly applicable in London is evident from a number of cryptic, but forceful, remarks scattered through Eliot's essays of this period. In *'Ulysses*, Order and Myth' he wrote that 'The novel ended with Flaubert and with James'. He ended his assessment of 'Swinburne as Poet' (1920) with the declaration that 'the language which is more important to us' was 'that which is struggling to digest and express new objects, new groups of objects, new feelings, new aspects' – such as that of Joyce and Joseph Con-rad.[11] In the *Egoist* for May 1918, writing as 'T. S. Apteryx' (one of his many pseudonyms at this time), he observed that 'the forces of deterioration are a large crawling mass, and the force of develop-ment half a dozen men,' among them 'Mr Pound, Mr Joyce, and Mr Lewis'.[12]

In a handful of retrospective statements, Eliot explained that his best criticism was written to forward his creative concerns and that its impact was inseparable from his impact as a poet. It was a 'by-product of my private poetry-workshop'.[13] His earlier essays, in reaction against Georgian poetry and criticism, were 'implicitly defending the sort of poetry that I and my friends wrote'.[14] 'Impli-citly' is no doubt the keyword here; there had been no 'Vortex: Eliot', or other manifesto to accompany Pound's and Lewis's manifestos in *Blast*, even though Eliot published his poems in the second number of that journal, and had to suffer the indignity of Lewis's rejection of a set of obscene verses, 'King Bolo and his Big Black Kween'.[15] The essays explicitly defending his friends' work, such as his 1918 review of *Tarr* and his many short articles on Ezra Pound, were among those deliberately omitted from his *Selected Essays*.

Eliot's early view of Pound is exemplified in his anonymous pamphlet *Ezra Pound: His Metric and Poetry* (1917). The stress throughout is on Pound's 'mastery' of technique, on the 'definite-ness' and 'concreteness' of his verse, and the arduousness of its method. Reading such verse is, in turn, a discipline to be 'mas-tered'. Pound, it is admitted, uses *'vers libre'*, but his free verse belongs in a different world from the 'bad free verse' of his contem-poraries: 'Pound's *vers libre* is such as is only possible for a poet who has worked tirelessly with rigid forms and different systems of metric'.[16] The attack on the vulgar proliferation of 'experimen-

tal' free verse is carried on in another contemporary essay, 'Reflections on *Vers Libre*', and Pound was very soon to paraphrase his
message with the words 'No *vers* is *libre* for the man who wants
to do a good job'.[17] Pound and Eliot were at one in championing
an ideal of hard, disciplined and technically masterful poetry
against the sloppier and more self-indulgent varieties of Imagism
and *vers libre*.

Eliot brought a very different emphasis to his discussion of Wyndham Lewis's work. What he found in *Tarr* was by no means formal
perfection – 'it is only in part a novel', he says – but rather a
'purely intellectual curiosity in the senses', a traditional English
humour (which Eliot likened to the humour of Ben Jonson and
Dickens) and a primitive energy. Lewis, he concluded, was 'the
most fascinating personality of our time rather than a novelist':

> The artist, I believe, is more *primitive*, as well as more civilized,
> than his contemporaries, but experience is deeper than civiliza-
> tion, and he only uses the phenomena of civilization in expressing
> it . . . In the work of Mr. Lewis we recognise the thought of
> the modern and the energy of the cave-man.[18]

Eliot looked for primitivism and 'rootedness' as well as for technique in avant-garde writing. Tzara's Dadaist verse, he wrote, 'does
not appear to have very deep roots in the literature of any nation'.[19]
Turgenev, Eliot remarked in reviewing Edward Garnett's study
of 1917, was a master-craftsman who 'recognised, in practice at
least, that a writer's art must be racial'.[20] It is hard to imagine
Eliot praising Pound for his Americanness or for his 'racial' quality;
the problem of rootedness, however, is one that he wrestled with
in his own work, and above all in his theory of tradition.

When, for example, he declares in *The Sacred Wood* that 'The
important critic is the person who is absorbed in the present problems of art, and who wishes to bring the forces of the past to
bear upon the solution of these problems,' Eliot seems to be equivocating between classicism and primitivism. The classicist holds that
the past offers the necessary formal models for poetry; and this
is the view that avant-garde groups such as the Futurists condemned
as hopelessly stale and *passéiste*. Eliot's tendency to authoritarian
classicism does not date, as has sometime been thought, from the
time of his religious conversion in the late 1920s, since he was
expressing these views in unpublished lectures as early as 1916.[21]
But for the poet of *The Waste Land* to write of utilising the 'forces
of the past' suggests that the choice of those forces and the use
that is made of them will be unexpected, to say the least. The

ultimate horizon of the 'past' for Eliot is no longer that of ancient Greece but of fertility rituals and cave-paintings, the neolithic and the paleolithic. Far from being poets just arrived from the New World, he and Pound are then made to seem the natural outcome of this past.

Eliot's dealings with issues of nationality and literary inheritance are tangled and self-contradictory. At one level, he is intent on establishing his dominance in his new (English) cultural environment. Writing in 1919 of his Harvard friend, the poet Conrad Aiken, he declared that 'If Mr Aiken were not so isolated, if he was in contact with European civilisation, he might go so very much further.'[22] He himself had gone further, yet how was he to avoid the rootlessness he had detected in Tzara's verse? In part this could be done by becoming, as far as he could, an Englishman, and by invoking seventeenth-century English precursors such as the Metaphysicals, Dryden, Webster and Tourneur. The criterion of nationality (English or American) could, however, do little to explain *The Waste Land*, which – particularly in its final form – must have seemed strange and unbidden even to its author. It is significant that the suppressed parts of the poem, most of them omitted at Pound's insistence, are not only comparatively laboured but are usually more conventionally and more recognisably English. In an essay on 'The Three Provincialities' of American, Irish and English writing (1921), he declared that 'literature is not primarily a matter of nationality, but of language; the traditions of the language, not the traditions of the nation or the race, are what first concerns the writer.'[23] Here he is stating that the poet acquires a 'home' and a cultural identity by means other than filiation or natural inheritance. In 'Tradition and the Individual Talent', however, Eliot argues that the tradition the poet must labour to acquire is not that of the English language but a very different conception, the 'mind of Europe'. Thus we may say that his most famous essay on these themes turns back to Matthew Arnold in the hope of resolving the confusions in his own thinking.

Eliot's 'tradition' – reversing the usual meaning of the word – is an intellectual construction which can only be assimilated by a deliberate programme of self-education. The principal constituents of the 'mind of Europe' in 'Tradition and the Individual Talent' are the dead poets whose works form an 'ideal order'. Eliot's use of the idea of tradition throughout his writings is an idealist one, leading him to posit the supreme authority of social institutions of the spirit much as Arnold had done. At the practical level of life, he would later affirm that culture and civilisation grew 'from the soil' and that, if possible, 'the great majority of human beings should go on living in the place in which they were born'.[24] If the uprooting of human beings had led (in certain circumstances) to higher levels of culture it must be because it was only through mobility and deliberate exchange that wider and grander conceptions – 'Christendom', the 'monuments' of art, the 'literature of Europe' – could be achieved. Eliot for the most part credits these abstractions with an organic life of their own. He sees the spiritual institutions of civilisation as growing, maturing and decaying like vegetables growing in the soil. Eliot's conception of the 'mind of Europe', however, cannot simply be represented by organic metaphors implying continuous growth. It is at once more primordial and more artificial than these metaphors suggest. In 'Tradition and the Individual Talent' he describes the growth of the European mind as a development 'which abandons nothing *en route*, which does not superannuate either Shakespeare, or Homer, or the rock drawing of the Magdalenian draughtsmen'. These are statements which could not have been made before the discovery of paleolithic art in the early twentieth century, a discovery in which Eliot, like the Vorticist sculptor Gaudier-Brzeska, seems to have taken a considerable interest.[25] If the draughtsmanship and intellectual energy of the 'cave-men' form part of the soil which fertilises modern artists, it can be seen how far Eliot's use of the terms 'tradition' and 'continuity' is from their normal implication of an uninterrupted historical process. What he referred to as the 'historical sense' – 'a perception, not only of the pastness of the past, but of its presence' – is in part Nietzsche's 'critical history', a radical revaluation of the past made possible by the modern world's unique interest in, and capacity for, historical research. But it is also more mysterious than this, and involves something we might call a prehistorical sense.

In an early article Eliot quotes J. B. Yeats on the 'dismay and consternation' felt by the poet as, without seeking originality, he 'finds the original, thereby to incur hostility and misunderstanding'. For Eliot, this is a thought which 'takes very deep roots; it strikes through the tangle of literature direct to the subsoil of the greatest – to Shakespeare and Dante and Aeschylus'. He adds that J. B. Yeats (the painter and father of W. B. Yeats) 'understands poetry better than anyone I have ever known who was not a poet, and better than most of those who have the reputation of poets'.[26] These are strong words which suggest that the older Yeats came close to Eliot's own sense of the creative process. 'Tradition and the Individual Talent' seeks to express this sense through the doctrine of the impersonality of poetry and the quasi-scientific analogy of the poet's mind as an unconscious agent or catalyst of imaginative creation. What Eliot calls the 'subsoil of the greatest' is not a deliberate creation like Arnold's 'grand style', but rather a dark and mysterious equivalent of his 'natural magic'.

The Sacred Wood and the dissociation of sensibility

The Sacred Wood, Eliot's first critical volume, was a collection of reviews and essays held together by his concerns with intellectual discipline, with poetic succession, and with an underlying primitivism. The title represents Eliot's most ostentatious acknowledgement of Sir J. G. Frazer's *The Golden Bough*. The 'sacred wood' metaphor has no obvious referent in Eliot's text, so that we can only make sense of it by referring to the priesthood at Nemi, with which Frazer begins his monumental account of civilisation as a sequence of fertility rituals. The new priest, an escaped slave, succeeds to his office by killing his predecessor. Eliot's rather modish invocation of the legend has been (I think, wrongly) interpreted as an attempt to present himself as Matthew Arnold's successor.[27] Arnold, once the High Priest of English criticism, is dismissed at the beginning of *The Sacred Wood* as 'rather a propagandist for criticism than a critic', but he had in any case died thirty-two years earlier. If Eliot is stalking a rather different victim, the first veiled clue to his identity is to be found in the somewhat feline epigraphs to *The Sacred Wood*. The first, in Latin, is from the *Satyricon*. The speaker is a shabbily dressed, white-haired old man, one of Eliot's familiar gerontocratic personae: '"I am a poet", he said, "and a poet of no mean ability, I like to think, at least if bardic crowns are to be trusted when favouritism confers them even on mediocrity."'[28] What this tells us, surely, is that succession to the 'bardic crown', not the chair of criticism, is being contested. By no stretch of the imagination was Arnold still the reigning poet in 1920; those commentators who see *The Sacred Wood* as dislodging Arnold's eminence have, I think, enrolled Eliot in the wrong competition. The second epigraph, 'I also like to dine on becaficas' (from Byron's *Beppo*), invites us to consider 'becaficas' as *sylvia* warblers, hence minor poets, small passage migrants in the sacred wood. Here is an early appearance by Eliot as Old Possum, or bird-catching Practical Cat. The major poet-turned-critic is a scourge of minor poets. After this rodomontade it would seem that Eliot's sacrificial victim must be a still prominent and influential poet who is also an important critic, and it is then not hard to identify him as Swinburne, who is the subject of two separate essays – 'Swinburne as Critic' and 'Swinburne as Poet'. As a critic, Swinburne had pioneered a good deal of the subject-matter of *The*

Sacred Wood, so that his name inevitably crops up when Eliot is writing on Jonson and Massinger, and might also have done in the essays on Marlowe and Blake. In 'Swinburne as Critic' Eliot judiciously debunks Swinburne's studies of Elizabethan drama, while deferring to the opinion that he may be a major poet. 'Swinburne as Poet' has an equally judicious air, allowing that its subject is a 'man of genius' whose poetry retains a 'singular life of its own'.

But the impression the reader carries away from this last essay is that Swinburne's art is a decadent product, leading nowhere – a dead-end. Eliot finds its self-enclosed world of words 'morbid', and argues that for 'language in a healthy state' – words focused on their referents – we must look elsewhere. 'The language which is important to us', he concludes, is that of two prose-writers, Conrad and Joyce. Though Eliot's view of poetic language is close to Pound's in his Imagist manifestos, Pound does not seem to have shared Eliot's intense hostility to Swinburne.[29] Pound had also preceded Eliot in calling attention to the 'prose virtues' in verse, but Eliot's invocation of the two greatest modern novelists at the end of his Swinburne essay is a superb rhetorical *coup de grâce*. After *The Sacred Wood* it was Swinburne's destiny to languish unread, while Eliot emerged as the unchallenged possessor of the bardic crown.

The self-confidence of this whole performance may be judged from the fact that *The Sacred Wood* begins with a discussion of 'The Perfect Critic' and a dismissal of 'Imperfect Critics', and ends with a brief essay on Dante, who for Eliot would remain the greatest of poets. In fact, the volume offers cryptic and premature statements of almost every theme that would come to seem characteristic of Eliot's criticism. There is, first of all, his insistence that the critic should be 'on the side of the artist', and that he should not be led astray by the search for theory and method – for 'there is no method except to be very intelligent'. What the critic should be intelligent *about*, Eliot suggests, is poetry itself – not the author's biography, or the reader's response. 'Honest criticism and sensitive appreciation is directed not upon the poet but the poetry'; and 'when we are considering poetry we must consider it primarily as poetry and not another thing'. This concern for the 'integrity of poetry' was Eliot's legacy to the New Critics, and the essays of *The Sacred Wood* are notable for their brilliant use of quotation and comparative illustration – all the more brilliant for being so compressed – to carry the force of the argument. But if 'Tradition and the Individual Talent' in particular insists on a separation between the finished poem and the 'feeling or emotion or vision in the mind of the poet', in a number of essays Eliot cannot resist moving from the one to the other. His doctrine of the impersonality of great poetry vies with his interest in the psychoanalysis of the artist.

The conflict is most evident in his notorious essay on 'Hamlet and His Problems'. Here Eliot's conviction that Shakespeare felt compelled to 'express the inexpressibly horrible', to make poetry out of 'some stuff that the writer could not drag to light, contemplate, or manipulate into art' leads to the overdetermined judgment that *Hamlet* must be an artistic failure. (Neither Freud nor Ernest Jones is mentioned in this essay, though Eliot must have been toying with the idea of a Freudian basis to the drama.) In the 'Hamlet' essay Eliot invented the phrase 'objective correlative' to denote the expressive power which, he felt, Shakespeare's play lacked. Elsewhere, however, Eliot invokes the mysteries of poetic communication in a rather different (though invariably quasi-scientific) terminology. In reading Ben Jonson, as opposed to the best of Shakespeare, he writes, 'unconscious does not respond to unconscious; no swarms of inarticulate feelings are aroused'. Guided by 'direct communications through the nerves', Shakespeare and Donne use words with 'a network of tentacular roots reaching down to the deepest terrors and desires'. Here poetry seems to be rooted not in the soil or in the 'mind of Europe' but in the individual or collective unconscious.

Throughout *The Sacred Wood* we meet the insistence that it was in the late sixteenth and early seventeenth centuries that poetic language was at its healthiest, and that feeling and sensibility were more finely tuned than they have ever been since. Here Eliot's concerns lead him not in the direction of psychoanalysis but of a still more influential literary sociology (or perhaps psychohistory). The decline, as he sees it, of English verse after the age of Elizabeth reflects the spiritual decline of the whole society. Elizabethan drama, with its framework of conventions uniting the artist and a popular audience, spoke to Eliot of a lost cultural unity such as Ruskin had found in the Gothic cathedrals. The second paragraph of Eliot's essay on Christopher Marlowe (the first paragraph being devoted to an attack on one of Swinburne's comments) sketches what was to become known as his 'dissociation of sensibility' theory:

The comparative study of English versification at various periods is a large tract of unwritten history. To make a study of blank verse alone, would be to elicit some curious conclusions. It would show, I believe, that blank verse within Shakespeare's lifetime was more highly developed, that it became the vehicle of more varied and more intense art-emotions than it has ever conveyed since; and that after the erection of the Chinese Wall of Milton, blank verse has suffered not only arrest but retrogression. That the blank verse of Tennyson, for example, a consummate master of this form in certain applications, is cruder (*not* 'rougher' or less perfect in technique) than that of half a dozen contemporaries of Shakespeare; cruder, because less capable of expressing complicated, subtle, and surprising emotions.

Here Eliot links the study of blank verse to the rise and fall of poetic drama in English. In this context the superiority of the Elizabethans over the nineteenth century is clearly uncontroversial. But Eliot's urge to legislate and generalise is also apparent. He ignores the generic and functional difference between blank verse in the Elizabethans, and in Milton and Tennyson. 'Complicated, subtle, and surprising emotions', however appropriate in playscripts written for actors to deliver, might destroy the rhythm of an epic narrative. Eliot could afford to disregard this because of his overmastering interest in achieving emotional complexity in his own early verse (though by the time of *Four Quartets* he would be handling blank verse in a very different fashion). Nor was it enough to register a general change in poetic language, since this had much wider implications. 'Every vital development in language is a development of feeling as well', he wrote in 'Philip Massinger', an essay which described the period of Webster and Donne as one in which 'the intellect was immediately at the tips of the senses'. Once that immediacy had been lost, *The Sacred Wood* implied, there was nothing but steady decline until the age of Swinburne. The 'dissociation of sensibility . . . from which we have never recovered' was – in the terms of Eliot's most famous formulation of his theory in 'The Metaphysical Poets' (1921) – 'something which had happened to the mind of England'.

In 1921, critical interest in metaphysical poetry was coming to the fore. Eliot began his review of Sir Herbert Grierson's anthology by restating the view of literary history which is implicit in *The Sacred Wood*. The main current of early seventeenth-century poetry (which, as he had said in 'Tradition and the Individual Talent', 'does not at all flow invariably through the most distinguished reputations') might, he now suggested, be seen as moving from the dramatists to the metaphysicals – thus eliminating the line from Spenser and Sidney to Milton. Eliot's unerringly chosen quotations from Donne, Bishop King, Crashaw, Chapman and Lord Herbert serve to establish the intellectual vitality, simplicity of diction, and rhythmic variety of metaphysical verse. When he contrasts the seventeenth century's 'direct sensuous apprehension of thought' with representative passages of Tennyson and Browning, it can be said that nothing so sharp and effective had appeared in English critical writing since Arnold's use of touchstones and Ruskin's contrast of true and false griffins.[30] Eliot then moves from illustration to generalisation as readily as Ruskin had done. Donne is the model of the intellectual poet, creating images out of disparate matter and constantly struggling to unify his experience. Yet the 'main current' represented by Donne seemed to have petered out almost as conclusively as prehistoric cave art had petered out – until, that is, its partial recovery at the end of the nineteenth century. Eliot's interest here is not in English poetry, but in the French symbolists – he includes quotations from Baudelaire and Laforgue. What he calls a main current might as well be re-named 'Influences on the Poetry of T. S. Eliot'.

In the English poetic tradition after Milton and Dryden, Eliot argues, the refinement and 'mastery' of diction outpaces complexity of feeling and thought. Poetry loses its worldliness, its qualities of alert observation and witty precision; the extent of the loss is brought home in 'Andrew Marvell', where Eliot pointedly contrasts Marvell and William Morris, two poets of comparable talent but very disparate achievement. Nineteenth-century poetry, he argues, loses itself in its 'effort to construct a dream world'. This historical scheme was highly influential, and was eventually to be popularised in two detailed studies by F. R. Leavis, *New Bearings in English Poetry* (1932) and *Revaluation* (1936). 'The Metaphysical Poets' and 'Andrew Marvell' represent the summit of Eliot's critical writing, and, therefore, of early twentieth-century criticism in English. Nevertheless, Eliot's view of poetic and cultural history is self-contradictory, much as T. E. Hulme's had been. Both writers combined an idealisation of the medieval world inherited from the nineteenth century (Eliot's most admired poet, it may be repeated, was Dante) with a belief in the ability of their own generation to reverse the course of the last three centuries *and* a wish to make discriminating judgments. So no sooner had Eliot set out his theory of the seventeenth century than he began to qualify it. In 'Andrew Marvell' Eliot (for all his display of courtesy towards Marvell's Puritanism) hints at a relationship between the 'dissociation of sensibility' and the Civil War. As a royalist, Eliot was naturally opposed to the generally favourable verdict on the Civil War and its outcome which had been passed by the nineteenth-century Whig historians. But in 'John Dryden', written in the same year and reprinted in pamphlet form with 'Andrew Marvell' and 'The Meta-

physical Poets', he urged the revaluation of a poet who had flourished after the Civil War, and after the 'dissociation of sensibility'.
Dryden, he suggested, should be studied by contemporary poets
because his diction was the complete antithesis of Swinburne's.
The next stage in Eliot's self-revisions is to be found in his unpublished Clark lectures of 1926 and in such essays as 'Donne in our
Time' (1931) where he spoke of a 'manifest fissure between thought
and sensibility . . . which was not the way of medieval poetry' in
Donne's work.[31] Eliot's later essays on Milton, often viewed as
recantations, further weakened his 'Chinese Wall' view of seventeenth-century poetry, though they came too late to have much
impact. By 1936, according to Leavis, the essays on the metaphysicals and Marvell were already the staple of 'university lectures
and undergraduate exercises',[32] and this was to remain true for
another three decades.

It is worth asking, whether the 'dissociation of sensibility' theory
can be re-formulated in a way that does not automatically involve
a Manichean notion of history. What Eliot values in poets, before
and after the supposed split, is their 'mastery', either in the narrow
technical sense of verbal craft or in their ability to express the
otherwise inexpressible in human experience. What he condemns,
by and large, is the prophetic and bardic tradition of verse (from
Milton to the Victorians) in which a rapt and incantatory manner
disguises vagueness and imprecision of feeling. And this leads him
to prefer dramatists and occasional poets to Milton and the subsequent exemplars of what might be called the Protestant sublime.
The poet, according to these influential essays, is an adroit technician rather than a seer; yet, as we shall see, Eliot views the greatest
poets in an entirely different light.

The later Eliot

Late in 1921, when he had completed his finest critical essays and
was writing *The Waste Land*, Eliot suffered a mental breakdown.
To make ends meet he was working hard at three careers, as a
poet, as a literary journalist (he wrote regularly for the *Times Literary Supplement* and was to launch his own review, the *Criterion*,
in the following year) and as an employee in a City bank. His
life could hardly have been more sharply contrasted with that of
such professional poets as Wordsworth, Shelley, Tennyson and
Browning. His championship of the Metaphysicals implicitly
defends and justifies, not only the poet of exacting technical standards, but the part-time poet who also happens to be a politician,
a courtier, a clergyman or a man of the theatre. The orotund open-

ing of the Marvell essay with its reference to the 'tercentenary of the former member for Hull' demonstrates not only Eliot's command of mannered prose but his interest in a poet who was active in public affairs and who was therefore well equipped to display 'a recognition, implicit in the expression of every experience, of other kinds of experience which are possible', and a 'tough reasonableness beneath the slight lyric grace'. In 'The Metaphysical Poets' Eliot stressed that it was the poet's task to bring together contingent and disparate experiences. The conditions of his own life, with its mixture of professional drudgery, cramped domesticity, and emotional frenzy, are evoked in the experiences of falling in love, reading Spinoza, and the 'noise of the typewriter or the smell of cooking' that he cites by way of illustration. Yet, in the terms of his theory, it is the poet struggling to survive in such bewildering circumstances who has the advantage over the cosseted professional. Eliot's early criticism is 'on the side of the artist' in arguing that the modern poet endowed with intelligence, toughness and an adequate sensibility – but capable of living on his wits and prepared to meet the world on its own terms – could become at least the equal of the dream-ridden bards of the nineteenth century.

Such a poet, if his gifts were not to be squandered, would need a 'tradition' to be aware of and a congenial intellectual climate to work in. Eliot in 1922 took on the editorship of the *Criterion* (1922–39), and soon afterwards he left his banking job and became a publisher. The *Criterion*, begun with high hopes, has been generally accounted a failure. By the time it closed the subscribers numbered no more than two hundred.[33] Eliot's work for Faber and Faber was less in the public eye, and it would be hard to stretch the definition of literary criticism to include the countless 'blurbs' that he wrote for the firm. Nevertheless, Faber's poetry list, extending from Pound and W. H. Auden to Sylvia Plath and Robert Lowell, was a noteworthy and lasting achievement. The *Criterion* struck an awkward balance between the literary avant-garde and the supposed interests of the general reading public. The first number included *The Waste Land* and Valéry Larbaud's authoritative exposition of Joyce's *Ulysses*, but began (as Eliot later recalled) with a contribution from that 'genial *doyen* of English letters, George Saintsbury'.[34] In 1924 Eliot began a regular editorial commentary, signed 'Crites', with a recommendation of T. E. Hulme as the 'forerunner of a new attitude of mind, if the twentieth century is to have a mind of its own'.[35] His 1926 manifesto, 'The Idea of a Literary Review', suggested that a review should have a 'tendency' rather than a 'programme' – 'Of messianic literature we have sufficient'.[36] Eliot at this time listed his intellectual heroes as

Hulme, Lewis, Charles Maurras, Julien Benda, Jacques Maritain and Irving Babbitt. The *Criterion* endorsed classicism, authority and the idea of order against the Fabian and liberal views of such writers as Shaw, Wells, and Bertrand Russell. In one attempt to attract new subscribers Eliot explained that it was its pure Toryism that would appeal to the younger generation.[37] However, other developments were to follow: Eliot became a practising Christian, while after 1930 the intellectual young turned, by and large, to Communism. The *Criterion* managed to avoid any Fascist taint, and gave much space to pro- and anti-Marxist debate, but it ceased to be a literary review of any real consequence. It could sustain neither the avant-garde experimental fervour of the magazine *transition*, (published in Paris), nor the critical rigour of such rivals and imitators as Edgell Rickword's *Calendar of Modern Letters* (1924–7) and F. R. and Q. D. Leavis's *Scrutiny*. In the end, it drifted; the 'new attitude of mind' became a thing of the past, at worst no more than a curiosity.

In 1932 Eliot's *Selected Essays* were published, and from that time he was a public celebrity, much in demand to grace academic occasions and give lectures. *For Lancelot Andrewes: Essays on Style and Order* (1928), with its declaration of faith and essays on the preachers Andrewes and Bramhall, had suggested a rather less literary Eliot; nevertheless, in the following years he completed his studies of Elizabethan dramatists, and wrote memorably on Baudelaire, Tennyson and Dante. His Charles Eliot Norton lectures at Harvard, published as *The Use of Poetry and the Use of Criticism* (1933), were the first of a series of strained and unhappy performances. *The Use of Poetry* begins with some extraordinarily acute perceptions about the relationship of criticism to poetry. Eliot announces that he will examine the history of criticism as a 'process of readjustment between poetry and the world in and for which it is produced', but despite the chronological progression this aim is never fulfilled, and the book becomes increasingly scrappy. Eliot's emotions were more engaged by his next venture, *After Strange Gods: A Primer of Modern Heresy* (1934), the Page-Barbour lectures given at the University of Virginia in 1933, and a work that he never allowed to be reprinted. Faced with a society 'worm-eaten with Liberalism', he speaks of the 'Forces of Evil' in contemporary literature and seems ready to abandon criticism and intelligence altogether. 'In our time, controversy seems to me, on really fundamental matters, to be futile', he wrote in his preface; the intellectual's task was not to acquire a tradition, but to maintain an orthodoxy. (Joyce was offered as an example of Orthodoxy, and D. H. Lawrence of Heresy, so that the literary-critical argument had been boiled down to one between a lapsed Catholic and a lapsed Protestant.)

It is tempting to say that in *After Strange Gods* we glimpse a facet of the 'real' Eliot, a stiff-necked, intolerant intellectual evangelist who had for twenty years been speaking of discipline, classicism and order and now meant to spell out these things in plain language. Much the most interesting aspect of the book is its adumbration of the themes of his later sociological works, *The Idea of a Christian Society* (1939) and *Notes towards the Definition of Culture* (1948). These are profoundly anti-utopian treatises; seldom can a desirable society have been sketched with so many qualifications and so little conviction or enthusiasm. 'A wholly Christian society might be a society for the most part on a low level; . . . It would require constant reform', intones Eliot in *The Idea of a Christian Society*. His prose here, and in the *Notes*, is pontifical in the extreme: 'It is my contention that', 'I should not like to have the reader supposing that', 'We can assert with some confidence that', 'it will not, I think, be disputed that', are typical of his endless opening gambits. Valuable points are certainly made, and Eliot, particularly in *Notes*, makes crucial allowances for pluralism, diversity, and 'friction' within cultures. On the central ideas of 'culture' and a 'Christian society', however, he is curiously evasive. He thinks all round these concepts, without ever confronting them head-on. Perhaps that is because he had done so baldly and tersely – and, it turned out, unacceptably – in *After Strange Gods*. It was in the latter book that he set out to revoke the theory of 'Tradition and the Individual Talent', describing a tradition in terms which must have been unrecognisable to readers of *The Sacred Wood* or the 1932 *Selected Essays*: 'What I mean by tradition involves all those habitual actions, habits and customs, from the most significant religious rite to our conventional way of greeting a stranger, which represent the blood kinship of "the same people living in the same place"'. He then sketches out the qualities of a good society as stability, locality, homogeneity of population, 'unity of religious background' (with an attack on the Jews), a balance of city and country, and narrow-mindedness if not bigotry ('a spirit of excessive tolerance is to be deprecated').[38] These points may have been tailor-made for his audience of Southerners, but they represent a permanent aspect of his thought. What is most striking is their utter negation of the erudite, rootless, cosmopolitan, expatriate life that he himself had led, and of his own position as an innovating artist and intellectual leader.

One explanation for this apparent contradiction is that Eliot firmly believed that his own age was one of cultural decline, and came to believe that the decline was irreversible,[39] so that his own life might well be taken as evidence for it. In *Notes towards the Definition of Culture*, however, he wrote of the inevitability of a stratified society, in which local culture would be nourished by the lower classes while the intellectuals would cultivate the higher ideas of Christian universality and European unity. (*Notes* is also the book in which he most blatantly hides behind the façade of his assumed 'English' identity.) His developed model of culture, then, reinstates the notion of the 'mind of Europe' which had been so important in 'Tradition and the Individual Talent', and which was one of the most honourable features of the *Criterion*. Eliot speaking on European culture in his later years sounds more and more like Matthew Arnold. 'We are all, so far as we inherit the civilization of Europe, still citizens of the Roman Empire', he pronounced in 'Virgil and the Christian World' (1951); but this was not the Empire of governors and legionaries, but 'something greater... which exists because Virgil imagined it'. In spiritual matters Europe was still one great confederation. But for Eliot this had two practical consequences, unforeseeable in Arnold's day. Despite the catastrophe of two world wars, he lived long enough to be able to cautiously anticipate Christian ecumenicalism, and to express his 'personal bias' in favour of Britain's joining the European Community.[40]

In his early criticism, Eliot is often at his most incisive when he is deliberately reworking and revising the terminology inherited from his predecessors: 'wit' from Johnson and Pope, 'feeling' and 'emotion' from Wordsworth, 'fancy' and 'imagination' from Coleridge, 'critical' and 'creative' from Arnold, 'sensibility' from Hulme, and so on. If much of his later criticism seems dull and verbose, it is partly because he seems obsessed with revising and restating his own pronouncements. Sometimes the results are almost comically bland. He had defined the function of criticism, in the 1923 essay of that title, as 'the elucidation of works of art and the correction of taste'; in his lectures on 'The Aims of Education' (1950), struck by the pomposity of this now classic formulation, he amended it to '[the promotion of] the understanding and enjoyment of literature'. His audience at the University of Chicago no doubt appreciated the magnanimity of this. Meeting Mr Eliot was no longer unpleasant.

Once upon a time, we might say, the only method had been to be very intelligent; the later Eliot, for much of the time, got by without being very intelligent at all. This is almost, but not quite, as damning as it sounds. What did Eliot mean by intelligence, and was it a quality he may have come to feel that he had pitched too highly? It was Charles Maurras, the founder of the right-wing Action Française, who converted 'intelligence' into a rallying-cry in his book *L'Avenir de l'intelligence* (1905), which Eliot bought in 1911. Maurras called for the intelligentsia to take a stand against the spread of materialism. He also championed Dante as the supreme exponent of 'latin culture'.[41] Eliot was deeply influenced by Maurras, as well as by T. E. Hulme, but their stance of bullying rationalism had much less appeal for him once he had converted to Christianity. In 'Religion and Literature' (1935) he wrote that 'the whole of modern literature is corrupted by what I call Secularism, . . . it is simply unaware of, simply cannot understand the meaning of, the primacy of the supernatural over the natural life'.[42] It is hard to see how 'intelligence' would help there. Perhaps this accounts for the ferocity with which, in *The Use of Poetry*, he demolishes Arnold's definition of poetry as a 'criticism of life':

> At the bottom of the abyss is what few ever see, and what those cannot bear to look at for long; and it is not a 'criticism of life.' If we mean life as a whole – not that Arnold ever saw life as a whole – from top to bottom, can anything that we can say of it ultimately, of that awful mystery, be called criticism? We bring back very little from our rare descents, and that is not criticism.

'Human kind cannot bear very much reality' – again, it is not 'intelligence' that is called for. In a very different context, it was Eliot who famously said, of the 'critical genius' of Henry James, that he 'had a mind so fine that no idea could violate it.'[43] There is something a little conventional in that remark – it is not from one of the essays that Eliot himself reprinted – but the implication is that intelligence at its best takes us beyond the concerns of the mere intellect, an implication that Eliot might more easily have attached to Flaubert (who is despite himself a more religious artist) than to James. Flaubert, at any rate, figures in a deeply disturbing passage in Eliot's 'Andrew Marvell':

> Gray and Collins were masters, but they had lost that hold on human values, that firm grasp of human experience, which is a formidable achievement of the Elizabethan and Jacobean poets. This wisdom, cynical perhaps but untired (in Shakespeare, a terrifying clairvoyance), leads toward, and is only completed by, the religious comprehension; it leads to the point of the *Ainsi tout leur a craqué dans la main* of Bouvard and Pécuchet.

That is Eliot himself looking into the abyss, as at certain moments in *The Waste Land*. One is reminded of the furious nihilism of the passage from *The Revenger's Tragedy* ('Does the silkworm expend her yellow labours / For thee? . . .') which, at this period, he so often quoted as an illustration of English verse at its most vital. The 'religious comprehension' is needed because the literature that Eliot admires most shows that human experience and human values have no permanent foundation; they crumble in one's grasp. Of *Ulysses* and *Tarr* he had written that 'Both are terrifying. That is the test of a new work of art.'[44] Following the 'roots that clutch' (where they exist) in a work of art we reach, it seems, a cave or empty space beneath the subsoil; perhaps an inferno.

At the intellectual level, Eliot's view of the limitations of mental perception should be related to his study of the philosopher F. H. Bradley, on whom he completed a doctoral thesis. In criticism, his celebration of some writers who might be described as nihilists (Webster, Tourneur, perhaps Baudelaire) is complemented by his fascination with two poets who do represent the 'religious comprehension', Blake and Dante. These poets are the subject of the last two essays in *The Sacred Wood*. In Blake Eliot found an illustration of the 'eternal struggle of art against education'; Blake was 'terrifying' because he viewed the world nakedly, without intellectual baggage of any kind. Blake's poetry, however, was almost destroyed by the 'Puritan thinness' of the version of Christian mythology that he inherited. He had to construct an all-but-impenetrable mythology for himself. Blake, however, 'presents only the essential, only, in fact, what can be presented, and need not be explained'; and this, in Eliot's eyes, allies him to Dante, who is the greatest Christian poet.

Eliot in *The Sacred Wood* describes Dante's achievement by means of visual metaphors. He 'succeeded in dealing with his philosophy, not as a theory . . . or as his own comment or reflection, but in terms of something *perceived*'. If we cannot do what he did, it is because 'our vision is comparatively restricted'. This makes the point that poetry is not, as Eliot's contemporary I. A. Richards considered, any form of 'pseudo-statement'; it is a mode of cognition, the thing itself. But Dante, who gazed unerringly on hell and purgatory, seems too composed, too exalted a visionary to serve as a model for the modern poet, for whom 'clairvoyance' is terrifying and comes, if it comes, in fits and starts. In 'The Metaphysical Poets' Eliot ridicules the suggestion that the poet should look into his heart; he must look into the 'cerebral cortex, the nervous system, and the digestive tracts'. This may be a modern equivalent of the soothsayer's inspection of entrails, and Eliot at least in his later criticism was prepared to admit that the poet was a kind of prophet.[45] But it is very far from Dante's sublimity. Dante, we may say, wrote in the full light of a Christian society; Eliot's criticism, both when it is prescribing and exemplifying intelligence and when it is undermining the intelligence, is an attempt to aid the modern poet poking around among the primitive horrors in his heart of darkness. Here it rejoins the sources of his own poetry. Among the English poet-critics, Arnold and Coleridge elaborated a critical outlook once their finest poetry was behind them. Each had, in Eliot's words, 'uttered something which he does not wholly understand'[46] and then sought to understand and perhaps to correct it. Eliot was equally conscious that his poetry arose from sources that he did not understand, but *The Sacred Wood* and the 1921 essays precede and accompany *The Waste Land*, while the tortuous, sometimes self-thwarting criticism and social theory of the 1930s precedes and accompanies *Four Quartets*. Eliot's best criticism will hardly lose its intellectual and imaginative appeal while he continues to command our attention through his poetry.

Poetry and the Age (1920–60)

Eliot had written in 'Tradition and the Individual Talent' that 'Honest criticism and sensitive appreciation is directed not upon the poet but upon the poetry'. In the 1920s there was a sustained attempt to bring more resources to bear on the study of poetry, which was itself seen to have become more difficult and more demanding. Several of the New Critics, including William Empson, John Crowe Ransom, Allen Tate, and Robert Penn Warren, were themselves accomplished poets in the modernist manner. What was perhaps the first detailed modern semantic analysis of an individual short poem (Shakespeare's Sonnet 129) was written by two professional poets, Robert Graves and Laura Riding, in their *A Survey of Modernist Poetry* (1928). Starting from the proposition that there was a technique of poetry peculiarly appropriate to the modern world, New Criticism set out to show that this entailed both a new version of literary history, and a method of verbal analysis which could be applied to the poetry of any period.

Since the 1890s, the principal vehicles of avant-garde writing had been the 'little magazines', which combined an acknowledgement of their own specialised and marginal status with an attitude varying from indifference to outright hostility toward the bourgeois public. Probably the scope, design and readership of the little magazines influenced the widespread conception of the modernist poem (and, to a lesser extent, the modernist prose piece) as a short work, an epitome of concentrated indirect expression, communicating by hints and allusions rather than by direct statement. In the magazine format, the short poem would invariably be surrounded by a good deal of white space. These were the 'specimens' that New Critics then subjected to clinical analysis, a proceeding which (again, thanks to the brevity and indirectness of the poem) had first been developed for use in the classroom.

The dissemination of the new analytic method and of the canon of modernist poetry can hardly be separated. Graves and Riding's influential *Survey* combined its examination of a Shakespeare sonnet with accounts of the poetry of Hopkins (whose late-Victorian poems had first appeared in Robert Bridges' edition of 1918), T. S. Eliot, Ezra Pound, John Crowe Ransom, e.e. cummings, Marianne Moore, and some others. F. R. Leavis's *New Bearings in English Poetry* (1932) had main chapters devoted to Eliot, Pound and Hopkins, with important subsidiary sections on W. B. Yeats and William Empson; W. H. Auden was the most notable absentee from the book, and Ronald Bottrall its most ill-judged inclusion. Among the American New Critics, R. P. Blackmur, Cleanth Brooks, Allen Tate and Yvor Winters all produced major critical books in the late 1930s on contemporary American poetry. Typically they set off Eliot and Pound against Robert Frost, Hart Crane, William Carlos Williams and (most of all) Wallace Stevens, as well as cummings and Moore.

I. A. Richards

I. A. Richards, the acknowledged pioneer of 'practical criticism' as a classroom technique, also played his part in shaping the modernist canon; by the end of 1926 he had written on Eliot, Hopkins, Hardy, Yeats, Lawrence and de la Mare. But above all Richards was the prototype of a new kind of philosopher–critic. His example is as pertinent to the current age of interpretation and theory as it was to his New-Critical successors. His great influence was due to his early work, though as a critic he had reversed most of his initial positions by the time he reached the end of a long intellectual odyssey. Richards's philosophy of language remained more consistent, as did his ideological views which were deeply opposed to those of most of his New-Critical followers. For Richards was a Wellsian rationalist who saw poetry as a useful ally in the struggle for a unified, technologically based and scientifically educated world community. His early work claimed as its point of view that of the 'men of the future' and even the 'men of A.D. 3000';[1]

later he wrote movingly about the global population problem, and campaigned for the adoption of Basic English (the invention of his friend and one-time collaborator C. K. Ogden) as an auxiliary world language.

Richards's emergence as a literary critic was due to the happy accident which made him the virtual founder of the English Faculty at Cambridge. (Around 1920, as he later recalled, he sounded out T. S. Eliot about joining him at Cambridge. Eliot, who had already refused a philosophy lectureship at Harvard, turned him down, preferring to stay in literary London.) Richards's pupils at Cambridge in the 1920s included both William Empson (whose work will be considered in Chapter 6) and F. R. Leavis, who attended his lectures, including the famous 'Practical Criticism' series. During these years Richards gave the discipline of academic literary criticism its modern identity, as well as many of its best-known terms and concepts. Not only such workhorses as *practical criticism, analysis* and *response* but the more recent terminology of *critical theory, interpretation, signs* and *discourse* features prominently in his writings.

Richards both reinforced and reinterpreted the revolutionary pretensions of modernist literature. In *Science and Poetry* (1926) he declared that 'some strange change has befallen man in this generation'. This change – the substitution of the scientific for the 'magical' world-view – had its origins in the seventeenth century, but had only been finally accomplished in the last seventy years. In the modern secular world, the art of all previous ages and cultures could for the first time communicate its meanings to any qualified reader or spectator; but these meanings, Richards added, were not quite the original meanings. Art was only accessible to the modern audience, as it were, in translation.

His first (collaborative) book, *The Foundations of Aesthetics* (1922), is based on a flamboyantly universal criterion of art. Though the majority of the literary quotations in the text are from English writers, its visual references are to ancient Egyptian, Indian, Chinese and African materials. The epigraph states the Confucian doctrine of mental equilibrium and harmony, which was to form a lifelong touchstone for Richards. Unlike *The Foundations of Aesthetics* his *Principles of Literary Criticism* (1924) has no illustrations, though it includes chapters on painting, sculpture and music asserting that the same critical principles apply to all the arts. These principles are psychological. The poem or work of art produces a complex emotional response, which can be characterised in the psychological and neurological vocabulary of 'attitudes', 'impulses' and 'stimuli', and whose path through the brain and nervous system can be charted with the aid of a diagram. The end-product, if the poem is successful, is a state of equilibrium. In *The Foundations of Aesthetics* the state of equilibrium is presented as if it were a cognitive experience, one which 'brings into play all our faculties', and through which the 'full richness and complexity of our environment [can] be realised'.[2] However, in *The Meaning of Meaning* (1923) Ogden and Richards proposed to distinguish between 'emotional' and 'referential' uses of language in such a way as to eliminate the cognitive function of poetry and art.

The Meaning of Meaning, subtitled 'A Study of the Influence of Language upon Thought and of the Science of Symbolism', was a pioneering attempt to bring an empirical scientific rigour to bear on the different uses of the concept of meaning. Sometimes the rhetoric of scientificity went to the authors' heads, and it is hard not to see their categorisation of poetry as an example of the 'symbolic or emotive' uses of language as being inherently dismissive and reductive. (The book carries an appendix by the anthropologist Bronislaw Malinowski which argues that primitive languages, too, are emotive and not scientific in nature.) From a utilitarian standpoint it would seem that poetry, the embodiment of the magical world-view *par excellence*, had been superannuated by the scientific and referential use of language and had lost its function. Nevertheless, Richards in the 1920s asserted *both* that poetry consisted of 'pseudo-statements' rather than of statements serving a cognitive intent, and that – far from being doomed to disappear, as one might have expected – it was supremely important for the modern world. Echoing Matthew Arnold, *Science and Poetry* went so far as to announce that poetry was 'capable of saving us'.

Richards's early literary-critical trilogy – *Science and Poetry, Principles of Literary Criticism*, and *Practical Criticism* (1929) – combines a messianic doctrine with a disinfected, no-nonsense clinical manner. In *Principles* the emergent science of criticism is freed from long-established superstitions such as the 'Revelation Doctrines' of poetry and the theories of what Richards labels the 'Phantom Aesthetic State'. The opening chapter, 'The Chaos of Critical Theories', is meant to clear out the clutter of the past. Richards enters in his white coat to expound a form of experimental psychology in which poetic value, measured in terms of the degree of emotional equilibrium it produces, could ideally be decided by electro-encephalograph. *Science and Poetry* likewise begins by asserting that, amid the 'wild speculations natural in pre-scientific enquiry', the actual nature of poetry has been lost sight of.[3] Richards then equates poetry with the 'poetic experience', which falls within the same framework as any other sort of experience; it takes time, say 'ten minutes of a person's life'. At no point, however, does Richards directly compare poetry and the sensation of equilibrium it produces with other possible ways of spending ten minutes of one's life; instead, the superiority of the poetic experience, and hence the culturally privileged status of writing and reading, are asserted in the very moment of seeming to question them. There is much in these two books to justify Richards's dismissal as something of a quack theorist, and, according to G. S. Fraser, their author was eventually to describe *Principles of Literary Criticism* as a 'sermon disguised in the fashionable scientific language of its time'.[4]

Practical Criticism, the third volume of the trilogy, is also a kind of sermon, though it attests much more directly than its predecessors to Richards's brilliance and inventiveness as a teacher. First he distributed sheets of anonymous and untitled poems to his audience, who were invited to think of themselves as taking part in a laboratory experiment. He then collected the audience's written responses (the 'protocols') which, he proceeded to show, were remarkable for their range of disagreement, as well as for their frequent inaccuracy and ineptitude. The book proceeds by discussing the protocols poem by poem, and finally unveils a technique of analysis which would, supposedly, reduce disagreement and eliminate the worst deficiencies in reading. Literary criticism, here, was magisterially linked to a broader educational project – the general improvement of reading and communication – which Richards was to pursue in two later books, *Interpretation in Teaching* (1938) and *How to Read a Page* (1942), devoted to the comprehension of prose passages. His aim was to conduct an 'extensive piece of natural history', a 'vast collective *clinical* study of the aberrations of average intelligence'.[5] Increasingly such work belonged to general education rather than to literary criticism, yet its plausibility evidently rested on his view of the nature of language, including poetic language, as a vehicle for the communication of beliefs and attitudes.

Richards's starting-point is the urgency of global communication; the catastrophe of the First World War had shown that we must understand one another or destroy ourselves. The practical means of communication in the modern world was a scientific use of language, producing unambiguous and empirically verifiable statements. But the commitment to language that was unambiguous and certifiable had itself been a contributory cause of the modern crisis. There had been, he wrote in *Science and Poetry*, a 'collapse of beliefs' which entailed 'psychological as well as . . . economic, social and political dangers'. Countless 'pseudo-statements', which had served for centuries, could no longer be believed, and the scientific knowledge which had replaced them, though capable of transforming human life, was 'not of a kind upon which an equally fine organization of the mind can be based'. Poetry, the supreme instance of emotive language, was the guardian of the 'supra-scientific myths' needed to preserve moral order and mental sanity. This relic of the old world was needed to redress the balance of the new.

In calling upon poetry to fill the emotional vacuum left by scientific advance Richards was following in the nineteenth-century tradition culminating in Mill and Arnold. The difference was that Richards seemed intent on denying the mythic potency of art in the very act of reasserting it. He described *Practical Criticism* as 'in part . . . the record of a piece of field-work in comparative ideology', but the 'arduous discipline' of analysis which he recommends at the end of the book is meant to transform the critical reading of poetry from an ideological activity into a science.[6] As a science, critical reading possesses its own means of determining error and of measuring the correct or appropriate response to linguistic stimuli, however emotive and ambiguous these stimuli may be. The scientific world-view, in other words, dictates not only the proper handling of referential statements but of emotive uses of language, such as poetry, as well.

Richards's belief that in the modern world our way of reading poetry – all poetry – has necessarily changed does not entail a historical approach to reading. Instead, his combination of scientific semantics and psychological aesthetics led him to view reading as an educational problem which could be solved by inducing the right sort of technical competence. This had the advantage of tidying up the study of language – which he saw, after all, as a prelude to 'linguistic engineering' for the good of the world[7] – but it led to his lifelong and inconclusive engagement with the problem of belief in poetry. An unsympathetic critic of Richards's version of historical determinism ('When attitudes are changing neither criticism nor poetry remains stationary', he had written in *Science and Poetry*[8]) could, indeed, claim that his attempts to aid linguistic comprehension were actually designed to reduce this comprehension. Few if any traditional poets can have regarded the poetic endorsement of Christian belief as a mode of 'pseudo-statement', and, as for modern poets, when Richards praised Eliot in *The Waste Land* for 'effecting a complete severance between his poetry and all beliefs', Eliot denied that this was so.[9]

But what actually happens to our beliefs when we confront a work of art? Each volume in the early trilogy has a chapter worrying away at this question. The short answer is that nothing ought to happen, since belief for the modern rationalist is an intellectual not an emotional matter. All that the work of art does is to tone up our mental organisation somewhat. In *Practical Criticism* and in a 1930 essay on 'Belief' he faced up to the problem that readers would often report that their response to devotional poetry was affected by their own religious belief, though other readers would deny this. 'The presence of the belief in the poet,' he wrote, 'seems to have been a condition of the poem. Is its presence in the reader equally a condition for successful reading – for full understanding?'[10] Either answer gave rise to considerable difficulties. Richards's invariable solution was to invoke a category of 'emotive belief' or 'imaginative assent'.[11] Emotive belief, he wrote in *Principles*, entails a 'provisional acceptance' of the doctrines set out in the poem, 'made for the sake of the "imaginative experience" which [it makes] possible'. The difference between such provisional acceptances and scientific beliefs was 'not one of degree but of kind'.[12] This could hardly be squared with a pragmatist or Popperian view of scientific belief, and in his extended discussion of 'Doctrine in Poetry' in *Practical Criticism* one senses a note of increasing desperation. It is here that he proposes a 'technique or ritual for heightening sincerity', in which the principal concerns of modern scientific-materialist cosmology are offered as a measuring-rod for the adequacy of the emotional belief to which the poem invites our assent. Having listed the main features of the materialist universe, he then recommends the following:

> Taking these not as targets for doctrine, but as the most incomprehensible and inexhaustible objects for meditation, while their reverberation lasts pass the poem through the mind, silently reciting it as slowly as it allows. Whether what it can stir in us is important or not to us will perhaps show itself then.

To the extent that it culminates in this secular spiritual exercise, the ideological basis of *Practical Criticism* is very transparent, as many of its earliest readers saw. What is perhaps equally interesting is the extent to which Richards's method presupposes the ideal literary object to be the short poem. His principal example of a 'doctrinal' work is one of Donne's Holy Sonnets. Such a poem's very brevity may contribute to the notion that reading it (or, rather, reading it *correctly*) has no lasting effects on our belief-systems.

When Richards spoke of the 'imaginative assent' that readers give to a poet's beliefs he was relying on a rather loose concept of imagination. In *Principles of Literary Criticism* he had enumerated six different senses of the term, one of which was the 'sympath-

etic reproducing of other people's states of mind'. The context
was a discussion of imagination as a property of the poem. The
poetic language, in its turn, sparked off 'imagery' in the reader's
mind; this might either be 'tied imagery', guided and shaped by
the poetic stimulus, or 'free imagery' which Richards dismissed
as the product of personal associations irrelevant to the aesthetic
response. The elimination of 'free imagery' was essential to the
discipline of reading as Richards conceived it; over-imaginative
reading, as practised by Pater and his successors, was bad reading.
Nevertheless, Richards restored imagination to a central place in
the poetic process (not the reading process) in *Coleridge on Imagination* (1934), a daring attempt to retrieve the Coleridgian theory
for modern poetics by separating imagination as a psychological
and linguistic technique from its supposed metaphysical origins.
The presence of imagination in poetry was to be attested not by
its effects of beauty or sublimity but by the phenomenon of 'verbal
interaction', or the mutual modification of meanings, which could
be revealed by semantic analysis. In *The Philosophy of Rhetoric*
(1936) he renamed this process as the 'interinanimation' of words.

According to Richards, metaphor is the central device of interactive poetic language. The analysis of metaphor rests on the division
between 'tenor' and 'vehicle'– in effect, the 'thought' expressed
by the figure and the language used to convey it – and it reveals
the semantic complexity arising from the relations between tenor
and vehicle. In a 1955 essay, Richards contrasted the fluidity of
poetic meanings with the 'assertorial clip' fixed upon them in scientific and factual discourse. 'In fluid language', he wrote, 'a great
many very precise meanings may be free to dispose themselves
in a multiplicity of diverse ways.'[13] The view that poetic language
combines complexity with precision of meaning – and that, therefore, the more vigilant and expert its readers, the less their assess-
ments of the poem should diverge – is, as we have seen,
fundamental to Richards's thought. What was changing in his outlook, however, had been prefigured in a small way by the substitution of 'interinanimation' for 'verbal interaction' in the mid-1930s.
It was as if poetic language, and ultimately poetry itself, was beginning to rise from the dissecting slab and take on a life of its own.

By the time that Richards returned to literary criticism after
many years in which his main concern was the theory and practice
of language teaching, there was some adroit intellectual manoeuvr-
ing to be done. The revival of structural linguistics in the 1950s
and 1960s naturally attracted his attention, and in essays on Roman
Jakobson's work he hailed the advent of a potential new science
of literary criticism, though with far more hesitations and qualifica-

Modernists and New Critics 241

tions than had accompanied his earlier enthusiasm for psychological aesthetics.[14] His commitment to Basic English had also cooled a little in his old age. 'Basic' was meant to reduce the quantity of global misunderstanding produced by the fluidity of language in contexts other than the poetic; and Richards recommended the exercise of translating from standard English into a drastically simplified vocabulary as a means of clarifying thought. In the early 1950s he and his co-workers had produced a series of modern-language primers adopting the methods of Basic for second-language learners. Nevertheless, he came to reject what he called the 'vulgar packaging view' of language (as a process of encoding and decoding information) put forward by the communications theorists. In a new edition of *Science and Poetry*, now retitled *Poetries and Sciences* (1970), he disowned his old view of a poem as a 'choice piece of experience': 'The poem knows more than we do about itself, and part of its business is to make us feel so'. In the original *Science and Poetry* he had asserted that the poet's command of language entailed 'The Command of Life'; now it was the poem's (not the poet's, or the reader's) tasks and responsibilities that he was choosing to stress.[15]

Finally – and, I believe, decisively – Richards came back to a species of 'Revelation Theory', the notion of poems not as bits of linguistic machinery but as scriptures, or as expressions of the prophetic imagination, which he had contemptuously rejected in his youth. In 1933, writing of D. H. Lawrence's poetry, he had observed that 'its reader cannot escape the problem of belief'.[16] That ought to have meant that Lawrence's poetry was bad poetry, unworthy of the new scientific age, though Lawrence was only the latest representative of the Protestant tradition of Milton, Wordsworth, and the Tennyson of *In Memoriam*, all of whom are visibly diminished by a theory which reduces the poetic domain to one of 'pseudo-statements'. Milton had set out to justify the ways of God to men, and Richards too had once invoked the language of missionary Protestantism to declare that poetry was 'capable of saving us'. It was not until his last major book *Beyond* (1974) that he faced up to the possibility that a culture is shaped by the beliefs of its writers, at a level that is more or less impervious to the modern intellectual's dismissal of these beliefs as comforting or spiritually enriching fictions. Turning from the short poem to such sacred epics as the Book of Job and the *Divine Comedy*, he now flatly refused the option of 'imaginative assent' leading to mental equilibrium which he had earlier favoured. A vehement imaginative dissent was the outcome of his reading.

Beyond, which is probably the least known of Richards's works, is the occasion of a truly awesome volte-face. The *Divine Comedy*, he now wrote, was an answer to 'one of the most important questions any mind must raise', and its answer was weighted with institutional authority: 'it is the only great poem still tied to an organized, active, and self-defensive system of religious teaching'.[17] In his early writings, he had scarcely considered the ideological role played by specific poetic statements of belief to be relevant to literary criticism. *Beyond*, however, invokes the scriptural status and doctrinal implications of Dante and the Book of Job in order to argue that, in the interests of human survival, we must reject their teaching. In place of their endorsement of Christian humility and submission to arbitrary power Richards pleaded the cause of 'Luciferian co-operation', the process of argument and elucidation of the nature of power initiated by Satan's questioning of divine authority. Richards compares his own rejection of the Christian epics to the Plato of the *Republic*, expelling Homer and his successors from the ideal state; though by way of tribute to Dante's poetic powers he states his objections to the doctrines of the *Divine Comedy* not merely in critical prose but in three cantos of *terza rima*. As a poem, the *Divine Comedy* was 'autonomous, self-governing', but its lessons, like those of the Bible, had for many been 'extraordinarily corruptive lessons'.[18]

Earlier Richards would have argued that these founding texts of Western culture had lost their power to do harm; now, less confident of the antiseptic power of modern reading methods, he argued that, if poetry was to save humanity, then new vital scriptures had to be found. *Beyond* ends with an enthusiastic endorsement of Shelley's vision in *Prometheus Unbound* and of Blake's vision in *Jerusalem*, concluding with a quotation from Blake and the comment that 'The last line, well understood, could be our key to Paradise'. Should all this be attributed – as doubtless some readers have done – to senile aberration, to the last, peevish throw of a theorist who all his life had been an inveterate juggler with ideas?[19] Certainly *Beyond*, as a militant and iconoclastic argument for world peace and mutual understanding, is no more free of self-contradictions than any of Richards's preceding books. Nevertheless, his attraction towards Eastern religions and towards alternatives to the Christian view of the good life had long been evident. *Mencius on the Mind* (1932) was a book-length attempt to appropriate the Confucian doctrines. Beginning with an exploration of Confucian 'equilibrium' as a psychological state, Richards had ended his career with an outspoken attack on the Christian tradition's fumbling attempts to imagine the heavenly.

He had remarked how often religions and philosophies present

us with self-contradictions as their central secrets.[20] Profound
insight or glib attempt at self-justification? Richards's long career
spent pondering the 'mystery of communication' has more than
its share of both these things. The growing eccentricity of his later
writing, its loss of lucidity and resort to idiosyncratic devices such
as the 'specialized quotation marks', testify to his sense of the loss
of the audience he had once so easily commanded. Richards is
certainly not a great English critic, though he has a strong claim
to be considered (for better or worse) as this century's paradigmatic
literary theorist. His intellectual radicalism and impatience with
narrowly literary concerns suggest that he has closer affinities with
the 'scientific schoolmen' to be discussed in the next chapter than
with the other New Critics. We can honour the integrity and
breadth of his ambitions, and his refusal after the 1920s to be confined within the band of professional exegetes – a 'very small special
crew'[21] – whose techniques he had done so much to pioneer. Taken
as a whole, however, his brave attempts to tackle the problems
of mutual understanding leave one with a sense of puzzlement.
He continues to be misunderstood.

Leavis and the Southern Agrarians

'*I* am not a moral hero,' Richards is once reported to have confessed
to F. R. Leavis.[22] Whatever we make of this, F. R. Leavis undoubtedly was a moral hero. Together with the quarterly journal *Scrutiny* which he edited from 1932 to 1953, Leavis came to symbolise
the literary-critical function in a Britain where literature was felt
to be by definition unpopular, and educated culture was no longer
seen as naturally leading public taste. Leavis's work, which began
as a militant assault on the cultural establishment, ended by secur-
ing widespread acceptance – at least in universities and schools
– though this did not prevent its author from pursuing his role
as a prophet and outcast to the end of his life. Criticism was for
him a means of bearing witness, of affirming the necessity for intelligence, creativity and compassion, and condemning the cultural disintegration that he saw around him. As a lifelong university teacher,
who nevertheless remained marginalised within the profession, he
was among the first modern thinkers to perceive that the university
had become not the home of unquestioned values but itself a prime
theatre of cultural conflict. Scorning academic quietism, he remained a mental warrior, one of whose last books had the Blakean
title *Nor Shall My Sword*.

Though 'Leavisism' was a peculiarly British phenomenon, nurtured in the University of Cambridge, American New Criticism

also set out with a socially committed, fighting stance. The ideological parallels between the two movements have, in fact, received less attention than one might have expected. In 1922 John Crowe Ransom, Allen Tate and five others describing themselves as 'amateurs of poetry living in Nashville, Tennessee' founded *The Fugitive*, a magazine devoted to poetry and criticism.[23] *The Fugitive* was a little magazine in the tradition of Harriet Monroe's *Poetry* (founded in 1912) and the *Little Review* (1914–29), disclaiming the broader cultural aims of Wyndham Lewis's *Blast* and of the *Egoist*. By 1930, however, the Nashville 'fugitives' had transformed themselves into a group of political ideologues, the 'Southern Agrarians'. Two years later, *Scrutiny* emerged in England to champion the social values of 'literary criticism' against the utilitarian, capitalist and Marxist spokesmen of the new technological and industrial order.

Like Leavis and his colleagues, the Southern Agrarians saw their own time as one of cultural disintegration which could only be resisted by a spiritual revival drawing its inspiration from earlier social forms. The Agrarians' position was set out by the twelve contributors to *I'll Take My Stand: The South and the Agrarian Tradition* (1930). In the South, John Crowe Ransom argued, it was still possible to maintain a 'seasoned provincial life', a 'world made safe for the farmers' and quarantined against the forces of deracination and 'Americanization' which rampaged unchecked elsewhere. Lacking the progressivism and pioneering spirit of the rest of the United States, the backward South remained closer to the rooted life of the English provinces.[24] The Agrarians did not hesitate to spell out the conditions needed to support this reactionary idyll. Agriculture must remain labour-intensive and must enlist the maximum number of workers, while, as Robert Penn Warren argued, racial segregation would continue indefinitely. The Agrarian vision of a unified Southern culture required, in actuality, two quite separate cultures, though both black and white were (needless to say) 'rooted in the soil'.[25]

Here the figurative rootedness of which T. S. Eliot (a near-Southerner by virtue of his birth in Missouri) had so often written had been given its literal application, and indeed the Agrarians numbered Eliot among their supporters. Eliot's pronouncement in 1931 that 'agriculture is the foundation for the Good Life in any society' was, in turn, soon to be quoted and endorsed by Leavis.[26] Leavis, too, characterised the 'old ways of life' as representative of 'human normality or naturalness', while the modern industrial world was seen to be abnormal. These writers' idealisation of the feudal and slave-owning past as an antidote to the rootless present drew on a long heritage of romantic thought, whose most influential contemporary representatives Leavis alone seemed concerned to acknowledge: they were D. H. Lawrence and Oswald Spengler. Leavis's 1930 pamphlet on D. H. Lawrence incorporates a plangently Lawrentian–Spenglerian statement of the modern predicament (the quoted passages here are actually from Lawrence rather than from Spengler):

> The traditional ways of life have been destroyed by the machine, more and more does human life depart from the natural rhythms, the cultures have mingled, and the forms have dissolved into chaos, so that everywhere the serious literature of the West betrays a sense of paralysing consciousness, of a lack of direction, of momentum, of dynamic axioms.

> 'We have no future; neither for our hopes nor our aims nor our art. It has all gone grey and opaque.'

> 'Vitally, the human race is dying. It is like a great uprooted tree with its roots in the air. We must plant ourselves again in the universe.'

> This is everywhere the cry of the sensitive and aware: Spengler merely voices the general sense.

Literary criticism, nevertheless, had a cure for this condition. Lawrence, whose writings opposed Spenglerian fatalism with their 'splendid human vitality', their 'passionate sense of responsibility' and their 'creative faith', stands in Leavis's work as the harbinger of a spiritual recovery based neither on the acceptance of Christian doctrine (as in Eliot) nor on the rose-tinted backwoodsmanship of the Agrarians. Such a recovery could, so the authors of the *Scrutiny* manifesto asserted in 1932, be actively pursued in the educational field.[27] Their commitment to educational activity meant that the agrarian ideal was to be upheld not as a political programme (such as the hopeless project of *I'll Take My Stand*) but as a cherished tradition, or sacred cultural memory. While evidence for the 'organic community' of pre-industrial England could be sought in the records of rural crafts and customs such as George Sturt's *Change in the Village* (1912), its principal deposits were linguistic ones, which could be brought to light in English lessons. Only the existence of an organic community, Leavis argued, could explain the rich colloquialism of English poetic language from Shakespeare to the last rural poets such as Hardy and Edmund Blunden. The 'spirit of the language', formed when the English people were 'predominantly rural', could still be handed down from one generation to the next through the vigilant teaching and writing of poetry.[28]

Leavis's first and most manifesto-like collection of essays was entitled *For Continuity* (1933), and it is instructive that cultural continuity was much less problematic for him than it had been for the Southern Agrarians. Shakespeare's language, Leavis argued in the course of an essay on 'Joyce and "The Revolution of the Word"', was the expression of a 'genuinely national culture . . . rooted in the soil'. If modern metropolitan writing was deracinated in these terms, so inevitably was the literature of colonised regions such as Ireland or the American South. Leavis, in writing of Joyce, in fact noted the vitality of those aspects of American English affected by 'pioneering conditions, which are as unlike those of the modern city as possible'; John Crowe Ransom, on the other hand, deplored the restlessness of American life and saw in industrialism the 'contemporary form of pioneering'.[29] Though the spiritual condition of the South was (so Ransom and his associates argued) superior to the 'state of arrested adolescence'[30] found in other areas of American life, it could hardly be expected to nurture a major literature on its own. Perhaps for this reason, the Agrarians' notion of the history of English poetic language was very different from Leavis's. In a 1925 essay, Allen Tate asserted that the flowering of poetic language in the Elizabethan period was due to its cross-fertilisation with foreign vocabulary and foreign ideas; Leavis, by contrast, would stress the vital cross-currents of an essentially homogeneous culture. Tate accepted that modern poetry had broken away from the immediate vitality of the spoken language; this break in continuity, and the opportunity it offered for drawing on the resources of the whole Western tradition, could bring a new Elizabethanism to English poetry.[31] Leavis, on the contrary, argued that Eliot, Pound and Hopkins had returned to the vitality of spoken English. Tate's argument here is the standard modernist one, where Leavis's affirmation of continuity in the national life and literature turns modernism on its head; he sets up a more parochial framework for literary criticism than the Nashville 'Fugitives', though they, for their part, seem to have made little attempt to reconcile their literary and their social views. They were 'children of the new epoch' in poetics, and Southern Agrarians in politics.

Leavis on poetry

F. R. Leavis was born in 1895, some seven years after John Crowe Ransom, the oldest of the American New Critics. Leavis served as a stretcher-bearer in the First World War, but did not find his critical voice for more than a decade after he returned to Cambridge. (During the 1920s, however, he became the first major literary critic to write a PhD dissertation.) Several factors may have contributed to his emergence from what he later called a 'dazed and retarded state' around 1930: D. H. Lawrence died, I. A. Richards's interests began to turn away from practical criticism to classical Chinese philosophy and world English, and Eliot announced his religious conversion and emerged as both an antagonist of Lawrence and a commentator on Church affairs. Also, at this time, the 1929 Wall Street crash was followed by economic depression and a pervasive political uncertainty which was soon to be echoed in Leavis's rhetoric. 'Even those who would agree that there has been an overthrow of standards, that authority has disappeared, and that the currency has been debased and inflated, do not often seem to realise what the catastrophe portends', he wrote in *Mass Civilisation and Minority Culture* (1930). Ostensibly a description of the state of literary culture, these sentiments owed much of their impact to the spectacle of disastrous monetary inflation and of Britain's imminent abandonment of the Gold Standard. Leavis was more aware than most of his commentators have been that his early criticism was a form of substitute politics.[32]

Leavis's early work was criticism conceived in response to a crisis, in the prophetic manner of Carlyle, Matthew Arnold and of course D. H. Lawrence. Such titles as *New Bearings in English Poetry* (1932), *For Continuity* (1933), *Towards Standards of Criticism* (1933), *Determinations* (1934) and *Revaluation* (1936) – not to mention the journal title *Scrutiny* – tell their own story of a reassertion of authority and critical guidance. At the same time, Leavis could hardly be unaware of the belated and secondary nature of his call to arms, and this may account for some of the stridency and exaggeration to which he was prone. He began *Mass Civilisation and Minority Culture*, for example, by invoking Arnold only to lament the 'so much more desperate plight of culture to-day'; faced by the shifting landmarks, bewildering signals and disappearing boundaries of the modern world it was necessary to 'face problems of definition and formulation where Arnold could pass lightly on'. The 'living culture' which was once the possession of a whole society was now confined to the tiny minority, not of readers of books, but of readers uncorrupted by the democratisation and commercialisation of literature itself. Leavis's heaviest fire was reserved for the newspaper critics, such as Arnold Bennett, Hugh Walpole and J. B. Priestley, who undertook to interpret literary developments to a mass public. The corruption of this public by popular novelists and reviewers was outlined in *Fiction and the Reading Public* (1932) by his wife and collaborator Q. D. Leavis. The 'minority', mean-while, were to be fortified by reprinted collections of critical articles from *Scrutiny* and from Edgell Rickword's *Calendar of Modern Letters* (1924–7), presented as *Scrutiny*'s immediate predecessor. For the next generation of readers there was *Culture and Environment* (1933) by Leavis and Denys Thompson, a school textbook on the training of critical awareness and the need to find substitutes, in modern living, for the rural 'organic community'.

Not surprisingly, Leavis's hectic critical output in these years incorporates a great deal of overlap. The most influential of the various books was *New Bearings in English Poetry*, an incisive primer of the modernist poetic. *For Continuity* (which, remarkably, has never been reprinted in Great Britain) stands, however, as Leavis's central literary manifesto. Here he dissociates himself from any specific artistic movement, on the grounds that 'there is no "modernist" poetry, but only two or three modern poets'; never-theless, in assembling an essay collection covering such writers as H. G. Wells, Arnold Bennett, Theodore Dreiser, John dos Passos, D. H. Lawrence, T. S. Eliot, W. H. Auden and James Joyce he was unmistakably fulfilling his programme of 'testing, nourishing and refining the currency of contemporary culture'.[33] In addition, no less than four of the essays are ripostes to the Marxist cultural criticism which (though it was still embryonic in Britain) he had identified as his principal ideological rival.

Marxist writers had failed, in Leavis's terms, to observe the two paramount responsibilities of literary criticism – responsibility to the 'concrete' and to the 'contemporary sensibility'. By the concrete was meant a strenuously empirical devotion to practical criticism, which was advocated by Leavis in a vocabulary heavily indebted to the technical and scientific biases of I. A. Richards. Criticism was charged with improving 'one's apparatus, one's equipment, one's efficiency as a reader'. Efficiency could be attained through the 'training of sensibility'[34] by means of pedagogical exercises which Leavis outlined in *Culture and Environment* and, later, in *Education and the University* (1943). Leavis's application of Richards had the effect of endowing the university 'English School' both with the professional mystique formerly reserved for the craft of poetry and with a kind of laboratory procedure, centring on the activities of 'reading' (a far more arduous process than was commonly assumed) and 'critical analysis'. Leavis's emphasis, how-ever, was on a discipline of literary response that was at once clinical and militantly evaluative. The sensibility that was to be trained was 'contemporary sensibility'; and though this implied a sensitivity (felt to be beyond the powers and prerogatives of Marxist literary criticism) to current developments, it also meant the reverse of a catholic appreciation of new movements and new writing. Leavis's judgment that the 'contemporary sensibility' required recognition of Eliot and Lawrence as the pivotal presences in modern English literature was set down in March 1933 and maintained unswervingly for the next forty years. Without such recognitions, he held, criticism and explication both of contemporary writing and of the literary tradition was an 'impotent', 'barren' exercise.[35]

Leavis's commitments thus led him to undertake the task of redrawing what he liked to call the chart or map of English poetic history, filling out the broad outlines laid down in Eliot's 1921 essay on 'The Metaphysical Poets'; the same task would be attempted, for the American New Critics, by Cleanth Brooks's *Modern Poetry and the Tradition* (1936). Leavis's new map, accompanied by professions of filial indebtedness to Eliot (who can scarcely have relished the compliment), was made with uncompromising boldness. *New Bearings* dismissed nineteenth-century poetry on the grounds that it was 'characteristically preoccupied with the creation of a dream-world',[36] and put forward Gerard Manley Hopkins, who had died in 1889, as a major modern on a par with Eliot and Pound. 'Hopkins has no relation to Shelley or to any nineteenth-century poet', Leavis affirmed. Among the twentieth-century figures discussed, Yeats was judged to have had more damaging affiliations to the Victorians than had Hopkins, but his later verse was redeemed by 'the equivalent of certain seventeenth-century qualities'; here one sees the tentative categories of Eliot's early essays hardening into unquestioned dogmas. In *Revaluation* Leavis startlingly announced Milton's 'dislodgement' from the tradition; thanks to Eliot's poetic achievement, it was the metaphysical 'line of wit' rather than the Miltonic grand style which now stood both as a model for practising poets and as the epitome of English poetic achievement. The 'concrete' analyses in Leavis's two books were forcefully set out and served a double purpose, that of expounding a way of reading difficult poetry and of affirming the qualities of poetic language that Leavis admired.

So far Leavis had followed in the footsteps of his master T. S. Eliot, but now he was challenged to justify his admirations on general, philosophical grounds. The author of the challenge, the Czech-American scholar René Wellek, invited Leavis to describe his ideal of poetry, his '"norm" with which you measure every poet'; and, in case Leavis would not do this, Wellek did it for him.[37] Leavis, who was already committed to resisting any abstract formulation of his poetic creed, responded by treating his difference with Wellek as a mere demarcation dispute, arising from a demand for philosophical clarity which, addressed to a literary critic, was simply inappropriate. A significant feature of this debate is that Leavis had never hesitated to employ a normative vocabulary, only he applied it to the whole drift of modern society, not to the analysis of poetry. *Culture and Environment*, for example, argued that the destruction of the organic community entailed the 'loss of a human naturalness or normality' manifested in the 'wanton and indifferent ugliness', the 'utter insensitiveness to humanity and the environment' of the urban landscape.[38] Yet in the literary-critical context Leavis refused to commit himself to abstract aesthetic values such as 'vitality' or 'life', arguing that valuation was inseparable from the 'realisation' of the individual poem and of its place in the literary system. His model of criticism was of an intuitional and interactive process (disagreement with other like-minded readers was an integral part of the process of developing and amending one's readings); curiously, he seemed to disavow the element of public advocacy which was such an irreducible feature of his own writing. Leavis's way of meeting an opponent would presumably be by reference to touchstones or concrete examples of valuable and less valuable poetry, but his own response to these touchstones was already endowed with the authority of the 'contemporary sensibility'.

One of the individual readings that Wellek questioned was Leavis's account in *Revaluation* of Blake's 'Hear the Voice of the Bard'. Leavis's determination to speak for the contemporary sensibility had led him to assert that Blake's poem had less in common with the orderly, discursive structures of eighteenth-century verse than it had with Eliot's *Ash Wednesday*, a poem hailed in *New Bearings* as still more 'disconcertingly modern' than *The Waste Land*. Though Leavis energetically defended his belief that grammatical ambiguities and multiple meanings contributed to the impact of Blake's poem, his invocation of Eliot's lustre in this context was bound to strike a more scholarly interpreter as a historical and logical absurdity. Leavis claimed for 'Hear the Voice of the Bard' an 'extraordinary precision' ('something like the extraordinary precision of *Ash Wednesday*')[39] which was imaginative and emotional, bearing no relationship to any paraphrasable philosophic context. This is one of many instances where the traces of symbolist aesthetics, transmitted by way of Eliot's early criticism, proved decisive in Leavis's writings on poetry.

For Leavis the poet's words are the 'objective correlative' of something beyond the poem. They evoke and gesture towards, rather than speaking directly of, the poet's experience at a profound level. We are most in contact with the poet's experience in places where 'the verse has such life and body that we hardly seem to be reading arrangements of words', as he wrote in a 1945 essay. Such moments of 'concreteness' or 'precision' are the fruit of 'deeply and finely experienced emotion poetically realized, . . . such as could come only of a profoundly stirred sensibility in a gifted poet'.[40] In Hardy's 'After a Journey', for example, the poet, 'with the subtlest and completest integrity, is intent on recapturing what *can* be recaptured of that which, with all his being, he judges to have been the supreme experience of life, the realest thing, the centre of value and meaning'.[41] However accurate as a response to Hardy, this comment (from a 1952 discussion of 'Reality and Sincerity') suggests that the ultimate role of Leavis's criticism is as an intuitive accessory after the poem which is, itself, only accessory. What his criticism most tangibly brings to the poem is a reverent reading coupled with historical nostalgia. The 'supreme experiences' of the 'centre of value and meaning' of which he speaks were formerly, Leavis holds, more generally available – which is to say more communicable – than they are today.

The most perfect medium of communication – arising out of social conditions which also claimed Leavis's admiration, though he never took a detailed interest in them – was Elizabethan English. In Shakespeare, the genius of the language encountered a poet able to use it for the most profoundly expressive purposes. Leavis's account of why, in Shakespearean drama, 'the words matter' was written in response to the challenge of Joyce's *Work in Progress*, representing an extreme stage in the modernist revolution in literary language. Leavis rejected Joyce's kind of verbal dexterity both on the grounds of its artificiality – its remoteness from any imaginable speech-situation – and its supposed lack of expressive power. Unlike *Ulysses*, which had a 'catholic' quality and an 'immediately personal urgency', *Work in Progress* had no 'commanding theme, animated by some impulsion from the inner life capable of maintaining a high pressure'. Shakespeare was different:

> in the mature plays, and especially in the late plays . . . , it is the burden to be delivered, the precise and urgent command from within, that determines expression – tyrannically. That is Shakespeare's greatness: the complete subjection – subjugation – of the medium to the uncompromising, complex and delicate need that uses it.[42]

This is a remarkably romantic and intuitionist account of Shakespeare, though it had been preceded by passages in Eliot's essays on Elizabethan drama speaking of the inner and visceral roots of verbal expression. As Leavis wrote elsewhere, 'Analysis leads us directly to the core of the drama, its central, animating interests, the principles of its life';[43] the secrets of the critical laboratory were not ultimately to be found in words and their manipulation, still less in artistic construction and technique, but in an irreducible human mystery that could still be recovered thanks to its precise symbolisation in great literature. 'The words matter because they lead down to what they come from.'[44]

Unfortunately, the spiritual odyssey prompted by Leavis's understanding of the 'contemporary sensibility' led him to uphold a standard of poetry unattainable by that sensibility. It was not only the style of the late Joyce that failed to pass muster. In *New Bearings* Leavis heralded the advent of two Cambridge poets, William Empson and Ronald Bottrall; later he had to concede that they had not developed as he had hoped. His essay on 'The Poetical Renascence' in *For Continuity* demolished the pretensions of the Auden group, and in his 1950 'Retrospect' to *New Bearings* Leavis observed that 'the history of English poetry since [1932] has been depressing in the extreme'. Eliot remained as the lone exemplar of modern poetic achievement, and, for all his gathering dislike of Eliot as critic and 'sage', Leavis stands out as one of the poet's most discerning and devoted readers. After *Revaluation*, nevertheless, Leavis's most influential criticism would be of prose fiction.

Leavis and Lawrence

The Great Tradition (1948), the first of his books on novelists, is as forceful and aggressive as anything he ever wrote. The opening chapter begins by exhibiting the kind of self-defensive manoeuvre ('Critics have found me narrow . . .') into which he was increasingly drawn; but he then notes that in the novel 'some challenging discriminations are very much called for', and proceeds to make them in thirty packed pages, ending with the following challenge:

> I have, then, given my hostages. What I think and judge I have stated as responsibly and clearly as I can. Jane Austen, George Eliot, Henry James, Conrad, and D. H. Lawrence: the great tradition of the English novel is *there*.

Here it is no longer short poems or verse passages, but the joint *oeuvre* of five novelists which is nominated as an Arnoldian 'touchstone'. Austen, Eliot, James, Conrad and Lawrence are distinguished by a 'vital capacity for experience, a kind of reverent openness before life, and a marked moral intensity'[45] – qualities which Leavis associates not so much with the 'organic community' as with the spiritual aspirations of English Puritanism. Indeed, one of the most striking features of this 'tradition' – contrasted, say, with Leavis's earlier 'line of wit' – is the solitude of each writer. Only the 'major novelists', or 'great geniuses', are admissible to a succession based far more on perceived moral affinities than on actual indebtedness. The oddity of some of Leavis's exclusions has attracted much comment; of these, the slight offered to Dickens was later to be corrected (though the authors never conceded that they had been at fault) in F. R. and Q. D. Leavis's *Dickens the Novelist* (1970).

Leavis consistently opposes the moral intensity of his chosen five to the 'disgust or disdain or boredom' of the high priest of modernist fiction, Flaubert, and by implication of Joyce as Flaubert's successor; and he convincingly relates George Eliot's Puritan inheritance to Henry James's New England ethos. For all this, the 'Englishness' of Leavis's great tradition remains its most contentious quality. Conrad must be silently excluded from many of the generalisations that link together the other four authors, though it is of course a mark of Leavis's originality that he chose to integrate the Polish writer into the tradition rather than, say, Hardy.

The Great Tradition marks a change in Leavis's analytical methods, as well as in his implicit reading of history. Though several chapters were first published in *Scrutiny* under the general title 'The Novel as Dramatic Poem', Leavis increasingly relies on moral and thematic commentary on the novel's characters, dramatic action and representation of experience instead of on close verbal analysis. The critic's devotion to the 'concrete' is now attested by the quotation of very long passages, from which the appropriate moral lesson (sometimes a very forced one) is then drawn. Though he regards the nineteenth-century novelists as the true successors of Shakespeare, the deeper meanings that he finds in their work are entirely different from those he had earlier found in Shakespearean drama. Henry James, for example,

> creates an ideal civilized sensibility; a humanity capable of communicating by the finest shades of inflexion and implication: a nuance may engage a whole complex moral economy and the perceptive response be the index of a major valuation or choice.[46]

Here Leavis's praise for the deliberate and constructive labour of the moral intelligence reveals his turning away from Eliot's influence, with its stress on the visceral communicative urge, to a valuation of aesthetic refinement which is much closer to James's own. Nevertheless, the latest member of the great tradition, and the 'great genius of our time', is the very un-Jamesian figure of

D. H. Lawrence. Leavis insisted in such late works as *English Literature in Our Time and the University* (1969) on the profound and fruitful contrast between Eliot and Lawrence, as the two dominant representatives of a 'contemporary sensibility' frozen in time and oblivious to the passing of decades; the contrast between Lawrence and James was one that he rigorously avoided.

D. H. Lawrence himself, though he never bothered to develop a consistent aesthetic, was an occasional literary critic of great distinction. His *Studies in Classic American Literature* (1923) not only brings to the reading of the American writers the imaginative energy and quirky emotional intensity that Lawrence more often reserved for his descriptions of nature and the human psyche, but is the first major study of its subject. The unfinished 'Study of Thomas Hardy' suggests Lawrence's subordination of critical analysis to his own creative compulsion to rewrite Hardy's novels, though some superb insights emerge from this visionary work. In an essay on John Galsworthy written near the end of his life, Lawrence expressed his scorn for 'all this pseudo-scientific classifying and analysing of books'; criticism stands or falls by the personal qualities of its author, since it can be no more than a 'reasoned account of the feeling produced upon the critic by the book he is criticising'.[47] Criticism forms a small part of Lawrence's prolific output as a prophet and journalist, so that one of his most characteristic – and endearing – performances in this mode is his description of an Alpine village performance of *Hamlet*, which arises naturally out of the travelogue material in *Twilight in Italy* (1915) and continues, by way of a brief consideration of Shakespearean tragedy, to the broadest of speculations about the development of civilisation since the Renaissance. It was Lawrence's prophetic ambitions, spread across a multitude of genres both imaginative and discursive, that Leavis, as he grew older, increasingly felt driven to incorporate within the narrower framework of contributions to academic English studies.

Leavis's long drawn-out last phase began with *D. H. Lawrence: Novelist* (1955), in which the author's virtually uncritical admiration for his subject subsides, to some extent, into tetchy self-admiration. The role of the critic as Messiah became an unhappy obsession in his last books, as the life of the university or 'English school' was offered as compensation for the loss of an organic culture, the literary-critical act became the prototype of all true understanding, and the undergraduate syllabus served as substitute for the shared knowledge of an educated public. A growing parochialism led him, for example, to turn his introductions to Marius Bewley's study of nineteenth-century American novelists and to the reprint of Mill's essays on Bentham and Coleridge into disquisitions on the final year of the Cambridge English course.[48] His engagements with other contemporary commentators resembled a *Peri Bathous* or *Dunciad* rather than a debate between intellectual equals, as in his notorious onslaught on the 'two cultures' theory of C. P. Snow. By the time of *Nor Shall My Sword: Discourses on Pluralism, Compassion and Social Hope* (1972) the criticism had become sermonising, the polemics laid waste to armies of pygmies, and the 'edged economy' of Leavis's early style had given place to verbose tub-thumping. His sword remained restless but, by the end, it was made of rubber.

At its best, however, Leavis's writing is worthy of the tradition in which he inserted himself (his wide range of critical essays includes considerations of the criticism of Johnson, Coleridge, Arnold, Eliot and James). The critic who wrote of Tennyson as follows –

> Actually, Tennyson's feeling for the sounds of words was extremely limited and limiting: the ear he had cultivated for vowel sound was a filter that kept out all 'music' of any subtlety or complexity and cut him off from most of the expressive resources of the English language. To bring English as near the Italian as possible could not have been the preoccupation of a great English poet, however interesting the minor poetry that might have come out of it.[49]

– was no stranger to the polemical and argumentative resources of English prose, so that whatever one thinks of such a judgement, one is compelled to take notice of it. In his own writing, however, the moral intensity and 'reverent openness' that Leavis admired in the novel was best displayed not so much in his incisive manner of delivering critical verdicts as in his choice of quotations from the writers he admired. Amid the inverted Philistinism of his attack on C. P. Snow there is offered, as a touchstone of the imaginative mind, the passage from Lawrence's *The Rainbow* describing Tom Brangwen 'watching by the fold in lambing-time under the night-sky: "He knew he did not belong to himself." '[50] At such moments Leavis's empathy with the Protestant strain in English literature reaffirms and recreates the continuity of a culture to whose prolonged crisis it was his chosen task to bear witness.

Williams, Caudwell and Orwell

Leavis had many associates, disciples and imitators, most of whom he eventually repudiated. Their names include respected academic

literary scholars but few critics of any real independence or originality. His early collaborators, such as L. C. Knights, D. W. Harding
and Q. D. Leavis, were (deservedly or not) entirely overshadowed
by their master. There is, however, one major English critic who
dominates the succession to Leavis, though he also reflects some
very different currents of thought: this is Raymond Williams. Born
in Wales in 1921, Williams entered Trinity College, Cambridge
in 1939. He joined the university Communist Party but was also
moved, as he later recalled, by the 'aggressiveness' and 'critical
radicalism' of Leavis's work, despite its unpalatable social views.[51]
Williams's first published books ten years later consisted of a primer
of practical criticism and studies of modern drama and film (areas
that Leavis had left unexplored, though his and Eliot's criticism
were potent influences on Williams's approach).[52] In 1947–8 Williams edited two short-lived journals, *Politics and Letters* and the
Critic, to which some of the regular writers for *Scrutiny* also contributed. His major works *Culture and Society 1780–1950* (1958), *The
Long Revolution* (1961) and *The Country and the City* (1973) dis-
card Leavisian nostalgia for the organic community in favour of
an optimistic commitment to the emerging common culture of
socialist democracies. The long crisis has become a 'long revolution'
towards democratic control of every aspect of social life, and,
despite all discouragements, Williams believed that he could see
such a progress taking place in Britain and throughout the world.

Williams inherits the Leavisian concern with literature as an
index of social and cultural health, but the Spenglerian pessimism
of Leavis's outlook is transformed, in his work, into a Marxist
utopianism. He had, in effect, resumed – at a much subtler and
more complex level – the cultural aspirations of the pre-war Marxist
criticism that Leavis had attacked in *For Continuity*. 1930s Marxism
had its own versions of what Leavis referred to as the 'concrete'
and the 'contemporary sensibility'. The contemporary sensibility
found its source of value in the socialist future, not in the past,
and the 'concrete' was the political struggle. These arguments were
put by A. L. Morton in an exchange with Leavis in the opening
volume of *Scrutiny*, but there was no serious Marxist criticism in
England until 1937, when Ralph Fox's *The Novel and the People*,
C. Day Lewis's symposium *The Mind in Chains*, Alick West's *Crisis
and Criticism* and Christopher Caudwell's *Illusion and Reality* all
appeared, the latter two books being published posthumously after
their authors had been killed in the Spanish Civil War.[53] The title
of Caudwell's second critical book, *Studies in a Dying Culture*
(1938), best sums up the mood of literary Marxists in those years.
The modernist revolution in literature which so preoccupied

Richards and Leavis was dismissed as a bourgeois phenomenon; similarly, the literature of the past, which (Richards argued) had to be read in new ways or not at all, was not yet superannuated, according to the Marxists, though they hoped that it would soon become so. Edward Upward's 'Sketch for a Marxist Interpretation of Literature' in *The Mind in Chains*, for example, suggests that even Macbeth's ambition and Othello's jealousy would come to seem merely barbarous in a socialist world.[54] Upward combines a Morrisian apocalypticism about the future of the arts with a banal party-line commitment to socialist realism.

Christopher Caudwell was not a recognised Party intellectual but a rank-and-file member of the Communist Party, which he did not join until 1935. A journalist of wide interests, he set out in *Illusion and Reality* to write a scientific history of literature, showing its subordination throughout the capitalist epoch to the interests of the dominant class. Caudwell is notable for his pioneering attempts to apply both Marxist and Freudian categories to literature, so that one can find accounts in his writings both of modern art as 'commodity fetishism' and of the 'dream-work' and the separation of manifest and latent content in poetry. Though his sociological reading of literature is usually based on rigid class categories and historical determinism, there are glimpses in his work of a more flexible view of social–literary relations. *Studies in a Dying Culture*, for example, argues briefly that there is 'interaction' between what Marx had called the cultural superstructure (including literature and language) and the material base; social consciousness can, therefore, act to change social being.[55] Such an interactive view forms the basis of Raymond Williams's analyses of society, ideology and cultural expression, though Williams was bitterly critical of the dogmatism and self-contradictions of Caudwell and his generation.[56]

Before Williams, the most effective opponent of Marxist simplifications from a left-wing standpoint was George Orwell. Orwell's ability to flourish in the late 1930s and 1940s as a literary journalist, independent in every sense, is probably the strongest counterexample one could bring against the Leavisian view of the irreversible commercialisation of the metropolitan literary world. Hence it is of some interest that the intellectual circles of Leavis and Orwell could very occasionally be seen to overlap. One of Orwell's most reliable outlets was the *Adelphi*, an independent radical journal edited by John Middleton Murry, and – though Leavis did not publish in the *Adelphi* – both men lectured at the summer schools that Murry organised. (Leavis's topic, in August 1937, was 'The Necessity of Literary Criticism'.) Two years later, when

Q. D. Leavis favourably reviewed Orwell's collection of essays *Inside the Whale*, she speculated that he 'might find his métier in literary criticism'.[57] Orwell's literary essays in fact display a far stronger sociological and ideological emphasis than the orthodox Cambridge critical analysis would permit. However unpredictable he may have seemed to the more disciplined Left (he glories in Dickens's individualistic bourgeois radicalism and, at the outset of the Second World War, makes a case for the aesthetic self-absorption of Henry Miller), Orwell as a critic is political to his fingertips. His influence too can be seen in Raymond Williams's work, above all in its concern with the plebeian, 'unofficial' areas of culture that Orwell had entered in his pioneering essays on thrillers, comic postcards and boys' weeklies.

Orwell, in a phrase that much irritated Williams, spoke of England as a 'family with the wrong members in control'.[58] Leavis, Orwell and Williams are united by their concern with the depth and texture of the English national culture, though Williams in his later work would stress both the unequal topographical and power relations within the British state and the insularity of its dominant ideological concerns in the second half of the twentieth century. The crucial feature of his writing is, perhaps, his abandonment of the narrow Leavisian notion of literary standards for broad political and social ones; his ideal 'common culture' was one in which the experience and wisdom of ordinary people who had never had access to artistic refinement or literary expression would play a crucial and recognised part. Williams offers the spectacle of a critic who had little to say about poetry, preferring to concentrate on the novel with its representation of 'knowable communities' and on the more collective genres of drama, television and film. Like many of his contemporaries he seems embarrassed by Leavis's intensely moral and evaluative vocabulary, so that his positive judgements are characteristically expressed in a metaphorical, oblique and subjective manner. Arguing for Thomas Hardy's rehabilitation in the tradition of the English novel, for example, he does not speak of 'great genius' or 'classic achievement' but affirms, instead, that 'Hardy is our flesh and our grass.'[59] After such a work as *For Continuity, Culture and Society 1780–1950* is overwhelmingly fair-minded and even-toned, especially in its meditative readings of the nineteenth-century cultural critics; it is only when he comes to Orwell and the 1930s that Williams's prose gives way to acerbity. His socialist vision is more generous and humane than Leavis's strident concern for the 'standards of criticism', while offering a firm democratic yardstick against which the cultural pretensions of any intellectual élite, including socialist ones, can be measured.

The New Critics: Ransom, Burke, Blackmur and Winters

What Leavis and *Scrutiny* did in England, the New Critics did in America. That is, their criticism consolidated and institution-alised the doctrines of modernist poetics, serving in the process to confirm Éliot's standing as the supreme modern poet and cultural theorist. Beyond this, parallels between Leavis and the New Critics as academic practitioners can be misleading. There was never the homogeneity among the New Critics that there was among the contributors to *Scrutiny*: for example, neither R. P. Blackmur, Kenneth Burke, nor Yvor Winters had any connections with the Nashville 'Fugitives' circle. A few years after *I'll Take My Stand*, the Fugitives themselves abandoned their pretensions to social and cultural criticism, so that when John Crowe Ransom invited Allen Tate to become an associate editor of his projected new journal, the *Kenyon Review*, in 1937 he wrote that 'our cue would be to stick to literature entirely'.[60] Even in its most influential phase Richard Foster has spoken of New Criticism's 'two voices', the first being that of 'impersonal textual and technical analysis', the second being impressionistic, speculative, essayistic and – we may add – consciously theoretical in its aims.[61]

It has been the fate of New Criticism to be mercilessly oversimplified in polemics directed against it by its successors. As practising poets (the major New Critics were all practising poets) they had a strong interest in poetic form, yet their reputation for formalism has to be set against their habit of publishing books with such stirringly 'ideological' titles as Burke's *Counter-Statement* (1931), Ransom's *The World's Body* (1938) and Tate's *Reactionary Essays* (1938). Nor was their work disabled by philosophical naivety as has so often been suggested. They were aware, for example, that the 'objective' status of the poem ('the words on the page') assumed for the purposes of analysis was not some metaphysical absolute but rather a necessary critical postulate: the poem 'in reality' was an act, not a thing.[62] Nor, Blackmur partially excepted, did they share Leavis's reluctance to spell out their aesthetic principles. Ransom, Winters and Burke were, quite consciously, literary theorists. It was Ransom who wrote that 'Theory, which is expectation, always determines criticism, and never more than when it is unconscious. The reputed condition of no-theory in the critic's mind is illusory, and a dangerous thing in this occupation, which demands the utmost general intelligence, including perfect self-consciousness.'[63] It is the New Critics, not those who came after them, who deserve recognition as the first school of deliberate literary theorists in twentieth-century writing in English.

Nevertheless, the heart of the matter is that, as R. W. Stallman wrote, 'Modern criticism was created to establish a new poetic convention, to explain it, and to make it prevail';[64] and that in this respect New Criticism was in the direct line of descent from Eliot, Pound and Hulme. Stallman's influential anthology *Critiques and Essays in Criticism 1920–1948* (1949) presented the movement in its most programmatic aspect. The opening section, on 'The Nature and Function of Poetry', includes Hulme's 'Romanticism and Classicism', Eliot's 'The Metaphysical Poets', Ransom's 'Poetry: A Note in Ontology', Tate's 'Tension in Poetry', and 'The Language of Paradox' by Ransom's former student Cleanth Brooks (who also supplied a foreword to the book). Each of these five essays treats the short poem as the epitome of the 'poetic', stresses its sinewy concentration and complexity, and affirms the centrality of early seventeenth-century poetry, and especially of Donne. For the New Critics, significant modern poetry constitutes what R. P. Blackmur would call a 'school of Donne'; thus Tate finds 'remarkable ties' between Donne and Emily Dickinson, and Blackmur himself calls Yeats the 'greatest poet in English since the seventeenth century'.[65] Yvor Winters, whose rationalist poetic is ostensibly based on a rejection of Eliot's theories, only slightly adjusts this standard. For him it is the 'plain style' of the sixteenth century and of George Herbert which approaches perfection. Winters resembles Eliot in finding a 'general deterioration of the quality of poetry since the opening of the eighteenth century',[66] though this does not prevent him from advancing his own, highly eccentric, canon of modern short poems. Like the other New Critics, he is adamant that the best Renaissance lyrics provide standards by which all poetry can be judged.

For the New Critics, then, the metaphysical or rational style of Renaissance poetry was distinguished by its modernity: and this meant that the poetry had to be abstracted from its historical context and subjected to a greater or lesser degree of intellectual processing. In Ransom's 'Poetry: A Note in Ontology' (1938) for example, metaphysical poetry is presented as the dialectical resolution of the conflicting poetics of Imagist and of Romantic and Victorian verse – the one approximating, in Ransom's view, to a purely 'physical' poetry, the other to a 'Platonic' poetry of abstract ideas. Neither Imagism nor Romanticism could succeed in its aims, but the seventeenth century had shown that a 'metaphysical' poetry embodying the physical substance or '*Dinglichkeit*' of ideas was a triumphant possibility. For a critic writing in Eliot's shadow this was, of course, a foregone conclusion; nevertheless, the cryptic and idiosyncratic philosophical terms of Ransom's argument lead to a theoretical redefinition of 'metaphysicality' in poetry which Eliot cannot have anticipated. Not only do Eliot himself, Emily Dickinson and Wallace Stevens now qualify as metaphysical poets: so does the Milton of *Lycidas* and *Paradise Lost*.

'Poetry: A Note in Ontology' is a particular statement of the general New Critical concern with the poetic enactment or 'incarnation' of thought and feeling. There are many formulations of this concern, which takes its urgency from the desire to present literature, typified by the short poem, as a mode of knowledge different from, but not inferior to, scientific knowledge. Science knows the world as a scheme of abstraction, while the task of poetry, Ransom argues, is to grasp 'the world's fulness'.[67] This is to be done – as he puts it in 'Poetry: A Note in Ontology' – through the correct use of poetic devices, and above all by means of 'the climactic figure, which is the metaphor'. Seventeenth-century poetry 'had the courage of its metaphors', imposing them 'imperially' on things so as to assert a full identification where to the rational mind there would be no more than partial analogy. Nineteenth-century poetry, by contrast, was half-heartedly metaphorical, being content with similes. The difference between the two periods, Ransom suggests, is the difference between the metaphor and the simile.

This goes beyond Eliot's 'dissociation of sensibility', in that it diverts attention from the poet's 'tough reasonableness' and sensuous alertness to the transcendental and religious dimensions of his verse (hence Ransom's ability to classify *Paradise Lost* as a metaphysical poem). Ransom accomplishes this move by returning to the seventeenth-century use of 'metaphysical' as a synonym for 'supernatural' or 'miraculous'. A poetry which is full-bloodedly metaphorical can then be said to possess the quality of 'miraculism', which is at the basis of mythical and religious thought. Ransom thus argues that religions themselves may be regarded as poetic creations, so that poetry in the modern world may reasonably take the place of religion. As we follow this series of brilliant but wholly academic manoeuvres it comes to seem largely accidental, in historical terms, that it is the seventeenth century which exemplifies the poetry Ransom admires, 'a poetry which is the most original and exciting, and intellectually perhaps the most seasoned, that we know in our literature'.

Ransom's reduction of virtually all poetry to a set of variations on the metaphor/simile distinction is a characteristically New Critical theoretical device, though it also brings to mind the later 'structuralist' theory which analyses literary language in terms of the polarity of metaphor and metonymy. That the New Critics were as strongly attracted to simplified linguistic models of explanation as their successors is suggested by Kenneth Burke's seminal essay on the 'Four Master Tropes' of metaphor, metonymy, synedoche and irony,[68] as well as by the innumerable essays in technical analysis by the camp-followers of New Criticism in which poetic structure is reduced to the art of metaphorical elaboration. Shakespeare's plays, in particular, were reinterpreted as complexes of 'echoing tropes and images' stemming from the dramatic enactment of a root metaphor.[69] Replacing A. C. Bradley's emphasis on character and 'atmosphere', image-analysis became the dominant mode of Shakespeare criticism, as can be seen from the parallel work in England of such commentators as L. C. Knights and G. Wilson Knight. *Macbeth*, the shortest and most tightly co-ordinated of the great tragedies, became the favourite exercising-ground for this approach, though it failed to satisfy the more austere demands of Ransom's poetics. For Ransom, the major poetic experience is to be found in what he somewhat contradictorily terms the 'minor poem', which alone presents the microcosm of the 'poetic object' (or, as others would say, the 'poetic experience') in its fullness. The minor poem for Ransom is the 'symbol of a major decision', 'as ranging and comprehensive an action as the mind has ever tried'. Macbeth's soliloquies are less admirable than the lyrics of Donne, being only 'dramatically, not metaphysically satisfying'.[70]

Here the divisions in New Criticism begin to emerge. On the one hand, for Ransom the poem offers knowledge of the world, while for Yvor Winters it is 'a statement in words about a human experience'.[71] For a critic such as Cleanth Brooks, however, the poem seems to represent, in the first place, knowledge about language, and Brooks pointed out that New Criticism was part of a 'general intensification of the study of language and symbolism'.[72] There is a further division between critics who tend to interpret the poem in spatial terms, as a complex metaphor, and those who regard it in temporal terms as an action. Though the two approaches are not irreconcilable, the tension between them is brought out by the contrast between Ransom's poetic theory and that of Kenneth Burke. For Burke the primordial poetic discourse is that of drama, not of the lyric, and the concept of drama is the key to the mode of knowledge that poetry offers.

Burke's highly individual development began from a strong interest, which he later repudiated, in late nineteenth-century aestheticism. *Counter-Statement* (1931) begins with a consideration of Flaubert, Pater and Rémy de Gourmont. There is still a Paterian flavour in the autobiographical essay, 'Curriculum Criticum', appended to the second edition of *Counter-Statement* more than twenty years later:

> He had early decided that, ideally, for each of Shakespeare's dramatic tactics, modern thought should try to find the corresponding critical formulation. But he soon came to see that any such orderly unfolding of the past into the present would be greatly complicated, if not made irrelevant or even impossible, by the urgencies and abruptnesses of social upheaval.[73]

The weird self-certainty of this is characteristic of Burke's thought. An early 'decision' transfers Shakespeare's universality, more or less effortlessly, to the would-be theorist, whose vision, thanks to his awareness of modernity with its 'urgencies and abruptnesses of social upheaval', is destined to become still more all-embracing. For Burke, language is 'symbolic action' and its analysis requires a terminology of 'dramatism' since the 'principle of form typified in drama' is diffused throughout all verbal expression. His two major studies, *A Grammar of Motives* (1945) and *A Rhetoric of Motives* (1950), are analyses of language and social life in terms of the variety of its tactics or 'motives'. Though they subsume literary criticism in much wider concerns, Burke's writings (which most readers have found too wayward and unsystematic to grasp as a whole) contain a number of highly influential, though scattered, insights into critical method.

In *Counter-Statement*, for example, he approaches Shakespearean drama not as a self-determined exercise resolvable to imagery and metaphor but as a linear structure revealing the dramatist's mastery of audience-expectations. The principle that form invites psychological analysis rather than the mere enumeration of patterns of meaning is then extended to lyric poetry, so that it is Burke rather than Ransom or his associates who pioneered the explication of the 'dramatic structure' of the short poem. Nevertheless, the ambition set out in 'Lexicon Rhetoricae', the longest of the essays in *Counter-Statement* – to produce 'a kind of judgment machine, designed to serve as an instrument for clarifying critical issues' – haunts his voluminous and sometimes chaotic later works. His later essay 'The Philosophy of Literary Form' (1941) draws on contemporary anthropology to argue that the ritual drama of primitive societies is the 'Ur-form' underlying all modes of human action. Burke has also published poetry and two novels, which he dismisses as mere source material for his impersonal 'analysis of motives'.[74]

Like some post-structuralist theorists, Burke effectively reduces the human world to a composite text and finds in literary categories

the key not merely to the analysis of literature but of all signification. He lacks the concern with the establishment of the modern
literary canon – and specifically that of modern American poetry
– which animates most of the other major New Critics. The canon-
making ambition is evident in some of Tate's *Reactionary Essays*,
in Cleanth Brooks's *Modern Poetry and the Tradition* (1939), in
Yvor Winters's *Primitivism and Decadence* (1937), and in the pre-
war writings of R. P. Blackmur. Blackmur, who held that criticism
was no more than the 'formal discourse of an amateur',[75] had perhaps the finest critical sensibility of his generation in America.
Language as Gesture (1954), the collection of his essays which
includes studies of Eliot, Stevens, Dickinson, Marianne Moore,
Hart Crane, e.e. cummings, William Carlos Williams and other
American poets, was fittingly described by Ransom as 'the official
classic, in exegesis of the poetry of an age'.[76]

The concept of language as gesture is reminiscent of Burke's
'symbolic action', and – since Blackmur himself differentiated his
approach from Burke's on several occasions – the contrast of the
two writers has become a standard item in American literary
theory.[77] Nevertheless, Blackmur scarcely invites treatment as a
theorist. His reiterated conviction was that criticism was a mode
of 'elucidation and appreciation', a pedagogical instrument whose
task was completed when text and reader were brought together.[78]
As he wrote in 'A Critic's Job of Work' (1935), 'Criticism must
be concerned, first and last, with the poem as it is read and as
what it represents is felt.' Later he found a model of scrupulous
literary attention in Henry James's critical prefaces to his own
novels; Blackmur described these as 'the most sustained and I think
the most eloquent and original piece of literary criticism in existence'.[79] Blackmur at his best achieved something of the Jamesian
intimacy with the modern poets he surveyed, writing as if he could
locate himself 'at the source of the poet's creativity'.[80] According
to the poet W. S. Merwin, Blackmur's idea of the good critic was
of a 'house waiting to be haunted'.[81]

Blackmur's best work is that in which he set out to become
the arbiter of contemporary poetry, or what he called the 'school
of Donne'. Each essay begins, as he says in 'The Later Poetry
of W. B. Yeats' (1936), by attempting 'a special approach, deliberately not the only approach, and deliberately not a complete
approach'; yet there is a strange contrast between the imperiousness of many of Blackmur's formulations and the show of diffidence
with which he surrounds them. 'The Later Poetry of W. B. Yeats',
written three years before the poet's death, provides as trenchant
and wide-ranging an assessment of the poet as can be found in

the half-century of Yeats criticism that has followed it. The essay views Yeats's reliance on magic as the foundation of his poetic craft, in the light of a reading of the modern cultural situation which is strongly reminiscent of Eliot's early essay on Blake. In the absence of the shared religious faith which sustained Dante's art – so Blackmur argues – the modern poet must wage his own isolated struggle towards the 'miracle of meaning'[82] by which the chaos of private experience becomes comprehensible. It was the 'rational defect of our society' that drove Yeats to his magical expedients, yet the reader, faced with the question of whether or not he can give imaginative assent to Yeats's poetry, must inevitably decide this by rational means. Blackmur thus pays tribute, in general terms, to the sensual immediacy of late Yeats – 'the words meet and move like speaking lips', he says (of 'Leda and the Swan'), in a striking evocation of 'language as gesture' – but his main concern is to present some of the materials required for the exegesis of particular poems, and to debate the general problem of Yeatsian exegesis. The movement from the particular to the general can be traced in virtually every paragraph of the essay. 'Possibly all poetry should be read as this poem is read, and no poetry greatly valued that cannot be so read', he comments, after quoting 'A Deep-Sworn Vow'. Blackmur's use of the pronoun 'we', his sense of the critic as forming a collective subject, has a genuine urgency:

> Thus more than any poet of our time [Yeats] has restored to poetry the actual emotions of race and religion and what we call abstract thought. Whether we follow him in any particular or not, the general poetic energy which he liberated is ours to use if we can.

This is the voice of the freelance critic and poet (Blackmur had no first degree and had not yet become a Princeton professor) writing to influence his poetic contemporaries.

Blackmur at this time saw himself as spokesman for the values of the 'school of Donne' – the authors of a 'court poetry without a court', as he put it[83] – and his negative criticism of romantic, expressionist writers such as Melville and Lawrence indicts them for failing to observe the necessary standards of poetic craftsmanship. Nevertheless, he was able to see beyond the poetic outlook of his own generation, predicting in 'Lord Tennyson's Scissors' (1950) that there might be a 'coming race of poets' who would regard Hardy, Housman and Frost, rather than Yeats and Eliot, as their true ancestors. Blackmur, it seems, would scarcely have been surprised by Philip Larkin's advent as Britain's major poet of the later decades of the twentieth century. But the meditative inwardness of his criticism lost some of its power to command attention when it was no longer directed to the task of contemporary canon-formation. In 1940 he moved to Princeton, initially as a temporary fellow in Creative Writing, and a year later he published his essay 'The Enabling Act of Criticism', which argues for a much more limited role for critical evaluation than the one that is implicit in his earlier essays.

Blackmur's concern in 'The Enabling Act of Criticism' is with the scrupulous attention, joined with the habit of submission to 'whatever authority your attention brings to light in the words', that criticism demands. 'Whether your submission is permanent or must be withdrawn will be determined by the judgement of all the standards and all the interests you can bring to bear', he adds; but criticism should be slow to bring such a judgment to bear, for Blackmur dreads the tendentiousness of the critic with a single approach or an *idée fixe*. The main function of critical evaluation, he now suggests, is as an 'enabling act', policing the boundaries of literature and determining which works are worthy of sustained attention. Once an author has been admitted to the canon, the determination of relative merit had better be left to posterity: 'Greatness is come up to, felt, discovered, not handled; ... a critic who attempted to establish the greatness of Joyce or Eliot or Yeats would be largely wasting his time'. What this evocation of the intuitive nature of perceptions of 'greatness' overlooks is the persuasive and even propagandistic function of criticism, which Blackmur had espoused only a few years earlier.

For all his insistence on 'unindoctrinated thinking', Blackmur's later criticism is founded on a mystique of the work of art as a privileged object, so that each essay becomes the public rationalisation of a private devotion.[84] Perhaps it could not be otherwise. The New Critics' intense awareness of the death of traditional religion opens their work to the suspicion of creating a substitute religion, 'the poetic imagining of a whole religion of poetry, complete with worshippers, images and holy objects, and a corps of spiritual fathers', as Richard Foster has put it.[85] Blackmur himself was conscious of the attractions of the scriptural analogy for literary study, and seems to succumb to them even as he repudiates them, as we see in 'A Burden for Critics' (1948):

> Critics are not fathers of a new church. I speak from a secular point of view confronting what I believe to be a secular world which is not well understood; and I suppose what I want criticism to do can as well as not be described as the development of

aesthetic judgment – the judgment of the rational imagination – to conform with the vast increase of material which seems in our time capable only of aesthetic experience.

The echoes of lost religion are powerful in this passage, since the ideal of 'aesthetic judgment' that it advances is implicitly a substitute for the theological judgement available in earlier periods. The notion of the 'burden' of criticism in a rationalistic age is an instance of what Edward W. Said has referred to as Blackmur's homegrown 'bourgeois humanism in a churchyard'.[86]

Phrases such as 'in our time' and 'of our time' convey that the burden of contemporaneity is as conscientiously shouldered in Blackmur's criticism as it is in that of Eliot, Richards, Leavis and the Southern Agrarians. The one deliberate heretic among the New Critics, who refused to consider that poetry was affected by the special needs of the modern age, was Yvor Winters. For Winters, belief in the uniqueness of the modern predicament was a typical romantic self-delusion. His critical notoriety, it has been said, rests largely on his rejection of the claims of the modernist or 'Poundian Revolution'.[87] As a theorist, he erected a rational standard according to which modern poets should be expected to write more or less exactly as poets had done two or three hundred years earlier. Winters's rigorous conservatism together with his geographical isolation at Stanford in California led him to adopt a stance of timeless detachment from the contemporary scene, though he did not thereby refrain either from provocative value-judgements or from academic in-fighting. The Winters canon of twentieth-century poets, which places the work of Robert Bridges, T. Sturge Moore, Elizabeth Daryush and Adelaide Crapsey above that of Yeats and Eliot, was ridiculed as early as Stanley Edgar Hyman's *The Armed Vision* (1948), so it scarcely needs to be at issue here. An underlying yearning for an uncomplicated Arcadian simplicity in intellectual matters received direct expression in some of his own poems, as in the following lines 'On Rereading a Passage from John Muir':

I might have been this man: a knowing eye
Moving on leaf and bark, a quiet gauge
Of growing timber and of climbing fly,
A quiet hand to fix them on the page –
A gentle figure from a simpler age.

Gentle, however, Winters was not, and there is no real analogy between his 'knowing eye' and that of the nineteenth-century Californian naturalist.

Winters has made most impact as the advocate of a plain style of poetry, unafraid of linguistic abstractions. His essay 'The 16th Century Lyric in England: A Critical and Historical Reinterpretation' (1939) was responsible for reviving such forgotten Elizabethan poets as Fulke Greville, George Gascoigne, and Barnabe Googe. These are poets who combine matter of factness with passion but who do not feel the need to 'clothe' or 'embody' their thought in a specially heightened diction. Winters's championship of the plain style continues to influence contemporary poets who believe in maintaining traditional standards of craftsmanship in verse; his wider achievement as a critic, however, is an embarrassment since it reveals the aberrations to which both a commitment to forthright evaluation and an outspokenly theory-laden approach to literature can lead. Rivalling Leavis in his belligerence, his judgements are more eccentric and his taste more austerely rationalistic than those of the *Scrutiny* school. But thanks to the clarity of his prose he remains one of the most bracing of critics to disagree with, as well as being committed in an exemplary way to the links between critical commentary and poetic practice, so that his best essays have been described as 'a kind of poet's education'.[88]

In the 1930s the New Critics set out to dislodge the mixture of historical and philological study which had dominated American English departments until that time. Despite their own freelance origins, they were anxious to make criticism academically respectable and to show that it was capable of being as systematically pursued as the forms of study it was to replace. Thus in 1938 Cleanth Brooks and Robert Penn Warren produced the first edition of their famous undergraduate textbook *Understanding Poetry*, while John Crowe Ransom advocated what he half-seriously called 'Criticism, Inc.', a collective and sustained effort to put criticism on a learned and semi-scientific basis. Ransom's programme was so speedily fulfilled that fifteen years later the poet and novelist Randall Jarrell, attacking the prestige-obsessed self-importance of run-of-the-mill academic criticism, was to claim that most of it 'might just as well have been written by a syndicate of encyclopedias for an audience of International Business Machines'.[89] What Jarrell failed to mention was that not only criticism but much of the profession of poetry in America had become absorbed into the universities.

In 1957 Allen Tate gathered together his selected essays under the title *The Man of Letters in the Modern World*. He and his contemporaries had shown that, in the occupations of critic, literary theorist, teacher and contributor to the academic quarterlies, a comfortable niche could be found for the poet in the modern world.

All that was missing was, perhaps, the sense of an audience – an audience motivated, that is, by reasons other than those of academic convention and deference to professorial authority. Tate perceived correctly that the aims of criticism were called into question by such conditions. The familiar explanation that each student generation was part of the educated reading public of the future could not disguise the fact that the students were encountered as a captive audience in the present. Teaching students to exercise the function of a reading public by passing judgement on literary works in the classroom had thus become something of a charade. As Tate wrote, in 'Is Literary Criticism Possible?' (1950–1), 'When I first taught a college class, about eighteen years ago, I thought that anything was possible; but with every year since it has seemed a little more absurd to try to teach students to "evaluate" works of literature, and perhaps not less absurd to try to evaluate them oneself.'

Most of the New Critics and their followers continued to regard evaluation as the first duty of the critic. Nevertheless, to leaf through the concluding paragraphs of academic literary essays published around the mid-century is to appreciate Tate's feeling of absurdity, since the final evaluative sentence (often preceded by some such phrase as 'in the last analysis') had become a convention as inert and merely decorative in function as the expressions of gratitude to one's friends and one's spouse on the acknowledgments page. Tate's confession of self-doubt about the process of evaluation in 'Is Literary Criticism Possible?' was laid to rest, however, by means of the sort of comfortable paradox which had also become a convention of routinised New Criticism. Literary criticism leading to evaluation, he concluded, was ('like the kingdom of God on earth') at once 'perpetually necessary' and 'perpetually impossible'. Blackmur, with his more probingly sceptical mind, had already suggested that the evaluative moment in criticism might be no more than an 'enabling act', a licence to begin the job of interpretation on a particular literary work. Thus New Criticism, which began as a campaign for new aesthetic and cultural values, ended by turning a quizzical glance on its own status as an instrument of pedagogic bureaucracy. But, if the New Critics had lost their way, there would be no commanding new artistic movement to provide the syllabus for the next generation of critics and theorists.

6 The Age of Interpretation

The Scientific Schoolmen

By mid-century not only was New Criticism the dominant mode of literary study, but criticism had become institutionalised in the universities. The new subject was growing fast – often at the expense of classics, philosophy and modern languages – within an educational system itself undergoing rapid expansion. In the United States, there was a dramatic rise in the proportion of the eligible population going to college, from 4 per cent in 1900 to 14 per cent in 1940 and then to 40 per cent in 1964.[1] Universities and colleges became the largest employers in many towns and cities, bringing with them a body of literature teachers who were expected to be active as critics and scholars. Literary research leading to the PhD was the main qualification for entry into the profession, and, once employed, most teachers were encouraged to publish regularly. The production of criticism and the range of its outlets in books and journals grew apace.

As criticism acquired the status of an academic discipline its by now customary sources of authority began to be questioned. Critics were nearly all pedagogues rather than journalists or poets, and for the first time there emerged new 'schools' which neither participated in, nor claimed allegiance to, contemporary developments in imaginative writing. The New Critics' close relationship to the modernist movement was not paralleled by any of their successors. Legitimacy, instead, was sought in the notion of an intellectual discipline, often modelled on the sciences. In Britain, following the example of Richards and Leavis, there was perhaps greater emphasis on the educative function of the 'close reading' of poetry; in America there was a more philosophical interest in the status of literature as an object of knowledge. In the 1940s W. K. Wimsatt and Monroe C. Beardsley published their theories of the 'intentional fallacy' and the 'affective fallacy', while René Wellek and Austin Warren's *Theory of Literature* (1949) – a survey covering a wide variety of valid critical approaches and methods – viewed literary criticism as a branch of aesthetics. Many critics agreed with Wellek and Warren in opting for a pluralistic framework in which to pursue their professional routines, but criticism remained a fairly turbulent discipline, frequently plunged into acrimonious crisis.

The search for authority in criticism is not, and never has been, entirely a matter for rational argument. It is significant, therefore, that just as James Joyce, emerging from his Jesuit college at the beginning of the century, sought to base a theory of aesthetics on Aristotle and Aquinas, so the first purely academic modern critical school was the 'neo-Aristotelianism' which arose at the University of Chicago in the 1930s. Though not noted for their reluctance to engage in controversy, R. S. Crane, Elder Olson and their fellow-Chicagoans were professed pluralists. Yet they, like their neoclassical forebears, chose to buttress rational argument with ancestor-worship. An alternative was to seek a strictly modern basis for a poetics, or critical science. There is, however, a third possibility, which locates the authority of the critical discipline not in the objective apparatus it brings to literary analysis but rather in the act of interpretation itself – the mutual encounter, as it were, between canonised text and disciplined reader.[2]

If criticism is to be a science, it must be able to specify what the objects it studies have in common. This quality which separates literature from non-literature is what the Russian Formalists – the originators of the modern 'science' of criticism – defined as 'literariness'. One view of literariness is that it is an intrinsic element of certain sorts of language-use, which can be identified and isolated by means of technical and structural analysis. The 'literary' effect, it is argued, is the consequence of language drawing attention to its own substance, through the deliberate use of devices such as metre, rhythm, repetition, narrativity (story-telling), 'estrangement', and so forth. Alternatively, literariness may be conceived not as the unfailing consequence of certain devices but as a system of differential and hierarchical functions: what is literary at one time or in one culture is not necessarily so elsewhere. The first view leads to the notion of an ideologically neutral textual science, while the second leads to a comparative and historical study in which literariness is understood as a social convention. Both tendencies can be discovered in Russian Formalism as a whole, and in the work of individual Formalists such as Roman Jakobson, whose contribution to Anglo-American criticism will be discussed below. It is, however, the movement towards a science of literature based on linguistics, rather than towards a mode of literary history, that dominates the postwar movement in poetic theory drawing on the Formalist legacy.

A science of literature would be ostensibly – and ostentatiously

– value-free. Yet modern academic criticism has sometimes claimed to be value-free not on account of its status as science, but of its status as interpretation. Interpretation was distinguished from criticism in one of the most influential of early twentieth-century Shakespeare studies, G. Wilson Knight's *The Wheel of Fire* (1930), which appeared with a long preface by T. S. Eliot.[3] Eliot rather grudgingly argues that interpretation is necessary 'perhaps only in so far as one is passive, not creative oneself',[4] and in Wilson Knight's hands it is, in fact, a way of paying homage to the transcendent genius of a great poet. Criticism, he says, is a 'judgement of vision; interpretation a reconstruction of vision'. Interpretation, which is 'metaphysical rather than ethical', presupposes the greatness of the literature it analyses. Wilson Knight's own interpretative practice in its more mundane aspects was strongly influenced by A. C. Bradley, but he was also a flamboyant and would-be messianic figure whose claim to write of genius 'from *within*', to reveal the 'burning core of mental or spiritual reality' in literary works led to striking eccentricities in his later years.[5] As a forerunner of the more recent protagonists of literary interpretation he must be something of an embarrassment, though one of his students, during a wartime stint at the University of Toronto, was Northrop Frye.

The task of the modern interpreter, as it is usually conceived, is neither metaphysical nor ethical but sceptical and inductive. Today literary study often seems burdened with self-consciousness about its interpretative responsibilities. Interpretation lays claim to a dignified genealogy, tracing its descent from the long tradition of Biblical exegesis and scriptural commentary rather than from the secular history of criticism and literary education. In England the most influential advocate of literary hermeneutics after Wilson Knight has been Frank Kermode, who gives a remarkably candid account of the methods and horizons of academic interpretation. The practice of construing the 'hidden' meanings of literary works is in Kermode's view a kind of Kuhnian 'normal science' or conventional mode of the production of knowledge; but it is also a privileged and sacred task performed by scholars who like to see themselves not as employees of an educational system but as a kind of self-ordained priesthood.

According to Kermode, the works studied by literary academics have already been evaluated. The fact that they are felt to require exegesis means that they belong to the 'canon' of texts given quasi-scriptural status. The question why and how some texts become and remain canonical, while others do not, preoccupies him in a series of books beginning with *The Classic* (1975). A literary classic, Kermode argues, is (paradoxically) a work possessing 'permanent modernity' by virtue of its continual openness to reinterpretation. It is its linguistic complexity which makes this possible, though at the same time it must lose some of its appearance of peculiarity and uniqueness due to its membership of the canon; and one of the main functions of textual interpretation is to represent the canon as a systematic entity full of repetitions and interlinkages. To 'interpret' in its earliest sense meant to translate. The canon-creating function of literary interpretation is not unlike that of the principal sacred text in English, the Authorised Version of the Bible, with its evenness of style which, as a modern scholar observes, 'makes the large variety of biblical texts, written in many different periods, styles, and genres, all appear the same.[6]

The analogy between modern literary study and the study of the scriptures has been very widely invoked, often by critics who (like Kermode and like R. P. Blackmur) have declared themselves to be sceptical rationalists. Kermode uses the scriptural analogy to stress the inevitability, in academic criticism, of a professional mystique which cultivates reserved senses of the texts inaccessible to the laity. For him, literary interpretation now has a preservative, not a missionary role. The state in which 'the opinion of the laity is of no consequence whatever' is, as he notes, a new development in criticism.[7] The 'literary institution', like the Church (though less effectively), 'controls the choice of canonical texts, limits their interpretation, and attends to the training of those who will inherit the presumption of institutional competence'.[8] Kermode seems fairly content with the institutionalisation of criticism, though many other writers on the subject have expressed their unease. According to Gerald Graff, for example, the lengths to which academic critics have gone in suppressing evaluative judgements provide one index of the bureaucratisation of literary studies. Graff speaks of the elimination of the notion of artistic defect from textual interpretation, and of the 'sheer determination to rationalize that seems to be built into the dynamics of the explication industry'.[9] Frederick Crews, more angrily, compares the practice of formalistic analysis on writers who may have been scarcely able to contain their sensuality or savage indignation to the 'computerized pacification of a province'.[10]

When Matthew Arnold foresaw that literature would come to take the place of the scriptural canon, the last thing he intended was a new mode of scholasticism. Today the gulf between the missionaries and the professional interpreters has become very wide. Yet some of the founding figures of modern criticism are particularly associated with the notion of a value-free practice of textual interpretation which has overtones both of religious devotion and of investigative science: these are William Empson, Northrop Frye, and Roman Jakobson.

William Empson

Of the three, Empson is the most paradoxical, but then he would be so in almost any company. He is usually classified as a pioneer of New Criticism, and in the 1930s he was sometimes mistaken for an intellectual Marxist. I. A. Richards, Empson's teacher at Cambridge, recalled the younger man's response to Robert Graves and Laura Riding's *A Survey of Modernist Poetry* soon after its publication:

> At about his third visit he brought up the games of interpretation which Laura Riding and Robert Graves had been playing with the unpunctuated form of 'The expense of spirit in a waste of Shame'. Taking the sonnet as a conjuror takes his hat, he produced an endless swarm of lively rabbits from it and ended by 'You could do that with any poetry, couldn't you?' This was a Godsend to a Director of Studies, so I said, 'You'd better go off and do it, hadn't you'.[11]

The result was *Seven Types of Ambiguity* (1930). Unlike Wilson Knight's form of interpretation, Empson's unravelling of verbal ambiguities is potentially applicable to all poetry. The same is true of Frye's and Jakobson's systems of literary analysis. Moreover, when a recent historian writes that 'Reuben Brower's *The Fields of Light* (1951) was probably the first major work of the New Criticism that explicated poems without an accompanying cultural thesis', he has presumably forgotten *Seven Types of Ambiguity*, in which the only cultural thesis advanced is a belief in the verbal and emotional richness of poetry and the desirability of submitting it to rational analysis.[12] Empson's commitment to analysis is strictly pragmatic and relativist. Analysis is a good thing if you are a person like Empson, but it does not have a 'unique value': 'The object of life, after all, is not to understand things, but to maintain one's defences and equilibrium and live as well as one can'.[13]

Looking back on Empson's career, *Seven Types of Ambiguity* with its dazzling relativism might be seen as an expression of the critic as *enfant terrible*. The author of *Milton's God* (1961) is a fighting critic with a strongly held set of cultural dogmas and prejudices to defend. But the temptation of simply reading the later Empson back into the earlier should be resisted. He was aware

of the conflict between Richards's scientism and Eliot's neo-Christianity during his period as a Cambridge undergraduate, but
remained open-minded about it (or so he later recalled) and 'would
probably have said that I was on the side opposed to [Richards].
I am not sure when I decided that he had been quite right.'[14]
Empson's early pluralism was reinforced by the interest in Oriental
thought that he inherited from Richards, and by his years teaching
in China and Japan. The manuscript of a book on Eastern religion,
The Faces of the Buddha, was apparently lost during the Blitz,
when he was working for the BBC in London.[15] Only after 1953,
when he returned from China to the chair of English at Sheffield
in his native Yorkshire, did Empson's creed as a militant rationalist
begin to dominate his writing.

In 1950, when asked to contribute to a symposium on 'My Credo'
in the New Critical *Kenyon Review*, he replied that having a credo
was not really the critic's business at all. What emerges most clearly
from the baffling twists and turns of his answer is his unrepentant
empiricism. 'A critic ought to trust his own nose, like the hunting
dog, and if he lets any kind of theory or principle distract him
from that, he is not doing his work', he declares at the outset.
Later he modifies this position a little, but claims that analysis
and judgment are wholly separable processes. The poem in analysis
should be treated as a kind of machine. What interests him is to
'show all its working parts in turn', though this aim has the effect
of turning criticism too into a mechanical process:

> There is a tendency to feel that, if the critic is offering a really
> efficient machine, it ought to be able to say whether marmalade
> is better than sausages; but even the most expert cook cannot
> say that; sometimes you want one, sometimes the other.
> Especially in our own age, the first to make a serious effort
> to appreciate the whole variety of good literature, this kind of
> absolutism seems to me comical.[16]

The bluff, Squire Western-like images – marmalade and sausages
after an early-morning run with the hounds – are an essential part
of Empson's manner: later, in *Milton's God*, he would present
Satan with his Northern Command in Heaven as a kind of honorary
Yorkshireman.[17]

Asked by the *Kenyon Review* to define the social responsibilities
of the critic, he replied that 'Even in so humble a walk of life
as literary criticism, it seems to me, a man might feel [that] the
best thing for him to do as a critic is to do his work as best he
can.'[18] Perhaps more enlightening is the comment which concluded

his controversial account of a speech from *Macbeth*, in the first
edition of *Seven Types*: 'Personally I am pleased and given faith
by this analysis, because it has made something which seemed to
me magical into something that seems to me sensible.'[19] That is
the nearest we ever get to the settlement of what Empson would
call a 'philosophic issue' in his earlier work. He tends to raise
such issues, only to dance around them and finally to brush them
aside. To adapt one of his canine metaphors, he can never resist
taking an interested sniff at an abstract ideal, but then, his curiosity
satisfied, he trots off without even bothering to lift his hind leg
at it.

Things are very different when he is confronted by a line of
verse. *Seven Types* begins with the famous confession that, coming
upon the flower of beauty, the analyst not only relieves himself
against it but feels compelled to scratch it up afterwards. 'Beauty'
in Empson means verbal richness; the scratching process reveals
the interplay of semantic possibilities which, he believes, gives the
poem its fascination and complexity. The situation in which a word
or grammatical structure takes effect in several ways at once 'covers
almost everything of literary importance', he writes. The ordinary
reader must scan the words very quickly, so that the ambiguities
Empson reveals are supposedly a subliminal part of his response.
What is most attractive in Empson's analyses, however, is their
exhibition of the intellectual virtuosity and vigour that a modern
sensibility can bring to (and that it also demands of) the reading
process.

While he converts the 'magical' into the 'sensible' wherever possible, Empson is also very willing to suggest that the full richness
of poetic language defies analysis. The meanings of a single English
sentence, he argues, could never be exhaustively explicated. For
this reason it is fitting that the structure of 'seven types' of ambiguity
is a convenience without much logical necessity or precision. In
general the book progresses from the relatively superficial to the
profoundly disturbing levels of poetic ambiguity; the result is an
exploration of the 'Depth Psychology' of authorship. Empson starts
from the loosely Freudian assumptions that no instance of ambiguity is merely trivial or accidental, and that by pursuing the thread
of linguistic 'slips' he can penetrate into a sort of poetic Unconscious. After a long and rambling introduction to the seventh type
(including a disquisition on mathematics and primitive languages),
he pauses to make the following pronouncement:

I have been searching the sources of the Nile less to explain
English verse than to cast upon the reader something of the

awe and horror which were felt by Dante arriving finally at the most centrique part of earth, of Satan, and of hell . . . We too must now stand upon our heads, and are approaching the secret places of the Muse.

The 'secret places' turn out to be those of the ambivalences and self-contradictions of English devotional verse. The final analyses deal with Crashaw, Herbert and Hopkins, and in the first two instances they hint at a deep connection between Christianity and sado-masochism. Herbert's 'Sacrifice', where the ambiguities hint at the sexual feelings aroused by the risen Christ, deals, Empson writes, with the 'most complicated and deeply-rooted notion of the human mind'.

In successful poems like Herbert's, the ambiguities are welded together in an artistic unity. The alternative meanings 'must in each case arise from, and be justified by, the peculiar requirements of the situation'. But many readers have wondered whether the depth of ambiguity displayed in Empson's seventh type is compatible with poetic unity. Empson does not confront this problem directly. In general, he maintains that the range of semantic possibilities he reveals is no greater than that implied by earlier methods of exegesis: after some brilliantly tortuous readings of *Macbeth* and the Sonnets, for example, he observes that 'most of what I find to say about Shakespeare has been copied out of the Arden text'. This leads in turn to a series of generalisations about the Elizabethans, who 'minded very little about spelling and punctuation' and had a different attitude to the written page from ours. Analysis tries to restore the 'body' to the words, to 'give back something of the Elizabethan energy to what is at present a rather exhausted language'. The member of Shakespeare's audience, he suggests, was 'prepared to assimilate words with a completeness which is now lost'. (It may be argued, of course, that the actor's speech would tend to resolve many potential verbal ambiguities before they could reach the audience.)

There is a historical dimension to the argument of *Seven Types*, but it does not receive much prominence. In any case, it is entirely compatible with the outlook of Eliot and *Scrutiny*. His next book, *Some Versions of Pastoral* (1935), repeats this historical view, though with some very idiosyncratic twists. The Elizabethan court pastoral, in which sophisticated poets put on the simple air of shepherds and shepherdesses, was felt to imply a beautiful relation between rich and poor; but this could not survive the Civil War and the rise of the middle classes. Puritanism and class consciousness were the 'fence' over which 'pastoral came down in England after the Restoration'. Empson, however, discusses pastoral not in its original manifestation but in various underground versions, as the device of 'putting the complex into the simple' reappears in Milton's Garden of Eden, in the criminal world of *The Beggar's Opera* and the child's world of *Alice in Wonderland*, and finally in the supposedly vanguard literature of the modern proletariat.

In 1935 the doctrine of proletarian literature had already been repudiated by Stalin and his henchmen, though few in the western communist parties were aware of this. Empson's personal sympathies were undoubtedly left-wing; at the same time, his chapter on 'Proletarian Literature' (originally published in *Scrutiny*) falls far short of revolutionary commitment. Proletarian literature, he tells us, is usually 'Covert Pastoral', and what Empson values in the pastoral mode is its reflection of the 'permanent truths' of social and personal inequality, together with its imaginative softening of class antagonisms. 'Clearly it is important for a nation with a strong class-system to have an art-form that not merely evades but breaks through it, that makes the classes feel part of a larger unity or simply at home with each other', he writes with *Don Quixote* in mind. The extent to which English literature expresses a national consciousness, and the extent of the critic's own implicit patriotism, are tacit themes of *Some Versions of Pastoral*. The essay on proletarian literature invokes the Marxist formulas of the time only to dazzle the reader with a comical display of English eccentricity and empiricism.

A careful reading of *Some Versions of Pastoral* would, then, disclose a social agenda very different from the one that its rather baffled early readers found there. It is not, as Kenneth Burke and others have thought, evidence of a Marxist phase in Empson's writing.[20] His complacency towards pastoral as a social ideology may, for example, be measured against the bitter denunciation of the form in Raymond Williams's *The Country and the City* (1973). For all his irreverent and subversive manner, Empson tends to concentrate on relatively trivial instances of the pastoral mode and to underline the stoically conservative outlook that he finds in them. Gray's 'Elegy in a Country Churchyard', which must strike Marxists as a crude statement of bourgeois ideology, is shown by Empson to outline a 'permanent truth'; and of the snobbery of the *Alice* books he writes that 'The two main ideas behind [it], that virtue and intelligence are alike lonely, and that good manners are therefore important though an absurd confession of human limitations ... would be recognized in a degree by any tolerable society'. Empson's permanent truths in this brilliantly entertaining book are usually sad ones, hitting an elegiac note although he fails to point out that the most influential of the classical pastoral forms is the elegy.[21]

The Structure of Complex Words (1952) forsakes social and historical generalisation for a niggling and formidably intricate process of semantic analysis. This is Empson's most technical and scientific work, beginning with professions of admiration for I. A. Richards's contribution to linguistics (in the book as a whole, Richards's name appears more often than any other writer except Shakespeare) and ending with suggestions for greater precision in lexicography. Empson's observation that the full meaning of a single sentence could never be analysed may have been the germ of this book: at its centre is a series of chapters tracing the complex feelings attached to such simple words as 'all', 'fool', 'dog', 'honest', and 'sense' in writers from Shakespeare to Jane Austen. The use of 'fool' in *King Lear*, for example, allows us to 'peer into the abyss for knowledge about the bases of the world', whereas the eighteenth-century slang use of 'dog' – Voltaire, doubtless revelling in his command of English idiom, spoke of Samuel Johnson as a 'superstitious dog' – implies the pastoral idea that there is a complete copy of the human world among dogs (and vice versa), giving grounds for some optimism about human life: 'if the worst is the dog, humanity is still tolerable', according to Empson. The doctrines implied by a writer's use of colloquial or joke phrases like those about dogs are, he adds, 'more really complex than the whole structure of his official view of the world'. Whether or not he had in mind Noel Coward's song about mad dogs, the effect of putting together Empson's chapters on 'Fool in Lear' and 'The English Dog' is to suggest the full range of the human predicament between the supposed extremes of madness and despair on the one hand, and Englishness on the other. There is much more rich and curious matter in *The Structure of Complex Words*, though its concluding chapter on dictionaries seems oddly uncertain after so much erudition. The book shows Empson at his most pedantic, but also at his most prolix and playful.

If *Complex Words* ends with a chapter on dictionaries, the very much more formidable last chapter of *Milton's God* sums up Empson's indictment of Christianity. Here and in other late essays he launched a counter-crusade against what he called the 'neo-Christian' critics, who included both Eliot's New Critical followers and more traditional English literary scholars such as C. S. Lewis, Helen Gardner and E. M. W. Tillyard. There is a sense, in this work, of Empson's returning to his intellectual roots in the late Victorian rationalism of such books as Frazer's *The Golden Bough*, and Winwood Reade's *The Martyrdom of Man*. 'When I was young' – as in 'the idea that there actually couldn't be a moral debate in a literary work amounts to a collapse of the Western mind, quite unforeseen when I was young' – becomes a constant refrain.[22] Empson now claimed to regret that readers had found his beliefs 'evasive or illogical', asserting that at bottom they could not have been more simple:

> I think the traditional God of Christianity very wicked, and have done since I was at school, where nearly all my little playmates thought the same. I did not say this in my earlier literary criticism because I thought it could be taken for granted, and that to fuss about it would do no good.[23]

Another statement of Empson's casts some light on his later work. This is his reported opinion that 'with periodic sanitary efforts ["Eng. lit."] can probably be got to continue in a sturdy, placid way, as is needed.'[24] A sanitary effort was now required. Neo-Christianity, he believed, had corrupted not only literary interpretation but the textual editing of poets such as Coleridge and Donne who had recanted their youthful unorthodoxies. The principle of respecting an author's final revisions led, in these cases, to what Empson regarded as transparent imposture. Setting out to rescue some famous poems from their authors' later insincerities, he launched into far-reaching and highly speculative biographical and textual reconstruction. Coleridge's 'Ancient Mariner', for example, was a 'splendid poem which was much mangled by its author for reasons of conscience'; it was 'fudged in 1815 to make it Christian', but then it 'had already been fudged in 1800 to make it Pantheist'.[25] Empson's critique of the established texts of Coleridge and Donne was a salutary demonstration of the role of ideology in the supposedly neutral area of textual scholarship; at the same time, he was invariably forced to rely on intricate, largely conjectural (and of course themselves ideological) arguments.

In *Milton's God*, the prime exhibit is Milton's Latin treatise *De Doctrina Christiana* which revealed that the author of *Paradise Lost* also had his struggles with theological orthodoxy. As a monument of the Christian tradition *Paradise Lost* was both 'horrible and wonderful', like Aztec or Benin sculpture. Empson views Milton both as the proto-Romantic who sympathised with Satan's rebellion and as the authoritarian poet who, in *Samson Agonistes*, glorified an act of divine genocide or mass murder. There is a curious sub-theme to the book: Empson had been forced to leave China as a result of the communist takeover, and, returning to the West, he found that neo-Christianity was widely endorsed as a necessary bulwark against communism. Empson views both creeds with equal distaste, showing (in the course of a digression on George Orwell) that one of the lessons of *Animal Farm* and *Nineteen Eighty-Four* is that 'a neo-Christian critic could easily be toppled over and turned into a Communist one'. At least two features of Marx's doctrine are clearly in his mind as he discusses *Paradise Lost*. Communism, like Christianity, calls both for militant activism and for a belief in historical inevitability. God's omnipotence makes victory in the War in Heaven a foregone conclusion, yet he must deploy his angelic fire power (like the Red Army) in battles which, in Milton's account, are absurdly one-sided. In addition, Empson deduces that Milton's God was planning for his eventual abdication. The angelic dictatorship would outlive its function, and the divine State would wither away. If his Milton is a great and even a sympathetic poet, despite his role as an apologist for unspeakable wickedness, it is probably because Empson attributed to him some of the tragic and tortuous dilemmas experienced by intellectuals committed to communism.

Empson, so far as we know, had no such commitment. Born in 1906, he was several years older than the 'Marxising' generation of Cambridge undergraduates with their quota of communist poets and spies. For all its niggling skirmishes and moments of self-parody, *Milton's God* marks the return of a strongly ethical criticism, concentrating on questions of character, motive and theological justification rather than on verbal ambiguities. Perhaps in the end the creed of value-free verbal analysis which he had spelt out in his *Kenyon Review* article of 1950 simply bored Empson? In *Seven Types of Ambiguity* he had confessed to the intense excitement of an interpretative procedure which seemed to cast new light on the nature of language. In the later criticism he surrenders to excitements of a different sort, reacting to the disappointing and humdrum world of postwar academic criticism with a noble rage.

Northrop Frye

When in *Seven Types of Ambiguity* and elsewhere Empson pauses to acknowledge the difference between the procedures of verbal analysis and the ordinary reader's response to poetry, he often sounds curiously apologetic. 'Teasing out the meanings of the text' is, he explains, helpful to himself, and with luck it may be helpful to us too.[26] Modesty of this sort is entirely alien to the criticism of Northrop Frye, who is the most influential purely literary critic of the generation that began writing immediately after the Second

World War. Frye makes no apology for the rigours of textual study, and appears to hold the ordinary reader's response to literary works in contempt. Critical thinking, he argues, begins *after* all the words of the text have been read. It sets out to construct an 'ideal experience' of the work, in which 'A great mass of additional detail that we missed in the sequential reading ... becomes relevant, because all the images are metaphorically linked with all the other images, not merely those that follow each other in the narrative.'[27] The model for such a process of study, in Frye's view, is the typological reading of the Bible. Such a reading is not analytical but synthetic. Its aim is to reveal not the diversity but the unity of the work, as a 'single archetypal structure', a poem completely consistent in its imagery and symbolism.[28] Nor is such consistency restricted to individual poems or plays or works of scripture. We do not need to go very far in Frye's writings to find that internal consistency, interlinkage and typological repetition are properties that he attributes to literature as a whole, and then to the still larger structures of knowledge, language, culture and history. Frye's version of modern scholasticism attempts not mere literary criticism but what he characteristically refers to as a 'higher' criticism, an encyclopaedic view of the real or essential nature of human society. Dwarfing Aristotle, what he sometimes refers to as his 'poetics' is the most ambitious intellectual system ever to have emerged from literary theory. It aspires to scientific status, and its true counterparts are to be found in the social sciences such as anthropology and sociology – not to mention metaphysics and philosophy of history – rather than in the study of literature.

In one of the very few personal asides in his writing, Frye has remarked that a favourite book of his childhood was H. G. Wells's *Outline of History*.[29] Later he doubtless absorbed other synoptic modern historians such as Spengler and Toynbee, as well as the anthropology of Sir J. G. Frazer. Like Frazer's *The Golden Bough*, Frye's life's work has been to produce a 'key to all mythologies', though his historical vision is cyclical rather than potentially progressive. Frye's historiography is cobbled together from various sources stretching from Vico's *The New Science* to such twentieth-century mythopoeic systems as Yeats's *A Vision* and Joyce's *Finnegans Wake*. Like all its predecessors, it points to the modern age as the moment of supreme crisis or apocalypse which marks the end of a completed cycle and, possibly, the beginning of a new one: Frye has argued that society has moved from a primitive stage to a 'decadent' one in its attachment to the arts, that the modern poet is belated in respect of his cultural tradition, that we have completed a 'gigantic cycle of language' from Homer's time and are about to go round again, and so forth.[30] The most famous of his cycles is the fivefold sequence of fictional modes set out at the beginning of *Anatomy of Criticism* (1957): here we are told that western literature during the Christian era has 'steadily moved its center of gravity down the list' from the mythical to the ironic mode. The next stage – as in the new form of science fiction which Frye fits effortlessly into his theory – is, it is suggested, 'the return of irony to myth'.

Though it has many of the trappings of intellectual modernity, Frye's system is also a blatantly archaic, almost medieval construct. Frank Kermode has noted its 'theological rigour'.[31] Its author's Canadian origins are doubtless relevant, for it is in Canada and the United States that the most avid consumers of twentieth-century non-Marxist theories of world history are to be found.[32] Yet, as we shall see, it is precisely the anxious modernity of his inspiration and outlook that Frye cannot possibly admit. His major book was called an 'anatomy', after the loosely encyclopaedic prose form epitomised by Burton's seventeenth-century *Anatomy of Melancholy*. His constant reference to the Bible as 'the world's greatest work of art'[33] and the central expression of western civilisation suggests an attitude closer to Dante's or Milton's than to other modern secular literary critics. Throughout his writings, he interprets reality in terms of the hierarchy of temporal appearance and spiritual substance. Such matters as political change and changes in literary taste – above all, those associated with the modernist revolution – are relegated to the temporal realm. Referring, for example, to the challenges to Milton's reputation mounted by such major critics as Eliot, Pound and Leavis, Frye has stated that 'Milton's greatness as a poet is unaffected by this: as far as the central fact of his importance in literature is concerned, these eminent critics might as well have said nothing at all.'[34] The assumption of timeless authority in statements like these is often puzzling to his readers, but in Frye's own view it derives from his position as a humanist and literary scholar. The universities are the social embodiment of the spiritual realm in modern society, he believes. His confidence might seem enviable, but it is also self-serving and narcissistic.

Frye has always distinguished the scholarly activity of literary interpretation from criticism in the sense of value-judgment. The only legitimate form of value-judgment he will admit is the 'recognition' of new works, but this he regards as a trivial and journalistic task, preliminary to the genuine act of scholarly understanding. *Anatomy of Criticism* begins with a 'Polemical Introduction', first published in 1949 under the Arnoldian title 'The Function of Criticism at the Present Time'. Polemical it certainly is. Frye describes the critic according to existing conceptions as a 'parasite', a 'jackal' and an 'educated shrew'; he dismisses Wordsworth's Preface to *Lyrical Ballads* with the comment that as criticism 'nobody would give it more than about a B plus', and speaks of the 'high percentage of sheer futility in all criticism' and the utter ignorance of its practitioners. In later works he has been equally shrill, accusing the evaluative critic of paranoia, self-advertisement and anxiety-projection.[35] In place of evaluative criticism Frye seeks to promote an impersonal science of literary understanding, such as is already implicit in the institutions of scholarship, but has yet to be realised in the form of a 'systematic study, the elementary principles of which could be explained to any intelligent nineteen-year-old'. All Frye's books are in a sense 'teachers' manuals' expounding the principles of mythopoeic or archetypal thinking for such students, as well as for their equally ignorant teachers.[36]

Frye's intricate yet rigid system received its first embodiment in a study of Blake's Prophetic Books, *Fearful Symmetry* (1947), and in an essay on 'The Archetypes of Literature' published four years later. *Fearful Symmetry* presents Blake not as a madman or eccentric but as a 'typical poet' in lineal succession to Chaucer, Spenser and Milton. Like his predecessors, Blake is the author of a national epic drawing on the romance tradition but referring back ultimately to the Bible as the archetype or 'great code' of Western culture. 'The Archetypes of Literature', however, refers to cultural anthropology rather than to Biblical criticism: here Frye outlines his conception of the whole of literary history as a 'complication of a relatively restricted and simple group of formulas that can be studied in primitive culture'. Frye's notion of a mythical formula differs from that of the structuralists and Russian Formalists who tried to subject all narrative to functional linguistic analysis. His formulas refer directly to the nature of 'real' (as opposed to merely temporal) society. They are located, above all, in the encyclopaedic myths he calls 'myths of concern', the central, culture-sustaining narratives which comprise 'everything that it most concerns [their societies] to know'.[37] Such myths are not, as was often thought, superannuated by the growth of rationality and science; instead, they are re-created in every age by the poets.

In *Anatomy of Criticism*, Frye with vast erudition divides western literature into the central classical genres of tragedy, comedy, romance and satire, which in turn are related to the immemorial rhythm of the seasons. Early in the book he introduces the medieval fourfold system of Biblical interpretation, and finally he comes to the archetypal 'myth of concern' itself, the Bible. The Bible, like everything else here, has a cyclical structure – a 'gigantic cycle from creation to apocalypse' – in terms of which modern man appears distinctly belated. All secular literature is necessarily related to it (a conception that Frye seems to have absorbed from Vico). The *Anatomy* is also held together by frequent analogies with music, grammar and mathematics, though the fact that the latter three disciplines (unlike literature) have been codified for centuries does not seem to bother Frye. The 'Tentative Conclusion' suggests that other social discourses such as law, theology, metaphysics and the social sciences could be brought within the same compass, and a later book, *The Critical Path* (1971), attempts to do this.

Frye's synoptic view of literature offers a valuable corrective to the historical parochialism of institutionalised New Criticism. It recaptures the epic and narrative dimensions of the literature of the past, with a bias towards the recognition of ironic and romance elements which allows Frye to take notice of contemporary popular fiction as well. Central to his vision, however, are his conceptions of the poet – the inspired figure who in every generation revives the mythological archetypes – and of poetics, or the study of poetry. Frye's conception of the grand mission of the poet links him to the romantics, especially Blake and Shelley, while his view of poetics as a theoretical endeavour leading to a total explanation of society and history underlies more recent attempts to promote literary theory as an all-embracing discipline. Once poetics has emerged, indeed, it is not clear that society needs to go on producing poets, and in the 'Polemical Introduction' he wrote that, even if new literature ceased to be written, literary study would proceed unaffected. The notion of studying a 'dead language' seems congenial to Frye – he already knows where everything fits – but he insists on an absolute distinction between scholarship and poetry. Perhaps his gravest charge against evaluative criticism is that the critic himself is trying to create a 'myth of concern'. He 'wants to get into the concern game himself, choosing a canon out of literature and so making literature a single gigantic allegory of his own anxieties'.[38]

For all his assertions that what he himself offers is poetics rather than poetry, Frye's oeuvre contains many statements which invite a narcissistic reading, drawing attention, implicitly, to his own resemblance to the poets he discusses. His books, too, can be seen to form a deliberate and self-conscious canon, full of the repetitions and interlinkages that denote typological unity, and possessing its own fearful symmetry. It is in his first book on Blake that the self-definitions begin. Blake, Frye argues, is a visionary not a mystic, and a visionary 'creates, or dwells in, a higher spiritual world in which the objects of perception in this one have become transfigured and charged with a new intensity of symbolism'. The function of the epic, he writes, is to teach, to members of the social unit that the poet is addressing, their own traditions. Frye's criticism transfigures the literary objects it encounters for a very similar pedagogic purpose. Later he argues that a study of archetypes could produce 'the missing piece in contemporary thought which, when supplied, will unite its whole pattern'. Once again he seems to be celebrating his own future achievement.

Other statements could be read not as self-praise but as self-diagnosis. For all his asperity towards the type of evaluative critic who tries to 'get into the concern game himself', the negative aspects of 'myths of concern' are readily recognizable in his own writing. 'The vice of concern', he writes in *The Stubborn Structure* (1970) 'is anxiety. We have anxiety when a society seizes on one myth and attempts to pound the whole of knowledge and truth into a structure conforming to it.' In an essay 'On Value-Judgements' (1968) he sounds still more lofty and vindictive, observing that 'Every age, left to itself, is incredibly narrow in its cultural range, and the critic, unless he is a greater genius than the world has yet seen, shares that narrowness in proportion to his confidence in his taste.' (Frye's own self-confidence allows for so little humility that one cannot resist the suspicion that he himself must be the 'greater genius' referred to.) Other critics do no more than exercise their personal taste, and so are condemned to temporal narrowness, while he claims the impersonal spiritual authority vested in his system. He even manages on occasion to sound superior to poets as well as to other critics, teachers and ordinary readers. Poets, he has written, 'are a competitive and traditionally an irritable group; their genius is one of intensity rather than wisdom or serenity'.[39] Once again, this passage invites a narcissistic reading. Even if we fail to grant Frye the qualities of wisdom and serenity, we can hardly deny him a poet's intensity, competitiveness and irritability.

Northrop Frye has written that there are three levels of criticism – criticism militant (the lowest), literary understanding, and 'criticism triumphant, the inner possession of literature as an imaginative force to which all study of literature leads, and which is criticism at once glorified and invisible'.[40] Works of literature are 'not things to be contemplated but powers to be absorbed'.[41] We can have a scientific understanding of a thing, but not of a power that we absorb. And when Frye is forced to abandon a scientific terminology of literary interpretation he invariably has recourse to theological vocabulary. Because of his assertions of the permanence and disinterestedness of academic scholarship, and of the subordination of critics to poets, and of students to their teachers, he has seemed to stand for humanist ideals. His absolute commitment to traditional notions of intellectual authority is of a kind that all the newer movements in criticism, from neo-Marxism to feminism and post-structuralism, have brought under attack. The connection between Frye's own view of culture as a spiritual realm and Matthew Arnold's is one to which he has himself drawn attention.[42] But he is both more and less than an Arnoldian humanist. If – as the various signs of anxiety and visionary stubbornness in his writings suggest – he has himself produced a poetic 'myth of concern' uniquely adapted to, yet rising above, the condition of modernity, then that is his glory. But once it loses only one of its supports – such as the hard-fought distinction between scientific knowledge and mythopoeic vision – the whole system collapses, and Frye's magisterial poetics becomes revealed as the grandest of literary impostures.

Roman Jakobson

When a large edifice lies in ruins, it yields good building stone for other projects. There are bits and pieces of Frye's system from which almost every subsequent critic has profited – notably, his characterisations of genres and modes. Other traditional concerns of criticism barely enter his writings. Not only does he forswear evaluation but he is the least verbal of critics: even literary quotations are excluded from three of the four essays which make up the *Anatomy of Criticism*. Though he maintains that 'Literature, like mathematics, is a language',[43] this does not commit him to examining the linguistic structures of individual literary works in any detail. Frye's criticism here is at the opposite pole from that of the structuralists, who aim to develop a universal literary science by applying the principles of theoretical linguistics and semiotics (the general science of signs). Linguistics and semiotics are accustomed to deal with very brief texts – typically, the sentence and the message – so that, in literary studies, this form of analysis has been most elaborately developed with respect to the short poem. Contemporary semiotics draws mainly on the pioneering work of two turn-of-the-century thinkers, the Swiss linguist Ferdinand de Saussure and the American philosopher C. S. Peirce. It has had a major impact on such disciplines as anthropology, psychoanalysis, and film and media studies as well as literary criticism. The major modern semioticians – continental thinkers such as

Emile Benveniste, A. J. Greimas, Roland Barthes, Claude Lévi-Strauss, and Umberto Eco – are largely peripheral to the history of English criticism, with one crucial exception. This is the Russian-born linguist Roman Jakobson, who became an American citizen and, late in his life, applied his analytic techniques in a series of commentaries on specific English poems.

Jakobson's essay 'Linguistics and Poetics' (1960) begins by reject-ing the label of 'critic' for the scholarly analyst of literary works. Literary scholarship, instead, aims at a 'poetics' which is an integral part of linguistic science. The division between poetic analysis and criticism corresponds to that between pure and applied linguistics; the former, in each case, is clearly the higher and more philosophi-cal activity. For Jakobson, the 'poetic function' is one of six differ-ent functions involved in the construction of verbal messages; the others are the referential, the emotive, the conative, the phatic and the metalingual functions. Poetic function, defined as a 'focus on the message for its own sake', is potentially present in any act of verbal communication; in literary works, however, it is the dominant function. ('Dominant', as we shall see, is one of Jakob-son's key terms.) Poetic function is manifested in the linguistic features which Jakobson groups under the general heading of 'equi-valence' or 'parallelism', enumerating their multiple varieties by reference to bodies of poetry in every major world language, as well as American Indian songs and African riddles. The underlying principle of parallelism, however, is said by Jakobson to derive from Robert Lowth's account of the texture of ancient Hebrew poetry (1778). It was first suggested as a general principle of all poetry in the notebooks of the Victorian poet Gerard Manley Hop-kins. Jakobson's innovation, then, is the systematic analysis of vari-able and invariant modes of parallelism and repetition at each linguistic level of the poem. Beginning with clear-cut and stereo-typed forms of poetry, he aimed to produce a descriptive frame-work which could be applied to any instance of the poetic function in language.

In order to understand his developed linguistic theory, we need to return to his intellectual origins. Jakobson was a leading member of the Moscow Linguistic Circle in the early 1920s, sharing the Formalist aim of basing a literary science on the concept of 'literari-ness'. Later, when the Formalist movement was suppressed, he was a founder of the Prague Linguistic Circle with substantially similar aims. While in Czechoslovakia Jakobson redefined 'literari-ness' as 'poeticity',[44] and developed his concept of the 'dominant', which states the necessity of a hierarchy of functions in any commu-nicative system. He then moved to New York, teaching at the

Ecole Libre des Hautes Etudes together with Claude Lévi-Strauss during the years 1942–6. Twenty years later, Jakobson and Lévi-Strauss were to collaborate in a famous structuralist analysis of Baudelaire's poem 'Les Chats'.

Jakobson's career forcefully illustrates the multinational character of contemporary literary theory. He is one of a group of twentieth-century critics (Paul de Man is another) whose careers were formed by a more or less accidental pattern of emigration in response to revolution and world war. The geographical isolation of the United States, together with the wealth of its universities, led large numbers of European intellectual emigrants to seek a home there. Once in the New World, cut off from the cultures which had nurtured them and from participation in the more public aspects of American life, some settled down to pursue the dream of a global 'science' of linguistic and literary study which would supersede the nationalistic traditions of literature and history in Europe. Obviously, there are strengths and weaknesses in the vision of a universal literary theory detached from the particular circumstances that produced the literature in the first place; what should be noted, however, is the extent to which a scholar such as Jakobson came to inhabit a museum-culture in which every form of poetry, including the contemporary poetry with which he had been intimate as a young man, was seen as belonging to the past and capable of being spread out for scientific inspection like a butterfly in a glass case.

During his Moscow years, Jakobson had been associated with some of the most original artists and thinkers of the twentieth century. His widow has written that his 'entire spiritual orientation must be viewed as both the result and the corrective of the art and science of the avant-garde'.[45] This is one reason why Jakobson remains a towering figure in literary studies, as well as in the professional domains of linguistics and semiotics. The Russian avant-garde, however, failed to survive the post-revolutionary period and the onset of the Stalinist era. Jakobson reflected on its fate in his moving essay 'On a Generation that Squandered Its Poets' (1931), written shortly after the suicide of his friend Vladimir Mayakovsky. Here Jakobson recalls how, in 1920, he returned to Moscow (where books and information were exceedingly scarce) with details of Einstein's discovery of relativity. Mayakovsky was fascinated by the news, and pressed his friend for further details.

I'd seldom seen him so interested and attentive. 'Don't you think,' he suddenly asked, 'that we'll at last achieve immortality?' I was astonished, and I mumbled a skeptical comment. He thrust his jaw forward with that hypnotic insistence so familiar to anyone who knew Mayakovsky well. 'I'm absolutely convinced,' he said, 'that one day there will be no death'.

This story becomes the key to Jakobson's interpretation of Mayakovsky's poetic themes, but it is revealing for a rather different reason. Jakobson was intimate with the avant-garde, he had a deep understanding of the poetic function and the poetic manner, yet in certain respects he could never really speak their language. It offended his rational sensibility. This should be remembered when we read the elegiac conclusion to 'On a Generation that Squandered Its Poets':

All we had were compelling songs of the future; and suddenly these songs are no longer part of the dynamic of history, but have been transformed into historico–literary facts. When singers have been killed and their song has been dragged into a museum and pinned to the wall of the past, the generation they represent is even more desolate, orphaned, and lost – impoverished in the most real sense of the word.[46]

Exiled from the 'dynamic of history', Jakobson himself would henceforth be concerned with the songs of dead poets as 'historico–literary facts'. In his exhaustive technical inventories of the linguistic richness of certain poems he perhaps found a kind of substitute world, a place of settled perfection that the world outside could not squander. The 'orphan' metaphor reappears in his structuralist analyses of verse, since there are, as he wrote in a 1966 essay, no 'orphan lines' or phrases in the poetry of pervasive parallels. Any word or clause entering such a poem is 'immediately incorporated into the tenacious array of cohesive grammatical forms and semantic values'.[47]

Semiotic theories such as Jakobson's are based on the dogma of the absolute unity and coherence of great poetry. Jakobson accepts the Formalist theory of literary change as a process of dynamic interaction between the various elements of the poetic 'system', leading to their regrouping under another 'dominant'; nevertheless, in practice he is concerned with fixed structures, and his principal analyses are of short poems in strict metrical forms such as Shakespeare's and Baudelaire's sonnets. To some extent he builds on New Critical practice, endorsing Empson's and Ransom's approaches to poetic language, though he reproves Ransom for confining his account of the structure of a sonnet to its strictly logical organisation. Jakobson holds both that the poem is a unified system and that this unity expresses the author's individual purpose (whether deliberate or intuitive).

A Jakobsonian analysis aims, then, at an exhaustive demonstration of the systematic coherence of the poetic text. 'Pervasive parallelism' is a language-game permitting an infinite number of permutations and combinations, but played with the fixed counters that Jakobson lists as constituting 'all the levels of language: the distinctive features, inherent and prosodic, the morphological and syntactic categories and forms, the lexical units and their semantic classes in both their convergences and divergences'.[48] Not only is the language of his semiotic analyses highly technical, but the poem's 'referential function' is for the most part reduced to formulae. The Jakobson–Lévi-Strauss analysis of 'Baudelaire's "Les Chats"' (1962), for example, refers in a curiously perfunctory way to the miraculous quality and mythological associations of the cats in the poem. The essay's one strongly interpretative suggestion – that the cats in Baudelaire's sonnet take the place of women – appears to be taken from an article by Michel Butor. The fact that a first-time reader is likely to misinterpret some of Baudelaire's lines – taking them as referring to human beings rather than to cats – is also passed over in silence.

A later theoretician, Michael Riffaterre, has tried to remedy these deficiencies by developing a more genuinely interpretative semiotics. Riffaterre's *Semiotics of Poetry* (1978) argues not only that poetic language differs from common linguistic usage but that 'a poem says one thing and means another'. The second, hidden meaning can only be discovered by retroactive reading.[49] Riffaterre's terminology is both denser and much more eclectic than Jakobson's. In both writers there is a contrast between the universal and scientific claims of the theory and a certain narrowness in the examples: short French poems of the nineteenth and twentieth centuries in Riffaterre's case, and short poems dealing with disappointed love or its magical sublimation in the case of Jakobson's articles on English and French poetry. Narrowness of a different kind is rather dramatically revealed in Jakobson's 'Language in Operation' (written in 1949 but not published until 1964), where he tackles Poe's 'The Raven'. A crucial point in Jakobson's theory is the opposition between poetic function (language focused on the message for its own sake) and metalinguistic function (language focused on the code in order to clarify it). Without some such opposition, structuralism could not claim to offer a scientific theory of poetry, for there would be no analytical language wholly separable from poetic language.

Poe, however, used both languages. 'The Raven' exhibits poetic function, but his essay 'The Philosophy of Composition' purports to give an exhaustive account of the logical and deductive process by which the poem was composed. According to Jakobson, Poe 'formulated perfectly the relationship between poetic language and its translation into what would now be called the metalanguage of scientific analysis'. The only problem is that, Baudelaire excepted, few readers have taken Poe's account of how he composed 'The Raven' entirely seriously. Jakobson professes himself mystified by the long line of critics who have referred to 'The Philosophy of Composition' as a 'mischievous caprice', as 'unparalleled effrontery', or simply as a leg-pull.

Jakobson's analysis of 'The Raven' is in some ways extremely perceptive. He notes, for example, that parallelism in the text extends to the near-palindromic relationship between the name of the bird itself and its famous refrain: *raven* is almost a mirror-image of *never*. For Jakobson, however, the raven appears simply as a name without an object. Its referent is not a bird but an abstract position in the thwarted communication-system which (he believes) the poem constitutes. The resulting analysis of 'The Raven' as a 'tragically one-sided' pseudo-dialogue cannot give anything more than perfunctory recognition to the grotesque and supernatural element in the poem. Poe's lover may see himself as tragic, but he is also manifestly absurd. 'The Philosophy of Composition' reduces 'The Raven' to a mathematical problem or emotional machine, which is more or less what Jakobsonian analysis does to poetry in general. But Poe's use of a scientific metalanguage in 'The Philosophy of Composition' and many other essays and tales is almost invariably parodic. Parody is of course a species of metalanguage, whether or not it belongs to 'poetic function'. It would seem that Jakobsonian analysis is powerless to distinguish between parody and non-parody, whether in the context of a poem or a scientific essay.

Roman Jakobson's critical methods have been widely influential, notably because of their insistence on the fundamental importance of binary pairings. One of his favourite binaries – the distinction between metaphor and metonymy – has been adopted by some critics as a universal principle of literary language. Recent semioticians, however, have turned to other sources. C. S. Peirce's semiotics offers one way out of the binary straitjacket.[50] But perhaps the sharpest contrast to Jakobson's sensitive and precise, if limited, approach is to be found in his Russian contemporary Mikhail Bakhtin.

Bakhtin was a lifelong outsider, excluded from the Formalist circles to which Jakobson belonged, and condemned to decades of pedagogic drudgery and internal exile by his refusal to emigrate from the Soviet Union. His writings are, none the less, joyous celebrations of the anarchic and carnivalesque aspects of literature, in which the central genre is not the short poem, but the sprawling, undisciplined novel. Bakhtin values the novel as the great antisystematic and anticanonical literary form, overflowing the boundaries of 'literariness' or 'poeticity' according to the Formalists' definitions.[51] In *Morphology of the Folktale* (1928) the Formalist Vladimir Propp outlined what he saw as the repetitive and schematic character of all prose narrative. For Bakhtin, however, the novel is characteristically 'dialogic', undermining literary and social hierarchies with the diversity of its linguistic codes and discourses. There is an implicit contrast in Bakhtin between monoglot poetry and an ideal 'heteroglossia' which finds its medium in the novelist, the reveller, the clown and the parodist. 'Parodic stylizations of canonized genres and styles occupy an essential place in the novel', he wrote. 'In world literature there are probably many works whose parodic nature has not even been suspected.'[52] Perhaps in the end his thought is too clearly oppositional, too much the expression of an open revolt against Formalist perspectives to be satisfying; but where Jakobsonian analysis seems incapable of detecting parody, Bakhtin would see parody everywhere.

Theory and Interpretation: The Text and the Dream

One of Roman Jakobson's most daring papers was 'Two Aspects of Language and Two Types of Aphasic Disturbances' (1956). Here he linked the two kinds of linguistic confusion suffered by mental patients with what he saw as the two grand opposing principles of linguistic organisation: similarity and contiguity, or metaphor and metonymy. Calling for joint research by experts in psychology, linguistics, poetics and semiotics, Jakobson suggested a hectic series of interdisciplinary applications for the similarity/contiguity distinction, which was, he hinted, fundamental both to Freud's classification of dream symbolism and to Frazer's analysis of the principles underlying magic rites. Indeed, the distinction was 'of primal significance and consequence for all verbal behaviour and for human behaviour in general'.[1]

These claims of Jakobson's have been much debated within the field of contemporary literary theory. 'Literary theory', in its newer sense, principally consists of theories that use literary and linguistic models as jumping-off points in order to posit fundamental insights into vast areas of social life. The philosopher Richard Rorty has written of literary theory's claim to 'preside over the rest of culture', backed up by an 'exhibition of its ability to put the other disciplines in their places'.[2] It asserts its power over other disciplines through its commitment to what has been called 'pantextualism', the view that all social phenomena are to be understood as 'texts', or systems of codes, to be interpreted. Pantextualism is a feature of deconstructionist doctrine and also of the cultural theories of social scientists like Clifford Geertz (to be discussed in Chapter 7). Nevertheless, its greatest appeal is, understandably enough, to those involved in the study of literature.

A universal theory of texts must be potentially aimed at a universal readership. Literary theory is thus necessarily a multinational enterprise, reuniting the different national traditions of criticism much as multinational capitalism is reuniting the world's industrial economies. The two developments show certain parallels, and both have flourished in the epoch of America's emergence as a great power policing the 'Free World' – the 'freedom' concerned being, of course, intellectual as well as economic. Not only does literary theory give a new twist to the cultural imperialism of an Arnold or a Leavis; it also reveals many of the up-to-date characteristics of capitalist competition. The academic 'market-leaders' of theory, writing at a more popular level than Jakobson or Frye, have shown remarkable dexterity in re-furbishing their product-lines, launching new brightly packaged intellectual models and consigning yesterday's theories to the remainder shop. The main casualty of such built-in theoretical obsolescence has been the ambition of founding a critical science offering not mental excitements but reliable knowledge.

The change of tempo in literary studies which began in the 1960s is captured by Elizabeth Bruss's phrase 'Suddenly, an Age of Theory'.[3] It was less like a 'paradigm shift' in literary criticism – since, as one writer put it, 'bright and promising theoretical paradigms'[4] seemed to come and go with awesome rapidity – than a sudden access of wealth. At one extreme, there was the rapid succession of translations of the major early twentieth-century European works of philosophy and cultural theory, often the work of authors who had suffered decades of silencing, persecution and neglect. At the other extreme was the belief, or the hope, that intense theoretical activity somehow made up for the perceived deficiencies of contemporary imaginative writing in England and America. The 'dominant mode of literary expression', according to the editor of an academic journal founded in 1974, was now criticism and theory of the kind published in the new academic journals.[5] Theory flourished particularly in the United States, where the very existence of an audience for literature outside the universities was now being questioned; and theory in America was often supposed to be more innovative, and more adequate to the needs of the time, than poetry or fiction. Yet the canon of earlier literature to which American literary theorists tended to refer became increasingly narrow and predictable.

Structuralism and semiotics had reduced the text to a set of linguistic devices or formulae rather than a communication of feelings between author and reader. Like the modernist poets, these methods 'placed the lyrical monologue in quotes and disguised the "ego" of the lyric poet under a pseudonym', as Jakobson put it.[6] The growing recognition that this was a partial and inadequate approach is reflected in the widely accepted distinction between structuralism and hermeneutics or interpretation. The practice of interpretation today is itself the subject of an intricate theoretical discourse, which has become increasingly important to literary criticism. Traditionally, hermeneutics was conceived as a 'resumption of meaning' involving the imaginative reconstruction of the past and the intuitive convergence of the reader's with the writer's understanding.[7] This notion, however, has been undermined by the doctrines of 'deconstruction' which license playful interpretation giving rise to a deliberate plurality of meaning, and also by political modes of criticism which stress the reader's responsibility to reinterpret the text against the grain of what the author may have put there. At a time when proposals for a textual science and attempts to circumscribe the text's possible meanings are widely discredited, the activity of interpretation has come to be regarded as the core of literary study and, indeed, of the reading of literature in general.

Freud and deconstruction

The modern prestige of 'interpretation' as a model of understanding can be traced back to one of the twentieth century's seminal books, which has now influenced at least four generations of literary critics. This is Sigmund Freud's *The Interpretation of Dreams* (1900). The first extended psychoanalytic interpretation of an English literary text was the study of *Hamlet* by Freud's disciple Ernest Jones, originally published in 1910. The impact of psychoanalysis lurks unacknowledged in T. S. Eliot's essay on 'Hamlet' (1919), and from this date onwards Freudian and Jungian ideas were eagerly taken up in artistic and intellectual circles. Yet, although *The Interpretation of Dreams* had appeared in English translation in 1913, the full recognition of its implications for literary criticism did not come until after the Second World War.

The two traditional methods of interpreting dreams were what Freud calls the 'symbolic' method and the 'decoding' method. Both are, to some extent, subsumed in the method of dream-analysis proposed by Freud. His basic principle is that the dream is a form of wish-fulfilment whose content is distorted by the phenomenon of mental censorship. The process of dream-construction, which Freud calls the 'dream-work', takes place in the unconscious mind and shows enormous ingenuity in its efforts to thwart and circumvent the internal 'censor'. The analyst's task is to use the methods of decoding and symbolic reading to move from the manifest to the latent content of the dream.

The relation between dream and linguistic expression is crucial to *The Interpretation of Dreams*.[8] The therapeutic basis of psychoanalysis is reflected in the notion of interpretation with its heavy emphasis on the content, rather than the form, of the dream; but some features of Freud's work tend to counteract this emphasis. In the first place, dream-interpretation is an open-ended process since it is never possible to be sure that a dream has been completely interpreted.[9] Secondly, Freud examines the nature of the dream-work in very great detail, outlining such processes as 'condensation' and 'displacement' by which a large number of unconscious trains of thought can be combined together in a single 'overdetermined' image or narrative element. Condensation includes the devices of verbal ambiguity, punning and the construction of portmanteau-words, all of which may occur in the process of dreaming. Displacement involves a redistribution of emphasis among the dream-ideas, to produce a version distorted enough to evade the operations of censorship. As a means of unravelling the condensed and displaced dream-thoughts, Freud recommends the technique of 'free association' to relax the critical and rational faculties of the mind. Both the free associations and the dreams themselves must be put into words if they are to be available to the analyst; and the specimen dreams in *The Interpretation of Dreams* are necessarily presented to the reader in the form of written texts. Freud's analysis uncovers what in traditional literary terminology might be called the grammar, the syntax, the vocabulary and rhetoric of dreaming. Not surprisingly, literary critics have adopted his principles to explore the 'latent' meanings and structures of poems and novels.

The earliest, and still the most widespread, use of Freudian methods in literary interpretation is for biographical ends. The author of the text to be analysed is treated as in some sense a psychoanalytic patient, and the text itself is the dream. Though often criticised for their reductiveness, the results of such analyses are frequently illuminating. They depend, however, on a very literal adoption of the nineteenth-century principle that art is fundamentally self-expressive. The problems to which this can lead are rather amusingly exemplified in a passage in which Freud speculates on the relationship between the 'neurotic symptoms' exhibited in *Hamlet* and the death of Shakespeare's father in 1601. 'It can of course only be the poet's own mind which confronts us in *Hamlet*', Freud observes. A later footnote, however, records his conversion to the theory that the real author of Shakespeare's plays was the Earl of Oxford.[10] Ernest Jones is equally vociferous in claiming that a psychoanalyst's reading of *Hamlet* gives access to the deeper levels of its author's mind, though in fact the reference to the biographical Shakespeare is extrinsic to the interpretation itself. What *is* of permanent interest is Freud's and Jones's contention that both *Hamlet* and Sophocles' *Oedipus Rex* deal in different ways with the buried matter of the male child's wishful fantasy of killing his father and marrying his mother.

Lionel Trilling argues in 'Freud and Literature' (1947) that the difference between the artist and the neurotic is that the artist is in command of his fantasy, not possessed by it. Trilling acknowledges, however, that the Freudian mechanisms of condensation and displacement come very close to the making of poetry. He suggests that psychoanalysis can be reincorporated into humanistic thought by stressing, first, that Freud's insights into the hidden conflicts of human nature had long been anticipated by the poets, and second, that the creative process, though analogous to the 'dream-work', is subject to the artist's conscious control. Trilling, who divides his attention between the Freud of *The Interpretation of Dreams* and the later Freudian doctrines of the 'death instinct' and the reality principle, argues that the underlying contention of psychoanalysis is to highlight the 'figurative' nature of all human thought. The new science of mind is a 'science of tropes, of metaphor and its variants, synecdoche and metonomy'.[11] This remark of Trilling's now seems strikingly prescient, for there is a close connection between the Freudian influence on recent literary theory and the rehabilitation of some of the terminology of traditional rhetoric.

Recent criticism has inherited the notion of psychoanalysis as a science of tropes while throwing out, in many cases, the humanistic ballast of the well-adjusted mind and the controlling author. Frederick J. Hoffman, a contemporary of the New Critics, had written of literary forms as providing 'the means of inhibition, the ways of containing creative energy, of balancing its tensions'.[12]

In current theory literature is usually seen not as an index of psychic balance but of imbalance, a theatre of warring codes and conflicting signs. Freud's splitting of the self into the separate entities of id, ego and superego destroys (or so it is said) the myth of the unified and deliberate author: writers have little more control over the texts they produce than dreamers have over their dreams. The French psychoanalyst Jacques Lacan and his followers have stressed the playful and pluralistic aspects of Freudian interpretation and its ability to undermine all orthodox notions of moral responsibility and individual integrity. For Roland Barthes, for example, the aim of interpretation is not to 'find the meaning' but to 'live the plurality of the text', while Michel Foucault views the 'authorial function' as an ideological figure used to limit the proliferation of meanings.[13] In Jacques Derrida's writings, Freud's dismemberment of selfhood and consciousness is brought together with Nietzsche's and Heidegger's critiques of the metaphysics of 'presence'. The figure of the author then becomes not only the manifestation of a (self-contradictory) latent content but the scene of an absence, a hypothetical, irrecoverable notion which the rational mind is constantly forced to reinvent in the very moment of discovering its non-existence. The deconstructionist movement in American literary criticism is heavily influenced by this conjoining of Freudian discourse with an intense metaphysical scepticism.

In 'Structure, Sign and Play in the Discourse of the Human Sciences' (1966), Derrida contrasted the notion of interpretation as decipherment with the notion of 'textual play' – the 'affirmation of a world of signs without fault, without truth, and without origin'.[14] This world of irresponsible signals reflects both Freud's pleasure principle (the dream as fulfilment of a wish) and the structuralist doctrine of the arbitrariness of the linguistic sign. The text for Derrida is no longer a 'finished corpus of writing, some content enclosed in a book or its margins', but a 'differential network, a fabric of traces referring endlessly to...other differential traces'.[15] One of the classes of signs thus divested of their fixed meanings is the class of the names of authors, such as Shelley: Shelley, as J. Hillis Miller writes in the Yale Critics' manifesto *Deconstruction and Criticism* (1979), becomes no more than a rhetorical device within a field of intertextual play:

> Who, however, is 'Shelley'? To what does this word refer if any work signed with this name has no identifiable borders, and no interior walls either? It has no edges because it has been invaded from all sides as well as from within by other 'names', other powers of writing.[16]

The passage begins by putting the name of Shelley within quotation marks: itself a rhetorical device, this both underlines the arbitrariness of the name given to a body of poetry and alludes to the Freudian doctrine that any element in a discourse may stand, in displaced and distorted form, for something else less admissible by our mental censorship. Deconstructionists hold that meaning as such is always displaced, that meaning is not inherent in words; they 'refuse to identify the force of literature with any concept of embodied meaning'.[17]

According to Freud, dreams (and also literary texts) are over-determined and therefore need to be 'over-interpreted': 'All genuinely creative writings are the product of more than a single motive and more than a single impulse in the poet's mind, and are open to more than a single interpretation'.[18] Deconstruction has been described by one of its American advocates simply as a means of identifying – or rather generating – new and unsuspected meanings in literary texts which are already constantly subject to interpretation.[19] This helps to account for the enthusiastic response to this critical movement in the English-speaking world. Almost any expression of impatience with the scientific pretensions of earlier critical schools or with the surface reading of a literary classic can be described as deconstructionist if one wishes. As competition between rival interpretations has become more intense, deconstruction has claimed to outflank its rivals by at once questioning them all and holding them all in suspense. Paul de Man, indeed, argued that texts are 'unreadable' in the sense that they entail both the possibility and the impossibility of a fixed reading: the text undoes whatever reading it permits, including the reading that says it is unreadable. Such criticism, however, has more or less abandoned the promise of rational disentanglement held out by Freudian interpretative practice. The celebration of the open-endedness of texts and the multiplicity of readings collapses into a nihilistic metaphysics which merely ties up the critic in further knots. If all interpretation is self-deluded and if it cannot be corrected (but only superseded) by rival interpretations, then all interpretation is also pointless.

Interpretation in the wake of deconstruction is strikingly eclectic: it attacks the same texts, again and again, with different methods. In Marxist and feminist readings, the text's distortion and displacement is attributed to the operations of social ideology (whether bourgeois or patriarchal): by exposing the activities of the mental Thought Police, we may recover repressed possibilities of meaning. In poststructuralist rhetorical criticism the various levels of figuration in the text are exposed to reveal an underlying disconnection and confusion which is the true material of interpretation. 'Reader-response' criticism argues that it is the reader, not the text or the author, who produces interpretative disagreements: texts are 'constructed', not construed. These critical movements all show a deconstructionist impulse, but deconstruction is also a narrower and more sectarian doctrine, the preserve of a handful of avant-garde groups each claiming privileged access to Derridean thought. By far the most influential of these has been the so-called 'Yale school' of Geoffrey H. Hartman, Paul de Man, J. Hillis Miller and (as a somewhat dissident member) Harold Bloom. The Yale critics take a strongly metaphysical stance, holding that modern culture is pervaded by the death of God and the disappearance of the sacred. Paul de Man, for example, argues with his customary rhetorical subtlety that the 'act of faith' and the 'act of reading' are incompatible; though we cannot read without faith of a sort, readings are inherently pluralistic and thus render the text 'unreadable'.[20] Harold Bloom sees an inescapable choice between de Man's nihilism and his own advocacy of a 'magical theory of all language'.[21] He would see Derrida's dismantling of the 'logocentricity' of Western civilisation as a kind of carnivalesque obsequy for the Judeo-Christian tradition in which, as the scripture says, 'The Word was God'. The deconstructionists are much closer to Nietzsche than they are to the positivistic Freud of *The Future of an Illusion* (1927); for Freud, religion, the 'universal obsessional neurosis of humanity', was in the process of being superseded by science which was, of course, no illusion.[22] It is partly to escape from scientific rationalism that the Yale deconstructionists have returned again and again to English romantic poetry, which asserts the transcendent and prophetic status of the imaginative act while at the same time (or so it is argued) revealing its impossibility. Deconstruction points out the self-interested and self-deluding character of a scientific ideology such as the one that Freud endorsed, while licensing a new kind of intellectual extravagance as the critics themselves try to invent a philosophical language that avoids the pitfalls of rationalism.

Harold Bloom

Harold Bloom's early criticism, though a trace flamboyant, is academically orthodox. He began with a study of the romantic poets, *The Visionary Company* (1961), and with monographs on Shelley (1959), Blake (1963) and Yeats (1970). Bloom's own romanticism is evident from these books, but their lack of theoretical ambition may be deduced from the author's statement in the preface to

The Visionary Company that 'in matters of critical theory, I have been guided by Frye's *Anatomy of Criticism* and by Abrams's *The Mirror and the Lamp*.'[23] Bloom's indebtedness to Frye is acknowledged elsewhere in his early work, and recently he has referred to the Canadian writer as 'the major literary critic in the English language'.[24] It was only with his short book *The Anxiety of Influence: A Theory of Poetry* (1973) that Bloom emerged as a theorist whose own influences and 'precursors' were of more than passing interest.

Bloom's theory of poetry began as a theory of nineteenth- and twentieth-century English poetry; subsequently it was much broadened. *The Anxiety of Influence* starts, more or less, at the point where Walter Jackson Bate had left off in *The Burden of the Past and the English Poet*. Its manner, however, is startlingly different from Bate's detailed scholarly humanism. The vatic prologue and epilogue suggest Bloom's immersion in the occult traditions of Kabbalah and Gnosticism. The 'Manifesto for Antithetical Criticism' inserted roughly halfway through the book takes the form of a series of aphorisms meant to recall Wilde's preface to *Dorian Gray*, or perhaps Blake's Proverbs of Hell. The more conventional expository sections introduce an elaborate and idiosyncratic set of rhetorical terms which bring to influence-study (formerly one of the dustier and more pedantic areas of literary scholarship) the air of a sacred ritual. Bloom's theory has been elaborated, restated and often simply repeated in his subsequent books, most notably in the trilogy *A Map of Misreading* (1975), *Kabbalah and Criticism* (1975) and *Poetry and Repression* (1976). Baldly stated, it reduces literary creation to a trial of strength between the new poem or its author, seen as an 'ephebe' (the word originally meant a young military cadet) and a specific precursor in the literary canon. The new 'strong poet' must win his spurs by subduing his natural reverence for his predecessor sufficiently for him to find his own voice. Originality – a highly relative term for Bloom – is approached by way of a 'swerve' away from the precursor poem, following a path which is governed by the six 'revisionary ratios' or possible strategies of 'misreading'. All reading is misreading, according to Bloom; 'weak' misreading produces mere imitation, while strong misreading follows the revisionary ratios and permits the ephebe to inherit the precursor's power. Bloom's allegory of a trial by poetic combat thus gives a new and unexpectedly gladiatorial twist to the traditional division between major and minor poetry and poets.

The Anxiety of Influence sketches the succession from romantic poetry down to the modern American verse of Wallace Stevens

and John Ashbery. Bloom refuses to consider the modernist movement as a new departure or break in the continuity which he traces
back to the romantics' need to emulate the epic achievement of
Milton's verse. Milton, not Shakespeare, is therefore the archetypal
'strong poet'. Bloom's introduction states that Shakespeare
'belongs to the giant age before the flood, before the anxiety of
influence became central to poetic consciousness' – an image which
recalls Eliot's 'dissociation of sensibility'. The relevant history of
English poetry, on this view, seems exceptionally brief: beginning
with Milton, it 'ends' (according to *Kabbalah and Criticism*) in the
year 1806, with the perfection of the Wordsworthian 'crisis-lyric'
which set a pattern that subsequent strong poems were doomed
to repeat. In *A Map of Misreading*, however, Bloom revised his
earlier presentation of the anxiety of influence as a romantic and
post-romantic phenomenon. He now saw the 'affliction of belatedness' as a permanent malaise of Western consciousness.

Belatedness has been a recurrent concern in the critical tradition
ever since neoclassicism with its struggle of the ancients and
moderns. The problem, as we have seen earlier in this book, was
to combine reverence for the past with the necessary scope for
creative innovation. Arnold's 'grand style', for example, is a trans-
historical entity supposedly accessible to modern poets, even
though its prestigious examples come from Homer, Virgil, Dante
and Milton. In *Fearful Symmetry*, Northrop Frye discusses belatedness as a factor in the English 'epic' tradition of Chaucer, Spenser,
Milton and Blake. Blake's *Milton*, in which the poet imagines himself to be a reincarnation of his predecessor, is a key text both
for Frye and for Bloom. For Frye, Blake's poem fulfils a visionary
possibility implicit in its precursor: the poet's 'real relation' to his
predecessor is not one of emulation or rivalry, but 'the common
relation of both to the archetypal vision'.[25] Bloom, however,
regards this as a 'beautiful idealization'. What is archetypal, for
him, is not a cosmological vision but the oedipal conflict of ephebe
and precursor. Milton is 'canceled rather than fulfilled' in Blake's
poem.[26] The argument suggests that belatedness, with its associated
neurotic conflicts, is an inescapable condition, since the ephebe
has no choice but to go on killing the precursor. All innovation
takes place in the shadow of this struggle, which cannot be transcended by a 'common relation' to an external standard.

Bloom has claimed Nietzsche and Freud as the prime influences
upon his theory of influence, and since he also describes them
as 'strong poets', the presumption exists that he is a strong poet
too. One of the elements of 'beautiful idealization' in Frye that
he seeks to undermine is, indeed, the subservient relation of the

critic to the poets. Bloom sees poetry-making as a critical act, since it is based on misreading, and criticism also as a form of creation. Frye, like all earlier critics, is thus guilty of a high-minded sublimation of the elemental facts of literary rivalry and conflict. Bloom's pervasive Freudianism is evident not only in his critique of literary sublimation but in his conception of the struggle between precursor and ephebe as an internalised battle characterised by anxiety and the employment of defence-mechanisms leading to psychic (and poetic) repression. The proof of literary influence, like the latent content of the Freudian dream, is to be found not in what the poem says but in 'what is missing in the poem because it had to be excluded'.[27]

As a literary critic, Bloom has popularised such Freudian notions as repetition-compulsion, the family romance and the primal scene. His most far-reaching references are to *Totem and Taboo* (1912–13), in which Freud adopted the standpoint of an armchair anthropologist to argue that the origins of religion, ethics, society and art could all be found in the Oedipus complex. Freud traced the beginnings of human culture to the mythological 'totem feast', a primal act of cannibalism in which the sons would slay and eat the father. Bloom has identified this 'mad piece of mythological literalism' as the most important page that Freud ever wrote.[28] Mad though it may be, it has its counterpart in Bloom's less graphic but equally ghastly account of the life-and-death struggle between precursor and ephebe by which poems get written. Since 'the strong imagination comes to its painful birth through savagery and misrepresentation,'[29] creation is also destruction and the new poem owes its life to its power of cannibalising or transuming its precursor.

If imaginative creation is trapped in this agonistic cycle, literary theory for Bloom is trapped in a logical circle by the interchangeability of its terms. It matters little whether we describe the Oedipal struggle in literature as being between poets or between poems. The 'revisionary ratios' are both psychic defence-mechanisms and rhetorical strategies. Since the writer reads and the reader writes, poetic creation and poetic interpretation are ultimately the same process, and so are interpretation and misinterpretation. Knowledge, which by definition is or can be made public, is also a private process since 'A reader understanding a poem is indeed understanding his own reading of that poem'.[30] The force of 'his own reading', however, is distinctly muted since, as Bloom has said elsewhere, 'I only *know* a text, any text, because I know a reading of it – someone else's reading, my own reading, a composite reading'.[31] Bloom's epistemological scepticism is all-corrosive at such moments; his statements only appear to convey meaning because we attribute to the concepts of knowledge, reading, the text, and so on, a status and significance that he himself appears to deny. In this Bloom is an adherent of the 'negative awareness' that he has identified in deconstructionist criticism, though he faces the abyss of endless negation only to turn his back on it, proclaiming the romantic myth of the strong poet and of his gladiatorial triumphs in a ceaseless battle of the books. Bloom's commitment to misreading, with its self-conscious echoes of Nietzsche and Emerson, is prophetic, transcendental, and also solipsistic. For all its ebullience, it is not so much a description of human creative activity as the formula of an all-textual world, in which warring automata galvanised with spiritual electricity strike sparks off each other for as long as (and only as long as) the reader, Bloom's reader, is reading them and being read by them. It is a closed system, overdetermined and suffused with literary entropy.

We live in a time of decadence, 'inescapable diminishment', Bloom has told one of his interviewers; nevertheless, there are 'new shades of awareness which come to birth'.[32] He has been an influential judge and advocate of contemporary verse, from Stevens to Ashbery and Geoffrey Hill. As editor and introducer of a long series of books under the title 'Modern Critical Interpretations', Bloom has extended the theory of influence-anxiety over virtually the whole range of the literary canon, including the novel and drama. In *Ruin the Sacred Truths* (1989) he begins with the Hebrew Bible and ends with Samuel Beckett, the 'last survivor' among the great modern writers in prose. Bloom's notion of literary history is catastrophic rather than evolutionary, yet his underlying presumptions are as conservative and archaic as Frye's. Great literature is 'disturbing' and 'uncanny', yet it forms an authoritative and unchanging tradition; belatedness is inescapable, and the future of literature is therefore foreclosed. Bloom's conservatism goes deeper than this, however, being linked to his identification with the Jewish inheritance. He is one of the first Anglo-American critics to wilfully assert his Judaism, rather than sublimating it as earlier intellectual generations had done.[33]

In *Kabbalah and Criticism* he argues that the thought of the sixteenth-century Kabbalists Moses Cordovero and Isaac Luria contains the germ not only of his own apparatus of defensive tropes and 'revisionary ratios', but of the broad range of Freudian and structuralist insights. The systems of Gnosis and Kabbalah are, he insists, 'the first Modernisms'; that is, unlike almost every other sort of traditional mysticism, they are systems of interpretation. Interpretation, in Bloom's version, comes to seem a peculiarly Jewish way of handling experience:

The great lesson that Kabbalah can teach contemporary interpretation is that meaning in belated texts is always wandering meaning, even as the belated Jews were a wandering people . . . What
governs this wandering, this errancy, is defense, the beautiful
necessity of defense.[34]

Since meaning is unfixed, Bloom will not allow any inherent distinction between sacred texts, such as the Bible and the Torah, and
secular literature and criticism. Sacredness implies magical and
scriptural authority, but that is attributed to texts by the politics
of canon-formation rather than being the sign of a transcendent
order. Canonisation, Bloom writes in *Kabbalah and Criticism*, is
'the most extreme version of what Nietzsche called interpretation,
or the exercise of the Will-to-Power *over* texts'. Strangely, however, though Bloom is a professed religious sceptic he expresses
no such scepticism about the established politics of literary canon-
formation. He seems fully satisfied with the academic incorporation
of poets and poetry.

It is tempting to suggest that Bloom's view of poetry as an inherently competitive mode, thriving on misreading, misrepresentation
and the disguised antagonism of ephebe and precursor, owes more
to conditions in modern American universities than it does to the
very varied historical circumstances in which poetry is written. The
agon of anxiety reads, at times, like a thinly disguised parody of
life in the American graduate school. In the academy students
have their work graded, and junior faculty members have their
claims to tenure decided, by the very teachers who have influenced
them most. The relationship of teacher and taught, the rewards
of successful imitation and the penalties of plagiarism are far more
immediate and intimate than is the case in the literary world at
large. Appropriately, Bloom's criticism implies an academic narrowing of poetic development, to the point where all influence
takes place within an unalterable and already institutionalised
canon. 'To write poetry these days in the United States is to read
Wallace Stevens', he has declared.[35] Yet for James Joyce to write
fiction did not mean to read Henry James, and the Brontë sisters
were able to write very satisfactorily without having read Jane
Austen. We are, however, told in *The Anxiety of Influence* that
'an ephebe's best misinterpretations may well be of poems he has
never read', so that the evidence of past writers' reading habits
is irrelevant to the consistency of Bloom's theory.

Bloom's theory is sustained by self-cancelling and self-serving
paradoxes. At times he seems willing to suggest that the true agon
outlined in his criticism is his own, not that of the poets in the

literary canon. He is the author of a novel, *The Flight to Lucifer* (1979), but if he has written any 'strong poems' they would seem to be contained in his criticism. His style of airy, hyperbolic, sweeping exposition often seems poised between intellectual conviction and an audacious whimsy that begs to be enclosed within quotation marks. Not only does he celebrate the romantic epic but his own prose constantly hints at the 'egotistical sublime' in which the authenticity of the thought is underlined by its rapt, first-person utterance. 'There is no method except yourself. Everything else is an imposture,' he has told an interviewer.[36]

Bloom's reply to the 'beautiful idealizations' of earlier critics is to idealise the necessity of tyrannical self-assertion. He has distinguished his theory from Thomas Kuhn's 'paradigm' theory on the grounds that what the strong poet has to overturn is not a paradigm but an individual precursor.[37] Paradigms exist, but they are generalisations with little relevance to the violent and savage creative act. Similarly, his theory remains unaffected by his rather flippant observation that the 'burgeoning religion of liberated Woman' could cause the first break with literary continuity in the West.[38] In 1979 Sandra M. Gilbert and Susan Gubar published *The Madwoman in the Attic*, a work of feminist criticism which showed some Bloomian influence. Gilbert and Gubar maintained that nineteenth-century women authors suffered from 'anxiety of authorship' rather than the patriarchal anxiety of influence. The existence of female precursors was perceived as a support, not a threat. Bloom, perhaps mindful of Gilbert and Gubar's use of his own theory, has responded that influence-anxiety could equally be found among contemporary women writers.[39] Gilbert and Gubar can be seen as returning to the common-sense view that the reading of precursors, and literary criticism itself for that matter, are a support rather than a threat to the writer's identity. Bloom, as a good Freudian, rejects such common-sense views precisely because they seem so manifestly obvious. The best critic, he asserts in his 'Manifesto for Antithetical Criticism', is the one who has 'misinterpreted more antithetically than all others'. Not only does he claim to unravel the latent meaning of poetic history but his is the darkly romantic ideal of the critic as Cain, who slew his brother Abel.

Paul de Man

In 1979 Harold Bloom, Paul de Man, Geofrey Hartman, J. Hillis Miller and Jacques Derrida appeared together in the Yale Manifesto *Deconstruction and Criticism*. To turn from Bloom's and Derrida's essays in that volume to Paul de Man's 'Shelley Disfigured' is, at first sight, to turn from self-preening histrionics to careful scholarly exegesis. First appearances (as de Man himself warns) are deceptive, however. 'Shelley Disfigured' begins as an attentive close reading of 'The Triumph of Life', but ends with a series of furiously nihilistic, self-cancelling gestures. By 'disfiguration' de Man means the 'repetitive erasures by which language performs the erasure of its own positions'. To trace these linguistic erasures is to question the status of Shelley's poem in the literary canon – since it practises a form of self-defeating expression – while at the same time teasing out the far-fetched implications of one of Shelley's own metaphors. If the poem is made to seem self-defeating, so is its exegesis:

> *The Triumph of Life* warns us that nothing, whether deed, word, thought, or text, ever happens in relation, positive or negative, to anything that precedes, follows or exists elsewhere, but only as a random event whose power, like the power of death, is due to the randomness of its occurrence. It also warns us why and how these events then have to be reintegrated in a historical and aesthetic system of recuperation that repeats itself regardless of the exposure of its fallacy.

The 'historicization' and 'aesthetification' of texts happens all the time, de Man wearily observes. Such texts are used by the critic to assert methodological claims 'made all the more pious by their denial of piety'. All we are left with is the steely nihilistic 'rigor' (the reverse of the qualities usually associated with Shelley) that de Man finds exemplary in his poem.

De Man, who had been a practising critic for forty years, had achieved fame as a literary theorist shortly before the publication of these self-lacerating sentiments. He had reasons for self-laceration that none of his admirers seem to have guessed and that, but for his fame, might never have come to light. In 1987, shortly after his death, a Belgian scholar working on a doctoral dissertation discovered a series of newspaper reviews written by the young Paul de Man during the Nazi occupation of Belgium. He had written pro-German articles (including one that was blatantly anti-semitic) for the collaborationist press in the confident expectation of a Nazi victory. Still worse, at Harvard in 1955 he had lied about the extent of his wartime journalism, in order to safeguard his academic standing.

De Man's critical achievement was already controversial. Some saw him less as a major critic than as a case-history of modern academic celebrity. The discovery of his pro-Nazi past revealed not only the strength of antagonism aroused by his work but the fanatical loyalty of his friends and fellow-deconstructionists. His range as a critic is notably restricted, and his thought, for all its subtleties, is often fuzzy and elusive. Nevertheless, he exemplifies many of the characteristics of the modern interpreter. He is a more multinational figure than any of his peers except for Roman Jakobson. Born in Antwerp, his working life was spent in Belgium, Switzerland and the United States, and he could as easily have become a leading French or German critic as an American one. A tireless exponent of the German idealist tradition of Hegel, Nietzsche, Heidegger and of the poetry of Hölderlin, the bulk of his critical writings between 1950 and 1970 consisted of accounts of French and other European writers for an American audience. His first book *Blindness and Insight* (1971) was a collection of essays on modern (mainly European) criticism from Nietzsche and Lukács to Derrida.

De Man had been a Flemish nationalist and then a pro-Nazi but his first intellectual objective in the postwar period, it now seems, was to obliterate the memory of these errors. Emigration to the United States would have helped in his project of disowning the past. Critical nationalism, he opined in 1966, was rare in the USA, though 'just as common in France and England as it is in Germany'.[40] When in the 1970s he again lent his name to the propaganda of a critical movement, it was one which poured scorn on all fixed beliefs and presuppositions and claimed to practise a rigorously undeluded and non-ideological mode of discourse, 'neither nihilism nor metaphysics but simply interpretation as such' as J. Hillis Miller put it.[41] Yet de Man could not entirely cut himself off from the intellectual movements which gave rise to modern nationalism, since his whole output as a critic and scholar (apart from a graduate-school essay on Montaigne) is concerned with the romantic period and its aftermath.

Still more explicitly than Bloom, de Man contended that romanticism was constitutive of modern culture and that early twentieth-century modernism was merely a 'moment' in that culture's growth.[42] Though he once spoke of the ' "waning" of modernity',[43] he had little interest in notions of postmodernism and was opposed to the fashionable view of literary theory as constituting a new paradigm or heralding a cultural revolution. The 'general trend in contemporary criticism', he remarked in a review of Bloom's *The Visionary Company*, was one in which 'the romantics are being reinterpreted as very close and immediate ancestors'.[44] Though this was written in 1962, it is not inconsistent with his later essays celebrating the 'advent of theory'. Deconstruction for him always seems to represent a twilight consciousness rather than a brilliant new dawn. Though he looks with scorn on historicising narratives, the unity of the literary and philosophical tradition linking the romantics to the contemporary predicament is taken for granted in his writings.

De Man was essentially an essayist. Only two books, *Blindness and Insight* and *Allegories of Reading* (1979), were published during his lifetime. More than half of *Allegories of Reading* consists of analyses of texts by Rousseau; the other authors considered are Proust, Rilke and Nietzsche. Since his death, three posthumous collections have appeared, while further volumes, including a study of aesthetic theory and ideology from Pascal to Marx, were left unfinished. De Man taught mainly French and comparative literature, so that his immense impact on Anglo–American criticism was achieved despite a set of interests that remained largely European. Though he also wrote on Wordsworth, Shelley, Keats and Yeats, it is notable that here, too, his choice seems to have been guided by the poets' European affiliations: Shelley's relation to Rousseau, Yeats's relation to Mallarmé, and Wordsworth's and Keats's affinities to Hölderlin.

In 'The Riddle of Hölderlin' (1970), de Man highlighted the German poet's 'negative insights' into the transitoriness of historical achievement and the difficulty of maintaining one's mental balance in an unaccommodating world. Only in poetry could 'some degree of lucidity' prevail about human life. A much earlier essay of De Man's had been devoted to Heidegger's exegeses of Hölderlin, and in it the author recalls Heidegger's image of the literary work as a bell, which interpretation causes to resound.[45] De Man can neither accept this passive and automatic view of interpretation, nor the view of Hölderlin as a great poet penetrating the very essence of Being that Heidegger's studies affirm; in fact, he alleges that Hölderlin says exactly the opposite of what Heidegger makes him say. Nevertheless, de Man remained content, at this time, to appraise Hölderlin and his fellow-romantics in the language of moral insight, stressing the prominence in their poetry both of self-division and of the separation of the inner consciousness from the external world. Later he would write of romantic negativity and self-division in a more radical terminology deriving from the splitting of the human subject in Heidegger and Freud. 'Literature can be shown to accomplish in its terms a deconstruction that parallels the psychological deconstruction of selfhood in Freud', he wrote in *Allegories of Reading*.[46]

Heideggerian rather than Freudian influence is evident in his essay 'Form and Intent in the American New Criticism' (1971). The reigning critical orthodoxy in the United States had, as he noted, rejected the author's intention as a guide to interpretation; hence it seemed very remote from the phenomenological perspective associated with Heidegger and Husserl. Nevertheless, de Man argues that the New Critics had inadvertently stumbled upon the 'hermeneutic circle' which is the guiding notion of interpretative theory. In other words, the organic 'unity' which the New Critics artificially located in the poetic text was to be found, instead, in the 'act of interpreting this text'; it was the interpreter's methodological intentions that imposed this unity. The proof of this, according to de Man, lies in the fact that, the more that it refined its interpretations, the more American criticism discovered a 'plurality of significations that [could] be radically opposed to each other'. New Criticism is thus made to illustrate the general principle of 'blindness and insight' which de Man finds in all the critical systems he surveys. The methodological blindness to which these systems are prone produces unrecognised and unpremeditated insights, which it is for the deconstructive critic to retrieve.

For de Man, what the interpreter has to work on is not the poetic text (as the New Critics mistakenly thought) but the experience of reading it. This 'problem of reading' is the burden of his mature criticism. Far from offering some sort of final assault on the New Critics' epistemological naivety, however, his emphasis on reading restates and reinscribes such favourite New Critical postulates as the impersonality of poetry, its separation from matters of ideology and belief, and the ubiquity of irony and poetic ambiguity. 'This unitarian criticism finally becomes a criticism of ambiguity, an ironic reflection on the absence of the unity it had postulated', he writes of the New Criticism. 'Finally', here, has no chronological force. The function of irony and ambiguity for de Man is to cut off the literary text from making referential assertions and, therefore, moving the reader with the force of its statements.

The problem of reading is at least twofold. First there is the fact that readers tend to differ from and to contradict one another. (In 'Literature and Language: A Commentary' (1972) de Man accused American and European literary analysts of an 'organized conspiracy' to suppress this fact, 'perhaps because the vested interests in literary studies as a respectable intellectual discipline are at stake or perhaps for more ominous reasons'.) Second, the causal mechanisms capable of producing the 'plurality of significations' that readers tend to find in texts must be described. De Man locates these not, as might have been expected, in the reader's hermeneutic apparatus but in the rhetorical strategies of language and discourse.

An essay such as 'Shelley Disfigured' speaks neither of a puzzled reader nor of Harold Bloom's agonistic author; instead, it outlines a world of animated linguistic abstractions. 'Rhetoric', implying persuasion, is the means by which the linguistic elements produce their effects on the reader. The interpreter disentangles these rhetorical effects, showing them to be characteristically self-contradictory and self-cancelling.

In distinguishing 'rhetorical' from 'linguistic' modes of textual analysis, de Man endorsed the objections to Roman Jakobson's structuralist methodology set out in Michael Riffaterre's *Semiotics of Poetry*. Structuralist analyses like the Jakobson–Lévi-Strauss account of Baudelaire's 'Les Chats' tend, in his view, to eliminate the reading experience.[47] In any case, textual significance cannot simply be revealed by grammatical analysis since the same grammatical structure serves radically different meanings. De Man turns, instead, to Nietzsche's posthumously published notes on rhetoric for a view of language which, he believes, does justice to its unstable and figurative character. De Man has been accused of misrepresenting Nietzsche by wrongly claiming the philosopher's authority for his own views on language, rhetoric and truth; his aim is, however, to represent language as a system of tropes, and truth as a 'moving army of metaphors, metonymies and anthropomorphisms'.[48] This means that language itself has a surface as fantastic and misleading as the Freudian dream. Not only the claims of literary language but those of any critical metalanguage are severely curtailed by this. The way is open for the deconstructionist contention that the struggle of discourse against discourse is unending, since no sooner has one 'master-trope' or key to interpretation emerged than it is 'troped' in its turn. Reviewing Derrida's *Of Grammatology*, de Man asserted that, far from transcending the perspectives of the text of Rousseau that he was claiming to interpret, Derrida's metalanguage was merely a 'discursive version' of Rousseau's own. Derrida had troped, or perhaps trumped, Rousseau, and de Man used Rousseau to overtrump Derrida.[49] De Man's deconstruction shares with Bloom's agonism its competitive ethos: language, for him, is not merely a game but a highly staked, constantly circulating card-game.

Nevertheless, de Man's view of language returns him (at the end of a cycle more or less peculiar to himself) to what is precisely the traditional position he claims to be subverting. For all its rigorous show of activity, De Man's version of deconstruction ends up by representing itself as passive interpretation – like Heidegger's commentator sounding the bell – since the strategies it pursues (or so it claims) are already present in the texts to be interpreted.

'Poetic language is the most advanced and refined mode of decon-struction', de Man claimed in *Allegories of Reading*. This means that any text can be interpreted as a quest containing at once the 'attempt of its own understanding' and the undoing of that attempt.[50] Rhetoric, which provides the terms of de Man's ana-lyses, is invariably revealed as the theme of the texts that he chooses to analyse. The resulting interpretations (like Bloom's) are mono-tonous, since certain rhetorical figures are pondered over and over again. A de Man essay is likely to turn on the figures of repetition, of prosopopoeia (by which the text can be said to 'speak to us') and of allegory and irony. Irony is the deconstructive trope of tropes, since it explicitly subverts and destabilises meaning, and de Man's tendency (outflanking the New Critics) is to celebrate irony in a mode that is itself sardonic, if not ironical.

The sardonic note is struck time and again in de Man's criticism. 'Autobiography veils a defacement of the mind of which it is itself the cause'; Proust's fiction 'narrates the flight of meaning, but this does not prevent its own meaning from being, incessantly, in flight'; 'the allegory of reading narrates the impossibility of reading'; 'all readings are in error because they assume their own readability':[51] de Man constantly subdues his intractable subjects with the aid of these disheartening paradoxes. 'What seems to be most difficult to admit,' he says of Nietzsche's work, 'is that this allegory of errors is the very model of philosophical rigour.'[52] There is an element of imposture in this, as in so many of de Man's prot-estations of rigour. Irony and paradox lead to an impasse, to a celebration of paralysis, in which the end of criticism is to assert that texts are 'unreadable' and their meanings 'undecidable'.

Asked about his attitudes to politics and ideology in an interview given when he was dying of cancer, de Man said that these problems were always uppermost in his mind. He could only approach them on the basis of a critical-linguistic analysis, and now, having mas-tered the means of such an analysis, he was more or less ready to do so.[53] Such masterly elusiveness is illustrated in another late essay, 'The Resistance to Theory' (1982), where he contemptuously dismisses opponents of modern literary theory in favour of a con-cept of inner resistance for which he seems directly indebted to Freud. De Man floats the conception of a 'universal theory of the impossibility of theory', and wonders aloud whether the current flourishing of literary theory is a 'triumph or a fall'. The question is undecidable, of course; de Man is alluding here to his analyses of Shelley's 'Triumph of Life' and Keats's 'Fall of Hyperion', whose very titles he has declared to be 'undecidable' so far as interpre-tation is concerned.[54] The essay concludes that 'Nothing can overcome the resistance to theory since theory is itself the resistance', Theory triumphs, that is, by triumphing over itself.

'The Resistance to Theory' might well have been entitled 'Is Literary Theory Possible?' Its concluding paradoxes more or less parallel the conclusion to Allen Tate's 'Is Literary Criticism Possible?' written thirty years earlier. The 'fall' of literary theory is a fortunate (triumphant) fall, since theory is as necessary and inevitable as it is impossible. Paul de Man's eminence belongs to the decadence of an age of literary interpretation; his writings outline a mysticism of interpretation, which no longer has any human goals except that of asserting its superiority over other modes of human thought. Where Harold Bloom reduced the literary tradition to a theatre of psychic agon and rhetorical combat, for de Man it becomes a conflict of abstract discourses, from which his own discourse always emerges with an air of smugly masochistic victory. Deconstruction would not have achieved the great influence it has exerted were this not, in some respects, a readily recognisable description of the modern critical process. Yet its nihilism loses contact with the purpose of criticism. It can no longer suggest any grounds on which criticism might appeal to, and exert its fascination upon, a lay audience of people not already involved in the toils and paradoxes of literary interpretation. For such a view we must go outside the narrowing and academic tradition that this chapter has surveyed, to other developments of twentieth-century criticism: the line of public critics or 'men of letters', feminist literary criticism, and cultural studies and cultural theory.

7   The Challenges to Interpretation

The Men of Letters: Wilson, Trilling and Steiner

In a lecture given at Princeton University on the centenary of Wordsworth's death in 1950, Lionel Trilling observed that 'If Wordsworth were not kept in mind by the universities he would scarcely be remembered at all'.[1] Whether this was true or false, it is not something that seems to trouble the deconstructive interpreters of Wordsworth's poetry. The fate of serious literature in the culture at large is, instead, a typical concern of the 'man of letters' who continues to champion the public function of criticism. Today's public critics are frequently academics, but they view literature as a criticism of life addressed to the non-specialist reader rather than as a body of dark texts requiring tortuous, esoteric and plural interpretations. At the same time, the self-conscious man of letters (the male noun is appropriate) cannot help appearing as in some sense a traditionalist, and even as the obituarist of a form of culture in terminal decline.

There have been almost as many nominations for the title 'last man of letters' as for the last romantic. The man of letters is not an innovator in criticism but a successor of Carlyle's literary heroes and of the Victorian sages and bookmen. Edmund Wilson, who exemplifies this dying species, saw himself as a successor to Saintsbury, Sainte-Beuve and Samuel Johnson. Lionel Trilling, whose first book was a study of Matthew Arnold, frequently echoes Arnold's terminology and canons of judgment. George Steiner deliberately adopts the style of cultural prophecy. It is perhaps hard to understand why criticism such as theirs seems to be losing its hold, since its sense of responsibility to the wider public, to the relations between literature and life, and above all, to the needs of the writers' own time would seem to be perennial necessities for literary discussion. In recent decades the case for and against public criticism has been more eloquently put in the United States than in Britain, where it simply seems threatened with genteel inconsequence. According to F. O. Matthiesson's 'The Responsibilities of the Critic' (1956), the critic's first duty is to be alive to the art of his own time; in addition, he should show a wide range of interests, be sensitive to the social relations of literature and to its cultural diversity, and be concerned with politics.[2] If prescriptions like these have lost some of their force it is not because they are intrinsically flawed but because the sphere of literature within the wider culture now seems somewhat diminished. Literature by itself clearly cannot support the whole framework of a 'criticism of life'; at the very least it must be supplemented by other disciplines and bodies of thought ranging from social and scientific theory to art, design and media studies. To be aware of the 'works of art of our own time' is to give an account of (rather than averting one's gaze from) the shifts in emphasis from verse to prose, from literature to music and recorded drama, and from the printed page to the screen and the videocassette. This appeal beyond literature as traditionally conceived is central to any form of criticism that would challenge the narrow horizons of academic interpretation, but it is also what has turned the 'man of letters' into an endangered species. In the long run, his survival is indissolubly linked to the cultural prestige associated with the writing and reading of books.

As yet there has been no diminution in the public demand for critical prose. Book-reviewing proliferates, though it is not as well paid as it used to be. Most leading modern writers have produced volumes of criticism, and – besides T. S. Eliot – there have been such influential 'occasional' critics as W. H. Auden, E. M. Forster, D. H. Lawrence, Edwin Muir, George Orwell, V. S. Pritchett, Virginia Woolf, and more recently, Chinua Achebe, Saul Bellow, Anthony Burgess, Donald Davie, Seamus Heaney, Gore Vidal and Angus Wilson. To make such a list, however, is to illustrate the decline of the metropolitan centres from which public criticism has tended to operate. This criticism needs the constant stimulus of a current of new and varied ideas, such as only metropolitan journalism can reflect; at the same time, if it is to be authoritative, it needs to convey something more than the knee-jerk response elicited by newspaper deadlines or the cut and thrust of a television studio. Not many modern critics have maintained this balance, and the places and times at which they were able to do so take on, in retrospect, a mythical quality.

Edmund Wilson

Edmund Wilson is the twentieth century's most consummate bookman. He was a learned critic of catholic tastes and scholarly interests who worked as a journalist and editor rather than as a professor of literature. He writes to communicate his understanding and enthusiasms as a reader, not to justify a discipline or defend a syllabus; unlike Lionel Trilling, he has no pedagogic situation in mind. Wilson is a strongly biographical critic, the master of a plain narrative style and the ancestor of more specialised biographers and historians of modernist writing such as Richard Ellmann and Hugh Kenner. As an essayist, and still more in his posthumously published letters and diaries, Wilson presents himself as the literary chronicler of the New York intellectual scene and not as an original thinker. Though he attacked the 'habitual blankness' of the scholar's outlook, his own range of knowledge and infectiousness of manner are not matched by any great richness of compelling ideas.[3]

As a journalist, his principal association was with the intellectual-political weekly the *New Republic*. He traced back his notion of criticism as a 'history of man's ideas and imaginings in the setting of the conditions which have shaped them'[4] to his undergraduate days at Princeton, and his debt to his academic mentors was frequently expressed. He dedicated *Axel's Castle* (1931), his classic survey of modernist literature, to the Dean of his old college, Christian Gauss. The prologue to his literary chronicle of the inter-war period, *The Shores of Light* (1952), consists of a long obituary essay on Gauss as a teacher of literature; in the same year he published a tribute to the Greek master at his preparatory school. Wilson, however, was never over-awed by an academic environment. Invited to Princeton in 1940 to lecture on 'The Historical Interpretation of Literature', he pressed the claims of Marx, Engels and Trotsky as literary analysts. Marxism led him to visit the Soviet Union and to write *To the Finland Station* (1940), a broad narrative of intellectual and political history stretching from Vico to Lenin; but his Freudian interests are more fully incorporated into his practice as a literary critic. His political independence, even at the height of his enthusiasm for Marxism, is characteristic of the stance of the 'man of letters'; so also is the conclusion to 'The Historical Interpretation of Literature', where he argues that Marxist and Freudian interpretative methods are irrelevant to the question of artistic value.

To say that historical interpretation is only secondary, since criticism is founded on value-judgments, makes an odd conclusion to a lecture evidently intended to win converts for Marxist and Freudian approaches. Wilson claims that if we understand literature in its historical context we will be able to appreciate what is genuinely new in art and human experience; yet this ability must stay confined to an élite of 'genuine connoisseurs who established the standards of taste'. In debate with John Crowe Ransom some years earlier he had conceded that 'no set of critical formulas can ever succeed in explaining a poem'; his own 'primary judgments' about poetry were no more than mysterious emotional responses.[5] He remained rather baffled by these matters. Turning his own methods back on himself, it is worth noting that Wilson's historicism is characteristic of other critics of his generation in America. For all his cosmopolitanism, he was an East Coast Protestant deeply versed in the writings of H. L. Mencken, Van Wyck Brooks and Vernon L. Parrington – contemporaries whose criticism was infused with a strongly national consciousness of American culture and history. Like many modern critics outside the tradition of academic interpretation, Wilson was torn between the role of the connoisseur and that of the socially committed cultural historian.

His value-judgments, especially in his shorter pieces, are often little more than reviewer's clichés: either a crude ranking of the 'first-rate' and the 'second-rate', or an equally straightforward affirmation of the vitality, lifelikeness, or maturity of the work in question. The major artist such as Joyce is the one who reflects all life, 'all human possibilities'.[6] But merely to write about all life is perhaps not enough, and the division between the creative and the active life haunts Wilson's criticism, as it haunts some of his favourite writers from Rimbaud to Hemingway. In 'Philoctetes: The Wound and the Bow' (1941) he interprets the Sophoclean drama as a parable of the modern artist, which also gives to the critic (more or less inadvertently) an active role in society. Overtly, Wilson's essay presents Philoctetes, the wounded Greek hero whose strength is symbolised by his magical bow, as the type of the great artist struggling to rise above his psychic disability. Genius and disease, as Wilson argues in influential psychological studies of Kipling and Dickens, are 'inextricably bound up together'.[7] (The suggestion of a causal link between mental disease and artistic power was later to be disputed by Lionel Trilling.) What is most interesting in 'The Wound and the Bow' is Wilson's account of the role of Neoptolemus, Achilles' son, whose task is to mediate between Odysseus and Philoctetes. The Greeks need Philoctetes' aid if they are to be victorious in the Trojan War, and Odysseus sets out to capture Philoctetes' magical bow by force or by fraud, knowing that the wounded warrior has a long-standing grudge against him. Aeschylus and Euripides had already written plays on this theme, but Wilson credits Sophocles with the invention of the third character whose task is to sympathise with Philoctetes:

> How then is the gulf to be got over between the ineffective plight of the bowman and his proper use of his bow, between his

ignominy and his destined glory? Only by the intervention of one who is guileless enough and human enough to treat him, not as a monster, nor yet as a mere magical property which is wanted for accomplishing some end, but simply as another man, whose sufferings elicit his sympathy and whose courage and pride he admires.

In order to overcome Philoctetes' stubbornness, Neoptolemus has to take the risk of identifying his own interests with those of the outlaw. The end-result is to cure Philoctetes and set him free, but also to re-enlist him on the side of the Greeks – thus reconciling the intractable artist with the military needs of the state. If Philoctetes stands for the artist in this parable, Neoptolemus is the humanistic and public-spirited interpreter who stands between artist and audience. Guilelessly and spontaneously recognising Philoctetes' true identity, he alone can help the artist to use his gift creatively. 'The Wound and the Bow' offers reassurance for the critic by representing a particular set of relations between artist, middleman and society as if they were universally and timelessly valid.

Neoptolemus can be moved to intense sympathy and admiration for Philoctetes, but he has a broader outlook than the bowman, and is more morally responsible and less self-centred. Wilson's attitude to Yeats, Valéry, Eliot, Proust and Joyce, the great modernist artists whose work he expounds in *Axel's Castle*, has something of the same duality. The book ends with a choice of parables. On the one hand is the life of Rimbaud, who forsook poetry for the life of action by becoming a Levantine trader; on the other hand is Villiers de l'Isle-Adam's hero Axel, who found his supreme aesthetic fulfilment in a suicide pact. Axel and Rimbaud together sum up the dead-end of the symbolist movement in art: they fascinate Wilson but they are also to be rejected as moral examples. Subtitled 'A Study in the Imaginative Literature of 1870–1930', *Axel's Castle* was written precisely at the point when modernist literature had run out of its initial momentum. Though he stresses the indispensability of symbolism to the most vital modern art, Wilson also portrays Yeats, Eliot, Valéry and Proust as self-absorbed, decadent writers, pedantically aloof from modern life and fighting a desperate rearguard action against technological, democratic society. Eliot's doomed attempt to revive the verse drama and Yeats's obscurantist theories of history are, he suggests, all too typical of the modernist movement. Yet most readers of *Axel's Castle* are less affected by the book's message that it is time to move on than by its prolonged savouring of symbolist illusions.

'The question begins to press us again as to whether it is possible to make a practical success of human society, and whether, if we continue to fail, a few masterpieces, however profound or noble, will be able to make life worth living even for the few people in a position to enjoy them', Wilson writes. In some ways the 'positive' hero of *Axel's Castle* is Bernard Shaw, the rationalist and socialist who 'shouldered the whole unwieldy load of contemporary sociology, politics, economics, biology, medicine and journalism', and whose writing Yeats had once compared to a cheerful sewing machine, yet it is the images of Valéry's M. Teste, of Joyce experimenting with words and of Proust in his cork-lined room which stand out as the embodiments of the artistic conscience. In fact, Wilson's expression of moral scruples tends to relieve what anxieties the reader may have felt about the anti-social tendencies of the modernist writers. Their revolutionary and reactionary force is somehow neutralised, just as in *To the Finland Station* Wilson's delighted absorption in the personal foibles of Marx and Engels makes it that much easier to consign their work to the retrospective judgment of history.

In T. S. Eliot Wilson found the 'American's peculiar combination of avidity and detachment', and his own writings on British and European literature and history share the same quality.[8] Near the end of *Axel's Castle* he suggests that 'we may live to see Valéry, Eliot and Proust displaced and treated with as much intolerance as those writers – Wells, France and Shaw – whom they have themselves displaced'. (His own book, however, has helped to prevent this.) His essay 'Marxism and Literature' (1938) concludes with the thought that revolutionary social transformation may be the prelude to 'the first efforts of the human spirit to transcend literature itself'. Perhaps he remained too much of an armchair critic ever to pursue intuitions such as these. One aspect of his criticism which was surely in advance of its time, however, was his registration of the shift of gravity from verse to prose. *Axel's Castle* insists that the modernist movement is at its weightiest not in the anachronistic Yeats and Eliot but in the novelists, especially Joyce. Wilson returned to the obsolescence of poetry in his essay 'Is Verse a Dying Technique?' (1938). His arguments were to be implicitly rejected both by the New Critics and by subsequent academic historians of modernist literature. The primacy of poetry in literary revolutions is, however, precisely the sort of shared ideological assumption that his historicism had set out to call in question.

Prose, according to Wilson, had already usurped most of the earlier functions of verse. Coleridge's and Arnold's redefinitions of 'poetry' had masked a growing unease about the future of verse as a medium. They made the highest claims for poetry, while tacitly reducing its essence to whatever could be concentrated in a phrase or a line. Eliot's essay on Dante continued this trend by valuing the *Divine Comedy* mainly for its momentary local intensities or 'Eliot-like fragments'. In reality, Wilson argued, it was not Eliot or Tennyson but the great modern prose artists who were the true successors of the classical poets. Once Flaubert and Joyce came to be seen as the heirs of Virgil and Dante, the notion of modern literary decline could be quickly dismissed. To Wilson, verse is not an end in itself but simply a literary technique like any other. Once again, he does not press this sort of argument as far as some other critics have done. He questions the traditional subordination of the novelist to the poet, but not that of the critic to the creative artist. The critic as Neoptolemus makes no claim either to Odysseus's power or to Philoctetes's magic.

Edmund Wilson wrote novels, plays and historical works as well as literary criticism. His achievement was to celebrate, to express his scruples about, and to weave a historical narrative around the major modernist writers and their works. His critical and personal relationships with Scott Fitzgerald, Hemingway, and other contemporary American writers are of great interest, and nowhere does he fulfil the role of the 'man of letters' more satisfyingly than in his various writings on Joyce. In *Axel's Castle* Joyce appears as 'the great poet of a new phase of the human consciousness'. *Finnegans Wake*, then known as *Work in Progress*, was the one central modernist experiment whose outcome was still uncertain when Wilson's first book was written. He continued to follow Joyce's work closely, writing a lucid and pioneering account of 'The Dream of H. C. Earwicker' (1939), and telling a perhaps sceptical readership in 1944 that 'The chance to be among the first to explore the wonders of *Finnegans Wake* is one of the few great intellectual and aesthetic treats that these last bad years have yielded'. Joyce's prose work, he added, was 'a very great poem'.[9] What Wilson lacked in critical subtlety or system he made up in zest.

Lionel Trilling

Lionel Trilling was the child of first-generation Jewish immigrants to the United States. In Greenwich Village in the late 1920s he was proud to rent an apartment across the street from Wilson, and, like his older contemporary he was associated with a leading political–intellectual journal. *Partisan Review*, founded in 1934 as an organ of the world communist movement, in time became the house-journal of the 'New York intellectuals' who dominated American liberalism. Trilling's first collection of essays, *The Liberal*

Imagination (1950), is, among other things, an assertion of the *Partisan Review* ideal of cultural politics. His association with other Jewish intellectuals of his generation, including the literary critics Philip Rahv, Alfred Kazin and Irving Howe, was close and complex.[10] While living in Greenwich Village, however, he was starting work on the PhD thesis, eventually to be published as *Matthew Arnold* (1939), which secured his tenure at Columbia University. The Trilling of the later essays is as closely identifiable with the English department at Columbia and its controversies as F. R. Leavis is with Cambridge. Often in his criticism he seems to be laying out a syllabus and pedagogic method in public. At no time does he tackle a major living writer as yet unmediated by critical commentary. Trilling's ideal of cultural politics led to select Arnoldian encounters with rival intellectuals (from Leavis and Vernon L. Parrington to the radical psychoanalysts Herbert Marcuse and R. D. Laing), rather than to an engagement with the profusion of contemporary writing.

The title of one of his best-known essays – 'On the Teaching of Modern Literature' (1965) – sums up the subject of all his criticism. His redefinition of modern literature is far-reaching. In the first place, and despite his declarations of intent in *The Liberal Imagination* with its image of the 'dark and bloody crossroads where literature and politics meet',[11] Trilling's view of modernity excludes any direct dealings with politics: what he means by the 'political' in his criticism is the battle of cultural ideas. He does not refer, except in the most glancing of ways, to such twentieth-century phenomena as Nazism, Zionism, or American power. In one of his last essays he wrote of the renewed appeal of William Morris's utopianism to the radical students of the time – 'Over the last decade many people, young people especially, have come to share Morris's certitude about the feasibility of extirpating aggression'[12] – without finding it necessary to advert to the nuclear arms race or to America's defeat in the Vietnam war. In 1974, he described the 'great sin of the intellectual' as being his failure to test his ideas 'by what it would mean to him if he were to undergo the experience that he is recommending'.[13] But Trilling's aloofness from social practice is at least as great as that of the people he criticises.

Where he did write of politics was in his novel *The Middle of the Journey* (1947), which was concerned with a liberal intellectual's flirtation with communism. When Trilling commented that there was a 'divorce between politics and the imagination', he meant that the great modernist writers were not liberal democrats.[14] Trilling's redefinition of modernity and its literary canon is an attempt to explain the ideas and sentiments that have led modern writers to embrace various notions of social apocalypse, including those associated with revolutionary politics. At the same time, his new canon reflects other pressures, such as his own specialisation in nineteenth-century literature and the fact that for many years the Columbia English department's teaching stopped at 1900. The 'modern' as he outlines it in *Beyond Culture* (1965) and *Sincerity and Authenticity* (1972) begins in the late eighteenth century. Trilling's is perhaps the most influential of the numerous formulations (beginning with Wilson's *Axel's Castle* and extending to the work of Paul de Man) of a pan-European, comparativist syllabus for contemporary criticism. His proposed canon extends from fictions of the 'anti-hero', such as Diderot's *Rameau's Nephew* with its expression of class envy and Conrad's *Heart of Darkness* with its exploration of savagery, to the philosophical and scientific diagnoses of modern malaise in Nietzsche and Freud.

Freud, Nietzsche and the fictive characters of Conrad and Diderot are what Trilling rather loosely calls 'cultural figures' – persons who, in addition to their intellectual or imaginative status, have taken on a metaphysical or symbolic role in cultural debate. The 'figure' emerges from the study of modern literature, yet he is of more than merely literary importance for us. 'Us' should perhaps be put in inverted commas, since Trilling was often mocked for his mandarin use of the first person plural. The 'we' in his writing is the voice not of a criticism that claims eternal validity but of one that asserts its authority over a particular community of readers, in time and place. The method has its dangers, however. Trilling tends to take for granted the primary artistic impact of the works he discusses, since his aim is to pronounce on their figural status and meaning. Time and again he manipulates the works he discusses in order to serve a particular set of contemporary interests.

The dilemmas of modernity stem, in his view, from the assertion of individual consciousness and of the autonomy of the self. Modern literature gives expression to an 'opposing self', which resists ideology and sets itself against the determining forces of its cultural formation. What worries Trilling, however, is that the oppositional self has gradually become an ideological construct, a badge of membership in the 'adversary culture' (or counter-culture) which offers a ready welcome to those in rebellion against bourgeois society. The opposing self has become bland and self-deceiving, while modern literature itself has become just one more academic subject. Wryly reflecting on his own teaching of modernism, he offers the following parable:

I asked my students to look into the Abyss, and, both dutifully and gladly, they have looked into the Abyss, and the Abyss has greeted them with the grave courtesy of all objects of serious study, saying 'Interesting, am I not? And *exciting*, if you consider how deep I am and what dread beasts lie at my bottom. Have it in mind that a knowledge of me contributes materially to your being whole, or well-rounded, men'.[15]

Obviously a form of ventriloquism is at work here, with Trilling projecting onto the Abyss the words of the teacher. With great ingenuity, he turns his own complicity in the domestication of modernism into a manifestation of the modernist dilemma and the modernist anguish.

Trilling's list of international modern 'cultural figures' includes Goethe, Rousseau, Hegel, Flaubert, Emerson, Marx, Dostoevsky, and Thomas Mann – all of them, he suggests, the authors of 'prolegomenal books' which should be read by anyone approaching the study of twentieth-century literature. It also includes some less predictable writers, such as Jane Austen who scarcely addresses us with the voice of the Abyss. Trilling devoted three major essays and a section of *Sincerity and Authenticity* to expounding Austen's modernity. In her novels, he writes, the 'archaic ethics' of honesty and sincerity is in love with the 'consciousness that seeks to subvert it' – that is, the self-dramatising 'modern' personality of an Emma or a Mary Crawford.[16] Trilling's own closeness to the 'archaic ethics' can be seen in his fondness for these novels. His book *The Opposing Self* (1955) begins by outlining the modern oppositional stance, but then examines a series of 'cultural figures' notable for passivity and resignation. Dickens's Little Dorrit represents the 'negation of the social will', Wordsworth's 'Judaic quality' is reminiscent of the humility of Joyce's Leopold Bloom, and Flaubert's last novel is set in the context of its author's saintly and self-sacrificing behaviour towards his niece. *The Opposing Self* concludes with a famous tribute to Jane Austen's Fanny Price, who may offend our 'conscious pieties' as modern persons but speaks intimately to our 'secret inexpressible hopes'.[17]

Mark Krupnick has written of *The Opposing Self* as the work of a 'monkish Trilling', who turns away from the modern world in despair at its futility and waste.[18] Trilling later wrote that the truth that we seek in literature is 'the truth of the self, and also the truth about the self'.[19] His authority as a public critic came from his ability to use criticism as a way of exploring and generalising intellectual and moral dilemmas. Trilling himself achieved the status of a 'cultural figure' for his times by making literary criticism the occasion of his own mental pilgrimage. In *The Opposing Self* he cites Hegel as the source of what he would call the 'cultural mode of thought', in which 'Not merely the deed itself [is] submitted to judgment, but also the personal quality of the doer of the deed'. This habit of judgment according to personality or style of life suggests that selfhood is a matter of deliberate choice, for which one should be held responsible; it verges on the mental world of fashion and the advertising industry. Even Leavis's criticism, he judged, was 'hampered and hidden by the defences of [his] own choice in life-styles'.[20] Certainly this was true of Trilling himself.

Trilling often spoke apologetically of the 'secret hopes' that modern readers invest in the plainer moral values of earlier novelists such as Jane Austen. Austen's popularity is a sociological fact of modern culture, and as such Trilling feels moved both to defend and to ponder it. We are cut off from archaic sentiments such as Wordsworth's delight in unaffected pleasure, he argued in 'The Fate of Pleasure' (1963), by the solicitations of cultural figures who insist on the duties of modern self-consciousness and modern self-pity; the 'specious good' of pleasure gives way to the higher good of anxiety. Trilling himself was one of these cultural figures whose solicitations he wryly noted. His essay 'On the Teaching of Modern Literature' offers, at its close, not to resolve the dilemmas it has raised but to 'confront those of us who do teach modern literature with the striking actuality of our enterprise' – in other words, to increase his readers' anxiety level. Trilling's masterful yet Olympian orchestration of cultural anxieties suggests a rather different role from that of the old-fashioned moral or political critic. At a 1974 forum he opposed the fighting, adversarial mode of criticism recommended by other New York intellectuals reacting against the intellectual radicalism of the young. In a bad time, he suggested, 'You become historical-minded'.[21] This is the contemplative, aestheticised historicism – Paterian rather than Arnoldian – of contemporary interpretation and cultural theory. Elsewhere he finds his source of value in Freud's notions of the death-instinct and of the inevitability of pain and frustration in human existence; these speak to Trilling of a biological self prior to its cultural constructions and deconstructions. He is a critic whose ultimate touchstones often seem to be not literary works but ideas, such as the idea of the 'Abyss'; the problem is that in the Abyss we hear our own voices echoed.

George Steiner

If Trilling is a man of letters who in the long run finds the world of letters profoundly deficient, it has been left to more recent critics to spell out these deficiencies. Of these, perhaps the most vociferous and intelligent is George Steiner. A cosmopolitan Jewish critic who holds university appointments in Geneva and Cambridge and writes for the *New Yorker*, Steiner shows no compunction in naming all the contingencies of modern life about which Trilling's self-defences obliged him to keep silent. Judaism, exile, the decline of the book, the decline of the West and the worst details of Nazi atrocities all figure, and are all interconnected, in Steiner's polemics. He insists that modern humanism and the teaching of literature must be weighed in the balance with the political terror of the twentieth century. The literary tradition is invariably found wanting, but the consequences of this are unclear. Perhaps, as with Trilling's more measured inquisitions, the outcome is mainly to raise the reader's anxiety level. 'Before we can go on teaching we must surely ask ourselves: are the humanities humane and if so, why did they fail before the holocaust?' Steiner concludes in 'To Civilize our Gentlemen' (1965). He does not actually propose not to go on teaching.

Though his early books *Tolstoy or Dostoevsky* (1959) and *The Death of Tragedy* (1961) belong to conventional literary criticism, Steiner's more recent work questions the fate not of literature in itself but of literacy and language. He takes a very limiting view of criticism, describing it as 'passionate, private experience seeking to persuade' which 'has about it neither rigour nor proof'.[22] It is curious, then, that he judges criticism and the teaching of literature by more exacting standards than the ones he brings to bear on the sciences. Taking scientific assertions of the moral and political neutrality of 'positive knowledge' at face value, he never stops to ask why these disciplines, too, have failed at the bar of modern political reality.

The trope of death and the death-instinct in his writings begins with Nietzsche's 'death of God' and extends to what he has called the 'death of language'. The retreat from the word is the retreat from the Word, and vice versa. *The Death of Tragedy* argued that without the 'intolerable burden of God's presence' certain dimensions of thought and creativity could no longer be attained, and by the time of *Real Presences* (1989) this line of argument had become openly theological. His essay 'The Hollow Miracle' (1959) offended many readers by suggesting that the German language was dying in the wake of Nazi barbarities; this was perhaps influenced by George Orwell's essay on 'Politics and the English Language', which linked the decay of language to its abuse by political propagandists. In later essays such as 'The Retreat from the Word' (1961) and 'The Distribution of Discourse' (1978), however, Steiner outlines the broader sociological and cultural trends that may be said to determine modern literacy. The primacy of language has been broken, he argues, by the destruction of social hierarchies which had relied on the 'wealth and dignity of speech', and by the growing importance of non-verbal discourse. The instant relaying and recording of sound have led to a loss of 'linguistic internality', to the death of silent language: the result is that 'where much more is, in fact, being heard, less is being said'.[23] It is true that such changes in language-production and language-use must have drastic effects on literary culture, but Steiner's assertions that we live in a 'post-culture' in which literature is dying remain incorrigibly speculative.

Steiner is a writer of high exuberance, touching in the course of an essay on matters as diverse as the sense of smell in the sixteenth century, the binding of Regency albums and the structure of pronouns in Thai – all matters essential, in his view, to the history of consciousness but requiring much more investigation than he has time for. In view of the decline of the man of letters in this century it was perhaps inevitable that literary culture would throw up its self-appointed obituarists. Steiner is the most millennial of these, though the very facility and rhetorical power of his writings suggests that the literary essay still has its uses. Very likely it is only a particular tradition or framework that is ending. The critique of modernity comes full circle in Steiner's writings, with his endorsement (or apparent endorsement) of the modernist writers' own intimations of apocalypse. To undergo fully the experience that Steiner recommends would mean either renouncing literature and its criticism, like Rimbaud, or committing suicide like Axel.

Virginia Woolf and Feminist Criticism

The hero of Villiers de l'Isle-Adam's *Axel* scorns erotic fulfilment and repulses the advances of Sara, a young French noblewoman. Nevertheless, he succeeds in persuading her to join in a suicide pact. Wilson in *Axel's Castle* does not remark on the presence of misogyny and female masochism at the heart of one of the 'sacred books' of the French symbolists, and this aspect of modern literature was largely taken for granted until the establishment of feminist criticism in the 1970s. The very notion of the 'man of letters', stemming from Carlyle's *On Heroes*, speaks of male domination: the 'woman of letters' sounds as though she might be an inferior species. Carlyle was writing at a time when the profession of female authorship was coming to be widely acknowledged, and when a few advanced intellectuals were beginning to advocate equal rights for both sexes. The tradition of 'men of letters', remained, however, a male preserve. John Gross in his history of *The Rise and Fall of the Man of Letters* (1969) unceremoniously debars the most distinguished modern female critic from the company he is celebrating. 'The typical Virginia Woolf essay is a brilliant circular flight, which, as criticism, leads nowhere', he writes.[1] This seems to imply that men of letters think in straight lines, like Woolf's own character Mr Ramsay in *To the Lighthouse*, whereas women, however gifted, flap around in circles.

Though women writers were a powerful force in Victorian fiction and poetry, they normally had to submit their work to male judges. Apart from Mary Shelley's edition of her husband's poems, George Eliot's review of 'Silly Novels by Lady Novelists' (1856) and Elizabeth Gaskell's biography of Charlotte Brontë, very little work by nineteenth-century female critics is easily accessible today. Certainly there were women reviewers in Victorian England, and at least one fictional heroine, Marian Yule in George Gissing's *New Grub Street*, briefly supplements her income with literary journalism; though Marian, a bookman's daughter, begins the novel as her father's unpaid research assistant and ends it as a provincial library assistant. The line of twentieth-century women novelists who were also famed, and feared, as critics begins with Virginia Woolf and Rebecca West. Of these, Woolf's reviews before the First World War were published anonymously, while West's appeared at first in minority feminist and socialist papers such as the *Freewoman* and the *Clarion*. For a long time women were much less conspicuous as critics than as teachers and students of literature, since the rise of English studies in the late nineteenth century coincided with the pioneering ventures in higher education for women. Excluded from the classical curriculum, they took to the university study of English with an enthusiasm that continues to this day. Women scholars and women professors of English literature were a small but significant presence from the 1920s on. The notion of critical authority, as well as of creative achievement, fostered within the profession remained, however, overwhelmingly male. When feminist criticism at last emerged as a separate presence, it gave expression to long-restrained feelings of frustration and anger.

It was in the 1970s that Virginia Woolf's *A Room of One's Own* (1928) achieved due recognition as the 'sacred book' of feminist criticism in English.[2] Earlier, Woolf's very considerable reputation

as a critic had centred on the two polemical essays – 'Modern
Fiction' (1919) and 'Mr Bennett and Mrs Brown' (1924) – in which
she set out a programme for 'Georgian' (that is, modernist) fiction.
Woolf had been a prolific literary journalist since 1905 when,
shortly after her father's death, she was asked to contribute to
the newly founded *Times Literary Supplement*. It is with her father,
Leslie Stephen, and with her contributions to the *TLS*, that an
assessment of Woolf as a critic ought to begin.

Woolf's first volume of critical essays was *The Common Reader*
(1925). There is a delicate allusion to Leslie Stephen's *Hours in
a Library* in the prefatory essay in which she imagines the common
reader sitting in one of 'those rooms, too humble to be called
libraries, where the pursuit of reading is carried on by private
people'. The common reader 'reads for his own pleasure rather
than to impart knowledge or correct the opinions of others'.[3] Woolf
is a successor to the nineteenth-century bookmen in speaking on
behalf of such 'private people'. The room she has in mind is the
'room of one's own' where, as she later argued, a woman would
be free to develop her literary potential. Libraries were gentlemen's
preserves, and at the beginning of *A Room of One's Own* she
describes her exclusion from an Oxbridge college library. As a
public critic rather than a 'common reader', Virginia Woolf of
course did spend hours in libraries, and a later chapter of *A Room
of One's Own* shows her at work in the Reading Room of the
British Museum. Entering her two major critical books we have
to negotiate the complexities of Woolf's self-consciousness about
her social and personal status: she is at once a profound insider
in literary culture, and a representative of the great majority of
people who are marginalised or excluded by it. She is, in fact,
a bookman's daughter.

Woolf is most conscious of this in writing of her father's favourite
century, the eighteenth. When, in a 1919 essay, she quotes Joseph
Addison's hopelessly patronising views on the 'fair sex' we might
remember that Leslie Stephen often expressed his distaste for
literary 'effeminacy'. Rather poignantly, Woolf goes on to fantasise
a filial literary relationship with Addison:

> It would have been, so one imagines, a great pleasure to take
> him a manuscript; . . . in spite of Pope, one fancies that his would
> have been criticism of the best order, open-minded and generous
> to novelty, and yet, in the final result, unfaltering in its stan-
> dards.[4]

Such whimsy is largely absent from the essays in *The Common*

Reader dealing with her predecessors in the female tradition of the novel: Jane Austen, the Brontës and George Eliot. In her essay on Eliot (which must surely have influenced Leavis's *The Great Tradition*) she describes *Middlemarch* as a book which 'with all its imperfections is one of the few English novels written for grown-up people'. 'Maturity', however, is not for Woolf the ultimate standard it would be for the *Scrutiny* critics. At her best she writes with an eye to the future of literary creation, and champions the excitement and impatience of youth. The critic's task, she asserted in 1917, is to 'keep the atmosphere in a right state for the production of works of art'; in a later essay, it is 'to see the past in relation to the future' and to 'prepare the way for masterpieces to come'.[5] In 'Mr Bennett and Mrs Brown' she declares that 'we are trembling on the verge of one of the great ages of English literature'. When the great age begins, it is plain, she intends to be there.

'Modern Fiction' and 'Mr Bennett and Mrs Brown' are celebrated for their liberating, if somewhat vindictive, attacks on the novelists of the immediately preceding generation. 'Modern Fiction' sets out Woolf's ideal of a 'spiritual' or psychological realism as opposed to the external, 'materialist' realism of Wells, Bennett and Galsworthy. The 'spiritual' novelists are Hardy and Conrad and, to a lesser extent, Joyce. ('Modern Fiction' was written while the earlier episodes of *Ulysses* were appearing in the *Little Review*.) For Woolf, Joyce's strength is that he is 'concerned at all costs to reveal the flickerings of that innermost flame which flashes its messages through his brain'. Woolf's phrase the 'innermost flame' suggests the empiricist psychology of William James, who was the first to speak of a 'stream of consciousness', but it also alludes to the 'inner light' of Quaker spirituality. She later described *Ulysses* as a 'memorable catastrophe – immense in daring, terrific in disaster'.[6] Joyce in his later episodes had abandoned the 'innermost flame' and had failed, presumably, to underwrite the cult of private experience and personal relationships to which Woolf, along with the other Bloomsbury intellectuals, subscribed. 'Modern Fiction' outlines a notion of individuality as an elusive, flickering essence which cannot be approached through outward attributes. In 'Mr Bennett and Mrs Brown', again, the Edwardian novelists are convicted of writing impurely didactic works of art and of creating characters whose inner lives are mechanically determined by external circumstances. To Woolf, consciousness is not sociologically induced but idiosyncratic and free. Her starting-point in the later essay is Arnold Bennett's charge that her own generation of novelists had failed to create characters who were 'real, true,

and convincing'. Woolf does not deny that such realism is the primary aim of fiction; instead, she imagines the figure of Mrs Brown,
the elderly lady in the railway carriage who represents 'the spirit
we live by', and she concludes with the determination 'never, never
to desert Mrs Brown'. For all its iconoclasm, 'Mr Bennett and
Mrs Brown' belongs in the tradition of humanistic criticism of fiction concerned with the representation of 'people' in the novel.
E. M. Forster's famous distinction between 'flat' and 'round' fictional characters in *Aspects of the Novel* (1927) is another version
of Woolf's contrast between extrinsic and intrinsic portrayal.[7]

'Mr Bennett and Mrs Brown' predicts a 'season of failures and
fragments', as novelists struggle to come to terms with the realisation that 'in or about December 1910, human character changed'.
Mrs Brown, however, represents eternal human nature, 'life itself'
which does not change. *A Room of One's Own* also centres on
figures of imaginary women who stand outside the (male) literary
tradition; in the latter essay there are two such women, Judith
Shakespeare – the unknown and frustrated sister of the great poet
– and a contemporary novelist, Mary Carmichael. Mary Carmichael
writes naturally as a woman – 'merely giving things their natural
order, as a woman would, if she wrote like a woman' – but the
result is a baffling modernist experiment. The description of Carmichael's novel recalls Dorothy Richardson's *Pilgrimage* as well
as Woolf's own earlier fiction; unsatisfying in itself, *Life's Adventure* (as it is very transparently called) is a forerunner of the
women's novels that will emerge in a hundred years' time.

A Room of One's Own originated in two talks on women and
fiction that Woolf gave to the women's colleges in Cambridge;
it is also literally a preamble to such a talk.[8] Straying into one
of the men's colleges as she tries to arrange her thoughts, the narrator is warned off the grass and barred from entry to the library.
It is not exactly that she is *persona non grata* in the college, since
the next scene shows her attending a private lunch party there.
She is no Jude the Obscure, but, as a daughter of the social and
intellectual élite, she is excluded from its most privileged bastions.
Realising this, she abandons any thought of a bland talk on the
nineteenth-century women novelists, done in the spirit of bookmanship. Instead, she reflects on the shabby plainness of the
women's college and of its most famous scholar, and on the misogy-
nistic bullying of Professor von X, author of *The Mental, Moral,
and Physical Inferiority of the Female Sex*. Here the essay moves
toward a psychopathology of masculinity in the age of imperialism
and scientific progress. Woolf touches on the connection, which
she was to develop at length in *Three Guineas* (1938), between

dictatorship in the public arena and in the home, between Fascism and contemporary patriarchy. At the same time she cunningly and wittily transfers her own anger onto her opponent, the frowning professor: 'Had he been laughed at, to adopt the Freudian theory, in his cradle by a pretty girl?' she mockingly asks.

After this prelude we come to the main part of the essay, which sets out to reconstruct an excluded and silenced female tradition, and develops a range of suggestions and strategies which would be taken up by feminist criticism half a century later. Judith Shakespeare, the imaginary sister whose literary potential was never fulfilled and who finally committed suicide, becomes the symbol of a new vision of social history or, as it would eventually be called, 'herstory':

> When ... one reads of a witch being ducked, or a woman possessed by devils, of a wise woman selling herbs, or even of a very remarkable man who had a mother, then I think we are on the track of a lost novelist, a suppressed poet, of some mute and inglorious Jane Austen, some Emily Brontë who dashed her brains out on the moor or mopped and mowed about the highways crazed with the torture that her gift had put her to. Indeed, I would venture to guess that Anon, who wrote so many poems without signing them, was often a woman.

The suppressed mystery of women's lives links Judith Shakespeare to Mrs Brown; but Woolf is equally aware of another direction she must take, which is to explore the actual output of women writers from the seventeenth century onwards. She touches briefly on Lady Winchilsea, Margaret Cavendish, Dorothy Osborne, Aphra Behn, and then the novelists. She was not quite the first in the field; for example, there was the work of her aunt, Anne Thackeray Ritchie (W. M. Thackeray's daughter), who wrote a number of essays on nineteenth-century women writers, and there was R. Brimley Johnson's *The Women Novelists* (1918), which Woolf had reviewed for the *TLS*. Her reconstruction of the female tradition is both an act of piety, and a declaration of the partial independence of women's writing from men's writing: 'for we think back through our mothers if we are women', she observes, and it is 'useless to go to the great men writers for help'. Women writers have had to fight against external mockery and suppression ('Women can't write, women can't paint', says Charles Tansley in *To the Lighthouse*), but also against the timidity and self-censorship which afflict anyone whose identity is denied by the social conventions around them. Here the very partial achievements of the women authors whose works have survived – like the talented Dorothy Osborne who 'wrote nothing' apart from her letters to her future husband – join on to the purely speculative history of Judith Shakespeare and the female Anon.

But Woolf implies that there may be natural as well as socially induced differences between men's and women's writing. Men and women differ, she asserted in 1918, over 'what constitutes the importance of any subject'.[9] In *A Room of One's Own* she states that Jane Austen and Emily Brontë write 'as women write, not as men write'. The notion of natural difference is highly contentious for more recent feminists. French theorists like Julia Kristeva and Hélène Cixous have set out to define an *écriture féminine*, but also to detach this from biological womanhood. Virginia Woolf was strongly attracted by notions of literary androgyny, and to-wards the end of *A Room of One's Own* she sketches a 'plan of the soul' divided between male and female: 'in the man's brain the man predominates over the woman, and in the woman's brain the woman predominates over the man'. The purely masculine or purely feminine mind 'cannot create', Woolf adds, and she notes that male writers of the imperialist age like Galsworthy and Kipling (and like Professor von X) tend to be aggressively masculine, lack-ing in androgynous balance. Such masculine aggression leads not to art but to power-hungry politics. Woolf links the 'self-assertive virility' she finds in the letters of Sir Walter Raleigh, Professor of English at Oxford, to the rise of Fascism in Italy. Later, however, she would claim that the threat of Fascism had revealed to the younger generation 'the need for emancipation from the old con-ception of virility'. Cultural change, she believed, could bring about a slow alteration in the 'hereditary constitution' of gender.[10]

There is some awkwardness in the transition in *A Room of One's Own* from the past to the present, from the recovery of a suppressed tradition to the experimental aims of Woolf's own writing. Mary Carmichael is the figure of the contemporary woman novelist con-cerned not with androgyny but with the realisation of her own female creative power, which may involve treating 'forbidden' sub-jects such as lesbianism or at least women's friendship. For all the achievements of the nineteenth-century women novelists, Woolf agrees, the 'poetry' of women is still denied outlet. (She has, however, nothing to say about Victorian and modern women poets.) She condemns the didactic strain in the women's novel much as she had done in her attacks on the Edwardians. Quoting an eloquent passage from *Jane Eyre*, Woolf charges that Charlotte Brontë has 'left the story, to which her entire devotion was due, to attend to some personal grievance'. Later the point is put in more general terms:

> It is fatal for a woman to lay the least stress on any grievance; to plead even with justice any cause; in any way to speak consciously as a woman. And fatal is no figure of speech; for anything written with that conscious bias is doomed to death. It ceases to be fertilized.

These considerations arise from Woolf's ideal of androgyny and from an almost mystical notion that 'creativity' arises from an act of male–female fertilisation within the brain. They reflect her commitment to 'telling the truth about my own experiences as a body' (as she put it in a 1931 essay[11]) within the confines and decorum of Bloomsbury aestheticism. In 'Mr Bennett and Mrs Brown' she had written of the 'incompleteness' of the fiction of Bennett and his contemporaries: 'In order to complete them it seems necessary to do something – to join a society, or, more desperately, to write a cheque.' Later she would devote a whole book (*Three Guineas*) to the writing of three cheques, but she refused to allow such propagandist writing to contaminate the work of fiction considered as a deliberate art form. It may be as a result of this rigid separation that *A Room of One's Own*, which is both a manifesto and a work of art, was for a long time one of the least regarded works in the Woolf canon.

Finally Woolf looks prophetically towards the future. Recalling the fiction of Judith Shakespeare, she suggests that women's writing is preparing the way for a second coming, the resurrection of that 'dead poet who was Shakespeare's sister'. The vision of the great woman poet expressed in these Biblical metaphors recalls Arnold's conclusion to 'The Function of Criticism at the Present Time'. The critic, as the voice of the intellectual community, is granted a vision of the promised land, but it is not hers to enter. Arnold wrote that 'we shall die in the wilderness', and Woolf writes of the female Shakespeare as follows:

> Drawing her life from the lives of the unknown who were her forerunners, as her mother did before her, she will be born. As for her coming without that preparation, without that effort on our part, without that determination that when she is born again she shall find it possible to live and write her poetry, that we cannot expect, for that would be impossible.

So the critic is still preparative to the creative artist; *A Room of*

One's Own ends with this very traditional notion of authorship and authority.

Virginia Woolf's essay is revered by contemporary feminist criticism, but it also sometimes overshadows it. In Mary Eagleton's *Feminist Literary Theory: A Reader* (1986), for example, three of the five sections begin with extracts from *A Room of One's Own*, while a fourth, entitled 'Do Women Write Differently?' features intense debate around Woolf's conflicting positions. The first chapter of a widely read survey of feminist theory by Toril Moi is called 'Who's Afraid of Virginia Woolf?'[12] One reason for being afraid of Virginia Woolf might be that she said so much, so eloquently but also contradictorily; another might be that her closing vision of the 'female Shakespeare' is a vision of a future that has not materialised and that many more recent feminists would repudiate.

Woolf believed that there were general literary standards – the 'unfaltering standards' she glimpsed in Addison – by which female writers could fairly be judged. A feminist criticism is bound to question whether such standards actually exist. If, as Moi asserts, 'feminist politics is the basis for feminist criticism', then criticism becomes overtly political.[13] The politics of cultural self-assertion entails not only the struggle between feminist and patriarchal ideologies but also the demand for 'equal rights' for all modes of writing seen as the expression of particular classes or minority groups. Plurality within feminism then becomes inevitable, as black feminist and lesbian feminist writers challenge the hegemony of the white middle-class majority. In the United States, a new curriculum can be discerned in which literary anthologies grant virtually automatic rights of representation to each vociferous sociological subgroup of writers or critics. Writing as democratic expression supplements (if it does not altogether supplant) the notion of a canon based on intrinsic value. It was by a similar process of self-assertion that American literature itself gained full recognition, and we should not underestimate the tendency of canonical structures to re-emerge, within a slightly altered framework.

Woolf's own criticism forcefully blames the weakness of traditional women's writing on the denial of expression to women. She also employs the class–race–gender analogy, which is central to contemporary feminist writing: women, she observes, have now 'less intellectual freedom than the sons of Athenian slaves'. The class–race–gender analogy would suggest that the most important precedents for contemporary feminist criticism lie in the campaigns for proletarian literature in the 1920s and 1930s, and for black writing in the 1960s. Feminism inherits the intellectual and political militancy of these movements and their claim to speak for the oppressed. At the same time, because women are more numerous and have historically been closer to the cultural centres of power, feminism promises a bigger upset to established intellectual and literary values than black writing or proletarian literature have been able to achieve.

In Britain, the emergence of gender as a literary category was promoted by feminist collectives and publishing houses.[14] An off-shoot of the political movement has been the rediscovery of the female 'common reader', providing a ready market for contemporary feminist writers and for reprint series of women's 'classics'. In America, the challenge to the male literary canon has been more academic than market-led. Sandra M. Gilbert, for example, has written that feminist courses raise the possibility that 'through literary study we can renew our lives'.[15] Elaine Showalter advocates 'feminist critique' as 'in essence a mode of interpretation', which any 'complex text' can accommodate.[16] Both writers are senior professional academics pursuing feminist aims in the field of literary theory. Showalter, the author of several critical manifestos, argues in 'Toward a Feminist Poetics' (1979) for a cultural project which she calls 'gynocritics' – the construction of a 'female frame-work' for the analysis of women's literature. Gynocritics demands 'models' and 'theories' based on the 'study of female experience'; it has been challenged by other feminists for its adherence to familiar social-scientific patterns. One of the tasks of gynocritics is to seek cultural rather than biological explanations for the suppression of women's creativity in the past. It can lead, therefore, to the exposure of institutional prejudice, including the hegemony of 'male critical theory' in the study of English.[17] An alternative approach is to turn to Freud and post-Freudian interpretative theories in order to probe the inner dynamics of female creativity.

In their studies of nineteenth- and twentieth-century women writers, *The Madwoman in the Attic* (1979) and *No Man's Land* (3 volumes, 1987–), Sandra M. Gilbert and Susan Gubar adopt the 'Bloomian premise' that literary history is a history of psychological conflict.[18] Revising Harold Bloom's theory of influence-anxiety (and incidentally revealing its complacent male-centredness), Gilbert and Gubar propose a model of female authorship based on the nurturing relationship of mother and daughter. Literary conflict takes place between the two sexes rather than between generations. The reason for the female 'anxiety of authorship' is outlined in the deeply Freudian rhetorical question which opens *The Madwoman in the Attic*: 'Is a pen a metaphorical penis?' In

No Man's Land Gilbert and Gubar revise their earlier model a little; one crucial aspect of their work, however, is their ability to interpret the literary works they discuss as dream-narratives disclosing through image and symbol (such as the Victorian motif of domestic imprisonment) the latent preoccupations of the female imagination.

A construct such as the 'female imagination' requires a cultural gender theory as its basis. In the 1980s, as the influence of French feminist theorists such as Kristeva, Cixous and Luce Irigaray became increasingly pronounced, feminist literary criticism tended to merge into a broader movement of cultural theory deriving from semiotics and psychoanalysis, and ranging in the objects of its attention from scientific and medical texts to advertising, pornography, popular fiction, the visual arts, television and film. The same period has seen a large output of feminist literary scholarship, writing the history of female authorship and of images and representations of women in both female and male writers, and investigating the demands and expectations of women readers. Women have provided the majority readership for the novel since its inception; today they constitute virtually the whole market for mass-produced romantic fiction, but also the majority of students of English literature. The woman reader and the woman student remain marginalised, however, both in the study of fiction and in the constitution of academic English. Until this state of affairs is changed, feminist criticism is likely to retain its polemical edge.

Of all current literary movements, feminist criticism is among the most insistently self-conscious. This can be seen in the proliferation of manifestos, anthologies, and symposia, and in feminist critics' readiness to theorise the history of their own discourse. One influential model is Elaine Showalter's suggestion of three inevitable stages, which she has named feminine, feminist and female; these are the stages of imitation of the dominant tradition, of protest and the demand for cultural autonomy, and (finally) of self-discovery or the search for identity, through which any literary subculture would need to pass.[19] Other writers object that it is unrealistic to suggest that the militant feminist stage could be comfortably outgrown. But is there a fourth stage, in which the subculture rejoins the main culture? It can be argued that a subculture is always part of a main culture, but the possible alternatives are not simply those of absorption or mutual opposition since both main culture and subculture may come to be seen as complex, fragmented and mutually overlapping. In *The History of Sexuality*, Michel Foucault claims that this is always the case:

we must not imagine a world of discourse divided between accepted discourse and excluded discourse, or between the dominant discourse and the dominated one; ... Discourses are not once and for all subservient to power or raised up against it, any more than silences are.[20]

The further development of feminist criticism perhaps depends on its ability to reconcile or to sustain a productive tension between two conflicting goals. The first is the political appropriation of literary works and cultural history for feminist purposes. The second is to reveal those characteristics of all writing, and of all human subjectivity, which are foregrounded by the study of women's literature and experience.[21] Both projects were powerfully foreshadowed in *A Room of One's Own*.

Literary Criticism and Cultural Theory

When she imagined the figure of Shakespeare's sister Virginia Woolf was implicitly questioning the universality, or cultural transcendence, attributed to Shakespeare's art. The Shakespeare celebrated by the nineteenth-century critics did not need an imaginary sister, for he was, as a character tells us in James Joyce's *Ulysses*, 'all in all'. Many forces besides feminism have recently challenged the cultural privilege accorded to literature and its texts. Measured quantitatively and by the intensity that some of its academic practitioners bring to it, literary criticism is flourishing today as never before; measured in terms of its ability to dominate and set the terms of intellectual discussion, it has seemed to many to be in decline. Criticism, it has been said, has lost the 'tone and temper of real authority' that it enjoyed in the heyday of Eliot and Leavis.[1] In 1976 a new journal, *Poetry Nation Review*, was launched in Britain with a manifesto undertaking to reclaim for contemporary literature and its readers 'a little of their lost authority'.[2]

The sense of lost authority (sometimes referred to as the 'crisis of criticism' or the 'decline of English') takes a number of different forms. It is argued, for example, that 'the book' is in decline, or that contemporary imaginative writing is weak and has been displaced by academic criticism, or that criticism itself has been displaced or absorbed by literary theory and cultural studies. The first of these claims is manifestly the most far-reaching. Books, once the near-sacred objects of veneration and study, have had their social role profoundly altered by growth of a secular and affluent society, by the spread of mass education, and by radio, the cinema, television and computers. From being prized because of their rarity, books became increasingly commonplace articles which have long lost the aura of technological novelty. At the same time, the theories of a 'post-literate' society reflect our own period's intellectual anxieties. What has been called the 'postmodern condition' is one in which the 'grand narratives' associated with the age of the book have lost their hold, to be followed by a new electronic or cybernetic consciousness in which intelligence is no longer felt to depend on the arduous, literary training of the mind. 'Literacy' as we know it will be outmoded in a culture where whole libraries can be accessed at the press of a button and encyclopedias have given way to data-banks.[3] And yet beliefs such as these continue to rely on literary narrative and the forms of the book and the newspaper for their transmission. Our age which has developed the myth of the obsolescence of the book continues to find writing and reading the most efficient methods of disseminating complex ideas.

But if writing in some form is certain to continue it may be that it is deserting the traditional imaginative genres. Gerald Graff has referred to a 'loss of belief – or loss of interest – in literature as a means of understanding'.[4] The literary artist, we are told, is no longer in touch with the most representative experience of our time, and this experience cannot be rendered in poetry or the novel as we have known them.[5] For Elizabeth Bruss, there is a direct link between the alleged weakness of creative writing in England and America and the hypertrophy of criticism and theory.[6] Alternatively, this alleged weakness may have more directly political causes. Raymond Williams, who detects a 'tragic misdirection' in modernist writing, points out that 'the lives of the great majority of people have been and still are almost wholly disregarded by most arts.'[7] Yet many of the theorists (Williams excepted) who hold views like these are themselves not truly concerned with the contemporary arts. A recent writer on popular culture has observed that most of the art produced today goes virtually uncriticised, just as most of the criticism goes virtually unread.[8]

Disillusionment with contemporary literature necessarily leads to disillusionment with criticism. Perhaps it is when a forceful new movement is emerging that the arts of evaluation and judgment are most seen to matter, and if not to command agreement, to command attention. Today, however, it is argued that the 'standards of taste' are arbitrary and that the pluralism of modern culture means that they cannot possibly be enforced. The subjectivity of critical judgment, William E. Cain has written, is 'both the discipline's menace and its justification'.[9] A comment such as this equates the fortunes of criticism with those of the academic study of literature, where 'pluralism' takes the form of a conflict between entrenched intellectual positions. Increasingly, these positions have to be explained and defended before they are applied. Judgment and evaluation are then brought to bear on the theories, rather than on the literary works themselves; but the judgment of theory turns out to be no more stable or progressive than the 'standard of taste'. 'No academic discipline currently produces as many theories as the study of literature', wrote one observer in 1979. Each new theory 'presents itself as the only sensible alternative to those that preceded it. But its predecessors remain stubbornly alive, and the new theory stimulates the production of still others intended to rectify the errors *it* has introduced.'[10] Literary theories, in fact, are disposable commodities. The unfolding narrative of theory-construction and theory-deconstruction has its own excitement, but often it appears less as a narrative of intellectual advance than an ideological pilgrim's regress in which we are always coming back to the place we thought we had just left.

Far from constituting a new 'Copernican revolution' or paradigm-change as is sometimes claimed, the theory 'boom' appears to be a symptom of deeper, underlying changes in literature and its academic study. Literature, in the sense of the masterpieces of the canon or the 'great tradition', has come to seem too narrow an object to be viewed in isolation from other social forms. The movement for the unification of the social sciences under the rubric of semiotics and discourse theory, the study of 'signifying systems' or of 'discursive practices' necessarily includes the study of literature in its aims. Literary criticism has been struggling to become cultural just as cultural theory was struggling to become, if not more literary, at least more alive to the categories of language and narrative. Before moving on to assess these developments, some more will be said of the social and academic context in which they have occurred.

Literary criticism today is largely identified with academic scholarship, and academic scholarship, referred to as 'my research' or 'my own work', is produced in time left at the university teacher's disposal in respite from the demands of pedagogic and bureaucratic routine. The scholar-critic is usually a teacher of English, who has been trained in the study of English literature; but the study and teaching of English literature are changing rather rapidly in response to local conditions in different parts of the world. Already the term 'Anglo–American', applied to generalisations about the state of criticism and teaching in both Britain and America (and, by extension, in the other English-speaking countries) is in most

340 Authors and Authority

cases an empty formality. It is becoming misleading to assume that criticism and English literature have the same status in British culture as they have in the United States, to go no further. This is clearly visible in the criticism itself. Most good criticism published in America is addressed in the first place to an exclusively American reader, and much good British criticism is addressed to a British reader, with some strenuous exceptions. (The bad criticism often has no reader at all in mind.) Book publishing in Britain and America is increasingly unified, but this is not the case with book reviewing, and still less with the actual reading of contemporary fiction and poetry. Nor are the two cultures as closely interrelated as might appear from the fact that, by and large, they acknowledge and study the same literary tradition. Great Britain is no longer the centre of English-speaking culture, and is in some (though not all) respects politically and culturally subordinate both to America and Europe. The United States has a national language and literary culture which it happened to acquire from one of the many European nationalities which make up the vast bulk of its population. In both countries it can be claimed that 'much of English literature up to the threshold of modern times is now as remote as the ancient classics'.[11] Few British undergraduates have studied medieval church architecture or have listened to a nightingale, and fewer still feel comfortable in the stately homes that are opened at the weekend to hushed parties of tourists. Nevertheless, these things and the literature that celebrates them are felt by the majority to be national possessions, at least in Leopold Bloom's sense of the nation as 'The same people living in the same place'.[12] In America the link is not primarily to the people or the place but only to the language. There is a distance, and a wider choice of potential classics, and as time goes on most of 'British literature', as it is now called, will come to seem increasingly optional to American readers. But for modern communications it would by now be written in a dead language; but then, if the Romans had invented television we should probably still all be speaking Latin.

It is ironic, then, that the major investment of energy and resources in the scholarly study of 'British literature' is to be found not in Britain but in the United States. Theory and scholarship remain international in scope but this is rather less true of literary teaching. Significantly, the recent histories of English studies such as D. J. Palmer's *The Rise of English Studies* (1965), Chris Baldick's *The Social Mission of English Criticism* (1983) and Gerald Graff's *Professing Literature: An Institutional History* (1987) are all monocultural. The preferred style of critical theory and academic popularisation is rather different on either side of the Atlantic. For

example, it is hard to imagine an American scholar surveying critical theory with the verve, lucidity and histrionic talent of Terry
Eagleton's *Literary Theory: An Introduction* (1983). American
critics, more long-winded and more circumspect, too often write
sub specie aeternitatis and as if they were giving evidence to some
interminable congressional inquiry on Mount Parnassus. They
write for their colleagues and for the graduate-school audience
of future colleagues, while the British are probably hoping to dazzle
their undergraduate students. American criticism, in the Germanic
tradition, is closer to philosophy and theology; the present-day
British style owes much to the debating chamber, to comic fiction
and political journalism. There is cross-fertilisation in plenty but,
apart from Wilson, Trilling, Steiner and Woolf, it is hard to think
of any important critic since T. S. Eliot whose writings have had
an equal impact in both countries.

In *English in America* (1976) the radical scholar Richard Ohmann
argued that 'There is just no sense in pondering the function of
literature without relating it to the actual society that uses it, to
the centers of power within that society, and to the institutions
that mediate between literature and people'.[13] In the United States
this sounded more novel than it would have done in Britain, where
Raymond Williams had been working on similar assumptions for
nearly two decades. Williams and the British Marxist historians,
E. P. Thompson and Christopher Hill, had written extensively of
the social relations and class ideologies embedded in particular
literary texts. Their work had a centrality in British intellectual
life, connecting with the writings of Leavis and Empson, and
appealing not only to socialist values but to a national sense of
historical memory. The American Marxist scholarship of the same
period had very little connection with American life, and was
usually theoretical and internationalist in outlook. When a much-
heralded movement for 'new historicism' emerged in America in
the 1980s, its initial concern was not with the bitter historical conflicts of the New World, but with reinterpreting the literature of
the English Renaissance.

New historicism denies the 'cultural transcendence' of literary
works, returning them to the cultural situations from which they
emerged; and these cultural situations are at once discursive and
political, being composed of a web of discourses shot through with
the workings of power.[14] The movement is deeply indebted to
Michel Foucault's 'archeologies of knowledge' and to his insistence that, as well as being concentrated in the state and its agencies,
power is diffused in 'ideological structures of meaning, characteristic modes of expression, recurrent narrative patterns'.[15] But if they

deny cultural transcendence to literary texts, new historicists are understandably anxious to claim transcendence, or at least contemporary relevance, for their own delvings into the operations of censorship in Elizabethan London or the architecture of Jacobean palaces. Stephen Greenblatt's study of *Renaissance Self-Fashioning* (1980), for example, turns the liberal view of the emergence of selfhood in the Renaissance inside out: the self is to a large extent 'fashioned' from outside. Greenblatt's book opens and closes with essays in cultural generalisation, arguing that the texts he surveys reveal, not moments of identity freely chosen, but the imprint of 'systems of public signification' which are themselves ideological products. What we have inherited from the Renaissance is thus not the experience but the delusion of unfettered subjectivity. Greenblatt's underlying thesis (it has been said) is that 'the Renaissance is *our* culture because it is the origin of our disciplinary society'.[16] Some American adherents of new historicism have become alarmed by the radical quasi-Marxist implications of such a position,[17] and the standard defence of the movement (one which reflects the underlying anxieties of the study of English, particularly in America) is that it 'revitalizes the canon', 'enlarges the interpretive scope' of literary criticism, and, in other words, keeps interpretation going.[18]

Behind both new historicism and the newer British developments in cultural history lies not only the work of Foucault but the theory and practice of 'cultural semiotics', as advocated by the American anthropologist Clifford Geertz and, in Britain, by the later Raymond Williams. Williams in the 1970s announced his 'rejection of literary criticism ... not only as an academic subject but as an intellectual discipline'.[19] In his earlier work (discussed in Chapter 5) he had set himself against the Arnoldian tradition by adopting the sociological and anthropological concept of a 'culture' as the identifying characteristic of a society or community seen as a whole. An outline of cultural sociology written a few years before his death defines a culture in semiotic terms as a 'signifying system through which ... a social order is communicated, reproduced, experienced and explored'. Cultural analysis undertakes to investigate not only the arts but the whole range of 'signifying practices' in a society.[20] Clifford Geertz's approach is very similar: one of his most influential anthropological essays treats the Balinese cockfight as a semiotic medium. Both Williams and the Geertz of *The Interpretation of Cultures* (1975) present cultural analysis as an interpretative science, not as a mode of evaluative critique. It is, moreover, a textual science, in which 'signifying systems' and 'signifying practices' take the place of the old literary apparatus of the language of poetry and the words on the page. Geertz frankly promotes textuality (or 'pantextualism' as it is sometimes called) as the *grande idée* or intellectual open sesame of the contemporary mind. For him a culture is an 'ensemble of texts', and doing ethnography means learning to read them.[21]

Like most post-structuralist thinkers, Geertz and Williams differ from earlier semioticians in their assertion that a text cannot be understood by simply unravelling its internal relationships. The task of interpretation, according to Williams, is not one of formal but 'formational' analysis, specifying the text's position within, and contribution to its cultural network. Each act of expression reflects and reproduces, but also informs, the structures and experiences of the society in which it takes place. Geertz also rejects formalist analysis in favour of a larger and more amorphous, but still structural, science. His essay 'Thick Description: Toward an Interpretive Theory of Culture' endorses Gilbert Ryle's notion of 'thick description' in which the meaning and purpose, not merely the formal structure, of each cultural act is investigated. Art and most other instances of human behaviour are for Geertz, following Kenneth Burke, forms of 'symbolic action'. The function of art is in general to 'display' and to 'reflectively address' the tensions of the social order.[22] Like some of Williams's concepts, Geertz's acknowledgement of the experiential quality and sensory appeal of art forms seems designed to avoid the reductiveness of structural linguistics without abandoning its basic notions of language and code. Both thinkers see artistic works and performances as, in effect, privileged events in the articulation of a common cultural language.

For Geertz, 'judgmental' questions have a place, but only a limited one, in the sociology of art.[23] Williams, as a cultural sociologist, goes much further in arguing for the complete separation of criticism from judgment. In an article on the term 'criticism' in *Keywords: A Vocabulary of Culture and Society* (1976) he notes that a 'habit (or right or duty) of judgment' is almost invariably associated with criticism; this, however, is now outmoded. Instead of promoting the 'abstraction of response', we should be aware of the specificity of criticism, or response, as a cultural practice. But Williams's assertion (which comes oddly in the quasi-lexicographic context of *Keywords*) of the need to 'get rid of' the habit of judgment is itself a judgment, presented in the reasoned form in which literary judgments should also be couched. As it happens, his own essays on literature and culture are evaluative through and through. His attempt to limit literary criticism, in the future, to an awareness of response is an assertion of the territorial claims

344 Authors and Authority

of the 'science' of cultural analysis over what he takes to be a diminished and discredited form of intellectual activity.

Clifford Geertz, from his ethnographic standpoint, describes the culture of a people as 'an ensemble of texts, themselves ensembles, which the anthropologist strains to read over the shoulders of those to whom they properly belong'.[24] The over-the-shoulder reader is privileged to read off their broader and more universal meanings. Like some of his predecessors in anthropology, Geertz is the author of a number of essays which range very widely from culture to culture. In 'Art as a Cultural System' (for example), bearing out Pater's contention that the modern spirit takes as its province 'all modes of thought and life', Geertz refers in some detail to Yoruba sculpture, Italian Renaissance art, Islamic poetry, and Abelam painting from New Guinea.

The horizon of Williams's writing is openly political. His cultural sociology or 'cultural materialism' is a revision and retranslation of Marxist literary theory. Yet Marxist theory during its history has veered unstably between scientific pretensions and political aims, and the same seems to be true of Williams's later thought. 'Cultural materialism' is both a discipline which claims the authority of a science, and a determined attempt by radical intellectuals to stoke the fires of change. Tony Bennett in *Formalism and Marxism* (1979) argues that the texts on which literary criticism works are already 'occupied', 'filled with interpretations' which the political critic is obliged to combat.[25] Literary analysis is a 'battle of readings', he has more recently written.[26] Terry Eagleton in *Literary Theory* (though not in his earlier *Criticism and Ideology*) takes a very similar line, and both writers tend to describe the critic's task in a Clausewitzian language bristling with military metaphors. The insistence that criticism ought to be politically motivated, and that the form of politics in which it engages is a battle of ideas, is not as new as the cultural materialists seem to imagine. In fact, it was present (as we have seen) in Trilling's *The Liberal Imagination*. Yet literary critics of all people should be able to recognise the view that 'all criticism is political' as a piece of jejune sloganising; and politically motivated criticism can serve as a safe, well-paid and glamorous substitute for political militancy.

A more complex view of the political and cultural dimensions of criticism is to be found in the writings of the American critic and Palestinian political activist Edward W. Said. Said's *Beginnings: Intention and Method* (1975) reaffirmed the capacity of authors to inaugurate or initiate a text, in a series of running arguments with the anti-humanist tendencies of structuralist and deconstructionist thought. In *Orientalism* (1978) he set out to expose the imperialist and colonialist assumptions underwriting Western discourses about the Orient and orientals, including the discipline of Oriental Studies. Said's demonstration that a supposedly objective and impartial science of cultural analysis could function as an instrument of Western ideological hegemony has been widely influential, especially in the Third World. At the same time, he is a defender of intellectual freedom who has asserted that the doctrine of 'solidarity before criticism' means the end of criticism. Said advocates an ideal of critical 'worldliness', which argues that critics should be aware of their political and moral responsibilities and privileges while conceding their 'institutionalized marginality' with respect to the centres of power.

Criticism striving to be worldly is bound to go beyond textual analysis in the narrow sense. In *Formalism and Marxism*, for example, Bennett outlined a research programme which has been widely heeded by British proponents of 'cultural materialism'. Shakespeare criticism, he suggested, should examine 'the way in which Shakespeare's texts are used in schools, the way in which they are appropriated by the "culture industry" at large, their place within the theatre and the social role and function of the theatre itself'.[27] Bennett also called for a reassessment of the pedagogic aims and institutional history of literary teaching. Most of the recent books attempting these tasks have been written from a controversial, politically committed point of view; in effect, to say that criticism should be political has become the most fashionable way of saying that it should be evaluative. Interpretation, on this view, is not an end in itself; the question to be asked is not 'what does a literary work mean' but 'what does it mean to us', where our needs as well as the work's possible meanings are brought into the argument. What is discreditable and demeaning to criticism is the kind of ideological manipulation which assumes that we are the only people for whom the text might have a worthwhile meaning.

To extend the ideal of critical discourse, as it has developed within the literary tradition, to other cultural 'texts' is obviously desirable. But should the label of 'criticism' and the idea of judgment still be attached to such a discourse? Said declared in 1976 that 'All of us can tell a good critic no matter what banner he carries: similarly, all of us *know* that it is possible genuinely to *learn* from one critic and not from another. It's not a partisan matter finally'.[28] Some would doubt whether such an intuitive consensus still exists, or whether it ever existed; at the very best, in every generation it has to be remade. Today it seems worth pointing out the limitations both of cultural analysis and cultural politics as potential sources of the kind of authority criticism has exercised. To do this, we need to recall Clifford Geertz's example of the Balinese cockfight. The cockfighter and ringside spectator are immersed in the Clausewitzian world of cultural politics, though it is the cock and not its owner whose life is at risk. The ethnographical analyst, or 'over-the-shoulder' reader, must necessarily pretend that taking part in cockfights is a matter for the Balinese, but that his analysis of the cockfight is potentially of universal interest. At the same time, the ethnographer himself can be subjected to ethnographic analysis; it is quite possible to interpret Western anthropology, for example, as a form of metaphorical cockfighting. In each case we believe we know to whom the cultural system in question 'properly belongs'. All the moves open to the over-the-shoulder reader are variations on what Trilling called the cultural mode of thought, a mode which denies the possibility of cultural transcendence and insists on the fact of belonging.

The historical strength of English criticism lay not in its philosophical, scientific or political rigour but in its affiliation to the creative process. Today the split between creator and critic has never seemed wider. We can, for example, debate the question whether literary works can transcend their cultures of origin and achieve universality without feeling it necessary to refer (let alone defer) to the intrinsic claims made by the works themselves. Yet these claims also represent the critical beliefs of their times. Within the tradition surveyed in this book, we have seen that both neoclassical and romantic literature and criticism assert their own universality. Neoclassicism remains committed to an ordered and rule-bound human nature, while romanticism puts its faith in the poet as prophet and in the literary work as a species of revelation. The major modernist writers also claim universality for their works, sometimes by repeating their predecessors' notions: thus Eliot calls for a revival of classicism and Yeats pursues poetic inspiration by dabbling in the occult and taking dictation from his 'spirit masters'.

Yet I shall argue that modernism, too, introduces new grounds for claiming transcendence. At their most characteristic, modernist writers set out to turn their own intellectual rootlessness and homelessness into a source of authority. This is the most revolutionary component of their writing. In James Joyce's *A Portrait of the Artist as a Young Man*, for example, there is a crucial moment when Stephen Dedalus realises that, as an Irishman, he is alienated from the language in which he has learned to speak and write. The words 'home', 'Christ', 'ale', and 'master' belong more naturally to the English dean of studies than they do to himself, he reflects. For him they are an 'acquired speech'. Within the political context of his times (and ours), we should expect Stephen, once he has reached this awareness, to embrace cultural nationalism. The Celtic revival is at its height, and many of his fellow-students are learning Gaelic, but Stephen shows no interest in 'Irish Studies' and begins, instead, to learn Italian. Joyce's major works reflect the Ireland which produced him, to which he may have 'properly belonged' and which, some have said, he never fully left; but their claim to universality is unmistakable, and it involves the repudiation of the beliefs about language at which Stephen arrived as a young man. *Ulysses* and *Finnegans Wake* suggest that we all – whatever our nationality – have to live and write through the medium of an acquired, not a natural language. No culture is closed to outside influence, and there is no 'pure' mother-tongue. Modernist literature – whether we think of the writings of Joyce, Eliot, Pound, Lawrence, Conrad or Beckett – is a 'detribalised' literature, so that we can never say to whom it properly belongs.

Some critics would argue that the detribalisation of modernist writing is its great weakness. In England, successive generations beginning with F. R. Leavis (and with the later Eliot himself) have expressed a profound distaste for modernist rootlessness. Postwar English writing is well known for its reassertion of a local English identity, notably in Philip Larkin's poetry. A number of postwar critics have portrayed the modernist movement as a brief and alien intervention in English literature; Graham Hough, for example, declared in *Image and Experience* (1960) that an author should, as far as possible, write for 'those whom he knows, whose habits and experiences he shares', and many more recent writers have echoed this view.[29] Raymond Williams, in a posthumous collection of essays, tries to subject the rootlessness of modernist writing to cultural analysis. For Williams, this literature with its experiences of 'visual and linguistic strangeness', its broken narratives and transient encounters, is a kind of sociological aberration reflecting the 'endless border-crossing' of the writers themselves.[30]

Edward W. Said argues that not belonging, the 'standing outside of cultures', is the great fact of modern life.[31] If this is so, it may of course be said that modernist writers take part in the common cultural language of their times, but modernist literature itself makes higher claims. It is not only in the twentieth century that life has been transient, unequal, migratory and multilingual. Perhaps, even, the settled community is not the predominant experience of people in society, but an idealisation of that experience and an expression of human desire. Complete monolingualism, for example, is much rarer than we have been taught to assume. Learning a new language is very much easier than it seems to chauvinist citizens living at the heart of great empires. Within a few decades of Columbus's voyage, huge numbers of native Americans had been forced to learn to communicate with their new conquerors. Many were doubtless already experienced translators. The myth of a lost settled community communicating freely in the same language is a pervasive ideological assumption of the twentieth century, which has left its mark on linguistic and anthropological models of culture.

For example, what Greenblatt calls a 'poetics of culture' seeks to understand literature as a 'part of the system of signs that constitutes a given culture'; yet, paradoxically, Greenblatt acknowledges a profound social and cultural mobility among the writers and thinkers of the English Renaissance.[32] Clifford Geertz argues in *Works and Lives* (1988) that the recent entrance of decolonised peoples onto the stage of world culture calls into question the position of the outside observer, or transcultural theoretician, that is taken for granted in most ethnographical writing. Cultural anthropology itself now appears less as a branch of semiotic science than as a literary genre open to rhetorical analysis. Thus the attachment of recent trends in cultural theory to notions of a 'system' and a 'given culture' is incompatible with their own best insights, as well as with those of modernist literature. Either these notions reflect a nostalgia for scholastic and scientific certainties that literary criticism cannot provide, or they are undermined by an acknowledgment of paradox and instability which itself may have been learned from the modernist writers.

Literature in English today reflects the growing diversity and rich cultural vigour of the English-speaking world. Global in its extent, it also seems faced and perhaps threatened by cultural decentrement and dispersal. The growth of cultural studies reflects this dispersal. There is, however, a kind of narcissism inherent in a study which nourishes local and sectional identity. The desire to know other cultures beside our own, and the recognition that there is not any one culture to which we simply and wholeheartedly belong, reflect the notion of a detribalised discourse and a global tradition. The models for this are to be found in literature, art, philosophy and science. At the extremes of contemporary scepticism it is sometimes argued that the universality claimed for all these discourses is necessarily false. Some new historicists have alleged that works survive because they continue to serve powerful interests that have a stake in their survival; far from transcending their cultures, they are continually reinscribed in ever-changing relations of power.[33] The difference between transcendence and 'continual reinscription', however, is largely theological in character, like that between resurrection and reincarnation. Moreover, the new historicists' position claims the universal validity that it denies to other products of the human intellect, while simultaneously failing by the very criteria it invokes: it serves the interests of those who utter it while asserting a knowledge of causality which (as they themselves testify) they cannot attain.

Literary criticism in the sense in which this book has described and defended it differs from other intellectual modes in that its authority is inescapably linked to that of the writings it comments upon. Once it becomes absorbed into political or social–scientific discourse it abandons universalistic claims for the works its studies, but not for the statements it makes about them; or these claims may be invested in the meta-statements it makes about its own statements. The relationship between literary and critical authority, however, is not one of irreversible domination and subservience. The power relations between text and reader and between literature and criticism are, or ought to be, intimate, dialectical and fluid. Criticism articulates the field of discussion, persuasion, reasoning and judgment within which the text is written and read. A poem, Archibald MacLeish said, must not mean but be; criticism lends the poem meaning in order to make it a thing about which we can agree and disagree.

Having begun with Joyce, I will end with Swift:

> Neither is reason among them a point problematical as with us, where men can argue with plausibility on both sides of the question, but strikes you with immediate conviction, as it must needs do where it is not mingled, observed, or discoloured by passion and interest. I remember it was with extreme difficulty that I could bring my master to understand the meaning of the word *opinion*, or how a point could be disputable; because reason taught us to affirm or deny only where we are certain; and beyond our knowledge we cannot do either. So that controversies, wranglings, disputes, and positiveness in false or dubious propositions, are evils unknown among the *Houyhnhnms* ... I have often reflected what destruction such a doctrine would make in the libraries of Europe; and how many paths to fame would be then shut up in the learned world.

The survival of criticism depends on two things. Opinions must differ and arguments must remain problematical and disputatious; and authors' words must continue to be found worth quoting.

Notes

(Many of the critical essays discussed in this book are well known and relatively brief. Often they are available in various modern editions and anthologies. Where this is the case, page references or references to a particular edition have been omitted.)

INTRODUCTION

1　See J. W. H. Atkins, *Literacy Criticism in Antiquity* (Cambridge, 1934), I, pp. 11ff.
2　T. S. Eliot, 'Imperfect Critics', in *The Sacred Wood* (1920).
3　Paul Feyerabend, 'Consolations for the Specialist', in *Criticism and the Growth of Knowledge*, ed. Imre Lakatos and Alan Musgrave (Cambridge, 1970), pp. 197ff. See also the contributions of Kuhn and Lakatos to the same volume.

1　SAMUEL JOHNSON: THE ACADEMY AND THE MARKET-PLACE

Neoclassicism: Dryden and Pope

1　R. S. Crane, 'English Neoclassical Criticism: An Outline Sketch', in *Critics and Criticism Ancient and Modern*, ed. R. S. Crane (Chicago, 1952), pp. 372ff.; and 'On Writing the History of Criticism in England 1650–1800', in *The Idea of the Humanities* (Chicago, 1967), pp. 157ff. See also J. W. H. Atkins, *English Literary Criticism: Seventeenth and Eighteenth Centuries* (London, 1966).
2　W. J. Bate, *The Burden of the Past and the English Poet* (London, 1971), pp. 16ff.
3　René Wellek, *The Rise of English Literary History* (New York, 1966), pp. 35–6.
4　Johnson, 'Life of Dryden'.

5 There are more serious grounds for the equivocating Augustan attitude to Shakespeare. A great work of art in the heyday of neoclassicism existed less as an uplifting cultural monument than as a model to be copied. Shakespeare seemed a highly misleading model for the very reason that the possibility of imitating him was still there. Poetic drama still held the stage; it did not yet need to be revived in the poet's study out of piety towards a vanished heroic age.
6 George Watson, *The Literary Critics* (Harmondsworth, 1962), pp. 43–4.
7 Addison, *Spectator* no. 409 (19 June 1712).
8 Reported by Spence in the last year of Pope's life. This is mentioned by Ian Jack, *Augustan Satire* (Oxford, 1966), p. 5.

Minim, the Dictionary *and the* Life of Savage

1 See the notes to the text in the *Yale Edition of the Works of Samuel Johnson* (New Haven, 1963), II, pp. 185ff.
2 Johnson, *Idler* no. 76 (29 September 1759).
3 There are many anecdotes of this, particularly in Mrs Thrale's memoir reprinted in *Johnsonian Miscellanies*, ed. G. Birkbeck Hill (Oxford, 1897), I, pp. 141ff.
4 Boswell, *Life of Johnson* (Oxford, 1953), p. 939. See also p. 798.
5 See Paul Fussell, *Samuel Johnson and the Life of Writing* (London, 1972), pp. 183ff.
6 Johnson, Preface to *A Dictionary of the English Language* (London, 1755).
7 Johnson, *Idler* no. 66 (21 July 1759).
8 See Johnson, *Rambler* nos 156 and 158 for classic statements of this.
9 Edmund Burke, *A Philosophical Enquiry into ... the Sublime and Beautiful*, 5th edn (London, 1767), p. 91.
10 Raymond Williams, *Culture and Society 1780–1950* (London, 1958), Introduction.
11 The phrase is from Fussell, *Samuel Johnson*.
12 Johnson, *Rambler* no. 93 (5 February 1751).
13 David Hume, 'Of the Standard of Taste' in *Philosophical Works* (Edinburgh, 1826), III, p. 263.

Milton, Shakespeare and the Lives of the Poets

1 Johnson, *Rambler*, nos 2 (24 March 1750) and 106 (23 March 1751).
2 Johnson, journal entry for 2 April 1779, in *Yale Edition*, I, p. 294.
3 Boswell, *Life*, p. 442.
4 Johnson, *Rambler* no. 208 (14 March 1752) and 'Preface to Shakespeare' respectively.

2   WILLIAM WORDSWORTH: THE POET AS PROPHET

Sublimity and transcendence: the later Eighteenth Century

1   Johann Peter Eckermann, *Conversations with Goethe*, trans. John Oxenford (London, 1930), p. 32. The passage is quoted in Bate, *The Burden of the Past and the English Poet*, p. 6.
2   Cf. M. H. Abrams, *The Mirror and the Lamp* (New York, 1958), pp. 240ff.
3   Joan Pittock, *The Ascendancy of Taste* (London, 1973), p. 65.
4   Wellek, *The Rise of English Literary History*, pp. 70ff.
5   Cf. Lawrence Lipking, *The Ordering of the Arts in Eighteenth-Century England* (Princeton, 1970), p. 11.
6   Quoted in Pittock, *The Ascendancy of Taste*, p. 175.
7   Hume, 'Of the Rise and Progress of the Arts and Sciences' in *Philosophical Works*, III, p. 154.
8   E.g. Stephen A. Larrabee, *English Bards and Grecian Marbles* (New York, 1943), p. 119. Larrabee argues that 'Blake accepted the Platonic elements of Neo-classical theory.'

The Preface to Lyrical Ballads

1   See Stephen Gill, 'The Original *Salisbury Plain*', in *Bicentenary Wordsworth Studies*, ed. Jonathan Wordsworth (Ithaca, New York, 1970), pp. 142ff., for a text of this poem.
2   See E. P. Thompson, 'Disenchantment or Default? A Lay Sermon', in *Power and Consciousness*, ed. Conor Cruise O'Brien and William Dean Vanech (London, 1969), pp. 149ff.; and Kelvin Everest, *Coleridge's Secret Ministry: The Context of the Conversation Poems 1795–1798* (Sussex and New York, 1979).
3   Hazlitt, 'On the Living Poets' in *Lectures on the English Poets*.
4   See W. J. B. Owen, *Wordsworth as Critic* (Toronto and London, 1969), pp. 112–13.
5   Ibid., p. 12.
6   Coleridge, *Biographia Literaria*, chapter 18.
7   'An original may be said to be of a vegetable nature; it rises spontaneously from the vital root of genius; its grows, it is not made; Imitations are often a sort of manufacture wrought up by those mechanics, art, and labour, out of pre-existent materials not their own' (Edward Young, *Conjectures on Original Composition*).
8   See Raymond Williams, *Culture and Society 1780–1950* (Harmondsworth, 1961), especially pp. 48ff.
9   Wordsworth, Preface to *The Excursion*.

Poetic power: Wordsworth and de Quincey

1   Owen, *Wordsworth as Critic*, p. 151.
2   Charles Lamb, review of *The Excursion* in *Quarterly Review* (1814),

reprinted in *Lamb's Criticism*, ed. E. M. W. Tillyard (Cambridge, 1923), p. 106.
3 Shelley, *Defence of Poetry*, and de Quincey, *Reminiscences of the English Lake Poets*, ed. John E. Jordan (London, 1961), p. 99.
4 Thomas de Quincey, 'Letters to a Young Man ...', in *Works* (Edinburgh, 1863), XIII, p. 55. De Quincey's distinction was first put forward in 1823 and elaborated in several other places. See especially the essays on Wordsworth (1839), Goldsmith (1848) and Pope (1848).
5 It was the utilitarians, however, who played a major part in the establishment of the study of literature in the universities. The irony of this has been noted by D. J. Palmer, *The Rise of English Studies* (London, 1965), p. 15. See also Chapter 4 below.

3 THE ROMANTIC CRITICS

Reviewers and Bookmen: from Jeffrey to Lamb

1 Table-talk, recorded by T. Allsop, in *Coleridge: Select Poetry and Prose*, ed. Stephen Potter (London, 1962), p. 476.
2 *The Poetical Works of Lord Byron* (London, 1945), p. 910.
3 William Hazlitt, 'Mr. Jeffrey' in *The Spirit of the Age*.
4 J. O. Hayden, *Romantic Bards and British Reviewers* (London, 1971), p. ix.
5 Samuel Taylor Coleridge, *Biographia Literaria*, ed. George Watson (London, 1956), p. 34. (Hereafter as *Biog. Lit.*)
6 For discussion of this episode, see *Coleridge's Shakespearean Criticism*, ed. Thomas Middleton Raysor (London, 1930), I, p. xxxi. (Hereafter as *Shak. Crit.*); and Norman Fruman, *Coleridge: The Damaged Archangel* (London, 1972), pp. 141ff.
7 *Shak. Crit.*, II, p. 260n.
8 A. W. Schlegel, *A Course of Lectures on Dramatic Art and Literature*, trans. John Black (London, 1846), p. 343.
9 William Hazlitt, *Complete Works*, ed. P. P. Howe (London, 1931–3), VI, p. 176.
10 *Shak. Crit.*, I, p. 140.
11 John Gross, *The Rise and Fall of the Man of Letters* (Harmondsworth, 1973), p. 23.
12 *Shak. Crit.*, I, p. 200; *Biog. Lit.*, p. 169.
13 *Shak. Crit.*, I, p. 129.
14 Schlegel, *Lectures*, pp. 38ff.
15 Introduction to *Jeffrey's Literary Criticism*, ed. D. Nichol Smith (London, 1910), p. xxi.
16 De Quincey, *Reminiscences of the English Lake Poets*, ed. John E. Jordan, pp. 172 and 173.

354   *Authors and Authority*

Samuel Taylor Coleridge

1 See John Colmer, *Coleridge: Critic of Society* (Oxford, 1959), pp. 52ff., for an account of Coleridge at this period.
2 Quoted by George Whalley, 'The Integrity of *Biographia Literaria*', *Essays and Studies*, VI n.s. (1953), pp. 87ff.
3 Letter to Robert Southey, in Coleridge, *Select Poetry and Prose*, p. 728.
4 *Biog. Lit.*, pp. xiiff.
5 See M. H. Abrams, *Natural Supernaturalism* (London, 1971), pp. 236ff.
6 *Biog. Lit.*, p. 88.
7 For discussions of Schelling, Coleridge and pantheism, see J. Shawcross's Introduction to his edition of *Biographia Literaria* (London, 1907); J. A. Appleyard, *Coleridge's Philosophy of Literature* (Cambridge, Mass., 1965), p. 205; and Thomas McFarland, *Coleridge and the Pantheist Tradition* (Oxford, 1969), which provides an exhaustive treatment of the whole question. For the religious tensions in Coleridge's life and work as a whole, see William Empson's Introduction to *Coleridge's Verse: A Selection*, ed. William Empson and David Pirie (London, 1972).
8 J. R. de J. Jackson, *Method and Imagination in Coleridge's Criticism* (London, 1969), p. 115. For the orthodox view, see Shawcross, *Biographia*, p. lxvii.
9 McFarland, *Coleridge*, p. 308.
10 *Biog Lit.*, p. 179. The reader may compare the discussions by Shawcross, Appleyard and Jackson cited above.
11 Letter to Southey, in Coleridge, *Select Poetry and Prose*, p. 729.
12 See his lecture 'On the Relation of the Plastic Arts to Nature', reprinted as an appendix to Herbert Read, *The True Voice of Feeling* (London, 1968).
13 *Biog. Lit.*, p. 182.
14 *Biog. Lit.*, p. 213.
15 Cf. Fruman, *Coleridge*, pp. 199ff.
16 Quoted in Hayden, *Romantic Bards*, p. 171.
17 *Biog. Lit.*, p. 257. On 'The Thorn', see pp. 194 and 202.
18 Ibid., p. 251.
19 *Biog. Lit.*, p. 180.
20 *Shak. Crit.*, II, p. 171.
21 *Shak. Crit.*, I, p. 91.
22 *Shak. Crit.*, I, p. 136.
23 Shawcross, *Biographia*, p. lxxiii.
24 Quoted by Jackson, *Method and Imagination*, p. 149.
25 Coleridge, *The Friend*, ed. Barbara E. Rooke (London, 1969), I, p. 507.

Shelley, Hazlitt and Keats

1 Coleridge, *Miscellanies, Aesthetic and Literary*, ed. T. Ashe (London, 1892), p. 6.
2 *The Letters of John Keats*, ed. Maurice Buxton Forman (Oxford, 1935), p. 52.
3 Ibid., p. 31.
4 Ibid., p. 384.
5 Quoted in *Peacock's Four Ages of Poetry, Shelley's Defence of Poetry, Browning's Essay on Shelley*, ed. H. F. Brett-Smith (Oxford, 1921), p. xiii.
6 See J. Bronowski, *The Poet's Defence* (Cambridge, 1939), p. 82, for an interesting examination of this point.
7 Hazlitt, *A Letter to William Gifford, Esq.* in *Complete Works*, IX, p. 50.
8 Hazlitt, *Complete Works*, XVI, p. 137.
9 Ibid., p. 268.
10 Ibid., XVIII, p. 101.
11 For Hazlitt's derivation of this idea, see his essay 'Schlegel on the Drama', *Complete Works*, XVI, pp. 62–4.
12 On Keats and Hazlitt, see Ian Jack, *Keats and the Mirror of Art* (Oxford, 1967); Stephen A. Larrabee, *English Poets and Grecian Marbles* (New York, 1943), pp. 223ff.; and Kenneth Muir, 'Keats and Hazlitt', in *John Keats: A Reassessment*, ed. Muir (Liverpool, 1958), pp. 139ff.
13 Jack, *Keats*, p. 72.
14 Hazlitt, 'On Poetry in General', in *Lectures on the English Poets*.
15 Hazlitt, *Complete Works*, VI, p. 49.
16 Hazlitt, 'On Criticism' in *Complete Works*, VIII, p. 217.
17 Charles Lamb, *Specimens of English Dramatic Poets* (London, n.d.), p. 158n.
18 Hazlitt, *Complete Works*, VI, p. 301.

4 VICTORIAN CRITICISM: THE REPUBLIC OF LETTERS

The Definition of Literary Culture

1 'Present System of Education', in *Westminster Review*, IV (1825), p. 166. See also II (1824), pp. 334ff.
2 'Belles Lettres', in *Westminster Review*, XXXIV (1968), p. 259.
3 Thomas Carlyle, 'Voltaire', in *Critical and Miscellaneous Essays* (London, 1899), II.
4 Carlyle, 'Goethe', in ibid., I.

5   Quoted in *Mill's Essays on Literature and Society*, ed. J. B. Schnee-wind (New York, 1965), pp. 351–2.

6   Ibid., p. 407.

7   J. H. Newman, *On the Scope and Nature of University Education*, Everyman edn (London, 1915), p. 82.

8   Carlyle, 'The Hero as Man of Letters', in *Sartor Resartus and on Heroes*, Everyman edn (London, 1908), p. 384.

9   Carlyle, 'Burns', in *Critical and Miscellaneous Essays*, II.

10 Arthur Hallam, review in the *Englishman's Magazine* (1831), reprinted in *Tennyson: The Critical Heritage*, ed. John D. Jump (London, 1967), p. 41.

11 J. S. Mill, 'What is Poetry?' in *Essays on Literature and Society*, p. 109.

12 Ibid., p. 122.

13 I. A. Richards, *Science and Poetry* (London, 1926), p. 59.

14 George Saintsbury, *A History of English Criticism* (Edinburgh, 1936), p. 452.

15 On Dallas, see Alba H. Warren, Jr, *English Poetic Theory 1825–1865* (Princeton, 1950), pp. 129ff.; and Jenny Taylor, 'The Gay Science: The "Hidden Soul" of Victorian Criticism', *Literature and History*, X. no. 2 (1984), pp. 189–202.

16 Ralph Waldo Emerson, 'Literary Ethics', in *Miscellanies* (London, 1896), pp. 129, 136.

17 Ibid., p. 138.

18 *Mill's Essays on Literature and Society*, p. 135.

19 Henry Timrod, 'A Theory of Poetry' (1863), in Daniel G. Hoffman, ed., *American Poetry and Poetics: Poems and Critical Documents from the Puritans to Robert Frost* (Garden City, N.Y., 1962), p. 318.

20 Walt Whitman, 'Edgar Poe's Significance,' in *American Poetry and Poetics*, p. 392.

21 John Ruskin, 'Of the received Opinions touching the "Grand Style"', in *Modern Painters*, III.

22 See Harold Bloom, *The Ringers in the Tower* (Chicago, 1971), p. 174; and Chapter 6 below.

23 Karl Marx and Frederick Engels, *The German Ideology*, quoted in *On Literature and Art*, ed. Lee Baxandall and Stefan Morawski (New York, 1974), p. 71.

24 William Morris, *Collected Works*, ed. May Morris (London, 1914), XXII, p. 132.

25 Cf. E. P. Thompson, *William Morris: From Romantic to Revolutionary* (London, 1955), p. 768.

26 See the discussions by Patrick Brantlinger, '*News from Nowhere*: Morris's Socialist Anti-Novel', in *Victorian Studies*, XIX (1975), pp. 35ff.; and Patrick Parrinder, '*News from Nowhere*, *The Time Machine* and the Break-Up of Classical Realism', in *Science-Fiction Studies*, X (1976).

Matthew Arnold

1 Reprinted in Matthew Arnold, *Essays, Letters and Reviews*, ed. Fraser Neiman (Cambridge, Mass., 1960), p. 199.

2 On this question see Lionel Trilling, *Matthew Arnold* (London, 1949), pp. 158 and 160.

3 Quoted in John Holloway, *The Victorian Sage* (New York, 1965), p. 202.

4 Geoffrey Tillotson, *Criticism and the Nineteenth Century* (London, 1951), p. 52.

5 Quoted in Trilling, *Arnold*, p. 157.

6 *The Poems of Matthew Arnold 1840–1867* (London, 1913), p. 9.

7 Holloway, *Victorian Sage*, p. 222.

8 Trilling, *Arnold*, p. 161.

9 *Literary Criticism of George Henry Lewes*, ed. Alice R. Kaminsky (Lincoln, Nebraska, 1964), p. 62.

10 Francis W. Newman, 'Homeric Translation in Theory and Practice', in Matthew Arnold, *Essays Literary and Critical*, Everyman edn (London, 1906), p. 312.

11 George Saintsbury, *Matthew Arnold* (Edinburgh, 1911), p. 67.

12 From the first section of *On Translating Homer*: ' "The poet", says Mr Ruskin, "has to speak of the earth in sadness; but he will not let that sadness affect or change his thought of it. No; though Castor and Pollux be dead, yet the earth is our mother still, – fruitful, life-giving." This is a just specimen of that sort of application of modern sentiment to the ancients, against which a student, who wishes to feel the ancients truly, cannot too resolutely defend himself. It reminds one, as alas! so much of Mr Ruskin's writing reminds one, of those words of the most delicate of living critics: "Comme tout genre de composition a son écueil particulier, celui du genre romanesque, c'est le faux." '

13 See Ruskin, *Modern Painters*, III, chapter 8.

14 T. S. Eliot, 'The Perfect Critic', in *The Sacred Wood*.

15 Marx and Engels, *On Literature and Art*, p. 117.

16 Matthew Arnold, *Complete Prose Works*, ed. R. H. Super (Ann Arbor, Michigan, 1960–), III, pp. 40ff.

17 Arnold, 'Joubert', in *Essays in Criticism* (London, 1865).

18 On Arnold and the Sainte-Beuve circle, see Christophe Campos, *The View of France: From Arnold to Bloomsbury* (London, 1965), p. 16.

19 Frederic Harrison, *Tennyson, Ruskin, Mill and Other Literary Estimates* (London, 1899), p. 132. Harrison's 'Culture: A Dialogue' was reprinted in *The Choice of Books* (London, 1917) pp. 97ff.

20 The first part was, in fact, originally called 'Culture and Its Enemies'.

21 Trilling, *Arnold*, pp. 277ff.

22 Quoted by Trilling, *Arnold*, p. 278.

23 On this point see Trilling, *Arnold*, pp. 259ff.

24 E.g. Arnold's denunciation of 'the hideous anarchy which is modern

English literature', in 'Tractatus Theologico-Politicus', *Complete Prose Works*, III, p. 64.
25 Trilling, *Arnold*, p. 375.
26 A. C. Bradley, *Oxford Lectures on Poetry* (London, 1909), p. 127; Bloom, *The Ringers in the Tower*, pp. 19–20.
27 T. S. Eliot, 'The Function of Criticism', in *Selected Essays*.

The later Nineteenth Century

1 Gerald Graff, *Professing Literature: An Institutional History* (Chicago and London, 1987), p. 124. For English studies in Britain see D. J. Palmer, *The Rise of English Studies*; for the United States see Graff's *Professing Literature*.
2 Quotations from Pater's essays 'Coleridge's Writings' are from the text reprinted in *English Critical Essays: Nineteenth Century*, ed. Edmund D. Jones (London, 1971), pp. 421ff.
3 Pater, Preface to *The Renaissance*.
4 On this point see Anthony Ward, *Walter Pater: The Idea in Nature* (London, 1966), p. 194.
5 'Poems by William Morris', in *Westminster Review*, XXXIV (1868), pp. 300–1.
6 On Pater and the Hegelians see Ward, *Walter Pater*, pp. 43ff.
7 Cf. Ian Fletcher, *Walter Pater* (London, 1971), p. 29.
8 Cf. Bernard Bergonzi, *The Turn of a Century* (London, 1973), p. 21.
9 Clyde K. Hyder, *Swinburne as Critic* (London, 1972), p. xi.
10 Ibid., p. 115.
11 Ibid., p. 75.
12 Reprinted in *Pre-Raphaelite Writing*, ed. Derek Stanford (London, 1973), p. 163.
13 A. C. Swinburne, 'John Webster', in Hyder, *Swinburne as Critic*, pp. 286ff.
14 Ibid., p. 308.
15 Oscar Wilde, 'The Critic as Artist', in *Intentions* (London, 1945), p. 111.
16 Ibid., p. 160.
17 Walter Pater, Postscript to *Appreciations* (London, 1927), p. 271.
18 Harrison, *The Choice of Books*, p. 6.
19 Ibid., p. 212.
20 George Saintsbury, *Dryden* (London, 1912), p. 31.
21 James Russell Lowell, *The Old English Dramatists* (Boston and New York, 1893), p. 31.
22 George Santayana, 'Dickens,' in *Selected Critical Writings*, ed. Norman Henfrey (Cambridge, 1968), I, p. 202.
23 Quoted by Hoffman, *American Poetry and Poetics*, p. 60.
24 Henry James, *Letters*, ed. Leon Edel (London, 1975), I, p. 76.
25 Henry James, *Hawthorne*, ed. Tony Tanner (London, 1967), p. 23.

26 *Henry James and H. G. Wells*, ed. Leon Edel and Gordon N. Ray (London, 1958), p. 267.
27 Henry James, *Selected Literary Criticism*, ed. Morris Shapira (London, 1963) p. 10.
28 James, 'Emile Zola' (1903), in ibid., p. 258.
29 James, 'Honoré de Balzac' (1902), in ibid., p. 211.
30 Leslie Stephen, 'Sterne', in *Hours in a Library* (London, 1892), III, p. 139.
31 Stephen, 'Sir Thomas Browne', in ibid., I, pp. 297–8.
32 Q. D. Leavis, 'Leslie Stephen: Cambridge Critic', reprinted in *A Selection from Scrutiny*, ed. F. R. Leavis (Cambridge, 1968), I, pp. 22ff.
33 'Thoughts on Criticism by a Critic' (1876), reprinted in Leslie Stephen, *Men, Books and Mountains*, ed. S. O. A. Ullmann (London, 1956), p. 68.
34 Noel Annan, *Leslie Stephen* (London, 1951) p. 276.
35 Ibid., p. 271.
36 Bradley, *Oxford Lectures on Poetry*, p. 395.
37 A. C. Bradley, *Shakespearean Tragedy* (London, 1974), p. 421.
38 W. B. Yeats, *Essays and Introductions* (London, 1961), p. 197.
39 Arthur Symons, *The Symbolist Movement in Literature* (London, 1908), pp. 8–9.
40 Morris, *Collected Works*, XXIII, p. 167.
41 Yeats, *Essays and Introductions*, p. 289.
42 Ibid., p. 128.
43 Ibid., p. 162.
44 Ibid., p. 245.

5 MODERNISTS AND NEW CRITICS

The Children of the New Epoch: Lewis, Pound and Hulme

1 Wyndham Lewis, 'The Children of the New Epoch', in *The Tyro* [1921], p. 3.
2 See John Goode, 'The Decadent Writer as Producer', in *Decadence and the 1890s*, ed. Ian Fletcher, Stratford-upon-Avon Studies 17 (London 1979), pp. 109–30.
3 Friedrich Nietzsche, *The Use and Abuse of History*, trans. Adrian Collins (Indianapolis, 1957), pp. 20–1.
4 Friedrich Nietzsche, *The Birth of Tragedy and The Genealogy of Morals*, trans. Francis Golffing (Garden City, N.Y., 1956), pp. 136–7.
5 See especially Frank Kermode, *Romantic Image* (London, 1957); Stephen Spender, *The Struggle of the Modern* (London, 1965); Graham Hough, *Image and Experience* (London, 1960); Tom Gibbons, *Rooms in the Darwin Hotel: Studies in English Literature and Ideas 1880–1920* (Nedlands, Western Australia, 1973).
6 See Spender, *The Struggle of the Modern*.
7 Hugh Kenner, *The Pound Era* (London, 1975), p. 444.

8 Wyndham Lewis, *Enemy Salvoes: Selected Literary Criticism*, ed. C. J. Fox (London, 1975), p. 181.
9 T. S. Eliot, Introduction to *Literary Essays of Ezra Pound* (London, 1954), p. xi.
10 Gibbons, *Rooms in the Darwin Hotel*, p. 126.
11 Wyndham Lewis, 'Early London Environment', in *T. S. Eliot: A Collection of Critical Essays*, ed. Hugh Kenner (Englewood Cliffs, N.J., 1962), p. 31.
12 See Gibbons, *Rooms in the Darwin Hotel*, and Eric Homberger, 'Pound, Ford, and "Prose". The Making of a Modern Poet', in *American Studies* (1972), V, pp. 281–92.
13 Pound, *Literary Essays*, p. 32.
14 Ibid., p. 11.
15 Pound, *Gaudier-Brzeska: A Memoir* (Hessle, Yorks., 1960), pp. 126, 121.
16 Pound, *Literary Essays*, p. 4.
17 Ronald Schuchard, 'Eliot and Hulme in 1916: Toward a Revaluation of Eliot's Critical and Spiritual Development', in *PMLA*, lxxxviii, (1973), pp. 1083–90.
18 Foreword to T. E. Hulme, *Speculations: Essays on Humanism and the Philosophy of Art*, ed. Herbert Read, 2nd edn (London, 1936), p. viii.
19 T. E. Hulme, 'A Lecture on Modern Poetry', in *Further Speculations*, ed. Sam Hynes (Minneapolis 1955), p. 70.
20 Ibid., p. 69.
21 On the parallels between Hulme and Pound see John T. Gage, *In the Arresting Eye: The Rhetoric of Imagism* (Baton Rouge and London, 1981).
22 Hulme, *Speculations*, p. 168.
23 T. S. Eliot, 'Poetry in the Eighteenth Century' (1930) in *The Pelican Guide to English Literature, Vol. 4: From Dryden to Johnson*, ed. Boris Ford (Harmondsworth, 1957), p. 272.
24 Hulme, *Speculations*, p. 116.
25 See, e.g. John Harrison, *The Reactionaries* (London, 1966).
26 Hulme, *Speculations*, pp. 127, 97.

T. S. Eliot

1 Quoted in Hugh Kenner, *The Invisible Poet: T. S. Eliot* (London, 1965), p. 83.
2 Cf. C. K. Stead, 'Eliot's "Dark Embryo",' in *The New Poetic: Yeats to Eliot* (Harmondsworth, 1967), pp. 125–46.
3 Eliot, *For Lancelot Andrewes: Essays on Style and Order* (London, 1928), p. x. The title *The Disintegration of the Intellect* is found in the preface to Eliot's unpublished Clark lectures, given at Cambridge in 1926. See Edward Lobb, *T. S. Eliot and the Romantic Critical Tradition* (London, 1981), p. 56.

4 Stanley Edgar Hyman, *The Armed Vision: A Study in the Methods of Modern Literary Criticism*, revised edn (New York, 1955), p. 57.

5 Kenner, *The Invisible Poet*, pp. 85–6.

6 See F. R. Leavis, 'T. S. Eliot as Critic' in *Anna Karenina and Other Essays* (London, 1967), p. 179.

7 See T. S. Eliot, 'Thoughts After Lambeth' in *Selected Essays* (London, 1951), p. 368.

8 Hyman, *The Armed Vision*, p. 56.

9 '*Ulysses*, Order and Myth' in *Selected Prose of T. S. Eliot*, ed. Frank Kermode (London, 1975), pp. 175–8. Eliot first gave permission for this essay to be reprinted in *James Joyce: Two Decades of Criticism*, ed. Seon Givens (1948).

10 T. S. Eliot, 'The Lesson of Baudelaire', in *The Tyro*, no. 1 [1921].

11 Eliot, *The Sacred Wood* (London, 1960), p. 150.

12 *Egoist*, V no. 5 (May 1918), p. 69.

13 T. S. Eliot, 'The Frontiers of Criticism,' in *On Poetry and Poets* (London, 1957), p. 106.

14 T. S. Eliot, 'To Criticize the Critic', in *To Criticize the Critic and Other Writings* (London, 1978), p. 16.

15 Timothy Materer, *Vortex: Pound, Eliot and Lewis* (Ithaca, N.Y., 1979), p. 27.

16 T. S. Eliot, 'Ezra Pound: His Metric and Poetry', in *To Criticize the Critic*, pp. 167–8.

17 Ezra Pound, 'Re *Vers Librè*', in *Literary Essays of Ezra Pound*, ed. T. S. Eliot (London, 1954), p. 12.

18 T. S. Eliot, 'Tarr', *Egoist*, V no. 8 (September 1918), pp. 105–6.

19 T. S. Eliot, 'Reflections on Contemporary Poetry', *Egoist*, VI (July 1919), p. 39.

20 T. S. Eliot, 'Turgenev', *Egoist*, IV no. 11 (December 1917), p. 167.

21 See Ronald Schuchard, 'Eliot and Hulme in 1916: Toward a Revaluation of Eliot's Critical and Spiritual Development', *PMLA*, LXXXVIII (1973), p. 1089.

22 Eliot, 'Reflections on Contemporary Poetry', p. 40.

23 T. S. Eliot, 'The Three Provincialities', *The Tyro*, 11 [1922], p. 12.

24 Eliot, *Notes towards the Definition of Culture* (London, 1962), pp. 19, 52.

25 Gaudier-Brzeska was the first major modern artist to be influenced by palaeolithic art. According to Hugh Kenner, Eliot went on his own to visit a prehistoric cave (possibly the Grotte de Niaux) while holidaying with Pound in Southern France in 1919. Kenner, *The Pound Era* (London, 1975), pp. 333–4.

26 T. S. Eliot, 'The Letters of J. B. Yeats', *Egoist*, IV no. 6 (July 1917), p. 90.

27 See for example C. K. Stead, 'Eliot, Arnold, and the English Poetic Tradition', in *The Literary Criticism of T. S. Eliot*, ed. David Newton-De Molina (London, 1977), pp. 203, 213n; and Chris Baldick, *The Social Mission of English Criticism 1848–1932* (Oxford, 1983), p. 112. It should be added that the notion of the critic as sacrificial priest

pre-dates *The Golden Bough.* In *The Gay Science* (I, p. 13), E. S. Dallas writes that 'It seems as if, like Diana's priest at Aricia, a critic could not attain his high office except by the slaughter of the priest already installed.' Dallas then attacks Arnold with considerable vehemence.

28 Petronius, *The Satyricon and the Fragments*, trans. John Sullivan (Harmondsworth, 1965), p. 93.
29 This point is made by Lobb, *Eliot and the Romantic Critical Tradition*, p. 156.
30 Edward Lobb regards Ruskin's method of 'argument by images' as an anticipation of modern critical method. *Eliot and the Romantic Critical Tradition*, p. 86.
31 See Lobb, *Eliot and the Romantic Critical Tradition*, pp. 31–2.
32 F. R. Leavis, *Revaluation: Tradition and Development in English Poetry* (London, 1936), p. 10.
33 Peter Ackroyd, *T. S. Eliot* (London, 1984), p. 248.
34 *The Criterion 1922–1939*, ed. T. S. Eliot, 18 vols (London, 1967), I, p. v.
35 *Criterion*, II (1924), p. 231.
36 *Criterion*, IV (1926), p. 3.
37 Ackroyd, *T. S. Eliot*, p. 143.
38 T. S. Eliot, *After Strange Gods* (London, 1934), pp. 18, 20.
39 Cf. Ackroyd, *T. S. Eliot*, pp. 291, 330–1.
40 Roger Kojecky, *T. S. Eliot's Social Criticism* (London, 1971), p. 212n.
41 Kojecky, *Eliot's Social Criticism*, pp. 62–3.
42 T. S. Eliot, 'Religion and Literature,' in *Selected Prose*, ed. Kermode, pp. 104–5.
43 T. S. Eliot, 'Henry James' (1918) in *Selected Prose*, ed. Kermode, p. 151.
44 T. S. Eliot, 'Contemporanea', *Egoist*, V no. 6 (June–July 1918), pp. 84–5.
45 See T. S. Eliot, 'Virgil and the Christian World', in *On Poetry and Poets*, pp. 122–3.
46 Ibid.

Poetry and the Age: 1920–60

1 I. A. Richards, *Science and Poetry* (1935 edn.), in *Poetries and Sciences* (London, 1970), p. 17; *Principles of Literary Criticism*, 2nd edn (London: 1926), p. 4.
2 C. K. Ogden, I. A. Richards, and James Wood, *The Foundations of Aesthetics* (London, 1922), p. 91.
3 I. A. Richards, *Science and Poetry* (London, 1926), p. 9.
4 G. S. Fraser, *The Modern Writer and His World*, 3rd edn (Harmondsworth, 1964), p. 384.
5 I. A. Richards, 'Retrospect', in *Interpretation in Teaching*, 2nd edn (London, 1973), pp. xxiii–xxvi.

6   I. A. Richards, *Practical Criticism: A Study of Literary Judgment* (London, 1929), pp. 6, 351.

7   I. A. Richards, *Complementarities: Uncollected Essays*, ed. John Paul Russo (Manchester, 1977), p. 259.

8   Richards, *Science and Poetry*, p. 49.

9   Richards, *Science and Poetry* (1926), p. 76n., 2nd edn (London, 1935), pp. 70n.–71n.

10 Richards, *Complementarities*, pp. 30–1.

11 The term 'imaginative assent' is used in Richards's 1930 essay on 'Belief'. By then he would have read Eliot's 'Dante' (1929), which distinguishes between belief and assent.

12 Richards, *Principles*, p. 278.

13 I. A. Richards, 'Poetry as an Instrument of Research,' in *Speculative Instruments* (London, 1955), pp. 148–9.

14 See I. A. Richards, 'Jakobson's Shakespeare', *Times Literary Supplement* (28 May 1970), pp. 589–90.

15 Richards, *Poetries and Sciences*, p. 98; 'The Future of Poetry,' in *The Screens and Other Poems* (New York, 1960), pp. 118, 119.

16 Richards, *Complementarities*, p. 198.

17 I. A. Richards, *Beyond* (New York and London, 1974), pp. 106, 107.

18 Ibid., p. 177.

19 W. H. N. Hotopf had characterised Richards as an intellectual juggler well before the appearance of *Beyond*. Hotopf, *Language, Thought and Comprehension: A Case Study of the Writings of I. A. Richards* (London, 1965), p. 49.

20 Richards, 'Belief' (1930), in *Complementarities*, p. 33.

21 Richards, *Complementarities*, p. 266.

22 This remark is attributed to Richards by Francis Mulhern, *The Moment of 'Scrutiny'* (London, 1981), p. 201n.

23 'Caveat Emptor', *The Fugitive*, i no. 2 (June 1922), p. 34.

24 John Crowe Ransom, 'Reconstructed but Unregenerate', in Twelve Southerners, *I'll Take My Stand: The South and the Agrarian Tradition*, ed. Louis D. Rubin, Jr (Baton Rouge and London, 1977), p. 5.

25 Robert Penn Warren, 'The Briar Patch', in *I'll Take My Stand*, p. 264.

26 T. S. Eliot in *Criterion* (October 31, 1931), quoted in F. R. Leavis, *For Continuity* (Cambridge, 1933), pp. 167n–168n.

27 '*Scrutiny*: A Manifesto', *Scrutiny*, i no. 1 (May 1932), p. 6.

28 Leavis, *For Continuity*, p. 217.

29 Ransom, 'Reconstructed but Unregenerate', p. 15.

30 Ibid., p. 5.

31 'A.T.' [Allen Tate], 'One Escape from the Dilemma', *Fugitive*, iii no. 2 (April 1924), pp. 35–6.

32 Cf. Iain Wright, 'F. R. Leavis, The "Scrutiny" Movement and the Crisis', in Jon Clark *et al.*, *Culture and Crisis in Britain in the Thirties* (London, 1979), p. 39.

364 Authors and Authority

33 Leavis, *For Continuity*, pp. 48, 70.
34 F. R. Leavis, *For Continuity*, p. 69; 'How to Teach Reading', in *Education and the University*, 2nd edn (London, 1948), p. 120.
35 F. R. Leavis, *For Continuity*, pp. 183–4; 'The Standards of Criticism', in Eric Bentley, ed., *The Importance of Scrutiny: Selections from 'Scrutiny: A Quarterly Review'* (New York, 1964), p. 396.
36 F. R. Leavis, *New Bearings in English Poetry: A Study of the Contemporary Situation*, 2nd edn (London, 1950), p. 14.
37 René Wellek, 'Literary Criticism and Philosophy: A Letter' in Bentley, *The Importance of Scrutiny*, pp. 23–30.
38 F. R. Leavis and Denys Thompson, *Culture and Environment: The Training of Critical Awareness* (London, 1962), p. 93.
39 F. R. Leavis, 'Literary Criticism and Philosophy', in *The Common Pursuit* (Harmondsworth, 1962), p. 216.
40 F. R. Leavis, 'Imagery and Movement', in *A Selection from 'Scrutiny'*, ed. F. R. Leavis (Cambridge, 1968), I, pp. 233, 240.
41 F. R. Leavis, 'Reality and Sincerity', in *A Selection from 'Scrutiny'*, I, p. 256.
42 Leavis, *For Continuity*, pp. 211, 208.
43 Leavis, *Education and the University*, p. 80.
44 Leavis, *For Continuity*, p. 208.
45 F. R. Leavis, *The Great Tradition: George Eliot, Henry James, Joseph Conrad* (Harmondsworth, 1962) p. 17.
46 Ibid., p. 26.
47 D. H. Lawrence, 'John Galsworthy', in *Selected Literary Criticism*, ed. Anthony Beal (London, 1961), p. 118.
48 F. R. Leavis, 'The Complex Fate', in *Anna Karenina and Other Essays* (London, 1967), pp. 152–60, and 'Introduction' in *Mill on Bentham and Coleridge*, ed. F. R. Leavis (London, 1950), pp. 1–38.
49 F. R. Leavis, review of *Essays Ancient and Modern* by T. S. Eliot (1936), in Bentley, *The Importance of Scrutiny*, p. 284.
50 F. R. Leavis, 'Two Cultures? The Significance of Lord Snow', in *Nor Shall My Sword: Discourses on Pluralism, Compassion and Social Hope* (London, 1972), p. 56.
51 Raymond Williams, 'Our Debt to Dr. Leavis', *Critical Quarterly*, i (1959), p. 245.
52 For a detailed discussion see Jan Gorak, *The Alien Mind of Raymond Williams* (Columbia, Missouri, 1988), pp. 19–24.
53 Cf. Samuel Hynes, 'Introduction', in Christopher Caudwell, *Romance and Realism: A Study in English Bourgeois Literature*, ed. Samuel Hynes (Princeton, 1970), p. 15.
54 Edward Upward, 'Sketch for a Marxist Interpretation of Literature', in C. Day Lewis, ed., *The Mind in Chains: Socialism and the Cultural Revolution* (London, 1937), p. 48.
55 Christopher Caudwell, 'T. E. Lawrence: A Study in Heroism', in *Studies and Further Studies in a Dying Culture* (New York and London, 1971), p. 25.

56 Raymond Williams, 'Marxism and Culture', in *Culture and Society 1780–1950* (Harmondsworth, 1961), pp. 258–75.
57 Q. D. Leavis, review of *Inside the Whale* by George Orwell, *Scrutiny*, ix no. 2 (September 1940), p. 175.
58 See Raymond Williams, *Orwell* (New York, 1971), pp. 18, 23.
59 Raymond Williams, *The English Novel from Dickens to Lawrence* (London, 1970), p. 118. For Williams on value-judgments, see Chapter 7, 'Literary Criticism and Cultural Theory' below.
60 Quoted by Gerald Graff, *Professing Literature: An Institutional History* (Chicago and London, 1987), p. 157.
61 Richard Foster, *The New Romantics: A Reappraisal of the New Criticism* (Bloomington, Indiana, 1962), p. 197.
62 See W. K. Wimsatt, Jr, *The Verbal Icon: Studies in the Meaning of Poetry* (London, 1970), p. xvii.
63 John Crowe Ransom, *The World's Body* (New York and London, 1938), pp. 173–4.
64 Robert Wooster Stallman, 'Preface', in Robert Wooster Stallman, ed., *Critiques and Essays in Criticism 1920–1948* (New York, 1949), p. v.
65 Allen Tate, *Reactionary Essays on Poetry and Ideas* (New York and London, 1936), p. 17; R. P. Blackmur, *Language as Gesture: Essays in Poetry* (London, 1954), p. 123.
66 Yvor Winters, *In Defense of Reason*, 3rd edn (Denver, 1947), p. 13.
67 Ransom, *The World's Body* (Port Washington, N.Y., 1964), p. x.
68 Kenneth Burke, 'Four Master Tropes', in *A Grammar of Motives* (New York, 1945), pp. 503–17.
69 See for example Francis Fergusson, '*Macbeth* as the Imitation of an Action', in W. K. Wimsatt, Jr, ed., *Explication as Criticism: Selected Papers from the English Institute 1941–1952* (New York and London, 1963), pp. 85–97.
70 Ransom, *The World's Body* (1938), pp. 271–2, 302.
71 Winters, *In Defense of Reason*, p. 11.
72 Cleanth Brooks, 'Foreword', in Stallman, ed., *Critiques*, p. xix.
73 Kenneth Burke, *Counter-Statement*, 2nd edn (Los Altos, California, 1953), p. 213.
74 Ibid., p. 219.
75 Blackmur, *Language as Gesture*, p. 372.
76 John Crowe Ransom, 'More than Gesture', in *Poems and Essays* (New York, 1955), p. 102.
77 See, e.g., James T. Jones, *Wayward Skeptic: The Theories of R. P. Blackmur* (Urbana and Chicago, 1986), pp. 2–5, 112.
78 Blackmur, *Language as Gesture*, p. 378; R. P. Blackmur, *The Lion and the Honeycomb: Essays in Solicitude and Critique* (New York, 1955), p. 184.
79 Blackmur, *The Lion and the Honeycomb*, p. 241.
80 Edward W. Said, 'The Horizon of R. P. Blackmur', in Edward T. Cone, Joseph Frank, and Edmund Keeley, eds, *The Legacy of R. P. Blackmur: Essays, Memoirs, Texts* (New York, 1987), p. 99.

81 W. S. Merwin, 'Affable Irregular', in Cone *et al., The Legacy of R. P. Blackmur*, p. 173.
82 Blackmur, *Language as Gesture*, p. 326.
83 Ibid., p. 435.
84 Cf. Foster, *The New Romantics*, p. 103.
85 Ibid., p. 180.
86 Said, 'The Horizon of R. P. Blackmur', p. 102.
87 Dick Davis, *Wisdom and Wilderness: The Achievement of Yvor Winters* (Athens, Georgia, 1983), p. 201.
88 Ibid., p. 150.
89 Randall Jarrell, 'The Age of Criticism', in *Poetry and the Age* (New York, 1953), pp. 72–3.

6 THE AGE OF INTERPRETATION

The Scientific Schoolmen

1 Gerald Graff, *Professing Literature: An Institutional History* (Chicago and London, 1987), p. 155.
2 Cf. Jean Starobinski, 'Criticism and Authority', trans, A. Cancogni and R. Sieburth, *Daedalus*, 106 no. 4 (1977), pp. 15–16.
3 Cf. René Wellek, *A History of Modern Criticism: 1750–1950*, V (New Haven and London, 1986), pp. 129–30.
4 G. Wilson Knight, *The Wheel of Fire: Interpretations of Shakespearian Tragedy*, 4th edn (London, 1949), p. xviii.
5 G. Wilson Knight, *The Imperial Theme: Further Interpretations of Shakespeare's Tragedies*, 3rd edn (London, 1951), p. vi; Knight, *The Wheel of Fire*, p. 14.
6 Gerald Hammond, 'English Translations of the Bible', in Robert Alter and Frank Kermode, eds, *The Literary Guide to the Bible* (London, 1987), p. 651.
7 Frank Kermode, 'Institutional Control of Interpretation,' in *The Art of Telling* (Cambridge, Mass., 1983), p. 170.
8 Ibid., p. 176.
9 Graff, *Professing Literature*, pp. 232, 233.
10 Frederick Crews, 'Do Literary Studies Have an Ideology?' *PMLA*, 85 (1970), p. 284.
11 Quoted in Stanley Edgar Hyman, *The Armed Vision: A Study in the Methods of Modern Literary Criticism* (New York, 1955), p. 263.
12 Graff, *Professing Literature*, p. 150.
13 William Empson, *Seven Types of Ambiguity*, Peregrine edn (Harmondsworth, 1961), p. 247.
14 Quoted by James Jensen, 'The Construction of *Seven Types of Ambiguity*', *Modern Language Quarterly*, 27 (1966), p. 257.
15 Katheleen Raine, 'Extracts from Unpublished Memoirs', in Roma Gill, ed., *William Empson: The Man and His Work* (London, 1974), p. 16.

16 William Empson, 'My Credo IV: The Verbal Analysis', *Kenyon Review*, 12 (1950), pp. 594, 597–8.

17 William Empson, *Milton's God*, revised edn (London, 1965), p. 77.

18 Empson, 'My Credo', p. 601.

19 Empson, *Seven Types of Ambiguity* (London, 1930), p. 25.

20 See Kenneth Burke, *The Philosophy of Literary Form: Studies in Symbolic Action* (Baton Rouge, Ca., 1941), p. 424, and Hyman, *The Armed Vision*, p. 249.

21 Cf. Roger Sale, 'The Achievement of William Empson', in *Modern Heroism* (Berkeley and Los Angeles, 1973), p. 123.

22 Empson, *Milton's God*, p. 262.

23 Ibid., p. 10.

24 Quoted in C. H. Page, 'Professor Empson's "Sanitary Efforts"': Part 1', *Delta*, 49 (1971), p. 28.

25 William Empson, 'Introduction', in *Coleridge's Verse: A Selection*, ed. Empson and David Pirie (London, 1972), pp. 27, 60.

26 Empson, *Seven Types of Ambiguity* (1961), p. x.

27 Northrop Frye, *The Great Code: The Bible and Literature* (San Diego, New York and London, 1983), p. 63, Cf. Northrop Frye, *The Critical Path: An Essay on the Social Context of Literary Criticism* (Bloomington and London, 1971), p. 27.

28 Northrop Frye, *Anatomy of Criticism: Four Essays* (Princeton, N.J., 1971), p. 315; Northrop Frye, *Fearful Symmetry: A Study of William Blake* (Boston, 1962), p. 109.

29 Frye, *The Critical Path*, p. 86.

30 Northrop Frye, *The Stubborn Structure: Essays on Criticism and Society* (London, 1970), p. 86; *Fearful Symmetry*, p. 319; *The Great Code*, p. 15.

31 Frank Kermode, *Continuities* (London, 1970), p. 116.

32 Both H. G. Wells's *The Outline of History* and Arnold J. Toynbee's *A Study of History* were runaway best sellers in the United States, far outstripping their performance in Britain. Frye himself has exercised a much greater spell in the US than elsewhere.

33 Frye, *Fearful Symmetry*, p. 108.

34 Frye, *The Stubborn Structure*, p. 78.

35 Frye, *The Stubborn Structure*, pp. 71, 80; *The Critical Path*, p. 127.

36 Frye, *The Great Code*, p. xiv. For Frye on the ignorance of the teaching profession, see *The Critical Path*, pp. 144–5.

37 Frye, *The Critical Path*, p. 36.

38 Ibid., p. 127.

39 Ibid., p. 91.

40 Frye, *The Stubborn Structure*, p. 88.

41 Ibid., p. 82.

42 Eg., Frye, *The Critical Path*, p. 74; *The Stubborn Structure*, p. 256.

43 Frye, *Anatomy of Criticism*, p. 354.

44 Roman Jakobson, *Language in Literature*, ed. Krystyna Pomorska and Stephen Rudy (Cambridge, Mass., and London, 1987), p. 378.

45   Krystyna Pomorska, 'Afterword', in Roman Jakobson and Krystyna Pomorska, *Dialogues* (Cambridge, Mass., 1983), p. 160.
46   Jakobson, *Language in Literature*, pp. 285, 300.
47   Ibid., p. 179.
48   Ibid., p. 173.
49   Michael Riffaterre, *Semiotics of Poetry* (London, 1980), pp. 1, 5–6.
50   This has been argued by Robert Scholes, *Textual Power: Literary Theory and the Teaching of English* (New Haven and London, 1985), p. 90–1.
51   Katerina Clark and Michael Holquist, *Mikhail Bakhtin* (Cambridge, Mass., 1984), p. 276.
52   M. M. Bakhtin, *The Dialogic Imagination: Four Essays*, ed. Michael Holquist (Austin, Texas, 1981), pp. 6, 374.

Theory and Interpretation: The Text and the Dream

1   Jakobson, *Language in Literature*, p. 112.
2   Richard Rorty, *Consequences of Pragmatism (Essays 1972–1980)* (Brighton, Sussex, 1982), p. 155.
3   Elizabeth W. Bruss, *Beautiful Theories: The Spectacle of Discourse in Contemporary Criticism* (Baltimore and London, 1982), Chapter 1 (title).
4   Howard Felperin, *Beyond Deconstruction: The Uses and Abuses of Literary Theory* (Oxford, 1985), p. 41.
5   W. J. T. Mitchell, 'The Golden Age of Criticism: Seven Theses and a Commentary', *London Review of Books* (25 June 1987), p. 16.
6   Jakobson, *Language in Literature*, p. 293.
7   Gérard Genette, 'Structuralism and Literary Criticism', in David Lodge, ed., *Modern Criticism and Theory: A Reader* (London and New York, 1988), p. 70.
8   Freud noted this in a footnote added in 1911. See Sigmund Freud, *The Interpretation of Dreams*, trans. James Strachey (Harmondsworth, 1976), p. 173n.
9   Ibid., p. 383.
10   Ibid., pp. 368, 368n.
11   Lionel Trilling, 'Freud and Literature', in *The Liberal Imagination: Essays on Literature and Society* (New York, 1950), p. 53.
12   Frederick J. Hoffman, *Freudianism and the Literary Mind* (New York, 1959), p. 322.
13   Roland Barthes, 'Textual Analysis: Poe's "Valdemar"', in Lodge, *Modern Criticism and Theory*, p. 173; Michel Foucault, 'What is an Author?' in Lodge, *Modern Criticism and Theory*, p. 209.
14   Jacques Derrida, 'Structure, Sign and Play in the Discourse of the Human Sciences', in Lodge, *Modern Criticism and Theory*, pp. 121–2.
15   Jacques Derrida, 'Living On', in Harold Bloom, Paul de Man, Jacques Derrida, Geoffrey H. Hartman, and J. Hillis Miller, *Deconstruction and Criticism* (New York, 1979), p. 84.

16 J. Hillis Miller, 'The Critic as Host', in Bloom *et al.*, *Deconstruction and Criticism*, p. 243.
17 Geoffrey Hartman, 'Preface', in ibid., p. vii.
18 Freud, *The Interpretation of Dreams*, p. 368.
19 Miller, 'The Critic as Host', p. 252.
20 Robert Moynihan, *A Recent Imagining: Interviews with Harold Bloom, Geoffrey Hartman, J. Hillis Miller, Paul de Man* (Hamden, Conn., 1986), pp. 143, 148.
21 Harold Bloom, 'The Breaking of Form', in Bloom *et al.*, *Deconstruction and Criticism*, p. 4.
22 Sigmund Freud, 'The Future of an Illusion', in *The Standard Edition of the Complete Psychological Works of Sigmund Freud*, ed. James Strachey, XXI (London, 1961), p. 43.
23 Quoted by Wallace Martin, 'Introduction', in Jonathan Arac, Wlad Godzich, and Wallace Martin, eds, *The Yale Critics: Deconstruction in America* (Minneapolis, 1983), p. xxi.
24 Imre Salusinszky, 'Harold Bloom', in *Criticism in Society: Interviews* (New York and London, 1987), p. 62.
25 Frye, *Fearful Symmetry*, p. 356.
26 Harold Bloom, *Ruin the Sacred Truths: Poetry and Belief from the Bible to the Present* (Cambridge, Mass., and London, 1989), p. 123.
27 Bloom, 'The Breaking of Form', p. 15.
28 Moynihan, *A Recent Imagining*, p. 34.
29 Harold Bloom, *The Anxiety of Influence: A Theory of Poetry* (London, Oxford and New York, 1973), p. 86.
30 Harold Bloom, *Kabbalah and Criticism* (New York, 1975), p. 107.
31 Bloom, 'The Breaking of Form', p. 8.
32 Moynihan, 'A Recent Imagining', p. 25.
33 Cf. Salusinszky, 'Harold Bloom', pp. 46–7.
34 Bloom, *Kabbalah and Criticism*, p. 82.
35 Ibid., p. 102.
36 Salusinszky, 'Harold Bloom', p. 67.
37 Bloom, *Kabbalah and Criticism*, pp. 86–7.
38 Harold Bloom, *A Map of Misreading* (New York, 1975), p. 33.
39 Moynihan, *A Recent Imagining*, pp. 29–30.
40 Paul de Man, *Critical Writings, 1953–1978*, ed. Lindsay Waters (Minneapolis, 1989), p. 164.
41 Miller, 'The Critic as Host', p. 230.
42 De Man, *Critical Writings*, p. 139.
43 Paul de Man, *The Resistance to Theory* (Minneapolis, 1986), p. 27.
44 De Man, *Critical Writings*, p. 91.
45 Paul de Man, *Blindness and Insight: Essays in the Rhetoric of Contemporary Criticism*, 2nd edn (London, 1983), p. 253.
46 De Man, *Allegories of Reading*, p. 174. He later told an interviewer that 'I think that what was performed for Lacan, Derrida, and others by Freud was done for me by Heidegger'. Moynihan, *A Recent Imagining*, p. 158.
47 De Man, *The Resistance to Theory*, pp. 35–6.

48 Paul de Man, *Allegories of Reading: Figural Language in Rousseau, Nietzsche, Rilke, and Proust* (New Haven and London, 1979), pp. 105, 110. See also Brian Vickers, 'The Atrophy of Modern Rhetoric, Vico to de Man', *Rhetorica*, 6 (1988), pp. 48–50; Stanley Corngold, 'Error in Paul de Man', in Arac *et al.*, *The Yale Critics*, pp. 104–5.
49 De Man, *Critical Writings*, p. 217.
50 Moynihan, *A Recent Imagining*, p. 138.
51 Paul de Man, *The Rhetoric of Romanticism* (New York, 1984), p. 81; *Allegories of Reading*, pp. 78, 77, 17.
52 De Man, *Allegories of Reading*, p. 118.
53 De Man, *The Resistance to Theory*, p. 121.
54 For 'The Triumph of Life' see de Man's 'Shelley Disfigured'; for 'The Fall of Hyperion', see 'The Resistance to Theory'.

7   THE CHALLENGES TO INTERPRETATION

The Men of Letters: Wilson, Trilling and Steiner

1   Lionel Trilling, *The Opposing Self: Nine Essays in Criticism* (London, 1955), p. 118.
2   F. O. Matthiessen, 'The Responsibilities of the Critic', in Bernard S. Oldsey and Arthur O. Lewis, Jr, eds, *Visions and Revisions in Modern American Literary Criticism* (New York, 1962), p. 168.
3   Edmund Wilson, *Classics and Commercials: A Literary Chronicle of the Forties* (New York, 1962), p. 249.
4   Edmund Wilson, dedication to *Axel's Castle*.
5   Edmund Wilson, *The Shores of Light: A Literary Chronicle of the Twenties and Thirties* (New York, 1952), p. 210.
6   Edmund Wilson, *Axel's Castle: A Study in the Imaginative Literature of 1870–1930* (London, 1961), p. 188.
7   Edmund Wilson, *The Wound and the Bow: Seven Studies in Literature* (London, 1961), p. 259.
8   Wilson, *Axel's Castle*, p. 98.
9   Wilson, *Classics and Commercials*, pp. 182, 189.
10 See Mark Krupnick, *Lionel Trilling and the Fate of Cultural Criticism* (Evanston, Ill., 1986), pp. 11, 97, 129n.
11 Lionel Trilling, *The Liberal Imagination: Essays on Literature and Society* (London, 1951), p. 11.
12 Lionel Trilling, 'Aggression and Utopia: A Note on William Morris's "News from Nowhere" ', *Psychoanalytic Quarterly*, 42 (1973), p. 214.
13 Quoted in Krupnick, *Lionel Trilling*, p. 163.
14 Trilling, *The Liberal Imagination*, p. 100.
15 Lionel Trilling, *Beyond Culture: Essays on Literature and Learning* (Harmondsworth, 1967), p. 38.
16 Lionel Trilling, *Sincerity and Authenticity* (London, 1972), pp. 76–7.
17 Trilling, *The Opposing Self*, pp. 65, 123, 230.
18 Krupnick, *Lionel Trilling*, pp. 107–8.

19 Trilling, *Beyond Culture*, p. 98.
20 Ibid., p. 157.
21 Quoted in Krupnick, *Lionel Trilling*, p. 155.
22 *George Steiner: A Reader* (Harmondsworth, 1984), p. 56.
23 Ibid., p. 368.

Virginia Woolf and Feminist Criticism

1 John Gross, *The Rise and Fall of the Man of Letters: Aspects of English Literary Life since 1800* (Harmondsworth, 1973), p. 266.
2 The phrase 'sacred book' is used of *A Room of One's Own* by Barbara Hill Rigney, '"A Wreath upon the Grave": The Influence of Virginia Woolf on Feminist Critical Theory', in Jeremy Hawthorn, ed., *Criticism and Critical Theory* (London, 1984), p. 76.
3 Virginia Woolf, *The Common Reader: First Series* (London, 1968), p. 11.
4 Ibid., p. 140.
5 Virginia Woolf, *Contemporary Writers* (London, 1965), p. 62; *The Common Reader*, p. 305.
6 Woolf, *The Common Reader*, p. 297.
7 E. M. Forster, *Aspects of the Novel* (Harmondsworth, 1962), pp. 75–85. Two consecutive chapters of Forster's book are headed 'People'.
8 Cf. Rachel Bowlby, *Virginia Woolf: Feminist Destinations* (Oxford, 1988), p. 40.
9 Woolf, *Contemporary Writers*, p. 27.
10 Virginia Woolf, *Three Guineas* (Harmondsworth, 1977), p. 205.
11 'Professions for Women', in Virginia Woolf, *Women and Writing*, intro. by Michèle Barrett (London, 1979), p. 62.
12 Toril Moi, *Sexual/Textual Politics* (London, 1985). Cf. also Bowlby, *Virginia Woolf*, Chapter 2.
13 Moi, *Sexual/Textual Politics*, p. 74.
14 Cf. Janet Todd, *Feminist Literary History: A Defence* (Cambridge, 1988), p. 89.
15 Sandra M. Gilbert, 'What Do Feminist Critics Want? A Postcard from the Volcano', in Elaine Showalter, ed., *The New Feminist Criticism: Essays on Women, Literature, and Theory* (London, 1986), p. 44.
16 Elaine Showalter, 'Feminist Criticism in the Wilderness', in *The New Feminist Criticism*, p. 245.
17 Ibid., p. 247.
18 Sandra M. Gilbert and Susan Gubar, *The Madwoman in the Attic: The Woman Writer and the Nineteenth-Century Literary Imagination* (New Haven and London, 1979), p. xiii.
19 Elaine Showalter, '*A Literature of Their Own*' in Mary Eagleton, ed., *Feminist Literary Theory: A Reader* (Oxford, 1986), pp. 11–15.
20 Michel Foucault, *The History of Sexuality: An Introduction*, trans. Robert Hurley (Harmondsworth, 1984), pp. 100–1.

372   Authors and Authority

21 See, e.g., Cora Kaplan, 'Speaking/Writing/Feminism', in Eagleton, *Feminist Literary Theory*, pp. 180–1.

Literary Criticism and Cultural Theory

1   Gabriel Pearson, 'Prometheans', *Guardian*, 31 January 1974, p. 9.
2   Quoted by David Trotter, *The Making of the Reader: Language and Subjectivity in Modern American, English and Irish Poetry* (Basingstoke and London, 1984), p. 238.
3   Jean-François Lyotard, *The Postmodern Condition: A Report on Knowledge*, trans. Geoff Bennington and Brian Massumi (Minneapolis, 1984), esp. pp. 4, 37, 51.
4   Gerald Graff, *Literature Against Itself* (Chicago and London, 1979), p. 7.
5   Cf. Giles Gunn, *The Culture of Criticism and the Criticism of Culture* (New York and Oxford, 1987), p. 61.
6   Bruss, *Beautiful Theories*, p. 23.
7   Raymond Williams, *The Politics of Modernism: Against the New Conformists*, ed. Tony Pinkney (London and New York, 1989), p. 116.
8   Mary Pratt, 'Art without Critics and Critics without Readers *or* Pantagruel versus The Incredible Hulk', in Paul Hernadi, ed., *What Is Criticism?* (Bloomington, Ind., 1981), p. 178.
9   William E. Cain, *The Crisis in Criticism: Theory, Literature and Reform in English Studies* (Baltimore and London, 1987), p. 79.
10 Wallace Martin, quoted in Cain, *The Crisis in Criticism*, p. 71.
11 Graham Hough, quoted in Alan Sinfield, 'Give an Account of Shakespeare and Education . . .', in Jonathan Dollimore and Alan Sinfield, eds, *Political Shakespeare: New Essays in Cultural Materialism* (Manchester, 1985), p. 144.
12 James Joyce, *Ulysses*, 'Cyclops' episode.
13 Quoted in Richard Ohmann, *Politics of Letters* (Middletown, Conn., 1987), p. 5.
14 Richard Helgerson, contribution to 'Historicism, New and Old: Excerpts from a Panel Discussion', in Claude J. Summers and Ted-Larry Pebworth, eds, *"The Muses Common-Weale": Poetry and Politics in the Seventeenth Century* (Columbia, Miss., 1988), p. 211.
15 Stephen Greenblatt, *Renaissance Self-Fashioning: From More to Shakespeare* (Chicago and London, 1980), p. 6. Cf. Helgerson, 'Historicism, New and Old', pp. 211–12.
16 Frank Lentricchia, *Ariel and the Police: Michel Foucault, William James, Wallace Stevens* (Brighton, Sussex, 1988), p. 97.
17 Helgerson, 'Historicism, New and Old', p. 212.
18 Leah Marcus, contribution to 'Historicism, New and Old', p. 209.
19 Raymond Williams, contribution to Ronald Hayman, ed., *My Cambridge* (London, 1977), p. 68.
20 Raymond Williams, *Culture* (London, 1981), p. 13.
21 Clifford Geertz, *The Interpretation of Cultures: Selected Essays* (London, 1975), pp. 3, 10, 452.

22 Clifford Geertz, 'Art as a Cultural System', *Modern Language Notes*, 91 (1976), p. 1499.
23 Geertz, *The Interpretation of Cultures*, p. 451n.
24 Ibid., p. 452.
25 Tony Bennett, *Formalism and Marxism* (London and New York, 1979), pp. 135–7.
26 Tony Bennett, 'Text and History', in Peter Widdowson, ed., *Re-Reading English* (London and New York, 1982), p. 230.
27 Bennett, *Formalism and Marxism*, p. 136. See also Dollimore and Sinfield, *Political Shakespeare*.
28 Edward W. Said, 'Interview', *Diacritics* (Fall 1976), p. 32.
29 Graham Hough, *Image and Experience* (London, 1960), p. 70.
30 Williams, *The Politics of Modernism*, p. 34.
31 Edward W. Said, 'Media, Margins and Modernity' (with Raymond Williams), in Williams, *The Politics of Modernism*, p. 196.
32 Greenblatt, *Renaissance Self-Fashioning*, pp. 4, 7.
33 Cf. Helgerson, 'Historicism, New and Old', p. 211.

Guide to Further Reading

GENERAL HISTORIES OF CRITICISM AND LITERARY CULTURE

George Saintsbury's *A History of Criticism and Literary Taste in Europe* (3 vols, Edinburgh: Blackwood, 1900–4) was the earliest comprehensive history of the subject; the English chapters were reprinted separately as *A History of English Criticism* (Edinburgh: Blackwood, 1936). For criticism since 1750, Saintsbury has now been superseded by René Wellek, *A History of Modern Criticism 1750–1950* (6 vols, London: Cape, 1955–86). Two shorter histories are W. K. Wimsatt and Cleanth Brooks, *Literary Criticism: A Short History* (New York: Knopf, 1957), written from the standpoint of New Criticism, and George Watson, *The Literary Critics* (Harmondsworth: Penguin, 1962), advocating a combination of New Critical and historical analysis. For stimulating discussions of particular aspects of the history of criticism see R. S. Crane, ed., *Critics and Criticism Ancient and Modern* (Chicago: University of Chicago Press, 1952), and Terry Eagleton, *The Function of Criticism: From the 'Spectator' to Post-Structuralism* (London: Verso, 1984).

For the history of English literacy and literary culture see Richard D. Altick, *The English Common Reader* (Chicago: University of Chicago Press, 1957), and Raymond Williams, *The Long Revolution* (London: Chatto, 1961). For the history of cultural ideas and vocabulary see Raymond Williams, *Culture and Society 1780–1950* (London: Chatto, 1958), and *Keywords* (London: Fontana, 1976). John Gross, *The Rise and Fall of the Man of Letters* (London: Weidenfeld, 1969) tells the story of English reviewing and bookmanship.

GENERAL ANTHOLOGIES OF CRITICISM

Walter Jackson Bate, ed., *Criticism: The Major Texts* (2nd edn, New York: Harcourt Brace Jovanovich, 1970) is the best general anthology on historical lines, especially for pre-twentieth century material. See also Robert Con Davis and Laurie Finke, eds, *Literary Criticism and Theory: The Greeks to the Present* (New York and London: Longman, 1989). Raman Selden, ed, *The Theory of Criticism: from Plato to the Present* (London and New York: Longman, 1988) is thematically, not historically organised.

374

JOHNSON AND THE EIGHTEENTH CENTURY

Johnson's complete works are appearing in the *Yale Edition of the Works of Samuel Johnson* (New Haven: Yale University Press, 1958–   ). See also *Rasselas, Poems and Selected Prose*, ed. Bertrand H. Bronson (3rd edn, New York: Rinehart, 1971); *Selected Essays from the 'Rambler', 'Adventurer', and 'Idler'*, ed. W. J. Bate (New Haven and London; Yale University Press, 1968); and John Wain, ed., *Johnson as Critic* (London: Routledge, 1973). Critical studies of Johnson's criticism include Paul Fussell, *Samuel Johnson and the Life of Writing* (London: Chatto, 1972), and Jean H. Hagstrum, *Samuel Johnson's Literary Criticism* (Chicago: University of Chicago Press, 1967).

Modern editions of other eighteenth-century critics include Joseph Addison, *Critical Essays from the 'Spectator'*, ed. Donald F. Bond (Oxford: Clarendon, 1970); William Blake, *Complete Writings*, ed. Geoffrey Keynes (London: Oxford University Press, 1966); John Dryden, *Of Dramatic Poesy and Other Critical Essays*, ed. George Watson (2 vols, London: Dent, 1962), and *Selected Criticism*, ed. James Kinsley and George Parfitt (Oxford: Clarendon, 1970); Alexander Pope, *Selected Prose*, ed. Paul Hammond (Cambridge: Cambridge University Press, 1987); and *Memoirs of the Extraordinary Life, Works and Discoveries of Martinus Scriblerus*, ed. Charles Kerby-Miller (New York: Russell, 1966); Sir Joshua Reynolds, *Discourses on Art*, ed. Robert R. Clark (San Marino, Ca.: Huntington Library, 1959); and Thomas Rymer, *Critical Works*, ed. Curt A. Zimansky (New Haven: Yale University Press, 1956).

For a general history of criticism in the period see J. W. H. Atkins, *English Literary Criticism: Seventeenth and Eighteenth Centuries* (London: Methuen, 1966), and R. S. Crane's essay 'On Writing the History of Criticism in England 1650–1800', in Crane, *The Idea of the Humanities* (Chicago: University of Chicago Press, 1967). See also Howard Anderson and John S. Shea, eds, *Studies in Criticism and Aesthetics 1650–1800* (Minneapolis: University of Minnesota Press, 1967). For the sociology of eighteenth-century literary culture see Alexandre Beljame, *Men of Letters and the English Public in the Eighteenth Century*, ed. Bonamy Dobrée (London: Kegan Paul, 1948), and Pat Rogers, *Grub Street* (London: Methuen, 1972). Laurence Lipking, *The Ordering of the Arts in Eighteenth-Century England* (Princeton: Princeton University Press, 1970) and Joan Pittock, *The Ascendency of Taste* (London: Routledge, 1973) are concerned with eighteenth-century aesthetics. For the later eighteenth century see Walter Jackson Bate, *From Classic to Romantic* (New York: Harper, 1961), and *The Burden of the Past and the English Poet* (London: Chatto, 1971); also René Wellek, *The Rise of English Literary History* (New York: McGraw-Hill, 1966).

Two anthologies which remain serviceable are Edmund D. Jones, ed., *English Critical Essays: Sixteenth, Seventeenth and Eighteenth Centuries* (London: Oxford University Press, 1922), and D. Nichol Smith, ed., *Shakespeare Criticism: A Selection* (London: Oxford University Press, 1916).

THE ROMANTIC PERIOD

Wordsworth's criticism is collected in William Wordsworth, *Prose Works*, ed. W. J. B. Owen and Jane Worthington Smyser (3 vols, Oxford: Clarendon, 1973); see also *Selected Prose*, ed. John O. Hayden (Harmondsworth: Penguin, 1988); *Literary Criticism*, ed. Paul M. Zall (Lincoln: University of Nebraska Press, 1966); and Wordsworth and Coleridge, *Lyrical Ballads*, ed. R. L. Brett and A. R. Jones (London: Methuen, 1968). Critical studies include W. J. B. Owen, *Wordsworth as Critic* (Toronto and London: University of Toronto Press, 1969).

The standard modern edition of Coleridge is Samuel Taylor Coleridge, *Collected Works* (London: Routledge, 1971–); other editions include *Biographia Literaria*, ed. George Watson (London: Dent, 1956), and *Coleridge on Shakespeare*, ed. R. A. Foakes (London: Routledge, 1971). For studies of his criticism see, among others, J. A. Appleyard, *Coleridge's Philosophy of Literature* (Cambridge, Mass.: Harvard University Press, 1965); M. M. Badawi, *Coleridge: Critic of Shakespeare* (Cambridge: Cambridge University Press, 1973); John Colmer, *Coleridge: Critic of Society* (Oxford: Clarendon, 1959); J. R. de J. Jackson, *Method and Imagination in Coleridge's Criticism* (London: Routledge, 1969); Thomas McFarland, *Coleridge and the Pantheist Tradition* (Oxford: Clarendon, 1969); and I. A. Richards, *Coleridge on Imagination* (London: Kegan Paul, 1934).

Modern editions of the other romantic critics include William Hazlitt, *Complete Works*, ed. P. P. Howe (21 vols, London: Dent, 1920–4), and *Selected Writings*, ed. Christopher Salvesen (New York: Signet, 1972); Francis Jeffrey, *Jeffrey's Literary Criticism*, ed. D. Nichol Smith (London: Henry Froude, 1910); Charles Lamb, *Lamb's Criticism*, ed. E. M. W. Tillyard (Cambridge: Cambridge University Press, 1923); Thomas de Quincey, *De Quincey as Critic*, ed. John E. Jordan (London: Routledge, 1973). Critical Studies include Roy Park, *Hazlitt and the Spirit of the Age* (Oxford: Clarendon, 1967); and John E. Jordan, *Thomas de Quincey: Literary Critic* (Berkeley and Los Angeles: University of California Press, 1952).

Meyer H. Abrams, *The Mirror and the Lamp: Romantic Theory and the Critical Tradition* (New York: Norton, 1958), is a major scholarly study of the period. See also the same author's *Natural Supernaturalism* (London: Oxford University Press, 1971); J. Bronowski, *The Poet's Defence* (Cambridge: Cambridge University Press, 1939); Marilyn Butler, *Romantics, Rebels and Reactionaries: English Literature and its Background 1760–1830* (Oxford: Oxford University Press, 1981); Frederick Hilles and Harold Bloom, eds, *From Sensibility to Romanticism* (New York: Oxford University Press, 1965); Graham Hough, *The Romantic Poets* (London: Hutchinson, 1953); Jerome J. McGann, *The Romantic Ideology: A Critical Investigation* (Chicago and London: University of Chicago Press, 1983); and P. W. K. Stone, *The Art of Poetry 1750–1820* (New York: Barnes, 1967).

Critical anthologies include Edmund D. Jones, ed., *English Critical Essays: Nineteenth Century* (London: Oxford University Press, 1971), and

John O. Hayden, ed., *Romantic Bards and British Reviewers* (London: Routledge, 1971).

THE VICTORIAN PERIOD

The standard edition of Arnold is Matthew Arnold, *Complete Prose Works*, ed. R. H. Super (Ann Arbor: University of Michigan Press, 1962–). See also *Essays, Letters and Reviews*, ed. Fraser Neiman (Cambridge, Mass.: Harvard University Press, 1960), and *Selected Criticism*, ed. Christopher Ricks (New York: Signet, 1972).

Modern editions of the other Victorian critics include Henry James, *The Art of the Novel*, ed. R. P. Blackmur (New York: Scribner, 1950), *Literary Reviews and Essays*, ed. Albert Mordell (New York: Grove, 1957), and *Selected Literary Criticism*, ed. Morris Shapira (London: Heinemann, 1963); Ralph Waldo Emerson, *Literary Criticism*, ed. E. Carlson (Lincoln: University of Nebraska Press, 1980); George Henry Lewes, *Literary Criticism*, ed. Alice R. Kaminsky (Lincoln: University of Nebraska Press, 1964); J. S. Mill, *Mill on Bentham and Coleridge*, ed. F. R. Leavis (London: Chatto, 1950), and *Mill's Essays on Literature and Society*, ed. J. B. Schneewind (New York: Collier, 1965); William Morris, *Collected Works*, ed. May Morris (24 vols, London: Longman, 1910–1915); Walter Pater, *Works* (9 vols, London: Macmillan, 1900–1901), and *Essays on Literature and Art*, ed. Jennifer Uglow (London: Dent, 1974); Edgar Allan Poe, *Essays and Reviews* (New York: Library of America, 1984); John Ruskin, *Complete Works*, ed. Sir E. T. Cook and A. D. O. Wedderburn (39 vols, London: Allen, 1902–12), and *Literary Criticism*, ed. Harold Bloom (Garden City, N.Y.: Anchor, 1965); George Santayana, *Selected Critical Writings*, ed. Norman Henfrey (2 vols, Cambridge: Cambridge University Press, 1968); Leslie Stephen, *Men, Books and Mountains, Essays*, ed. S. O. A. Ullmann (London: Hogarth, 1956); A. C. Swinburne, *Complete Works*, ed. Sir E. Gosse and T. J. Wise (20 vols, London: Heinemann, 1925–27), and *Swinburne as Critic*, ed. Clyde K. Hyder (London: Routledge, 1972); and Oscar Wilde, *The Artist as Critic*, ed. Richard Ellmann (London: Allen, 1970).

Among the many studies of individual critics are Edward Alexander, *Matthew Arnold and John Stuart Mill* (London: Routledge, 1965); Lionel Trilling, *Matthew Arnold* (London: Allen, 1955); Morris Roberts, *Henry James's Criticism* (New York: Haskell, 1965); Alice R. Kaminsky, *George Henry Lewes as Literary Critic* (New York: Syracuse University Press, 1968); Ian Fletcher, *Walter Pater* (London: Longman, 1971); Noel Annan, *Leslie Stephen: The Godless Victorian* (London: Weidenfeld, 1984), and David D. Zink, *Leslie Stephen* (New York: Twayne, 1972); and Robert L. Peters, *The Crowns of Apollo: Swinburne's Principles of Literature and Art* (Detroit: Wayne State University Press, 1965).

Studies of the critical journals include Edwin Everett Mallard, *The Party of Humanity: The 'Fortnightly Review' and its Contributors* (New York:

Russell, 1971); and George L. Nesbitt, *Benthamite Reviewing* (New York: Columbia University Press, 1934).

General studies of Victorian criticism and literary culture include Jerome Hamilton Buckley, *The Victorian Temper: A Study in Literary Culture* (London: Cass, 1966); Christophe Campos, *The View of France: From Arnold to Bloomsbury* (London: Oxford University Press, 1965); David J. Delaura, *Hebrew and Hellene in Victorian England* (Austin and London: University of Texas Press, 1969); Kenneth Graham, *English Criticism of the Novel 1865–1900* (Oxford: Clarendon, 1965); John Holloway, *The Victorian Sage* (New York: Norton, 1965); Graham Hough, *The Last Romantics* (London: Duckworth, 1949); D. J. Palmer, *The Rise of English Studies* (London: Oxford University Press, 1965); Geoffrey Tillotson, *Criticism and the Nineteenth Century* (London: Athlone, 1951); and Alba H. Warren, Jr, *English Poetic Theory 1825–1865* (Princeton University Press, 1950). On Shakespearean criticism and scholarship see S. Schoenbaum, *Shakespeare's Lives* (Oxford: Clarendon, 1970).

Anthologies covering specific aspects of the period include Derek Stanford, ed. *Pre-Raphaelite Writing* (London: Dent, 1973), and the same editor's *Writing of the Nineties* (London: Dent, 1971); Graham Hough and Eric Warner, *Strangeness and Beauty: An Anthology of Aesthetic Criticism 1840–1910* (2 vols, Cambridge: Cambridge University Press, 1983); and Daniel G. Hoffman, *American Poetry and Poetics: Poems and Critical Documents from the Puritans to Robert Frost* (Garden City, N.Y.: Anchor, 1962).

MODERNISM AND NEW CRITICISM

As a rule, the individual volumes of criticism published by the major early twentieth-century critics remain in print or are otherwise easily available. These are listed in the text of this book, and are not repeated here. Subsequent editions and selections include T. S. Eliot, *Selected Prose*, ed. Frank Kermode (London: Faber, 1975); R. P. Blackmur, *Selected Essays*, ed. Denis Donoghue (New York: Ecco, 1986); Christopher Caudwell, *Romance and Realism: A Study in English Bourgeois Literature*, ed. Samuel Hynes (Princeton: Princeton University Press, 1970); T. E. Hulme, *Speculations: Essays on Humanism and the Philosophy of Art*, ed. Herbert Read (2nd edn, London: Routledge, 1936), and *Further Speculations*, ed. Samuel Hynes (Minneapolis: University of Minnesota Press, 1955); Wyndham Lewis, *Enemy Salvoes: Selected Literary Criticism*, ed. C. J. Fox (London: Visition, 1975); Ezra Pound, *Literary Essays*, ed. T. S. Eliot (London: Faber, 1954); John Crowe Ransom, *Beating the Bushes: Selected Essays 1941–1970* (New York: New Directions, 1972); I. A. Richards, *Complementarities: Uncollected Essays*, ed. John Paul Russo (Manchester: Carcanet, 1977); Allen Tate, *On the Limits of Poetry: Selected Essays 1928–1948* (New York: Swallow, 1948), and *The Man of Letters in the Modern World: Selected Essays 1928–1955* (London: Meridian, 1957).

Reprinted critical journals include *The Criterion*, ed. T. S. Eliot (18 vols, London: Faber, 1967); *The Fugitive* (4 vols, Gloucester, Mass.: Smith, 1967); and *Scrutiny* (20 vols, Cambridge: Cambridge University Press, 1963). Two editions of selections of *Scrutiny* have also appeared. These are *The Importance of Scrutiny*, ed. Eric Bentley (New York: New York University Press, 1964); and *A Selection from Scrutiny*, ed. F. R. Leavis (2 vols, Cambridge: Cambridge University Press, 1968).

Studies of T. S. Eliot's criticism include Roger Kojecky, *T. S. Eliot's Social Criticism* (London: Faber, 1971); Brian Lee, *Theory and Personality: The Significance of T. S. Eliot's Criticism* (London: Athlone, 1979); Edward Lobb, *T. S. Eliot and the Romantic Critical Tradition* (London: Routledge, 1981); Graham Martin, ed., *Eliot in Perspective* (London: Macmillan, 1970); David Newton-de Molina, ed., *The Literary Criticism of T. S. Eliot: New Essays* (London: Athlone, 1977); and Allen Tate, ed., *T. S. Eliot: The Man and His Work* (London: Chatto, 1967).

Individual studies of other early twentieth-century critics include Edward T. Cone, Joseph Frank, and Edmund Keeley, eds, *The Legacy of R. P. Blackmur: Essays, Memoirs, Texts* (New York: Ecco, 1987); James T. Jones, *Wayward Skeptic: The Theories of R. P. Blackmur* (Urbana and Chicago: University of Illinois Press, 1986); William Walsh, *F. R. Leavis* (London: Chatto, 1980); Ian F. A. Bell, *Critic as Scientist: The Modernist Poetics of Ezra Pound* (London and New York: Methuen, 1981); Timothy Materer, *Vortex: Pound, Eliot, and Lewis* (Ithaca and London: Cornell University Press, 1979); Reuben Brower, Helen Vendler, and John Hollander, eds, *I. A. Richards: Essays in His Honor* (New York: Oxford University Press, 1973); W. H. N. Hotopf, *Language, Thought and Comprehension: A Case Study of the Writings of I. A. Richards* (London: Routledge, 1965); John Needham, *The Completest Mode: I. A. Richards and the Continuity of English Literary Criticism* (Edinburgh: Edinburgh University Press, 1982); Pamela McCallum, *Literature and Method: Towards a Critique of I. A. Richards, T. S. Eliot and F. R. Leavis* (Dublin: Gill and Macmillan, 1983); and Dick Davis, *Wisdom and Wilderness: The Achievement of Yvor Winters* (Athens: University of Georgia Press, 1983). For studies of William Empson see pp. 380–1.

Among studies of the critical journals are Wallace Martin, *The 'New Age' under Orage: Chapters in English Cultural History* (Manchester: Manchester University Press, 1967); Francis Mulhern, *The Moment of 'Scrutiny'* (London: Verso, 1981); Louise Cowan, *The Fugitive Group: A Literary History* (Baton Rouge: Louisiana State University Press, 1959); and Lewis P. Simpson, James Olney, and Jo Gulledge, eds, *The 'Southern Review' and Modern Literature 1935–1985* (Baton Rouge and London: Louisiana State University Press, 1988).

Of the numerous general studies of modernist literature, those with a bearing on the critical ideas of the period include John T. Gage, *In the Arresting Eye: The Rhetoric of Imagism* (Baton Rouge and London: Louisiana State University Press, 1981); Tom Gibbons, *Rooms in the Darwin Hotel: Studies in English Literary Criticism and Ideas 1880–1920* (Nedlands: University of Western Australia Press, 1973); Graham Hough,

Image and Experience: Studies in a Literary Revolution (London: Duckworth, 1960); Hugh Kenner, *The Pound Era* (London: Faber, 1975); and Frank Kermode, *Romantic Image* (London: Routledge, 1957).

For the growth of academic literary criticism see Chris Baldick, *The Social Mission of English Criticism 1848–1932* (Oxford: Clarendon, 1983); Lesley Johnson, *The Cultural Critics: From Matthew Arnold to Raymond Williams* (London: Routledge, 1979); Margaret Mathieson, *The Preachers of Culture: A Study of English and Its Teachers* (London: Allen, 1975); Floyd Stovell, ed, *The Development of American Literary Criticism* (New Haven: College Press, 1964); René Wellek and Austin Warren, *Theory of Literature* (3rd edn., Harmondsworth: Penguin, 1963); and Gerald Graff, *Professing Literature: An Institutional History* (Chicago and London: University of Chicago Press, 1987). On the New Criticism, see John Crowe Ransom, *The New Criticism* (Westport, Conn.: Greenwood, 1979); John Fekete, *The Critical Twilight* (London: Routledge, 1977); Richard Foster, *The New Romantics: A Reappraisal of the New Criticism* (Bloomington: Indiana University Press, 1962); Stanley Edgar Hyman, *The Armed Vision: A Study in the Methods of Modern Literary Criticism* (2nd edn, New York: Vintage, 1955); and Murray Krieger, *The New Apologists for Poetry* (Minneapolis: University of Minnesota Press, 1956). For a late reappraisal of New Criticism and its rivals see Malcolm Bradbury and D. J. Palmer, eds, *Contemporary Criticism* (Stratford-upon-Avon Studies no. 12, London: Arnold, 1970).

General anthologies of early twentieth-century criticism include James Scully, ed., *Modern Poets on Modern Poetry* (London: Collins, 1966); Bernard S. Oldsey and Arthur O. Lewis, Jr, eds, *Visions and Revisions in Modern American Literary Criticism* (New York: Dutton, 1962); Robert Wooster Stallman, ed., *Critiques and Essays in Criticism 1920–1948* (New York: Ronald, 1949); Peter Faulkner, ed., *A Modernist Reader: Modernism in England 1910–1930* (London: Batsford, 1986); Graham Martin and P. N. Furbank, eds, *Twentieth Century Poetry: Critical Essays and Documents* (Milton Keynes: Open University Press, 1975); and David Lodge, ed., *Twentieth-Century Literary Criticism: A Reader* (London and New York: Longman, 1972).

THE AGE OF INTERPRETATION: STRUCTURALISM, DECONSTRUCTION AND INTERPRETATIVE THEORY

Scholarly editions and selections of the work of the individual English-language critics considered under this heading have barely begun to appear: see, however, William Empson, *Argufying: Essays on Literature and Culture*, ed. John Haffenden (London: Chatto, 1987); Roman Jakobson, *Language in Literature*, ed. Krystyna Pomorska and Stephen Rudy (Cambridge, Mass. and London: Harvard University Press, 1987); and Paul de Man, *Critical Writings 1953–1978*, ed. Lindsay Waters (Minneapolis: University of Minnesota Press, 1989).

Critical studies include Roma Gill, ed., *William Empson: The Man and*

His Work (London: Routledge, 1974); Christopher Norris, *William Empson and the Philosophy of Literary Criticism* (London: Athlone, 1978); Frederick J. Hoffman, *Freudianism and the Literary Mind* (2nd edn, New York: Grove, 1959); Murray Krieger, ed., *Northrop Frye in Modern Criticism: Selected Papers from the English Institute* (New York: Columbia University Press, 1966); Jan Gorak, *Critic of Crisis: A Study of Frank Kermode* (Columbia: University of Missouri Press, 1987); Jonathan Arac, Wlad Godzich, and Wallace Martin, eds, *The Yale Critics: Deconstruction in America* (Minneapolis: University of Minnesota Press, 1983); David Fite, *Harold Bloom* (Amherst: University of Massachusetts Press, 1985); and Christopher Norris, *Paul de Man: Deconstruction and the Critique of Aesthetic Ideology* (New York and London: Routledge, 1988).

For broad overviews of contemporary literary theory, beginning with the New Criticism, see G. Douglas Atkins and Laura Morrow, eds, *Contemporary Literary Theory* (Basingstoke: Macmillan, 1989); Terry Eagleton, *Literary Theory: An Introduction* (Oxford: Blackwell, 1983); Ann Jefferson and David Robey, eds, *Modern Literary Theory: A Comparative Introduction* (2nd edn, London: Batsford, 1986); Raman Selden, *A Reader's Guide to Contemporary Literary Theory* (Brighton: Harvester, 1985); Jeremy Hawthorn, ed., *Criticism and Critical Theory* (Stratford-upon-Avon Studies, 2nd series, London: Arnold, 1984); and Frank Lentricchia, *After the New Criticism* (London: Athlone, 1980). Taken together, many volumes in the 'New Accents' series under the general editorship of Terence Hawkes provide a cumulative guide to contemporary theory: see especially Catherine Belsey, *Critical Practice* (London and New York: Methuen, 1980); Terence Hawkes, *Structuralism and Semiotics* (London: Methuen, 1977); Christopher Norris, *Deconstruction: Theory and Practice* (London and New York: Methuen, 1982); and Elizabeth Wright, *Psychoanalytic Criticism: Theory in Practice* (London and New York: Methuen, 1984).

Jonathan Culler has written a series of guide-books to structuralist and post-structuralist theory, including *Structuralist Poetics: Structuralism, Linguistics and the Study of Literature* (London: Routledge, 1975); *The Pursuit of Signs: Semiotics, Literature, Deconstruction* (London: Routledge, 1981); and *On Deconstruction: Theory and Criticism after Structuralism* (Ithaca, N.Y.: Cornell University Press, 1982). Other commentaries on deconstruction and its aftermath are Howard Felperin, *Beyond Deconstruction: The Uses and Abuses of Literary Theory* (Oxford: Clarendon, 1985); and Christopher Norris, *The Contest of Faculties: Philosophy and Theory after Deconstruction* (London and New York: Methuen, 1985).

Some more individual – and often, in the long run, more rewarding – commentaries on contemporary theory and interpretation will be found in the following: Elizabeth W. Bruss, *Beautiful Theories; The Spectacle of Discourse in Contemporary Criticism* (Baltimore and London: Johns Hopkins University Press, 1982); William E. Cain, *The Crisis in Criticism: Theory, Literature, and Reform in English Studies* (Baltimore and London: Johns Hopkins University Press, 1987); Denis Donoghue, *Ferocious Alphabets* (London and Boston: Faber, 1981); Eugene Goodheart, *The*

Failure of Criticism (Cambridge, Mass. and London: Harvard University Press, 1978); Gerald Graff, *Literature Against Itself: Literary Ideas in Modern Society* (Chicago and London: University of Chicago Press, 1979); Geoffrey H. Hartman, *The Fate of Reading and Other Essays* (Chicago and London: University of Chicago Press, 1975), and *Criticism in the Wilderness: The Study of Literature Today* (New Haven and London: Yale University Press, 1980); Paul Hernadi, ed., *What Is Criticism?* (Bloomington: Indiana University Press, 1981); E. D. Hirsch, Jr, *The Aims of Interpretation* (Chicago: University of Chicago Press, 1976); Fredric Jameson, *The Prison-House of Language: A Critical Account of Structuralism and Russian Formalism* (Princeton: Princeton University Press, 1974); Paul de Man, *Blindness and Insight: Essays in the Rhetoric of Contemporary Criticism* (2nd edn., London: Methuen, 1983); Stein Haugom Olsen, *The End of Literary Theory* (Cambridge: Cambridge University Press, 1987); and Robert Scholes, *Textual Power: Literary Theory and the Teaching of English* (New Haven and London: Yale University Press, 1985).

Anthologies of multinational literary theory include David Lodge, ed., *Modern Criticism and Theory: A Reader* (London and New York: Longman, 1988); K. M. Newton, ed., *Twentieth-Century Literary Theory: A Reader* (Basingstoke: Macmillan, and New York: St Martin's, 1988); and Philip Rice and Patricia Waugh, eds, *Modern Literary Theory: A Reader* (London: Arnold, 1989).

THE CHALLENGES TO INTERPRETATION: CULTURAL CRITICISM, FEMINISM AND CULTURAL THEORY

Edmund Wilson's book reviews were collected as *The Shores of Light: A Literary Chronicle of the Twenties and Thirties* (New York: Farrar, 1952); *Classics and Commercials: A Literary Chronicle of the Forties* (New York: Vintage, 1962), and *The Bit Between My Teeth: A Literary Chronicle of 1950–1965* (London: Allen, 1965). See also *The Portable Edmund Wilson* (Harmondsworth: Penguin, 1983).

Lionel Trilling's volumes of criticism have been re-published as the *Collected Works* (12 vols, New York: Harcourt, 1978–80).

A selection of George Steiner's writings is available under the title *George Steiner: A Reader* (Harmondsworth: Penguin, 1984).

For a critical study of Trilling see Mark Krupnick, *Lionel Trilling and the Fate of Cultural Criticism* (Evanston, Ill.: Northwestern University Press, 1986).

A selection of Virginia Woolf's feminist criticism has been published as *Virginia Woolf: Women and Writing*, ed. Michèle Barrett (London: Women's Press, 1979). Books discussing feminist criticism and theory include Elizabeth Abel and Emily K. Abel, eds, *The Signs Reader: Women, Gender and Scholarship* (Chicago: University of Chicago Press, 1983);

Mary Ellmann, *Thinking about Women* (New York: Harcourt, 1968); Judith Newton and Deborah Rosenfeldt, eds, *Feminist Criticism and Social Change* (New York: Methuen, 1985); Maggie Humm, *Feminist Criticism* (Brighton: Harvester, 1986); Toril Moi, *Sexual/Textual Politics: Feminist Literary Theory* (London and New York: Methuen, 1985); K. K. Ruthven, *Feminist Literary Studies: An Introduction* (Cambridge: Cambridge University Press, 1984); Elaine Showalter, ed., *The New Feminist Criticism: Essays on Women, Literature, and Theory* (London: Virago, 1986); and Janet Todd, *Feminist Literary History: A Defence* (Cambridge: Polity, 1988).

Anthologies of feminist criticism include Mary Eagleton, ed., *Feminist Literary Theory: A Reader* (Oxford: Blackwell, 1986); and Catherine Belsey and Jane Moore, eds, *The Feminist Reader: Essays in Gender and the Politics of Literary Criticism* (Basingstoke: Macmillan, 1989).

Contemporary Anglo-American studies of the Marxist tradition include Tony Bennett, *Formalism and Marxism* (London and New York: Methuen, 1979); Terry Eagleton, *Criticism and Ideology: A Study in Marxist Literary Theory* (London: NLB, 1976), and *Marxism and Literary Criticism* (London: Methuen, 1976); John Frow, *Marxism and Literary History* (Cambridge, Mass.: Harvard University Press, 1986); Fredric Jameson, *Marxism and Form: Twentieth-Century Dialectical Theories of Literature* (Princeton: Princeton University Press, 1971); and Raymond Williams, *Marxism and Literature* (Oxford: Oxford University Press, 1977), and *Problems in Materialism and Culture: Selected Essays* (London: Verso, 1980).

For discussions of cultural politics, cultural theory and new historicism from a variety of perspectives see Paul A. Bové, *Intellectuals in Power: A Genealogy of Critical Humanism* (New York: Columbia University Press, 1986); Jonathan Dollimore and Alan Sinfield, eds, *Political Shakespeare: New Essays in Cultural Materialism* (Manchester: Manchester University Press, 1985); Giles Gunn, *The Culture of Criticism and the Criticism of Culture* (New York and Oxford: Oxford University Press, 1987); Frank Lentricchia, *Criticism and Social Change* (Chicago: University of Chicago Press, 1983), and *Ariel and the Police: Michel Foucault, William James, Wallace Stevens* (Brighton: Harvester, 1988); Richard Ohmann, *English in America: A Radical View of the Profession* (New York: Oxford University Press, 1976), and *Politics of Letters* (Middletown, Conn.: Wesleyan University Press, 1987); Patrick Parrinder, *The Failure of Theory: Essays on Criticism and Contemporary Fiction* (Brighton: Harvester, 1987); Edward W. Said, *The World, the Text, and the Critic* (London: Faber, 1984); Harold Veeser, ed., *The New Historicism* (London: Routledge, 1989); and Peter Widdowson, ed., *Re-Reading English* (London and New York: Methuen, 1982).

Index of Authors and Critics Cited in the Text